Aboriginal Peoples and the Law

Jim Reynolds

Aboriginal Peoples and the Law

A Critical Introduction

Purich Books, an imprint of UBC Press
2029 West Mall
Vancouver, BC, V6T 1Z2
www.purichbooks.ca

27 26 25 24 23 22 21 20 19 18   5 4 3 2 1

Printed in Canada on FSC-certified ancient-forest-free paper (100% post-consumer recycled) that is processed chlorine- and acid-free, with vegetable-based inks.

Library and Archives Canada Cataloguing in Publication

Reynolds, James I., author
   Aboriginal peoples and the law : a critical introduction / Jim Reynolds.

Includes bibliographical references and index.
Issued in print and electronic formats.
ISBN 978-0-7748-8021-3 (softcover).–ISBN 978-0-7748-8022-0 (PDF).–
ISBN 978-0-7748-8023-7 (EPUB).–ISBN 978-0-7748-8024-4 (Kindle)

   1. Native peoples–Legal status, laws, etc.–Canada. I. Title.

KE7709.R47 2018   342.7108'72   C2018-901658-2
KF8205.R47 2018   C2018-901659-0

Canadä

UBC Press gratefully acknowledges the financial support for our publishing program of the Government of Canada (through the Canada Book Fund), the Canada Council for the Arts, and the British Columbia Arts Council.

Printed and bound in Canada by Marquis
Set in DIN, Myriad, and Minion by Artegraphica Design Co. Ltd.
Copy editor: Audrey McClellan
Proofreader: Judith Earnshaw
Indexer: Judy Dunlop
Cover designer: Martyn Schmoll

This book is dedicated to my wife, **Pui-ah**, and our sons, **Christopher** and **Alistair**.

Contents

Preface

In his bitter, brilliant, and provocative polemic *The Unjust Society*, Harold Cardinal (then president of the Indian Association of Alberta) wrote: "Our people want, our people, the Indians, demand just settlement of all our treaty and aboriginal rights. To the Indian people, there can be no justice, no just society, until their rights are restored ... The question of Indian rights is the paramount question for all Indian people from the vantage point of the past, the present and the future."[1] Cardinal was writing in 1969 in response to Prime Minister Pierre Trudeau's proposal to terminate the special rights of Aboriginal peoples.

Almost fifty years later, Justin Trudeau followed in his father's footsteps as prime minister but declared a very different approach to Aboriginal policy, stating that no relationship was more important to his government than that with Aboriginal people. Clearly, much has changed, at least on the surface.[2] But is there now justice for Aboriginal people? Do we have a just society? Are Aboriginal and treaty rights now restored? The answers are found in modern Aboriginal law developed since *The Unjust Society*.

Anyone who pays attention to current affairs in Canada will have seen almost daily reports relating to this area of law. Take, for example, the Supreme Court of Canada's 2014 decision in favour of the Tsilhqot'in people, which found that they held Aboriginal title over almost 2,000 square kilometres; the final report of the Truth and Reconciliation Commission in 2015, which recommended greater knowledge of this area of the law; the Liberal government's repeated statements confirming its desire to implement the UN Declaration on the Rights of Indigenous Peoples; the Supreme Court's 2016 decision that Métis and non-status Aboriginal people are considered "Indians" for some purposes of the Constitution; and the Federal Court of Appeal's decision that same year to overturn the federal government's approval of the $7-billion Northern Gateway pipeline project because of the government's failure to adequately consult Aboriginal groups. You may have also noticed reports of the proposed treaty with the Chippewas of Ontario.[3] In February 2017, the prime minister announced a working group of ministers to review all relevant federal laws, policies, and operational practices to ensure they met constitutional obligations and international commitments to Indigenous peoples. In July 2017, the minister of justice, Jody Wilson-Raybould, released principles to guide the review, based largely on statements from recent decisions of the Supreme Court of Canada.[4] In October 2017, there were press reports of boats being burned in Nova Scotia, actions arising out of a dispute over the right to fish under a treaty.[5] February 2018 saw second reading of a bill to implement the UN Declaration and an announcement by the prime minister of Recognition and Implementation of Rights legislation and policy.

This book is intended as an introduction to Aboriginal law for law students; students of Aboriginal studies, politics, and the social sciences; and general readers interested in this fascinating and important topic. A major consideration has been to maintain a length appropriate to this objective (and demanded by the publishers!), and this consideration, as well as the desire to focus on the most important features of the law and the policy issues involved – the forest and not the trees – means that I have not attempted to make this a comprehensive introduction. Of necessity, I have omitted much that others already acquainted with the topic may feel to be important. I hope that my modest effort will help you find a route through the legal thicket, and I encourage you to continue on the journey by reading some of the books and articles mentioned in the notes on particular topics, or by reading a more detailed text for a comprehensive account.

Although legal writers and judges may use long and technical words, or words from dead languages like *sui generis, plaintiff,* or *defendant,* law should not be a mystery.[6] I attempt to avoid technical detail as much as possible and explain it when I must use it, but on occasion you will have to be willing to slog on in order to get an understanding of the law. The important thing is to keep in mind the words of Professor Wedderburn in the preface to his classic work *The Worker and the Law:*

> Technical law by itself is useless, at best an arid game played by keen
> minds in court rooms and academic ivory towers. To understand its sig
> nificance we must look at its historical and social setting, we must ques
> tion what are the value and policy judgements enshrined within the
> propositions of law, and we must ask what is done in other countries
> about the problems revealed.[7]

Despite the introductory nature of this book, my aim is to follow this approach. Value and policy considerations are especially important to our task because this is an area of law developed largely by judges of the Supreme Court of Canada, unelected and unrepresentative, with limited input from Aboriginal people, the general public, or their elected representatives. It enshrines the social and political views of those judges and is unlikely to be challenged or changed given the nature of the judicial process (with no further appeals from their decisions) and the constitutional protection from being reversed by Parliament, since judges effectively have the last word on the Constitution.

This is also a critical introduction. It goes beyond a description of what the law is, based on what the judges say it is, and includes commentary on that law. As might be expected in an area of law dealing with such sensitive political, social, and economic issues as whether Aboriginal title prevails over private property rights and whether Aboriginal fishers should have priority over others, there has been a great deal of commentary and criticism. Sometimes that has been from dissenting judges. More often it has come from academics in disciplines such as law, political science, and anthropology. Their perspectives range from libertarian conservatives such as Tom Flanagan, who decries what he calls "the aboriginal orthodoxy" reflected, in part, in judicial decisions,[8] to the views of advocates of Aboriginal sovereignty, who are critical of decisions that have upheld Canadian sovereignty over Aboriginal peoples and lands. I attempt to summarize the diversity of views. I also include comments based on my own experiences as a lawyer, especially in the concluding chapter.

I hope this book will correct some misunderstandings about the current state of the law and provide some perspective for critical thinking and discussion about both the reform and the limits of the law. I have been deeply involved for almost forty years in representing Aboriginal peoples (especially the Musqueam people of Vancouver) as a lawyer. I agree with Felix Cohen, the great pioneer of US Aboriginal law, that "law is the battlefield on which all great social struggles take place."[9] However, as a practising lawyer, I am also very aware of the limits of the law in dealing with the unfinished business of colonialism in Canada and bringing about genuine reconciliation between Aboriginal and non-Aboriginal Canadians.

I have been fortunate to have spent most of my professional career acting for the Musqueam, including many years working on reserves with community members. As I briefly summarize in Chapter 8, they have been at the forefront of developments in Aboriginal law since they went to court in what became the *Guerin* decision of the Supreme Court of Canada in 1984.[10] I had the honour to be part of the legal team in that case and in subsequent litigation, negotiations, and preparation of documents to record agreements with governments and businesses. This experience gave me a unique opportunity to participate in, and witness, what by any standards must be considered one of the most exciting aspects of Canadian law and politics in the last few decades. I have also come to learn something of the richness of Musqueam history, culture, and values. To all the Musqueam people, I express my best wishes and thanks, *hay chxw qʼa*.

The general scheme employed in this book is to consider some introductory issues in Chapters 1 and 2, giving background material to better understand the substantive legal issues covered in later chapters. Chapter 3 covers issues of Crown and Aboriginal sovereignties and the relationship between the governments and Aboriginal peoples. Aboriginal rights and title are the heart of Aboriginal law and are covered in Chapter 4. Treaties, which are the predominant legal means to terminate Aboriginal rights and title in exchange for treaty rights, are discussed in Chapter 5. The next chapter deals primarily with the topic of consultation in the context of claims of Aboriginal rights that have not been proven. In theory, such consultation is intended to protect unproven rights, pending negotiation of treaties or litigation to establish their validity. Chapter 7 looks at bodies of law that are not directly part of Canadian Aboriginal law but may influence and be adopted into it. The chapter is divided into sections on the Indigenous laws of Aboriginal groups in Canada and international law. Finally, Chapter 8 provides concluding comments, including my views on the limits of the law and the need for governments to show greater political will.

At the beginning of the book, I include a list of what I consider to be the leading cases in date order, using a short form for the name of each case. This list will help you understand the overall development of the law. At the end of the book, you'll find a list of all the cases mentioned, with complete names and citations.

A few points of clarification:

- I use "Aboriginal" rather than "Indigenous" because that is the term used in Canadian law and it is intended to be synonymous with "Indigenous," except when the distinction is made in Chapter 7 between "Aboriginal law" (the law of the Canadian legal system applying to Aboriginal peoples) and "Indigenous laws" (the laws of an Indigenous group). This term is used for consistency and not to deny that

"Indigenous" may be a better term or that some "Aboriginal" people identify only with their own tribe or nation.

- References to "governments" are to federal and provincial governments rather than Aboriginal governments. This is to avoid confusion and not in any way to deny the validity of Aboriginal governments, although it does reflect the general failure of Canadian law to recognize the powers of Aboriginal governments, as is discussed in Chapters 3 and 7.

- References to case names in the text are usually in a shortened form and are indicated by the use of italics. Full citations are given in the endnotes and in the list of cases cited at the end of the book.

- I have not included URLs for most references, but many of the materials cited can be found using a simple search. For all the Supreme Court of Canada cases, go to the website "Judgments of the Supreme Court of Canada by Lexum" (https://scc-csc.lexum.com/scc-csc/en/nav.do) and insert part of the case name. More recent decisions of other courts can be found at the Canadian Legal Information Institute website (https://www.canlii.org/en/). Many articles and some older books can also be found online.

I would like to acknowledge the assistance of the following people: my colleagues at Mandell Pinder LLP for their encouragement, and, in particular, Kris Statnyk and Aaron Wilson, who kindly provided me with materials on Indigenous laws; Don Purich, who reviewed a draft of this book and provided many helpful comments; Randy Schmidt, Lesley Erickson, Judith Earnshaw, Judy Dunlop, Nadine Pedersen, and Martyn Schmoll at UBC Press for their assistance during writing and production; Audrey McClellan for her careful copy-editing; and Haida artist Jim Hart, who allowed me to use a photo of part of his impressive Reconciliation Pole at the UBC Vancouver campus on the front cover.

Leading Cases

1823 – *Johnson v. McIntosh*

1831 – *Cherokee Nation*

1832 – *Worcester v. Georgia*

1888 – *St. Catherine's Milling*

1973 – *Calder*

1984 – *Guerin*

1985 – *Simon*

1990 – *Sioui; Sparrow*

1991 – *Bear Island*

1995 – *Blueberry River*

1996 – *Badger; Côté; Gladstone; N.T.C. Smokehouse; Pamajewon; Van der Peet*

1997 – *Delgamuukw*

1999 – *Marshall I; Sundown*

2001 – *Mitchell*

2002 – *Wewaykum*

2003 – *Powley*

2004 – *Haida; Taku*

2005 – *Marshall/Bernard; Mikisew Cree*

2006 – *Sappier*

2009 – *Ermineskin*

2010 – *Little Salmon; Rio Tinto*

2011 – *Lax Kw'alaams*

2013 – *Manitoba Métis Federation*

2014 – *Grassy Narrows; Tsilhqot'in*

2016 – *Daniels*

Note: A full list of cases cited in this book, including complete names and citations, can be found at the end of the book.

Aboriginal Peoples and the Law

What Is Aboriginal Law?

1

Aboriginal law deals with the legal situation of the Aboriginal peoples of Canada – in particular, their special rights, which may, of course, also have an impact on non-Aboriginal people. In order to understand substantive legal issues such as the content and limits of those rights and the basis for their recognition by the Canadian legal system, it is important to consider fundamental questions. For instance, why should Aboriginal peoples be treated differently from other groups? Who are the Aboriginal peoples of Canada? And what are the objectives and sources of Aboriginal law?

> Aboriginal law deals with the legal situation of the Aboriginal peoples of Canada under the laws of Canada; "Indigenous law" refers to the law of a particular Aboriginal group, developed within and applying to that group.

The Special Rights of Aboriginal Peoples

An immediate question is why should Aboriginal people be treated differently from other minority groups, such as Ukrainians or Italians? Prominent Aboriginal rights lawyer Thomas Berger has asked that question and sought to answer it: "Native people did not immigrate to Canada as individuals or families who expected to be assimilated to Canada ... The Native peoples ... were already here: they have been forced to submit to the laws and institutions of the dominant White society. They have never relinquished their claim to be treated as distinct peoples in our midst."[1] He has also suggested that Aboriginal peoples' attempt to preserve, on their own terms, a land-based culture and way of life distinguish them from other minorities. No other minority can assert a right to a land base and to distinct political institutions founded on Aboriginal sovereignty.[2] The remaining rights of Aboriginal peoples to their property and sovereignty are fundamental to the law. Patrick Macklem has suggested that four "complex social facts" account for the unique constitutional relationship that exists between Aboriginal peoples and the Canadian state:

- Aboriginal cultural difference
- Aboriginal prior occupancy
- Aboriginal prior sovereignty
- Aboriginal participation in a treaty process.[3]

Macklem argues that constitutional protection of "indigenous difference" promotes greater equality and a just distribution of constitutional power.

"Native peoples ... have been forced to submit to the laws and institutions of the dominant White society. They have never relinquished their claim to be treated as distinct peoples in our midst."

Thomas Berger, *A Long and Terrible Shadow*

A related question is whether special rights for Aboriginal peoples are objectionable as a form of racial discrimination. Since descent from the original population is a requirement (leaving aside exceptional cases based on marriage or adoption), ethnicity is an invariable factor. This can be regarded as a racial requirement; on occasion, courts have referred to "Indians" as a race.[4] And discrimination against them has been described as racial discrimination.[5] Some critics have complained that Aboriginal rights are themselves a form of race-based discrimination and are "at variance with liberal democracy" since "Indians did not do anything to achieve their status except to be born, and no one else can do anything to join them in that status because no action can affect one's ancestry."[6] The Supreme Court of Canada (SCC or "the Court") has struggled with this issue, noting in one case:

> In the liberal enlightenment view ... rights are held by all people in society because each person is entitled to dignity and respect. Rights are general and universal ... Aboriginal rights cannot, however, be defined on the basis of the philosophical precepts of the liberal enlightenment ... they are rights held only by aboriginal members of Canadian society. They arise from the fact that aboriginal people are aboriginal.[7]

The Court has resolved complaints from non-Aboriginal Canadians who claim they are being discriminated against – for example, when a licence to fish at a certain time and place is granted to an Aboriginal group but not to non-Aboriginal Canadians – by upholding special treatment for an Aboriginal group on the grounds that the Aboriginal group is disadvantaged and the favourable treatment can be justified as a form of affirmative action.[8]

Unless a law makes an exception, persons of Aboriginal descent are bound by the same obligations as other Canadian citizens. The SCC noted in one case: "Indians are citizens and, in affairs of life not governed by treaties or the Indian Act, they are subject to all the responsibilities ... of other Canadian citizens."[9] This means, among other things, that there is no general tax exemption for Aboriginal peoples. (The exemption in Section 87 of the *Indian Act* applies only to those people who are entitled to be registered as "Indians" under the act and only to property situated on a reserve. Modern treaties generally phase out this exemption.) In another case, the SCC noted that "Aboriginal people do not, by reason of their Aboriginal heritage, cease to be citizens who fully participate with other Canadians in their collective governance."[10] The Court has also stated, "Aboriginal peoples are part of Canada, and they do not have special status with respect to constitutional obligations owed to Canadians as a whole."[11]

Until relatively recently, "Indians" suffered from official discrimination. For example, they were denied the federal vote until 1960. Now, however, such discrimination would be illegal, and Aboriginal people are entitled to enjoy the same rights as non-Aboriginal people. For example, in 2016, the Canadian Human Rights Tribunal upheld a complaint that the federal government discriminated against First Nations children and families living on reserves and in the Yukon in the provision of child and family services.[12] The SCC has noted widespread prejudice against Aboriginal people, which has become greater because of land claims and fishing rights.[13] The question of discrimination within an Aboriginal group has been the issue in some litigation. The SCC overturned a provision that restricted voting in band council elections to those members resident on reserve.[14] In a recent case, the Court held that there was no evidence that a requirement for a minimum level of education to be elected chief or councillor was discriminatory.[15] Until 2008, the *Canadian Human Rights Act* did not apply to decisions made under the *Indian Act,* such as allocation of housing by band councils. The act was amended to remove the exemption, but the amendment states that it is to be interpreted and applied in a manner that gives due regard to the First Nation's legal traditions and customary law, particularly when it comes to balancing individual rights and interests against collective rights and interests to the extent that the traditions and law are consistent with the principle of gender equality.[16]

The Dispossession of Aboriginal Peoples and Supposed Justifications

An issue directly related to the special rights of Aboriginal peoples is their dispossession, since the limited extent of those rights today is the result of such dispossession. Generally speaking, current Aboriginal rights are rights dating from before the arrival of Europeans that have survived extinguishment, surrender, and infringement by government. It is vital to remember that they are rights that existed before European settlement and not rights conferred by non-Aboriginal governments. Likewise, most treaty rights are rights reserved by Aboriginal peoples when they agreed to surrender other Aboriginal rights. As noted by the Supreme Court of the United States, a treaty "was not a grant of rights to the Indians, but a grant of rights from them, a reservation of those not granted."[17] This fundamental point is often

Dispossession, Extinguishment, Surrender, and Infringement

"Dispossession" is the loss of use by Aboriginal peoples of their traditional lands.

"Extinguishment" is the termination of an Aboriginal or treaty right by a colonial or the federal government. It has not been possible since 1982 because Section 35 of the *Constitution Act, 1982* protects those rights.

"Surrender" is the voluntary termination by an Aboriginal group of an Aboriginal or treaty right.

"Infringement" is a limitation by a government of an Aboriginal or treaty right, and it is valid only if it can be justified under the test developed by the Supreme Court of Canada.

ignored, and people speak of reserve land being "given" to the Aboriginal group, when it is actually land that, in the vast majority of cases, was retained from their traditional territory, with the balance being taken from them. The SCC has been guilty of this error.[18] Retention may be on a diminishing basis: some treaties, such as the numbered treaties in the Prairie provinces, have provisions permitting the government to "take up" land from time to time, a provision that limits the area within which Aboriginal rights have been retained.[19] Both the federal and provincial governments may infringe Aboriginal and treaty rights if this can be justified under a test devised by the SCC, although outright extinguishment has not been possible since the passage of Section 35 of the *Constitution Act, 1982.*

> "[A treaty] was not a grant of rights to the Indians, but a grant of rights from them, a reservation of those not granted."
>
> US Supreme Court, *U.S. v. Winans*

Aboriginal and treaty rights have only been fully recognized since 1982 under Section 35 of the *Constitution Act, 1982.*[20] It must be acknowledged that the role of law has been to support the colonization of Canada, including the dispossession of Aboriginal peoples, disruption of their culture and legal systems, and limitation of their power to govern. The Truth and Reconciliation Commission described Canadian law as "a tool for the dispossession and dismantling of Aboriginal societies."[21] As stated by Justice Binnie in the *God's Lake* case, "The history of Indian peoples in North America has generally been one of dispossession, including dispossession of their pre-European sovereignty, of their traditional lands, and of distinctive elements of their cultures."[22] Law played a prominent part in this colonial process and continues to support its legacy by legitimizing it. Although fundamental legal principles recognized Aboriginal rights until they were surrendered by treaty or extinguished by clear legislation, some laws directly prevented Aboriginal peoples from enforcing those rights. For example, an amendment to the *Indian Act,* passed by the federal government in 1927, made it an offence to raise funds to pursue claims of Aboriginal title.[23] Other laws attacked Aboriginal culture. A prime example is legislation that made it an offence to carry on certain customs and governance practices, such as the West Coast gift-giving feasts and assemblies (potlaches).[24]

More commonly, and especially in British Columbia, the legislatures and courts simply ignored the Aboriginal interest in land and resources. As the SCC acknowledged in *Sparrow,* "For many years, the rights of the Indians to their aboriginal lands – certainly as *legal* rights – were virtually ignored," and "there can be no doubt that over the years the rights of the Indians were often honoured in the breach."[25] Laws that ignored Aboriginal rights (as with land laws passed in British Columbia under the policy of denial of such rights) effectively defeated those rights by giving title to others. In practice, "Aboriginal rights existed at the margins, meaningful only in geographical spaces left vacant by Crown or third-party non-use."[26] Even today, the law requires Aboriginal people to commence protracted and expensive litigation to prove their rights and have them recognized and enforced.[27] Special rights and recent developments in the law recognizing Aboriginal rights must be seen in this context.

A variety of justifications has been given for the dispossession of Aboriginal peoples: the religious excuses proffered by the Spanish that colonization would save souls; the racist views that Aboriginal peoples were "uncivilized" and inferior and should make way for a superior race; and the theory of "terra nullius" (the claim that the land was unoccupied or occupied by peoples without property rights), which was used in Australia. The view that the land was not being sufficiently used by Aboriginal peoples, who had no need for much of it, was the dominant theory in North America based on principles of "natural" or international law.[28] It remains alive today. Canadian author Conrad Black recently wrote:

> There remains the issue of the moral and legal justification for the occupation of the Americas by the Europeans. It was a rich and underpopulated area and the occupants were, from the standpoint of the potential of the human species underutilizing it ... Indian society was not in itself worthy of integral conservation, nor was its dilution a suitable subject for great lamentations. To the extent the Americas were underdeveloped, the arrival of the Europeans was a positive thing.[29]

This view still influences the law through the test of justification, which permits infringement of Aboriginal and treaty rights to achieve objectives considered more beneficial to "the broader society." The theory goes back to at least 1516, when Thomas More explained in *Utopia* that the Utopians were entitled by natural law to colonize another country if land in that country was not being sufficiently used, and to drive out the original inhabitants if they refused to follow Utopian laws: "For they count this the most just cause of war, when any people hold a piece of ground void and vacant to no good nor profitable use, keeping others from the use and possession of it."[30] *The Law of Nations* by Vattel, first published in 1758, put it forward as a legal justification for the colonization of the Americas, saying that hunters had "no reason to complain if other nations, more industrious and too closely

Aboriginal Peoples and the Law

confined, come to take possession of a part of [their] lands," and adding that Europeans "were lawfully entitled to take possession of it."[31] However, he described the conquest of the agrarian empires of Peru and Mexico as "a notorious usurpation."

The theory of the inferior claim of hunters and gatherers was widely used in Canada to justify the dispossession of Aboriginal peoples. This can be seen in a contemporary account from colonial British Columbia of a conversation between a settler and a chief, who said that he and his people did not want the white man, "who steals what we have." The settler replied that "the high chief of King George men [the English], seeing that you do not work your land, orders that you shall sell it. It is of no use to you." However, theory only went so far. Recognizing that "we had taken forcible possession of the district," the settler stated that the practical answer to the question of "the right of any people to intrude upon another and to dispossess them of their country" is "given by the determination of intruders under any circumstances to keep what has been obtained; and this, without discussion, we, on the west coast of Vancouver Island, were all prepared to do."[32] In the final analysis, the dispossession was explained and justified by "the loaded canon pointed towards the [Tseshaht] village."

The Supreme Court of Canada has confirmed [in *Haida*] that Aboriginal peoples were never conquered.

The Supreme Court of Canada has confirmed that Aboriginal peoples were never conquered.[33] However, duress and the threat of force if they failed to comply with the colonial authorities were always present. The historical treaties, which according to their English terms transferred much of the country to the Crown, were signed under conditions of great hardship that throw their validity into question.

These fundamental questions of fairness and justice should be kept in mind as we examine some of the legal rules.[34] In the final analysis, Aboriginal law and the special rights of Aboriginal peoples are about the continuing impacts of colonialism. In her recent book *Price Paid: The Fight for First Nations Survival*, Aboriginal author Bev Sellars quotes Chief Dan George: "We are a people with special rights ... We do not beg for these rights, nor do we thank you ... we do not thank you for them because we paid for them ... and God help us, the price we paid was exorbitant. We paid for them with our culture, our dignity and self-respect. We paid and paid and paid." In her own words, "The trauma of colonialism is still with us today."[35]

Related to the issue of justification for the historical dispossession of Aboriginal peoples is the question of the legal entitlement of the current occupants, who cannot claim Aboriginal title. Their entitlement is based on treaties (where they have been signed) and on the laws made under Crown sovereignty and upheld against Aboriginal title.

Who Are the Aboriginal Peoples of Canada?

According to the 2016 Census, there were 1,673,785 Aboriginal people in Canada, accounting for 4.9 percent of the total population, comprising 977,230 First Nation (or "Indian") people, 587,545 Métis, and 65,025 Inuit. This was an increase of 42.5 percent since 2006, due, in part, to more people identifying as Aboriginal.[36] Not all of these self-identifying Aboriginal people will be considered as "Aboriginal" under the current law, although some may be entitled to register as "Indians" (and so be included as "Aboriginal") under recent changes to the *Indian Act* to remove vestiges of sexism.[37]

The legal terms used to refer to Aboriginal people in Canadian law are inconsistent and confusing. In 1969, Harold Cardinal called them "legal hocus-pocus."[38] They certainly are a hodgepodge. As noted by Paul Chartrand, "In Canada, then, there are as many definitions of Aboriginal people as there are constitutional or legislative provisions that reflect particular purposes, and the relationship between the various terms has not been developed."[39]

Section 35 of the Constitution Act, 1982

35.(1) The existing aboriginal and treaty rights of the aboriginal peoples of Canada are hereby recognized and affirmed.

(2) In this Act, "aboriginal peoples of Canada" includes the Indian, Inuit and Métis peoples of Canada.

(3) For greater certainty, in subsection (1) "treaty rights" includes rights that now exist by way of land claims agreements or may be so acquired.

(4) Notwithstanding any other provision of this Act, the aboriginal and treaty rights referred to in subsection (1) are guaranteed equally to male and female persons.

He makes the important point that a distinction should be made between Aboriginal groups with collective Aboriginal rights and individuals of Aboriginal ancestry who share the same rights as other citizens, including the right to equal treatment, and who, where justified, may benefit from affirmative action to remedy discrimination based on their Aboriginal ancestry. As we'll see, Aboriginal law is concerned primarily with group and not individual rights.

Section 35 of the *Constitution Act, 1982* (which provides constitutional recognition for the "existing aboriginal and treaty rights of the aboriginal peoples of Canada") defines the aboriginal people of Canada to include "the Indian, Inuit and Métis peoples of Canada." Although offensive to some, "Indian" is the term used in legislation such as the *Indian Act* for those people who are entitled to be registered under that act and (especially if they live on a reserve) are subject to that act. "Inuit" refers to the Indigenous people living in northern Canada, especially Nunavut and northern Quebec. They may have Aboriginal title to their lands, although in many cases it will have been surrendered under one of the modern treaties. The term "Métis" has traditionally been associated with distinct historical communities formed as a result of marriages between European fur traders and "Indian" women, especially in western Canada, but it can also refer to anyone with some Indian or Inuit ancestry, however limited. The SCC has defined "Métis" for the purposes of Section 35 as follows:

- self-identification as Métis
- an ancestral connection to an historical Métis community
- acceptance by a modern Métis community.[40]

Section 91(24) *of the* Constitution Act, 1867

91. ... it is hereby declared that (notwithstanding anything in this Act) the exclusive Legislative Authority of the Parliament of Canada extends to all Matters coming within the Classes of Subjects next hereinafter enumerated; that is to say ...

24. Indians, and Lands reserved for the Indians.

Section 91(24) of the *Constitution Act, 1867,* which gives the federal government jurisdiction over "Indians" (as well as "lands reserved for the Indians"), has been interpreted to include within its scope Inuit,[41] Métis people, and "non-status Indians."[42] This last term refers to both Indians who lost status under the *Indian Act* and members of "mixed communities" who have never been recognized as Indians by the federal government and who identify with their Indian heritage rather than as Métis.[43] In the recent *Daniels* decision, the SCC declined to give a definition of Métis or "non-status Indians" for the purposes of Section 91(24), saying it was "a fact-driven question to be decided on a case-by-case basis in the future."[44] Unlike the *Indian Act* registry for "Indians," there is no government registry for Métis or Inuit.[45] As noted above, depending on the context, "Métis" can include all those who claim some "Indian" or Inuit ancestry or only those who are connected to a historical Métis community such as the Red River Colony in Manitoba. An individual may be both an "Indian" within the *Indian Act* and a "Métis,"[46] and an Aboriginal group may have both Inuit and Métis Aboriginal rights.[47] To add more confusion, the definition of "Indian" in the *Indian Act* excludes all Inuit[48] and some people who have ancestry in a First Nation but are not eligible to be registered as "Indians" (perhaps because an ancestor lost Indian status), and it includes some people without any First Nation ancestry (because of marriage before 1985 to an Indian man).

Certain other related terms appear frequently in this area of law. A "band" is defined in the *Indian Act* as "a body of Indians" for whose use and benefit in common lands have been set apart, for whose use and benefit in common moneys are held by the federal government, or who the federal government declares to be a band. In the last thirty or so years, the term "First Nation" has come into general use to replace "band" and has been used in recent legislation. Tom Flanagan maintains that this change was politically driven, given the implicit assumptions about sovereignty and nationhood in a phrase that includes the word "nation," and has helped achieve political victories.[49] Since the reform of the Constitution in 1982 and the addition of Section 35 recognizing and affirming existing Aboriginal and treaty rights, the term "Aboriginal" has been generally used to refer to the "Indian," Inuit, and Métis peoples. However, the term "Indigenous" has been used interchangeably with "Aboriginal" and is becoming more common. For example, the Department of Aboriginal and Northern Affairs Canada (formerly the Department of Indian Affairs) changed its name to Indigenous and Northern Affairs Canada in November 2015.[50] I use "Aboriginal law" to refer to the general law of Canada as it applies to the Aboriginal peoples of Canada and "Indigenous law" to refer to the law of a particular Aboriginal group developed within and applying to that group.

In practice, any attempt to distinguish between Aboriginal and non-Aboriginal individuals is complicated by the fact that many, if not most, Aboriginal people have some non-Aboriginal ancestry. This may be a difficult matter, as witnessed by the recent controversy over the entitlement of Joseph Boyden, a prominent writer on Aboriginal issues, to be considered Aboriginal.[51] Further, the cultural practices and day-to-day lives of Aboriginal peoples have been greatly influenced, and to some extent replaced, by those of the approximately 95 percent of Canadians who do not identify as Aboriginal in census responses. The SCC has observed that "Mixed identity is a recurrent theme in Canada's ongoing exercise of achieving reconciliation between its Aboriginal peoples and the broader population ... Yet lines must be drawn" to distinguish different groups for some legal purposes.[52] The Royal Commission on Aboriginal Peoples considered this issue in its 1996 report, and the conclusion was that Aboriginal peoples are not racial groups; rather, they are organic political and cultural entities: "Although contemporary Aboriginal groups stem historically from the original peoples of North America, they often have mixed genetic heritages and include individuals of varied ancestry. As organic political entities, they have the capacity to evolve over time and change in their internal composition."[53] The commission was, therefore, of the view that for a group to qualify as Aboriginal, it did not have to be composed of individuals with a certain quantum of Aboriginal blood.

In contrast, "blood quantum," or a specified degree of ancestry from an ancestral group, is a common requirement for membership in US tribes. Some call for a minimum of one-fourth degree of ancestry in the tribe, but others require as much as one-half.[54] Also, US law permits the right of entry into the United States of "American Indians born in Canada" if they "possess at least 50 per cent of blood of the American Indian race."[55] Generally, Canadian law does not require a minimum "blood quantum," although there have been exceptions. Early versions of the *Indian Act* referred to those "of Indian blood." In one case, Justice Wilson of the SCC described a former provision of the *Indian Act* as being "designed to impose a restriction on the dilution of Indian blood by excluding from Indian status the offspring of two generations of mixed parentage."[56] At times, the law has defined "Indians" as including those who "follow the Indian mode of life," but this was dropped in the 1951 *Indian Act*.

For practical purposes, Aboriginal peoples may generally be regarded as groups descended from those groups living in what is now Canada at the time of the arrival of Europeans who have retained some of their own social, economic, cultural, or political institutions.[57] Whether a particular group qualifies will depend on the facts and may be contentious.

What Is the Crown?

In Aboriginal law cases, there are numerous references to the Crown. Judges seem to assume that everyone knows what is meant by this term, implying that the meaning is clear. In fact, it is confusing and somewhat mystical. As one of the leading scholars on constitutional law wrote:

> There is one term against which I wish to warn you, and that term is "the crown." You will certainly read that the crown does this and the crown does that. As a matter of fact we know that the crown does nothing but lie in the Tower of London to be gazed at by sight-seers. No, the crown is a convenient cover for ignorance.[58]

For most people, references to the Crown are likely to conjure up images of the British monarch and perhaps her immediate family. Sometimes Aboriginal people in Canada personalize their relationship with "the Crown," as if it were with the Queen and her family. During the negotiation of historical treaties, there were references to the "Great White Mother," and since then there have been several unsuccessful attempts by Aboriginal groups to present their grievances to the monarch. In the 1980s, some Aboriginal groups went to London to lobby the monarch and British Parliament and to challenge the proposed patriation of the Constitution without adequate protection for Aboriginal and treaty rights. In 2013, Chief Theresa Spence unsuccessfully demanded that the Queen's representative in Canada, the governor general, participate in negotiations to end her hunger strike. In 2016, Aboriginal leaders urged Prince William during his trip to British Columbia to intervene with the Canadian government to address their concerns.[59]

Two points need to be kept in mind:[60]

- "The Crown," for our purposes, is not the monarch (whether of Britain or of Canada) but the relevant government of the day.
- The relevant government is not the British government but either the Canadian federal government or the government of the province.

As to the first point, it has been clear since *Calvin's Case* in 1608 that "the King hath two capacities in him: one a natural body ... the other is a politic body or capacity, so called because it is framed by the policy of man."[61] It is the political body called "the Crown" that concerns us. A broad summary of constitutional developments over the last thousand years was given by the Supreme Court of the United Kingdom in its 2017 ruling on leaving the European Union. The Court noted that "the Crown's administrative powers are now exercised by the executive, i.e., by ministers who are answerable to the U.K. Parliament."[62]

> "The Crown," for our purposes, is not the monarch ... but either the Canadian federal government or the government of the province.

Calvin's Case also made it clear that, in the political sense, there are different Crowns for different countries, including England, Scotland, and now, of course, Canada. Since Canada has a federal system, there are provincial Crowns as well as the central federal Crown. Depending on the context, references to "the Crown" in Canadian Aboriginal law can refer to the federal or provincial governments – specifically the federal or provincial cabinets, made up of representatives of elected politicians from the party that won the most seats in the most recent election, and all those who act under their authority, including the many employees of the federal and provincial governments. As a practical matter, "the Crown" meets daily across the country with representatives of Aboriginal groups, often with relative informality and without a tiara in sight.

As noted above, Section 91(24) of the *Constitution Act, 1867* listed "Indians, and Lands reserved for the Indians" as within federal rather than provincial jurisdiction. However, provincial governments are equally bound by the obligations of the Crown in their dealings with Aboriginal groups so far as Section 35 rights are concerned.[63] A 2014 decision of the SCC has changed the prior law and permits provincial governments to infringe those rights if such infringement can be justified under the *Sparrow* test.[64] Another 2014 decision permits the provinces to "take up" land under some treaties.[65] The law is changing and the role of provinces is becoming greater. There are situations where both federal and provincial governments together owe duties to Aboriginal peoples, such as treaty promises by the Crown.[66] In the case of the Trans Mountain pipeline expansion project, both governments consulted as "the joint Crown" following a court decision that invalidated an attempted delegation of powers by the Province of BC to the federal government.[67]

It is not always easy to determine if a body exercising government powers is "the Crown" that owes duties of the Crown to Aboriginal peoples. There are semi-government bodies running airports or transit systems and performing functions of government that would arguably make them "the Crown" for these purposes, although the semi-government bodies would dispute this. Lower courts have said that local governments, although created by provincial governments, are not part of the Crown. All depends on the particular legal status of the body in question.[68] The SCC has held that actions taken by the Crown through a body such as the National Energy Board are to be considered "Crown actions" subject to duties binding on the Crown.[69]

As we will see, the Crown (i.e., the federal or provincial government or both) is usually on the opposite side to an Aboriginal group, seeking to deny or limit Aboriginal and treaty rights.[70] This is despite an early ruling of the SCC that stated: "The relationship between the Government and aboriginals is trust-like, rather than adversarial."[71] It is a David-and-Goliath struggle with the awesome power of the state against small Aboriginal communities.

Collective versus Individual Rights

It is important to note that Aboriginal law deals mainly, and almost exclusively, with the legal situation of Aboriginal peoples as collectives rather than that of individuals of Aboriginal ancestry. Aboriginal societies are collectivist rather than individualistic,[72] and as the SCC has confirmed repeatedly, Aboriginal and treaty rights, including ownership of land, are held communally rather than by individuals.[73] Indeed, the Court has ruled that land held individually cannot be an Aboriginal interest.[74] The United Nations Declaration on the Rights of Indigenous Peoples recognizes in its recitals that the collective rights of Indigenous peoples are "indispensable for their existence, well-being and integral development as peoples."[75] We shall consider this issue in more detail. For now, it may be noted that, like the ethnic basis for Aboriginal rights, their collective nature is problematic for the prevailing liberal-democratic ideology, with its emphasis on individualism rather than the common good that is the focus of social democracy.[76] From the perspective of Aboriginal peoples, it is said that liberalism, as reflected in the law, fails to respect their autonomy and cultural differences.[77]

Aboriginal and treaty rights, including ownership of land, are held communally rather than by individuals.

Despite this general rule that Aboriginal law deals with collective and not individual rights, individuals with Aboriginal ancestry directly benefit from legislation that has been passed relating to employment and sentencing.[78] Other benefits that apply to individual "Indians" residing on a reserve, as well as to bands, are found in Sections 87 and 89 of the *Indian Act*,[79] which deal with certain exemptions from taxation and seizure of property situated on a reserve. The act also has provisions that permit individuals to have a right of possession to reserve lands and that regulate the making of wills and what happens if no will has been made ("intestacy"). Other provisions give the minister of Indigenous affairs the power to deal with the property of "Indians" who lack capacity to manage their property and the property of the children of "Indians." The *Family Homes on Reserve Act* deals with what happens to reserve lands on a breakdown of marriage.[80]

This book deals largely with SCC decisions and doesn't attempt to cover lower court decisions, but a decision of the British Columbia Supreme Court is of interest in the context of a consideration of collective and individual rights. *Thomas v. Norris* involved the Coast Salish practice of initiating members in spirit dancing. The plaintiff claimed he was seized for dancing, confined in a Long House without food and with limited water, forced to bathe in a creek, and whipped with cedar branches.[81] The judge said he found it difficult to accept the argument that, in the contest between alleged collective cultural rights and the rights of the plaintiff, the plaintiff's individual rights should give way to the communal rights. "He cannot be coerced or forced to participate ... by any group purporting to exercise their collective rights in doing so. His freedoms and rights are not 'subject to the collective rights of the aboriginal nation to which he belongs.'"[82]

Section 25 of the *Constitution Act, 1982* states that nothing in the Charter of Rights and Freedoms (which protects individual rights) is to be construed as taking away from ("abrogate or derogate") any Aboriginal, treaty, or other rights or freedoms of Aboriginal peoples. This provision is potentially very relevant to the topic of collective versus individual rights and favours the former. However, it has not yet been the subject of much clarification by the courts.[83]

Development of Aboriginal Law

Aboriginal people have opposed colonization and defended their rights from the time of the assertion of British sovereignty. However, this opposition took place mostly in the political arena with petitions to government, meetings with representatives of the British monarch, and delegations to parliamentary committees. Their main allies were missionaries and anthropologists. The results were disappointing. Legal proceedings were few and far between and equally ineffective. One of the earliest legal cases, involving the Mohegan Indians of Connecticut, began in 1704 and ended in 1773 with a decision of the Privy Council in London. Scholars still debate the correct legal interpretation of these protracted and complex proceedings. Some more recent decisions of the nineteenth century were essentially disputes between the federal and provincial governments about which level of government would get title to Aboriginal lands once the Aboriginal interest in them ended. The Aboriginal group was not represented.

However, since the SCC's *Calder* decision in 1973, on the Nisga'a's claim of Aboriginal title, there has been an explosion in the development of Aboriginal law. In 1966, the Hawthorn Report referred to "the comparative paucity of cases" and the lack of interest of legal scholars in the topic.[84] A pioneering book, *Native Rights in Canada,* published in 1970, summarized the situation: "Indians have, generally speaking, not gone to court to test or enforce their rights. Unfortunately, this has meant that their legal rights and aboriginal claims are very poorly defined in our law. Being poorly defined they could easily be disregarded by the government."[85] The second edition of that book, published in 1972, stated that it was "within the prerogative of Government to reject aboriginal and treaty rights" and that "the legal authority dealing with aboriginal rights is not readily found in Canadian case law ... we have only limited precedents on the question of the content of an aboriginal claim and on the rules respecting extinguishment and compensation."[86] The SCC observed, "By the late 1960s, aboriginal claims were not even recognized by the federal government as having any legal status."[87] Lawyers knew little or nothing about Aboriginal law. Aboriginal rights were not taught at law school.[88] *Calder* was a turning point.

In 1982, Section 35 of the *Constitution Act,* recognizing Aboriginal and treaty rights, was passed. Two years later, the Musqueam were successful in persuading the SCC that the federal government had a legal obligation to act in their best interests (a "fiduciary duty") and that it was not merely a political obligation unenforceable in the courts. The realization that they could seek legal remedies and were not dependent on the whim of politicians and government officials opened up new possibilities for Aboriginal people. Other key developments included a 1990 decision of the Court, also involving the Musqueam, which interpreted Section 35 for the first time.

These "breakthrough cases"[89] were followed by other cases that clarified the meaning of the section; the proof of Aboriginal rights, Aboriginal title, and treaty rights; the honour of the Crown principle; the duty to consult; and the legal situation of Métis people. The approximately one hundred decisions of the SCC which form the basis of this book have been supplemented by thousands of decisions of other courts.

This case law has been examined in and influenced by numerous articles and books on aspects of Aboriginal law. The SCC has relied to an unusual extent on the opinion of legal scholars, who have made significant contributions to the development of the law. In part, they looked back at other areas of the law – such as old English property law, imperial laws, and ancient cases – to point a way forward for Aboriginal rights and title.[90] Using this research, they developed innovative arguments to persuade courts to advance the law in directions they thought favourable. One commentator has observed, "The contemporary role of legal scholarship in ... seeking to put law at the service of Aboriginal aspirations can scarcely be exaggerated."[91] In recent years, legal scholars with Aboriginal ancestry have been both prominent and provocative.

Thomas Berger has summed up the current situation: "Today, the law schools teach Aboriginal rights. There is a thriving Aboriginal rights bar – many of whose members belong to First Nations – and major law firms advertise the fact that they employ specialists in Aboriginal rights."[92] It has been estimated that the number of Aboriginal lawyers grew from about six in 1973 to over a thousand in 2010.[93] In addition to specialist courses on Aboriginal rights, the subject is now increasingly recognized as a foundation course for all Canadian law students. One of the recommendations of the recent report of the Truth and Reconciliation Commission is that all law students and lawyers, as well as government officials and journalists, become familiar with this area of the law.

Objectives of Aboriginal Law

Aboriginal law has four main objectives:

- justice for Aboriginal people
- providing a peaceful solution to historical grievances
- recognition of Indigenous laws
- reconciliation.

Application of these objectives depends mainly on the views of the judges deciding cases, since this is largely a judge-made area of law.

Justice for Aboriginal people. A desire for justice is the motive of Aboriginal people and most lawyers acting for them. As noted by the SCC, "What is at stake is nothing less than justice for the Aboriginal group and its descendants."[94] The Court has recognized that the history of colonialism, displacement, and residential schools continues to translate into social problems that have been allowed to fester for too long.[95] As noted in another recent decision: "As the curtain opens wider and wider on the history of Canada's relationship with its Indigenous peoples, inequities are increasingly revealed and remedies urgently sought."[96] Law is seen as one way to partially address the historical injustices suffered by Aboriginal peoples. In particular, their dispossession, and the economic and social inequalities between Aboriginal and non-Aboriginal Canadians,[97] may be partially overcome by recognizing Aboriginal Canadians' ownership of land and other assets, and by giving them a greater say in what happens within their traditional territories.

> Law is seen as one way to partially address the historical injustices suffered by Aboriginal peoples ... their dispossession, and the economic and social inequalities between Aboriginal and non-Aboriginal Canadians.

Providing a peaceful solution to historical grievances. Peaceful solutions to historical grievances contribute to a more peaceful society, which minimizes the violent confrontation that has been an occasional feature of recent history. In a revealing comment, Michael Ignatieff, the former leader of the Liberal Party of Canada, wrote, "Federal and provincial review panels may approve pipelines and mines, but companies know that lines can be cut and shaft-digging stopped if Aboriginal resistance is sufficiently determined. The companies have the watches but Aboriginal peoples have the time."[98]

Recognition of Indigenous laws. Recognizing Indigenous laws is an example of the doctrine of continuity, a legal principle long applied by British imperial law and followed in Canada.[99] It means that the laws in effect in a new British colony are to be respected and continue to apply unless and until they were replaced by the imperial or colonial governments. Therefore, the Indigenous laws of the Aboriginal peoples of Canada should continue to be recognized by the Canadian law in the absence of contrary laws of the new governments.

Reconciliation. Reconciliation has been described by the SCC as "the fundamental objective,"[100] and "the grand purpose,"[101] of modern Aboriginal law. Chief Justice McLachlin listed it as one of five "constitutional moments" that have shaped what Canada is today.[102] The term has been used in three different, although related, senses. The first use was the reconciliation of the power of the federal government to limit Aboriginal rights with the duty to recognize them. In the view of the Court, "the best way to achieve that reconciliation is to demand the justification of any government regulation that infringes upon or denies aboriginal rights."[103] A few years later, the Court adopted a different and somewhat inconsistent approach to reconciliation, which it now described as "the reconciliation of the pre-existence of aboriginal societies with the sovereignty of the Crown."[104] Unlike the first use of "reconciliation," this use has been repeated many times subsequently. In effect, it upholds the paramount power of the Canadian state over any competing claim that an Aboriginal group may have to continued sovereignty. It might be seen as completing the process of legitimizing colonialism. Reconciliation in this sense has been rejected by many Aboriginal people.[105] John Borrows, a prominent Aboriginal law professor, describes reconciliation as "a flawed metaphor" that has problematically dominated the jurisprudence.[106] He warns that "any compromise with colonialism causes us to be compromised by colonialism."

A third and now more common use of "reconciliation" balances Aboriginal and treaty rights with the interests of non-Aboriginal people. Different decisions have expressed the entities being reconciled in different ways:

- "aboriginal societies with the rest of Canadian society"[107]
- "aboriginal and European perspectives"[108]
- "Aboriginal interests and the interests of the broader community"[109]
- "aboriginal peoples and non-aboriginal peoples and their respective claims, interests and ambitions"[110]
- "aboriginal entitlements with the interests of all Canadians"[111]
- "Aboriginal and non-Aboriginal Canadians"[112]
- "Aboriginal and non-Aboriginal communities"[113]
- "Aboriginal peoples and the broader population"[114]
- "the [Aboriginal] group and the broader society"[115]
- "Aboriginal rights with the interests of all Canadians."[116]

The flexible concept of reconciliation has often been used in court decisions, especially those permitting the infringement of established Aboriginal rights in the interests of the broader society. But should the courts be conducting the essentially political act of limiting Aboriginal rights for the perceived benefit of the broader society when Aboriginal peoples lack meaningful participation in that process? The SCC has stressed that reconciliation is an ongoing process,[117] which, for example, includes both treaty making and the implementation of treaties.[118] It noted in one case that "[r]econciliation in the Yukon, as elsewhere, is not an accomplished fact. It is a work in progress."[119]

Sources of Aboriginal Law

There are several sources of Aboriginal law:

- historical practice, both before and after contact
- Indigenous law
- the Canadian Constitution and statutes
- judicial law making
- imperial law
- international law
- law in other jurisdictions.

Historical practice, both before and after contact. To understand the current law, it is necessary to have some understanding of Aboriginal societies pre-contact as well as the post-contact historical background, which goes back as far as 1550 in Newfoundland and for centuries in all parts of Canada and will be explored further in the next chapter. As noted above, Aboriginal rights are essentially rights retained from pre-contact times. Proving Aboriginal rights requires proof of practices at the time of first contact (or at the time of effective control by the British in the case of Métis people), and proving Aboriginal title requires proof of exclusive occupation at the time of assertion of British sovereignty. Sometimes courts are called upon to interpret ancient treaties. The next chapter provides a very broad overview of the relevant history and especially developments that have influenced modern Canadian Aboriginal law. The basic issues of Aboriginal law have not changed greatly over the years. They remain the nature and extent of Aboriginal property rights and the question of who has jurisdiction to decide what may happen in traditional territories.

Indigenous law. The law of Aboriginal rights has been described as "intersocietal law" resulting from both the common law brought by the British settlers and the Indigenous laws of the Aboriginal peoples.[120] In my view, this greatly overstates the Canadian courts' recognition of Indigenous law. However, it is correct to say that there has been some recognition

Aboriginal Peoples and the Law

and much work done, especially by Aboriginal legal scholars, to increase that recognition.

The Canadian Constitution and statutes. Section 35 of the Canadian *Constitution Act, 1982,* which recognizes and affirms existing Aboriginal and treaty rights, plays a central role in modern Aboriginal law. This vague provision had a difficult birth, and it is unlikely that any of the politicians who were involved had any idea what they were approving. Section 35 forms part of the Constitution and "applies to both provinces and the federal government."[121] Section 52 of the *Constitution Act, 1982* states that the Constitution "is the supreme law of Canada, and any law that is inconsistent with the provisions of the Constitution is, to the extent of the inconsistency, of no force and effect." The words "any law" include federal and provincial statutes as well as judge-made law. The SCC stated in *Manitoba Métis,* "The Constitution is not a mere statute; it is the very document by which the Crown asserted its sovereignty in the face of prior Aboriginal occupation."[122] The same judgment also stressed the role of the courts in upholding the Constitution against inconsistent laws: "The courts are the guardians of the Constitution and ... cannot be barred by mere statutes from issuing a declaration on a fundamental constitutional matter. The principles of legality, constitutionality and the rule of law demand no less."[123] The Constitution can be amended, so Section 35 could be repealed or modified. However, under Section 38, constitutional amendment requires the consent of the Senate, the House of Commons, and the legislative assemblies of at least two-thirds of the provinces that have at least 50 percent of the population of Canada as a whole, which sets the bar for amendment pretty high.

In addition to constitutionally protected Aboriginal and treaty rights, an Aboriginal group or individual may have rights under legislation, such as exemption from taxation or seizure of property situated on a reserve under Sections 87 to 90 of the *Indian Act.* The *Indian Act* and its predecessor legislation have been a major part of Aboriginal law for over 150 years. More recent legislation has been passed that applies only to First Nations that wish to adopt its provisions – for example, the *First Nations Land Management Act,*[124] which governs management of reserve lands, and the *First Nations Elections Act.*[125] These provisions do not qualify as constitutionally protected Aboriginal or treaty rights and may be withdrawn or modified by the federal government at will. They are examples of delegated powers.

Since "Indians, and Lands reserved for Indians" are matters of federal and not provincial jurisdiction under Section 91(24) of the *Constitution Act, 1867,* most specifically applicable legislation will be federal rather than provincial. However, this is a confusing and confused area of the law, and many provincial laws will validly apply to Aboriginal peoples.

Judicial law making. There is much debate about the proper role of the courts and whether judges should make law or simply apply it. There is little doubt that judges do make law and do not simply declare it as if it had always existed, waiting to be discovered.[126] This role has increased. In the words of Chief Justice McLachlin of the SCC, "Courts are playing a more important role in governance and playing it more openly than ever before,"[127] and "Judicial lawmaking ... is invading the domain of social policy once perceived as the exclusive right of Parliament and the legislatures."[128] Judges are especially activist in the area of Aboriginal law. There has been almost no guidance from politicians on Section 35 to clarify the content of existing Aboriginal and treaty rights and how they are to be recognized and affirmed. Constitutional conferences intended to provide this guidance resulted in failure. By default, the SCC has given meaning to the section and developed related areas of the law, including Aboriginal title and the duty to consult in the case of as-yet-unproven rights. It has done so without prior authority, plucking important concepts (e.g., the inherent limit to Aboriginal title) out of the air or from the opinion of legal scholars. It has also effectively rewritten the Constitution to place limits on Aboriginal and treaty rights.[129] Judicial law making requires political decisions to be made, which is cause for concern, especially given the lack of Aboriginal participation in that process.

> Judges are especially activist in the area of Aboriginal law.

One important aspect of judge-made law is that it is retroactive. The philosopher Jeremy Bentham said that it was like training your dog – you wait for him to do something you don't approve of, and then you beat him for it.[130] Legislation is usually only applicable to future events. In contrast, judicial decisions are made today but deal with events that have occurred in the past – perhaps centuries ago in the case of Aboriginal law, such as entering into historical treaties. When judges make law, their decisions give rise to complaints that they are applying current values and new law to events that took place at a completely different time. A lively academic debate has been taking place on this issue.[131]

A brief word is in order about the SCC.[132] It has been the final court of appeal for Canada since appeals to the Privy Council in London were terminated in 1949. There are nine judges representing the different regions, appointed by the prime minister with little external input or review beyond (in some cases only) a token appearance before parliamentary committees without a vote. Most of the current judges were appointed by Conservative prime minister Stephen Harper and, given their relative youth and a mandatory retirement age of seventy-five, they will be in the majority for many years. A review in 2011 revealed broad legal education but limited social experience outside of law. There was nothing to indicate any experience with Aboriginal people or special expertise in Aboriginal law.[133] Justice Rowe, appointed in 2016, was the first candidate for nomination to the Court to complete and have published a detailed questionnaire, and this document indicated little experience in Aboriginal matters beyond sentencing Aboriginal offenders. However, although not Aboriginal, the second appointee of the Liberal government, Justice Martin, who was appointed in 2017, worked for the Assembly of First Nations on the residential schools settlement and became "immersed in learning and teaching about the Gladue principles in sentencing [of Aboriginal offenders], and ... read the Royal Commission on Aboriginal Peoples and the Truth and Reconciliation Committee Report."[134] Reflecting on the origin of Canada's legal system in the common law from England and the civil law from France, she noted, "[T]here is also a modern movement to go beyond a binary understanding of our nation's history and to incorporate Indigenous perspectives, laws, practices and customs into Canadian jurisprudence." There have been no SCC judges with Aboriginal ancestry despite many recommendations that such an appointment be made, especially given the role of the Court in developing Aboriginal law.

The general role of the Court was summarized by Justice Rowe in his questionnaire:

> The Supreme Court is not, primarily, a court of correction. Rather, the role of the Court is to make definitive statements of the law which are then applied by trial judges and courts of appeal. Through the leave to appeal process, the Court chooses areas of the law in which it wishes to make a definitive statement. Thus, the Supreme Court judges ordinarily make law, rather than simply applying it. The Court deals more with constitutional, public law and criminal matters, as well as aboriginal and treaty rights and less with private law.[135]

Justice Rowe makes it clear that, in his view, the Court's role is ordinarily to make law rather than simply apply it. This is refreshing honesty. Too often the Court gives the appearance that it merely applies existing law. As one critic has said, the Court sometimes writes as if the law "is what it is" without acknowledging that it has created it.[136] Appeals to the Court are not usually automatic; leave to appeal is required from the Court and is given in only about 10 percent of cases. In this way, the Court can decide what cases to hear and in what areas it wishes to make law.

Generally speaking, the Court will follow its earlier decisions (the doctrine of precedent or *stare decisis*) and will not lightly depart from them. But the Court has overruled some earlier judgments "based on compelling reasons" after conducting "a balancing exercise between the two important values of correctness and certainty."[137] In 2014, the Court reversed a 2006 decision in Aboriginal law.[138] In the same case, the Court effectively reversed another decision, decided in 2005, without acknowledging that it was doing so.[139] Lower courts are bound by decisions of higher courts, although the SCC has recognized two exceptions: "(1) where a new legal issue is raised; and (2) where there is a change in the circumstances or evidence that 'fundamentally shifts the parameters of the debate.'"[140] Although comments of the Court unnecessary to the actual decision (*obiter dicta*) are not strictly binding, it is a brave lawyer or lower court that does not treat them as authoritative.[141]

Imperial law. "Imperial law" refers to the law that previously applied to British colonies, including the doctrine of continuity mentioned above and the Royal Proclamation of 1763. Imperial law applied automatically to each colony when it was acquired, without regard to the prior law that may have applied, whether that was Indigenous law or the law of a prior colonial authority. Therefore, it applied to parts of Canada previously under French control, such as Quebec. This was made clear in the *Côté* case:

> The doctrine of aboriginal rights applied, then, to every British colony
> that now forms part of Canada, from Newfoundland to British Columbia.
> Although the doctrine was a species of unwritten British law, it was not a
> part of English common law in the narrow sense, and its application to a
> colony did not depend on whether or not English common law was
> introduced there.[142]

The Court rejected the contrary view as it "would create an awkward patchwork of constitutional protection for aboriginal rights across the nation, depending upon the historical idiosyncrasies of colonization over particular regions of the country."[143] Today, this former imperial law is part of what is referred to as "federal common law."[144]

International law. International law refers to the laws among nations and includes treaties with other nations, international conventions such as

Aboriginal Peoples and the Law

the International Covenant on Civil and Political Rights, and declarations such as the United Nations Declaration on the Rights of Indigenous Peoples. We shall consider relevant aspects of international law in Chapter 7. To date, international law has played only a marginal role in Aboriginal law, but this will change dramatically if the declaration is implemented in Canada as it is written.

Law in other jurisdictions. In early cases, the SCC relied somewhat on cases from the United States, especially the decisions of Justice Marshall of the United States Supreme Court of the 1820s and 1830s, which established the foundation of US Indian law. Cases from Australia and New Zealand are also relevant. Canadian Aboriginal law is now significantly different from that of those jurisdictions, and there are fewer references to their laws. English law is relevant in providing fundamental principles, such as trust principles, that have been adopted by Canadian courts.

TO SUM UP

- The source of Aboriginal peoples' special status lies in the fact that they never immigrated to Canada or relinquished their claim to be treated as special distinct peoples.

- Special rights for Aboriginal peoples raise the question of race-based discrimination.

- Special rights are rights that pre-existed colonialism and are not rights conferred by non-Aboriginal governments.

- The role of the colonial and Canadian legal system has been to support the colonization of Canada, including the dispossession of Aboriginal peoples and the disruption of their governments and legal systems.

- The dominant justification for the dispossession was that Aboriginal peoples were not using the land sufficiently. This justification continues today in the ability of governments to infringe Aboriginal and treaty rights to benefit non-Aboriginal people.

- Aboriginal law and the special rights of Aboriginal peoples are about the continuing impacts of colonialism.

- The legal definitions of Aboriginal peoples are inconsistent and confusing but important since they determine which Aboriginal groups enjoy special rights.

- For practical purposes, Aboriginal peoples consist of those groups descended from groups living in what is now Canada at the time of the arrival of Europeans.

- Federal and provincial governments usually represent non-Aboriginal peoples in legal disputes with Aboriginal groups and are referred to as "the Crown."

- The federal government has the primary jurisdiction over "Indians, and Lands reserved for the Indians," but the power of the provinces is increasing greatly.

- Aboriginal law deals mainly with the legal situation of Aboriginal peoples as collectives and not that of individuals. Aboriginal and treaty rights are communal and not private rights.
- Aboriginal law has developed explosively over the last forty years or so.
- The objectives of Aboriginal law include a peaceful solution to historical grievances, the recognition of Indigenous laws developed by Aboriginal groups outside the Canadian legal system, and reconciliation.
- Reconciliation has been described by the Supreme Court of Canada as the fundamental objective of modern Aboriginal law. It is defined in different ways but mainly to balance Aboriginal and treaty rights with the interests of non-Aboriginal people.
- There are several sources of Aboriginal law, including the prior occupation of Canada by Aboriginal groups; the relationship between those groups and non-Aboriginal governments; the Canadian Constitution; and judge-made law.
- Aboriginal and treaty rights have received constitutional protection since 1982 under Section 35 of the *Constitution Act, 1982*.
- Judge-made law is the primary source of Aboriginal law.
- It's impossible to understand Aboriginal law without understanding the history of colonialism in Canada.

Historical Background

2

An appreciation of history is of critical importance to understanding modern Aboriginal law. It is necessary to be familiar with developments, legal and non-legal, that may date back centuries.[1] In considering this history, it is worth bearing in mind the acidic but accurate comment by Aboriginal author Thomas King: "Native history in North America as writ has never really been about Native people. It's been about Whites and their needs and desires. What Native peoples wanted has never been a vital concern, has never been a political or social priority ... What do Whites want? ... Whites want land."[2]

The Four Main Stages of Canadian History

The Royal Commission on Aboriginal Peoples listed four stages of Canadian history: separate worlds; contact and co-operation; displacement and assimilation; negotiation and renewal.

The Royal Commission on Aboriginal Peoples (RCAP), which reported in 1996, divided the history of Canada into four main stages, and these stages overlapped and occurred at different times in different regions.[3]

The first stage of Canadian history, according to RCAP, was the era of separate worlds, which lasted until approximately 1500. Aboriginal and non-Aboriginal societies developed in isolation in the Americas and Europe: "On both sides of the Atlantic ... national groups with long traditions of government emerged, organizing themselves into different social and political forms according to their traditions and the needs imposed by their environments."[4]

The next stage, contact and co-operation, was a period when Aboriginal people provided assistance to the newcomers to help them survive in the unfamiliar environment. This stage also saw the establishment of trading and military alliances, as well as intermarriage and mutual cultural adaptation. There were some conflicts, an increase of the non-Aboriginal population, and a steep decrease in the Aboriginal population as people died from diseases to which they had no natural immunity. "Although there were exceptions, there were many instances of mutual tolerance and respect during this long period that lasted until the late eighteenth and early nineteenth centuries."[5] The social, cultural, and political differences between the two societies were largely respected: "Each was regarded as distinct and autonomous, left to govern its own internal affairs but co-operating in areas of mutual interest, and occasionally and increasingly linked in various trading relationships and other forms of nation-to-nation alliances."[6]

During the third stage, displacement and assimilation, non-Aboriginal society was for the most part no longer willing to respect the distinctiveness of Aboriginal societies and made repeated attempts to assimilate them into the mainstream society. Aboriginal populations were relocated to Indian reserves, children were taken from their families and placed in residential schools, and some Aboriginal cultural practices were banned. "Non-Aboriginal society made repeated attempts to recast Aboriginal people and their distinctive forms of social organization so they would conform to the expectations of what had become the mainstream."[7] This period lasted until the 1969 White Paper.

In 1887, the prime minister, Sir John A. Macdonald, said, "The great aim of our civilization has been to do away with the tribal system and assimilate the Indian people in all respects with the inhabitants of the Dominion, as speedily as they are fit for the change."[8] In 1920, the deputy superintendent of Indian Affairs, Duncan Campbell Scott, told a parliamentary committee, "I want to get rid of the Indian problem ... Our objective is to continue until there is not a single Indian in Canada that has not been absorbed into the body politic and there is no Indian question."[9] This philosophy of forced assimilation (or "cultural genocide," to quote a former chief justice of Canada) was accompanied by a belief that Aboriginal people would largely die out as separate peoples.[10] In the words of one of Canada's leading anthropologists, writing of West Coast Aboriginal peoples in 1935: "Socially, they are outcasts, economically they are inefficient and an encumbrance. Their old world has fallen into ruins, and helpless in the face of a catastrophe they cannot understand, they vainly seek refuge in its shattered foundations. The end of this century, it seems safe to predict will see very few survivors."[11] The prevailing attitude toward Aboriginal title was reflected by the famous humorist and political scientist Stephen Leacock, who wrote in 1941,

> We think of prehistoric North America as inhabited by the Indians, and
> have based on this a sort of recognition of ownership on their part. But
> this attitude is hardly warranted. The Indians were too few to count.
> Their use of the resources of the continent was scarcely more than that
> by crows and wolves, their development of it nothing.[12]

RCAP named the last of the four stages negotiation and renewal. This is the current period and, in the view of the commission, "is characterized by non-Aboriginal society's admission of the manifest failure of its interventionist and assimilationist approach ... From the perspective of Aboriginal groups, the primary objective is to gain more control over their own affairs by reducing unilateral interventions by non-Aboriginal society and regaining a relationship of mutual recognition and respect for differences."[13]

Contact and Co-operation

Four key events affected Aboriginal law during the first stage:

- treaties of peace and friendship
- the Mohegan Indians case, 1704–73
- the Royal Proclamation of 1763
- the Marshall decisions.

Treaties of peace and friendship. In the complicated relationship between Aboriginal groups and the French, Dutch, American, and English settlers, there were military episodes followed by ceasefire agreements and treaties designed to either neutralize Aboriginal people or gain their military support. The English text of the treaties sometimes acknowledged that the Aboriginal group had agreed that they were subjects of the Crown. However, the treaties did not purport to transfer any land, although they may have recognized possession of land. With the odd exception of a treaty subsequently being replaced or extinguished prior to 1982, these ancient treaties are still legally valid and enjoy constitutional protection under Section 35 of the *Constitution Act, 1982.* For example, a treaty of 1760 with the Mi'kmaq of the Maritime provinces has been the subject of two recent SCC decisions.[14]

One important alliance, concluded in 1613 between the Iroquois and the Dutch, and later assumed by the English, is known as the covenant chain. It was recorded in the two-row wampum (beads) belt, which symbolized the separate and equal nature of the relationship, which was aimed at peaceful co-existence and co-operation and is still referenced in discussions about Aboriginal sovereignty.[15] In one case, the Ontario Court of Appeal held that the covenant chain and the Treaty of Niagara, discussed below, were too general to support a claim of virtually unlimited self-government.[16]

> One important alliance, concluded in 1613 between the Iroquois and the Dutch, and later assumed by the English, is known as the covenant chain. It was recorded in the two-row wampum (beads) belt, which symbolized the separate and equal nature of the relationship.

The Mohegan Indians case, 1704–73.[17] This complex and protracted litigation from Connecticut was an early example of an Aboriginal group going to court to have its rights recognized. In 1640, the Mohegans transferred their lands to English settlers except for a portion reserved for them, which was subsequently transferred to an English official to be held in trust for them. The official then transferred those reserved lands to the colony on the basis that sufficient land for the Mohegans would be left after settlement. The Mohegans challenged this last transfer in a petition to the Crown in 1704 on the grounds that they had not been party to it. The dispute was not settled until 1773, when a decision was made in favour of the colony. The court decided that the transfer was valid. The proceedings were complex as well as protracted, and scholars still argue over the decision. The consensus seems to be that the litigation confirmed that, under imperial law, Indigenous laws (including those relating to government) continued to apply in the absence of relevant colonial laws. What is disputed is whether the Privy Council, the final court of appeal, upheld a ruling that the Mohegans retained their status as sovereign and that a third-party court should determine the outcome.

The Royal Proclamation of 1763. This proclamation is a key development in the history of Aboriginal law, and although it has been overtaken in more recent years by other developments, it is still relevant and relied upon as confirming the basic principles that the law recognizes Aboriginal rights and title and that only the Crown can purchase Aboriginal land, usually through a treaty. The proclamation has been called the "Indian Bill of Rights"[18] and is referenced in the Canadian Constitution. It was much discussed in the *Calder* case, the pioneer Canadian decision on Aboriginal title, in which the SCC split evenly on whether the proclamation applied to British Columbia. In that case, Justice Hall described it as "a fundamental document upon which any just determination of original rights rests."[19] In another case, the Court noted that the objective of the proclamation "was to find a solution to the problems created by the greed which hitherto some of the English had all too often demonstrated in buying up Indian land at low prices. The situation was causing dangerous trouble among the Indians."[20] It prohibited settlement in areas not yet settled by non-Aboriginal people and reserved those areas for "the several Nations or Tribes of Indians ... as their Hunting Grounds" until they were willing to agree to dispose of them to the Crown at a public meeting. Other people in those areas were required "forthwith to remove themselves." The prohibition failed in practice and was one factor leading to the American Revolution. Prior to the revolution, George Washington is said to have surreptitiously marked out land in breach of the prohibition, after dismissing the proclamation as "a temporary expedient to quiet the minds of the Indians."[21] At one time the proclamation was considered the source of Aboriginal rights,[22] but this is no longer the case as the courts now acknowledge that, except for the Métis, these rights are based on the pre-existence of Aboriginal peoples in Canada before the arrival of Europeans.[23]

The Royal Proclamation has been described by John Borrows, a prominent Aboriginal law professor, as straddling "the contradictory aspirations of the Crown and First Nations."[24] Although it recognized Aboriginal title and the requirement for Aboriginal consent to transfer land, it also created a process to take land away. Further, it reserved land "under our Sovereignty, Protection and Dominion, for the use of the said Indians," thus asserting British sovereignty. In one case, Justice Binnie commented, "The *Royal Proclamation* of 1763 was not a treaty, of course, but a unilateral declaration of policy by the Imperial Crown."[25] Tom Flanagan calls it "a monument to monarchy and imperialism."[26] Borrows challenges this view by describing the meeting at Niagara the year following the proclamation, attended by some two thousand chiefs invited by the Crown's chief representative. The proclamation was read out, the alliance constituted by the covenant chain was confirmed, and presentations were made of wampum belts and gifts in accordance with Aboriginal custom for treaties. The two-row wampum belt symbolized each party living side by side in peace with separate laws and customs. Borrows states that, in this way, the Royal Proclamation became a treaty, with each party agreeing it would not interfere in the affairs of the other. In his view it is wrong to rely only on the written terms of the proclamation since it does not reflect the agreement of the parties. This discrepancy between the written text and the Aboriginal understanding occurs in other contexts, such as the historical treaties, discussed below, and the Treaty of Waitangi in New Zealand. The Royal Proclamation also influenced the Marshall decisions.

The Marshall decisions. These decisions, given by Chief John Marshall of the Supreme Court of the United States in the 1820s and 1830s, have had a critical importance in the development of the law of that country and, to a lesser extent, the development of Canadian Aboriginal law. According to Thomas Berger, Marshall's "analysis has been the basis for asserting the claims of Native people not only in the United States but also in Canada and most of the countries throughout the world where indigenous peoples claim rights under legal regimes derived from English common law."[27] Marshall's decisions resulted from the determination of President Andrew Jackson and the State of Georgia to force the Cherokee Nation to move off their lands and relocate farther west (which ultimately happened, and the removal is known as the Trail of Tears).

The decisions consider the two main issues in Aboriginal law, which will be explored in more detail in later chapters:

- the remaining sovereignty of Aboriginal groups
- the remaining legal interest enjoyed by such groups in their traditional lands.

For present purposes, the judgments recognize Indian tribes as having a limited form of sovereignty as "domestic dependent nations" (a view not yet adopted in Canada) and that Aboriginal title survived colonization (adopted in Canada). These judgments, which were sympathetic to the Cherokee, created a constitutional crisis and supposedly resulted in the comment, attributed to Jackson, that "John Marshall has made his law; now let him enforce it." This may not be a correct quotation, but it underlines the point that judgments are only valid as far as governments are prepared to respect them or can be made to do so. In practice, government officials are often unwilling to accept duties imposed by the courts, and Aboriginal groups must take the necessary steps to ensure compliance.

Displacement and Assimilation

The following key developments affecting Aboriginal law took place during the displacement and assimilation stage:

- land treaties
- the *Indian Act*
- the *Manitoba Act, 1870*
- the Special Committee of the Senate and House of Commons, 1927
- the Hawthorn Report
- the White Paper.

Land treaties. Starting in the first half of the nineteenth century with treaties in southwestern Ontario and parts of Vancouver Island, followed by the eleven numbered treaties in western Canada from 1871 to 1930, the federal government entered into treaties with Aboriginal groups. These treaties differed significantly from the earlier peace and friendship treaties in eastern Canada because they were clearly intended, at least according to the written English-language versions, to be transfers of vast areas of land (except for small parcels of land, known as "reserves," that were set aside for the Aboriginal groups) in return for nominal payments and other benefits, such as agricultural supplies intended primarily to turn hunters into farmers.

The Indian Act. Commencing in the 1850s, and implementing the Bagot Commission report of 1844, the province of Upper Canada passed the first legislation that would ultimately become known as the *Indian Act*. The first act with that name was passed in 1876, and a consolidation of 1880 remained substantially in place until 1951, when it was replaced by a new act that is still in place subject to various amendments over the years. As amended, the 1880 act banned certain cultural practices such as the potlach. In 1927 a provision was added that made it illegal to raise funds in order to pursue land claims; this was not repealed until 1951. The act has been universally criticized over the last thirty or forty years because it "paternalizes and assimilates Aboriginal peoples and remains the single largest impediment to Aboriginal sovereignty and Aboriginal social and economic development within Canada."[28] However, attempts to repeal it have not been successful.[29] Among other things, the act provides for the registration of Indians, membership in bands, the management of reserve lands and band funds, election of chiefs and band councils, and the delegation of limited municipal-type

Aboriginal Peoples and the Law

powers to chiefs and councils.[30] The minister of Indigenous affairs has powers through the act to make decisions for individuals and bands, although administration is now often delegated. In recent years, other legislation has been passed that enables bands to opt out of some of these provisions and assume responsibility themselves.

One provision of the *Indian Act* had especially tragic effects. It made attendance at residential school mandatory for "Indian" children and imposed penalties on parents who refused to send their children to the schools. The intent of these institutions was to assimilate the children, who were forbidden to speak their languages. The recent report of the Truth and Reconciliation Commission, discussed below, contains a full history and account of the continuing trauma caused by abuses suffered at these schools.[31]

> One provision of the *Indian Act* had especially tragic effects. It made attendance at residential school mandatory for "Indian" children and imposed penalties on parents who refused to send their children to the schools.

Manitoba Act, 1870. This act resulted from the emergence of the Métis people as an Aboriginal people distinct from their Aboriginal and non-Aboriginal ancestors and, specifically, from the founding of the Red River Colony near today's city of Winnipeg. The Métis had been especially active in the fur trade, where they acted as intermediaries and interpreters. Section 31 of the act was aimed at extinguishing Métis Aboriginal rights in exchange for grants of land to Métis children. The difficult history of the implementation of this provision was recently considered by the SCC, which found there had been a breach of the honour of the Crown and issued a declaration to this effect.[32]

Special Committee of the Senate and House of Commons, 1927. In 1927, a committee of the Senate and House of Commons was appointed to look into land claims in British Columbia.[33] Despite all the evidence placed before it to the contrary, the committee found that the province had been acquired by conquest, denied the existence of Aboriginal title, and said that Aboriginal groups had accepted the policy of the government "without demur." The committee claimed that "designing white men" had deceived the Aboriginal groups "to expect benefits from claims more or less fictitious" and concluded that "the matter should now be regarded as finally closed." As noted above, legal restrictions preventing Aboriginal groups from pursuing land claims were introduced the same year to prevent any judicial determination of the validity of such claims.[34]

The Hawthorn Report. In the mid-1960s, the federal government held an inquiry into the socio-economic, political, and constitutional conditions of "Indians."[35] The resulting report broke with the assimilation policy and recommended that "Indians" should be viewed as "citizens plus," meaning they would continue to enjoy treaty and other rights while simultaneously sharing a common citizenship with other Canadians. This view has effectively been adopted by the SCC in its approach to Aboriginal law. Special attention was paid to the situation of urban Aboriginal people, and recommendations were made to support those who chose to leave their reserves to find opportunities elsewhere.

The Hawthorn Report ... recommended that "Indians" should be viewed as "citizens plus," meaning they would continue to enjoy treaty and other rights while simultaneously sharing a common citizenship with other Canadians.

The White Paper. The 1969 *Statement of the Government of Canada on Indian Policy,* popularly known as the White Paper, was issued by the Pierre Trudeau government as part of its "just society" program.[36] It ignored the recommendations of the Hawthorn Report, reasserted the policy of assimilation, and rejected any unique legal status for "Indians," which it saw as the cause of their disadvantaged position. This separate status "and the policies which have flowed from it have kept the Indian people apart from and behind other Canadians," the authors wrote, claiming Aboriginal people had travelled "the road of different status, a road that has led to a blind alley of deprivation and frustration." The White Paper proposed, instead, that they take "the road that would lead gradually away from different status to full social, economic and political participation in Canadian life":

- Indian status would be terminated in order to remove "the legislative and constitutional basis of discrimination."
- Services would "come through the same channels and from the same government agencies" (i.e., provincial agencies rather than the Department of Indian Affairs) as for other Canadians.
- "The control of Indian lands [would] be transferred to Indian people," with the possibility that reserve lands would later be transferred to non-Aboriginal people and the land base would be lost.
- The Department of Indian Affairs would be abolished.
- Section 91(24) of the *British North America Act* (now known as the *Constitution Act, 1867*), which gave the federal government the power

to legislate for "Indians, and Lands reserved for the Indians," would be repealed.

In a speech on August 8, 1969, in Vancouver, the prime minister summarized his government's proposed approach to "the Indian problem":

> So this year we came up with a proposal. It's a policy paper on the Indian problem ... [I]n our policy, the way we propose it, we say we won't recognize aboriginal rights. We will recognize treaty rights ... But aboriginal rights, this really means saying, "We were here before you. You came and you took the land from us and perhaps you cheated us by giving us some worthless things in return for vast expanses of land and we want to re-open this question. We want you to preserve our aboriginal rights and restore them to us." And our answer – it may not be the right one and may not be one which is accepted but it will be up to all of you people to make your minds up and to choose for or against it and to discuss with the Indians – our answer is "no."[37]

The 1969 White Paper rejected any unique legal status for "Indians."

Negotiation and Renewal

The years since 1970 constitute the formative period of modern Canadian Aboriginal law, and several developments have influenced the law:

- increased pressure from Aboriginal people
- the failure of attempts at constitutional reform
- the Royal Commission on Aboriginal Peoples
- the Kelowna Accord/Conservative government
- international developments
- modern treaties
- the Truth and Reconciliation Commission
- election of a Liberal government in 2015
- success in the courts.

Increased pressure from Aboriginal people. The pressure for more self-government powers and greater legal recognition of treaty and Aboriginal rights started as a protest against the White Paper and the federal government's attempt to remove special legal status for "Indian" people. This created momentum for Aboriginal people to seek constitutional protection for an inherent right of self-government and for Aboriginal rights and title. In *The Unjust Society*, a book that received much attention, Harold Cardinal, president of the Indian Association of Alberta, described the White Paper as "a thinly disguised programme of extermination through assimilation" and said that Indian people "will not trust the government with our futures any longer. Now they must listen to and learn from us."[38] The Indian Association of Alberta issued a counter-report, *Citizens Plus,* which became known as the Red Paper. It began: "Under the guise of land ownership, the government has devised a scheme whereby within a generation or shortly after the proposed Indian Lands Act expires our people would be left with no land and consequently the future generations would be condemned to the despair and ugly spectre of urban poverty in ghettos."[39]

Pierre Trudeau had met his match. Rarely has government policy backfired so badly. The White Paper, which was to end the special legal position of Aboriginal peoples and privatize their reserve lands, led, instead, to fundamental changes that have transformed Canadian Aboriginal law and brought constitutional recognition of collective Aboriginal and treaty rights. Trudeau had intended to be the undertaker, preparing emaciated Aboriginal and treaty rights for burial; instead, he became the reluctant midwife of a movement that gave them new life and a vigour they had never possessed.

Aboriginal peoples have had success in using the court system to gain greater recognition of their treaty and Aboriginal rights and a greater say in developments affecting their traditional territories. However, they have been less successful in gaining significantly greater powers of self-government through either the political or judicial process. Early signs of Aboriginal pressure for change were the legal decisions in *Calder* and *Guerin* in 1973 and 1984, which began the move to recognition of Aboriginal title and enforceability of the Crown's obligations to Aboriginal peoples. There was also successful opposition to the proposed hydroelectric and pipeline developments at James Bay and in the Mackenzie Valley in 1975 and 1977. The James Bay dispute was resolved by the first modern treaty. The Mackenzie pipeline was not built following an inquiry led by Thomas Berger.

Most of this pressure has been peaceful, consisting of lobbying, especially through the Assembly of First Nations, and either court proceedings or the exercise of the right of peaceful protest in the form of roadblocks and protest marches. Idle No More, a grassroots movement, has received a great deal of publicity for protests organized throughout Canada, including a hunger

Aboriginal Peoples and the Law

strike in December 2012 and January 2013 by Chief Theresa Spence to protest living conditions on the Attawapiskat reserve, a community that has become a symbol of the plight of many remote Aboriginal communities.[40]

On occasion there have been violent incidents, and it is probably safe to assume that these incidents have contributed to efforts to bring about peaceful methods of dispute resolution, including through judicial activism.[41] A dispute over land grants of 1718 and 1735 had been allowed to fester without resolution at Oka in Quebec. When the local municipality sought to expand a golf course on land claimed by the Mohawk containing a burial site, a violent confrontation erupted that led to the death of a Quebec provincial police officer. The confrontation lasted from July to September 1990 and involved nearly four thousand soldiers with mechanized equipment, armed Mohawk warriors in camouflage with AK47s, and many unarmed civilians. The gravity of the situation was captured in an iconic photograph of a determined Canadian soldier face to face with an equally determined, armed, and masked Mohawk warrior. One of the main bridges leading to Montreal was blockaded, causing chaos. Another death occurred in September 1995 when police shot Dudley George during a protest at Ipperwash Provincial Park in Ontario. The shooting was followed by blockades and protests across the country. Violence also erupted that year near Gustafsen Lake, British Columbia, during a dispute over an eviction notice served to keep protestors away from what was claimed to be a sacred site for a sun dance. Over seventy-thousand rounds of ammunition were fired by the RCMP to end the standoff. The protesters were represented by Bruce Allen Clark, an academically outstanding but controversial lawyer, who was himself jailed for contempt and ultimately disbarred, and who once attempted a citizen's arrest of the judges of the BC Court of Appeal for alleged complicity in genocide.[42] About ten years later, unrest at Caledonia in Ontario to stop a housing development on disputed land involved barricades, burned-out vehicles, blockades of rail lines, and counter-protests by non-Aboriginal residents.

The failure of attempts at constitutional reform. The failure of attempts at constitutional reform was a critical factor behind the modern state of Aboriginal law. The Trudeau government became focused on constitutional reform, especially in response to separatist pressure following the election of the Parti Quebecois in 1976. Negotiations took place with the provinces over issues such as official languages (French and English – not Aboriginal),

> The failure of attempts at constitutional reform was a critical factor behind the modern state of Aboriginal law.

a charter of rights, and an amending formula. According to lawyer Mel Smith, who participated in the constitutional negotiations for British Columbia, "aboriginal rights were not on the agenda."[43] However, from 1980 there was a parallel process being conducted simultaneously by a Special Joint Committee of Parliament. Initially, Aboriginal rights were not on the agenda of that committee either, but the New Democratic Party insisted on inclusion of a provision recognizing and affirming Aboriginal and treaty rights as a condition of their support for the proposed legislation to amend the Constitution. This provision was drafted by lawyers who had been active in representing Aboriginal groups,[44] and it was included in the formal proposal revised in January 1981 by the federal government following lobbying by Aboriginal leaders. This lobbying included the Constitutional Express, the journey of more than one thousand people from Vancouver to Ottawa on two trains organized by the Union of BC Indian Chiefs as a peaceful protest. The proposal contained an agreement to hold a constitutional conference to identify and define Aboriginal rights. However, provincial leaders, opposed to the proposal and the unilateral approach of the federal government, launched a court challenge.

On November 5, 1981, the prime minister and nine of the ten provincial premiers (Quebec was the exception) reached an agreement on the constitutional amendment. However, in a glaring omission or betrayal, the provision dealing with Aboriginal and treaty rights was not included. This led to a vigorous campaign by Aboriginal leaders to have it reinstated. It also led to a speech by Thomas Berger, by now a judge of the BC Supreme Court, criticizing the omission. When the chief justice of Canada and the prime minister publicly rebuked him for speaking out, he was forced to resign as a judge and eventually returned to legal practice in which he remains active at the age of eighty-four.[45] These efforts and sacrifice were successful, and the provision was subsequently restored to the draft constitutional amendment with the addition of the word "existing," so it now read "The existing aboriginal and treaty rights of the Aboriginal peoples of Canada are hereby recognized and affirmed." This is the wording of Section 35(1) of the *Constitution Act, 1982,* proclaimed in force on April 17, 1982.

It should be noted that not all Aboriginal people supported the proposed constitutional amendment. Several First Nation chiefs went to England to express their opposition. They were concerned that it would damage what they regarded as a special relationship with the English queen and that their rights might be taken away by a future Canadian government. Several court cases were unsuccessfully commenced in the English courts, which held that this was an issue to be resolved in Canada.[46]

What is clear is that there was a distinct lack of enthusiasm from the federal and provincial governments to provide constitutional protection for Aboriginal and treaty rights. They were not in the original proposal and were dropped from the November 1981 proposal. It took determined action by Aboriginal organizations and their supporters to get constitutional recognition for those rights. As noted by the SCC, Section 35 represents "the culmination of a long and difficult struggle."[47] What is equally clear is that there was a lack of understanding among politicians about what they were including in the fundamental and paramount law of the country – the Constitution – so far as such rights were concerned. In the words of Mel Smith, who was present during the negotiations, "Sad to say the full import of what they were agreeing to was not even understood much less discussed."[48] One writer who interviewed several participants noted that "elements of the package were not thoroughly discussed, there were few preliminary meetings, and there was little agreement on what the terms of the amendment meant."[49]

The lack of agreement on what the terms of Section 35 meant was understandable. They were so vague as to be almost meaningless. What "existing aboriginal and treaty rights" were being "recognized" and "affirmed"? How would they be determined? Would the same rules apply in each province, even in Quebec, which followed different rules based on French legal principles? Did "existing aboriginal and treaty rights" include Aboriginal title, on which the SCC had split evenly in *Calder*? If so, how was title to be proven, and what was its content? Did Section 35 include an "inherent right to self-government," as claimed by Aboriginal groups? What was the relevant date for determining Aboriginal rights? At the time of first contact? At the time of sovereignty? What about the Métis, who had both Aboriginal and non-Aboriginal ancestry and whose distinctive rights, therefore, could not have arisen until after contact? What did "existing" mean? Did it mean subject to regulations in force on April 17, 1982, the date the provision came into effect? Was it intended to mean "unextinguished"? Did it mean only those Aboriginal and treaty rights that had been upheld as of that date by a court? What about future treaties? Were they not to be protected equally?[50] Could governments still extinguish Aboriginal and treaty rights if their intent was clear? What did "recognize and affirm" mean? What protection did these words provide? In the light of subsequent developments, it is fascinating to read papers written at the time that discussed how Section

35 should be interpreted. Some of those early predictions turned out to be very wrong.[51]

The answers to some of these questions, including identifying and defining Aboriginal rights, were to be decided at a constitutional conference in 1983. This was set out in Section 37 of the 1982 act and became known as the Section 37 process. The first conference resulted in amendments that clarified that "treaty rights" included rights under both existing and future land claims agreements. Also, this conference determined that there had to be representatives of Aboriginal peoples at future conferences before amendments could be made to provisions directly referring to them. However, it became clear at this conference that reaching an agreement was going to be a difficult task, and three more First Ministers' Constitutional Conferences were scheduled, in 1984, 1985, and 1987.[52] The matter that dominated was whether Aboriginal peoples had a right of self-government. This issue then became whether any right of self-government was "inherent," as claimed by Aboriginal groups, or was delegated by, or "contingent on" (i.e., based on agreement with), the federal and provincial governments? Financing was also a major issue. The conferences failed to resolve the identification and definition of Aboriginal rights, including self-government.

Aboriginal anger at the federal and provincial governments' failure to reach an agreement on self-government for Aboriginal peoples (a failure they thought was due to a lack of will) was inflamed by the ease with which those governments agreed in 1987 on the Meech Lake Accord. This accord recognized Quebec's status as "a distinct society." To Aboriginal people, it appeared their concerns were being treated as secondary to those of Quebec.[53] However, they had the final say on the accord through the lone figure of Elijah Harper, a Cree-Ojibway member of the Manitoba legislature. Prime Minister Brian Mulroney had sought to put pressure on the provincial legislatures to approve the accord by effectively imposing a deadline for approval of June 1990. In his words, he had rolled the dice. The prime minister lost the gamble because Elijah Harper, holding an eagle feather in his hand, indicated in a soft voice that he would not give the necessary approval for Manitoba MPs to vote on the accord, time ran out,[54] and the Meech Lake Accord died. Another prime minister had underestimated the resolve of Aboriginal people.

In an attempt to appease Aboriginal people, the next stage in this constitutional saga saw the prime minister, the ten premiers, and national Aboriginal leaders meet to agree on a new constitutional package at Charlottetown in August 1992.[55] This detailed accord had provisions recognizing Quebec's distinct status, but it also proposed amendments to the Constitution that would

- recognize Aboriginal governments as one of the three orders of government, in addition to the federal and provincial governments
- recognize the inherent right of self-government.

The accord also contained provisions that would

- reserve special seats in the Senate for Aboriginal peoples
- negotiate the role of Aboriginal peoples in relation to the SCC
- give consideration to Aboriginal representation in the House of Commons
- include principles relating to interpretation of treaties
- clarify Métis rights
- commit the federal and provincial governments to the principle of providing the governments of Aboriginal peoples with fiscal or other resources, such as land, to help them govern their own affairs
- require future conferences on Aboriginal constitutional matters and require Aboriginal consent for any future amendments directly referring to them.

Aboriginal people went from being shut out of the Meech Lake Accord to having their wish list of constitutional amendments included in the Charlottetown Accord two years later. This shift almost certainly reflected the federal government's desperation to resolve the Quebec issue rather than any genuine desire to improve the situation of Aboriginal peoples. In any event, the new accord was defeated in a national referendum held on October 26, 1992, partly as a result of the opposition of the Native Women's Association of Canada, which was concerned about the accord's impact on equality rights.[56] Also adding his voice to the opposition was former prime minister Pierre Trudeau, who denounced the "vague project about a third order of [Aboriginal] government."[57]

The Charlottetown Accord was effectively the last attempt at constitutional reform, as fatigue had set in across the country. In 1990, shortly after the failure of the Meech Lake Accord, Keith Spicer, former commissioner of official languages, was appointed to chair the Citizens' Forum on National Unity, which would visit communities across the country and listen to

Canadians' thoughts on the future of Canada. Among other things, he reported on "the rage building in aboriginal communities" and the urgency to deal promptly with their needs and aspirations, including territorial and treaty claims; linguistic, cultural, and spiritual needs; and self-government.

The Royal Commission on Aboriginal Peoples summarized these years of attempted constitutional reform, stating that "government policies, attempts at legislative reform, and attempts at constitutional reform have failed." However, Aboriginal peoples and their rights had emerged from the shadows to occupy centre stage. Aboriginal people had "forced their way into the debate on the future of the country. It is hard to imagine that Aboriginal proposals for the future of Canada, including constitutional reform, can be ignored when discussions about the basic values of the country resume."[58] Those discussions have yet to resume.[59]

The one exception to the constitutional failures of the period that did emerge, however reluctantly on the part of the federal and provincial governments, was Section 35 recognizing and affirming existing Aboriginal and treaty rights. The SCC described its importance in its decision regarding Quebec's secession: "The protection of these rights, so recently and arduously achieved, whether looked at in their own right or as part of the larger concern with minorities, reflects an important underlying constitutional value."[60] In another case, the Court said, "The entrenchment of aboriginal ancestral and treaty rights in Section 35(1) has changed the landscape of aboriginal rights in Canada."[61] However, the section was vague and so lacking in content that it was often described as "an empty box," and constitutional conferences failed to fulfil the promise to identify and define Aboriginal rights and answer the many questions listed above. As we shall see throughout this book, it fell to the SCC to do so by default. The Court's success, as well as the limits of law making by judges, will be discussed as we continue our examination of this emerging area of law.

The Royal Commission on Aboriginal Peoples. In the words of the Royal Commission on Aboriginal Peoples, "In response to such events as Kanesatake [the Oka crisis], the failure of the Meech Lake and Section 37 processes, the Spicer commission, and the government of Canada's failure to resolve the growing rift in relations between Aboriginal peoples and the Canadian state, the federal government created this Royal Commission on 26 August 1991."[62] It was charged with finding ways to rebuild the relationship between Aboriginal and non-Aboriginal people in Canada. The commission (widely

Section 35 was vague and so lacking in content that it was often described as "an empty box."

referred to as "RCAP") had four Aboriginal members and three non-Aboriginal members, including a former justice of the SCC, Bertha Wilson. It took five years and 178 days of hearing to produce its massive final report, which was published in 1996 in five volumes and nearly four thousand pages.[63]

The report is encyclopedic in its coverage and includes detailed reviews of different aspects of the history and the contemporary relationship of Aboriginal and non-Aboriginal peoples. It is highly critical of the government's policies concerning Aboriginal peoples: "The main policy direction, pursued for more than 150 years, first by colonial then by Canadian governments, has been wrong."[64] There are 440 recommendations intended to result in a "renewed relationship between Aboriginal and non-Aboriginal people in Canada."[65] The commissioners called for a new Royal Proclamation to acknowledge past injustices, recognize the inherent right of self-government, and establish the renewed relationship. Institutional changes would include legislation setting up treaty commissions, an Aboriginal Lands and Treaty Tribunal, an Aboriginal Nations Recognition Act, and an Aboriginal Peoples

Main Recommendations of the Report of the Royal Commission on Aboriginal Peoples

- 440 recommendations for a "renewed relationship between Aboriginal and non-Aboriginal people in Canada"
- a new Royal Proclamation to acknowledge past injustices, recognize the inherent right of self-government, and establish the renewed relationship
- institutional changes, including legislation to set up treaty commissions, an Aboriginal Lands and Treaty Tribunal, an Aboriginal Nations Recognition Act, and an Aboriginal Peoples Review Commission
- a twenty-year timetable for the creation of the renewed relationship in order to redress economic and welfare inequities and bring about constitutional reform
- constitute existing Aboriginal groups into sixty to eighty new nations and provide them with adequate resources, including external funding and an enlarged land base, to discharge their self-government powers.

Review Commission to monitor progress. The commissioners estimated a twenty-year timetable for the creation of the renewed relationship in order to redress economic and welfare inequities and bring about constitutional reform. In order to be able to discharge their self-government powers, existing Aboriginal groups were to be constituted into about sixty to eighty new nations and provided with adequate resources, including external funding and an enlarged land base. (The discussions and recommendations in the report on specific issues such as Aboriginal sovereignty and treaties will be considered in the parts of this book devoted to those issues.)

The RCAP report has been described as the "most comprehensive and complete study of Aboriginal people, Aboriginal history and Aboriginal policy that has ever been done in North America."[66] It is fair to say that its recommendations reflected the hopes and aspirations of the national leaders of Aboriginal peoples. Critics have attacked it as "a monument to the new [Aboriginal] orthodoxy,"[67] and have challenged the underlying principles.[68] Writing before the publication of the final report, one prominent critic prophesied that the commission's proposals "will almost certainly be accepted by the political leadership in power and their elites as the conventional wisdom accompanied, no doubt, with a compelling urge to put as many of the recommendations into place as possible without counting the cost in dollars or in long-term implications."[69] In fact, as has been observed, "almost as soon as the report was released, it was placed on the shelf with all the rest of the reports from Royal Commissions."[70] Another writer has commented that the report "ran headlong into the deep constitutional fatigue that followed the Meech Lake and Charlottetown fiascos ... The RCAP report was ignored almost across the board due to its overly ambitious recommendations and unrealistic cost projections."[71]

There is little doubt that many of the recommendations are unlikely to ever find favour with the federal and provincial governments. However, the commission's attempt to address fundamental issues (unparalleled before or since) and the thoroughness of its research should not be underestimated. Its findings have been quoted with approval by the SCC, including in the 2016 *Daniels* decision.[72] It did not achieve its aim of renewing the relationship between Aboriginal and non-Aboriginal people and closing the economic and social gap between them by 2016, but it still remains highly relevant.

The Kelowna Accord/Conservative Government. To the list of failures in the political arena must be added the Kelowna Accord, signed in 2005 by Prime Minister Paul Martin, provincial governments, and the leaders of the main national Aboriginal organizations.[73] The main commitment was $5 billion over five years to fund educational and other programs for Aboriginal people. The accord seemed to indicate renewed efforts to resolve the disadvantages suffered by Aboriginal peoples in Canada. However, the election of a Conservative government in 2006 led to abandonment of the Kelowna Accord and the introduction of many programs that lessened environmental protection and upset Aboriginal peoples. Dependent on government financing, the national Aboriginal organizations gave only muted resistance. Opposition to the Conservative government came primarily from the grassroots Idle No More movement.

International developments. Greater international recognition of Indigenous rights has taken place in the last forty or so years. The United Nations established a Working Group on Indigenous Populations in 1982, which began working on a Declaration on the Rights of Indigenous Peoples in 1985 and produced a draft document in 1993. That document was adopted in September 2007. Its far-ranging provisions, and its status in Canadian law, are considered in Chapter 7.

Modern treaties. Although the Nisga'a lost the *Calder* case in 1973, it had an immediate impact, causing the federal government to introduce a policy to resolve comprehensive land claims outside the court system. The resulting agreements are known as land claims agreements or modern treaties. The first agreement to be reached was the James Bay Agreement in 1975 in Quebec; this was followed by the Inuvialuit Agreement in 1984, the Gwich'in Agreement in 1992, the Nunavut Agreement in 1993, the Sahtu Dene and Métis Agreement in 1993, the Yukon Umbrella Agreement in 1993, the Nisga'a Agreement in 1999, the Tlicho Agreement in 2003, the Labrador Inuit Land Claim Agreement in 2005,[74] and the Nunavik Inuit Land Claims Agreement in 2008. In 2016, the federal and Ontario governments signed an agreement in principle with the Algonquin of Ontario. British Columbia has had its own process to negotiate treaties since 1990. The Tsawwassen First Nation was the first to sign a treaty under that process in 2008, with three more signed since.

The Truth and Reconciliation Commission. Residential schools were a major component of the displacement and assimilation stage of Canadian history. The RCAP report contained a chapter on those schools and recommended a national inquiry. The federal government's response to that report in January 1998 included an apology and $350 million to facilitate healing. The issue remained a major concern to Aboriginal people, and many hundreds of criminal and civil cases were commenced against the federal government, the individuals who abused the children in those schools, and the institutions that operated the schools. In August 2005 the Assembly of First Nations launched a class-action lawsuit against the federal government on behalf of former students and their families. A settlement – the largest class-action settlement in Canadian history – was announced the next year and came into effect on September 19, 2007.[75] It included a common experience payment for all former students, who received $10,000 for their first year at a school and $3,000 for each additional year. An independent assessment process made awards to individuals based on the abuse they suffered. Other components of the settlement included a Truth and Reconciliation Commission (the TRC) to document the residential schools experience and make recommendations on reconciliation, funding to promote community healing, and an apology given by Prime Minister Stephen Harper in Parliament on June 11, 2008. Approximately 40,000 claims for compensation have been made to date, three times the original estimate, with payments totalling $3.137 billion.[76]

The TRC, chaired by Justice Murray Sinclair, spent six years travelling to all parts of Canada and heard from more than 6,500 witnesses. In December 2015 it released its six-volume final report.[77] The TRC defined "reconciliation" as "an ongoing process of establishing and maintaining respectful relationships."[78] In the report, the commission covered many topics related to reconciliation in addition to residential schools, including Canadian sovereignty, Aboriginal self-determination, Indigenous law, and the UN Declaration on the Rights of Indigenous People (UNDRIP). It made the following damning statement:

> In Canada, law must cease to be a tool for the dispossession and
> dismantling of Aboriginal societies. It must dramatically change if it
> is going to have any legitimacy within First Nation, Inuit and Métis
> communities. Until Canadian law becomes an instrument supporting
> Aboriginal peoples' empowerment, many Aboriginal people will con-
> tinue to regard it as a morally and politically malignant force. A com-
> mitment to truth and reconciliation demands that Canada's legal
> system be transformed.[79]

Bear in mind that the chair of the commission was a judge, and one of the other two commissioners was a lawyer.

There were ninety-four recommendations or "calls to action" in the report, designed to bring about reconciliation. The new federal government of Justin

Trudeau (son of Pierre Trudeau) agreed to all of them. They are far-reaching and include recommendations regarding child welfare, education, language and culture, health, and justice; an action plan to implement UNDRIP; a Royal Proclamation and Covenant of Reconciliation; and suggestions for educating lawyers, public servants, and journalists about treaties, Aboriginal rights, and related matters. One recommendation in particular would have great legal consequences if it were implemented:

> 47. We call upon federal, provincial, territorial, and municipal govern-
> ments to repudiate concepts used to justify European sovereignty
> over Indigenous peoples and lands, such as the Doctrine of Dis-
> covery and *terra nullius*, and to reform those laws, government poli-
> cies, and litigation strategies that continue to rely on such concepts.

This recommendation and its implications are considered in Chapter 3.

A recommendation more likely to be implemented is one calling on law schools in Canada to require all law students to take a course in Aboriginal peoples and the law. The SCC has already referenced the TRC report in its judgments.[80]

Calls to Action

The Truth and Reconciliation Commission's recommendations included calls to action on

- child welfare, education, language and culture, health, and justice,
- implementation of the UN Declaration on the Rights of Indigenous Peoples
- a Royal Proclamation and Covenant of Reconciliation
- the education of lawyers, public servants, and journalists about treaties, Aboriginal rights, and Indigenous laws.

It also called upon federal, provincial, territorial, and municipal govern-ments to repudiate concepts that had been used to justify European sovereignty over Indigenous peoples and lands.

Election of a Liberal government in 2015. The federal Liberal government elected in 2015 made much in its election promises of an improved relationship with Aboriginal peoples; acceptance of all the recommendations of the TRC, starting with UNDRIP; and a review of all federal legislation, policies, and operational practices in partnership with Aboriginal peoples to ensure that Canada was fully executing its constitutional obligations.[81] Prime Minister Justin Trudeau repeatedly said no relationship was more important to him than that with Aboriginal peoples. Two members of Parliament with Aboriginal ancestry were appointed to cabinet, including the minister of justice, a former leader of the Assembly of First Nations in BC. Expectations were high that relations would improve greatly. However, approval of projects opposed by many Aboriginal groups, such as the Kinder Morgan pipeline expansion in BC, and apparent backtracking on the commitment to fully implement UNDRIP have strained the relationship to some extent.[82] Time will tell when and how the election promises are fulfilled.

Success in the courts. The central role of the courts, and especially the SCC, in developing modern Aboriginal law has been already mentioned, and a close examination of this will form the bulk of this book. As already noted, this is a role that was forced on the courts by the determination of Aboriginal peoples to resolve their grievances and the failure of politicians to respond effectively. Other groups have also played important supporting roles in the transformation of the law over the last thirty to forty years, particularly pioneering lawyers who were willing to take cases despite the apparently limited prospects of success given the prevailing state of the law and legal scholars and experts from other disciplines (such as anthropologists, historians, and human geographers) who attempted to find innovative arguments.[83] Some people have been very critical of these developments and the "Aboriginal industry" that they say has arisen to promote Aboriginal interests.[84] P.G. McHugh refers to "an infestation of lawyers and, on their coat-tails and playing attendant to their toilsome legalism, legions of other professionals like anthropologists and (ethno-) historians ... The claims 'industry' ... became the target of criticism, some of it justified, much of it bordering on the hysterical and misinformed."[85]

Whatever one's views on this issue – and I will give mine later – there can be no doubt as to the overall favourable outcome of litigation for some Aboriginal people. Bill Gallagher, a lawyer who has experience acting for governments and industry, has written a book called *Resource Rulers* and for a time maintained a blog keeping track of "the native winning streak."[86] He writes that "Natives have amassed the longest running, most impressive legal winning streak over resource access in Canadian history."[87] As of March 2014 he had calculated 191 "wins" for Aboriginal groups in cases dealing with natural resources across Canada. In the words of Alan Cairns, a long-time scholar of Aboriginal issues in Canada and critic of the RCAP report who wrote the preface for *Resource Rulers,* Gallagher's survey "portrays a remarkable country-wide consistency in positive judicial findings supportive of native claims in resource development. In practical terms, this means that vast territories, especially in northern and western Canada, cannot be opened up without the support of the relevant First Nations. The latter have become key players whose support or opposition can determine the future of the proposed opening of a mine, or the construction of a pipeline." The truth of these words was shown in the June 23, 2016, decision of the Federal Court of Appeal, which quashed the federal government's approval of the Northern Gateway pipeline, a $7-billion project to transport oil from Alberta to Asian markets, because of the government's failure to adequately consult First Nations.[88] The new federal government later abandoned Northern Gateway altogether. Aboriginal peoples' success in the courts had killed it.

TO SUM UP

- The Royal Commission on Aboriginal Peoples divided the history of Canada into four main stages: separate worlds; contact and co-operation; displacement and assimilation; and negotiation and renewal.

- The contact and co-operation stage lasted until the late eighteenth and early nineteenth centuries and was characterized by Aboriginal and non-Aboriginal societies controlling their own internal affairs but co-operating in areas of mutual interest. The main legal events during this stage were treaties of peace and friendship, the Mohegan case, the Royal Proclamation of 1763, and the Marshall decisions.

- Several key developments took place during the displacement and assimilation stage that still influence modern Aboriginal law, including treaties intended by the federal government to transfer land to enable non-Aboriginal settlement; the *Indian Act*'s diminishment of Aboriginal self-government; and the White Paper of 1969, which proposed the termination of the special status of Aboriginal peoples.

- The years since the White Paper were described by the Royal Commission on Aboriginal Peoples as the stage of negotiation and renewal and were formative years for modern Aboriginal law. The period was characterized by increased pressure from Aboriginal peoples for political and constitutional reform; failed attempts at constitutional reform; the royal commission; modern treaties; the Truth and Reconciliation Commission; and success in the courts by Aboriginal groups.

- From 1980 to 1992, there were attempts to negotiate what Aboriginal rights were to be protected by Section 35 of the *Constitution Act, 1982*. These attempts failed largely because of disagreement over Aboriginal self-government.

- The comprehensive 1996 RCAP report recommended fundamental changes to bring about a renewed relationship between Aboriginal and non-Aboriginal people in Canada, but it has been largely ignored.

- Since the James Bay Agreement in 1975, there have been over twenty modern treaties signed.

- The TRC reported in 2015 on the history of residential schools and their continuing consequences and made recommendations to achieve reconciliation, including on Canadian sovereignty, Aboriginal self-determination, Indigenous laws, and the UN Declaration on the Rights of Indigenous Peoples.

- Litigation has been a major and, arguably, the most important development affecting Aboriginal peoples in recent years. A central role was forced on judges by the failure of politicians to respond to the challenges of constitutional change.

- Recent decades have seen tremendous development in Aboriginal law, commencing with the *Calder* case in 1973, which was followed by several other decisions of the SCC that have fundamentally changed the law.

Sovereignty and Aboriginal-Crown Relations

3

A fundamental issue in Aboriginal law is the relationship of Aboriginal groups with the Canadian state. This issue raises a number of questions. What powers to make law ("jurisdiction") does each have? In particular, what powers do Aboriginal groups still possess following the assertion and establishment of sovereignty by the British Crown? Are Aboriginal groups still "sovereign"? What is the legal justification for the sovereignty of the Canadian (and before it, the British) state? What is the nature of the relationship between the Crown and Aboriginal groups, and what obligations are owed?

Defining Sovereignty, Self-Determination, and Self-Government

There is a great deal of discussion and some confusion about what is meant by "sovereignty" and related terms such as "self-determination" and "self-government." Broadly speaking, they can refer to the following concepts:

- The full sovereignty of a nation state under international law. Some Aboriginal groups have claimed to have this status. For example, the Haudenosaunee unsuccessfully sought membership in the League of Nations in the 1920s and issue their own passports today.[1] According to Mohawk scholar Gerald Taiaiake Alfred, "The people of Kahnawake have allegiance solely to the Mohawk nation, and their view of the

Mohawk nation is one in the fullest sense of the term as it is used in international law."[2]

- The right of Aboriginal people to govern themselves within Canada with laws they have passed to the exclusion of, or having priority over, laws passed by other governments (this is more often the meaning today). This model is often described as a "nation-to-nation" relationship, with each side co-existing and pursuing parallel paths with separate sovereignties – the "two-row wampum."[3] It harkens back to the contact and co-operation stage in the history of Crown-Aboriginal relations, when Aboriginal groups were independent and the Crown entered into treaties with them as equals. This may be described as "shared sovereignty" or "treaty federalism,"[4] and variations of it were recommended by the 1983 Report of the Special Committee on Indian Self-Government (the Penner Report)[5] and the Royal Commission on Aboriginal Peoples (RCAP) in 1996.[6]
- Delegated self-government powers (like those of a municipality) that have been granted by the federal government and are subject to revocation.[7] The *Indian Act* has long provided for limited delegation of powers by the federal government, sometimes subject to approval or disallowance by the minister of Indian affairs. The Canadian Revenue Agency has stated in a recent interpretation bulletin that "the very nature of an Indian band and its council under the Indian Act is that of a local government, similar in nature to a municipality" and thus entitled to a similar exemption from income tax.[8]

Sovereignty, Self-Determination, and Self-Government

"Sovereignty," "self-determination," and "self-government" can refer to the following concepts:

- the full sovereignty of a nation state under international law
- the right of Aboriginal people to govern themselves within Canada with laws they have passed to the exclusion of, or having priority over, laws passed by other governments – a "nation-to-nation" relationship
- delegated self-government powers that have been granted by the federal government and are subject to revocation.

These are only basic distinctions. Many versions of sovereignty, self-determination, and self-government could exist.

An important disagreement during the constitutional talks that occurred in the 1980s, described in Chapter 2, was whether self-government powers were "inherent." The talks broke down over this issue. "Inherent" means not derived from anyone else. Aboriginal groups have insisted that their rights of self-government derive from their powers as groups existing before the arrival of Europeans, and so these rights are not powers granted by the federal government or by Section 35. The RCAP agreed with this position, concluding that Section 35 had recognized and affirmed the inherent right as an existing Aboriginal and treaty right. In RCAP's view, the inherent right of self-government was thus entrenched in the Canadian Constitution, providing a basis for Aboriginal governments to function along with the federal and provincial governments as one of the three distinct orders of government in Canada.[9] Proponents of inherent rights to self-government often imply or expressly state that these rights, being inherent, cannot be limited by other governments. However, US law recognizes both that "Indian" tribes in the United States have inherent sovereign powers and also that these powers are at the mercy of the "plenary" (absolute) power of the US federal government.[10]

Many commentators who object to self-government in the first and second senses are willing to support it in the third sense. For example, Michael Ignatieff, former leader of the federal Liberal Party, has said that he thinks the pursuit of "exclusive Aboriginal sovereignty" is "a dead-end," but he has no problem with Aboriginal communities acting as "responsible municipal governments" (which they have been doing for over a century under the *Indian Act*).[11] In British Columbia the provincial government held a referendum in 2002 to gain support for its position to limit Aboriginal self-government under treaties so it had the characteristics of local government, with delegation of powers from Canada and the province.[12] Over 80 percent of those who voted were in favour, but the referendum was very controversial, and only about a third of the ballots were returned.

It is important to note that sovereignty of a country is not necessarily the same as owning the land in it, except perhaps in a nominal sense. In technical terms, for those who like to use Latin, the distinction is between *imperium,* or sovereignty over a territory, and *dominium,* ownership of land.[13] This distinction will be discussed in more detail in Chapter 4 as part of the discussion of Aboriginal title. For now, we can note that although the assertion of British sovereignty to North America meant Britain claimed the right to make laws that would govern Aboriginal peoples and prohibit the sale of land by them to another country, it did not automatically deprive Aboriginal peoples of their interests in that land, which were to be recognized and continue. This critical distinction has not always been made. Justice Binnie observed in *Mitchell* that "the assertion of sovereign authority was confused with doctrines of feudal title to deny aboriginal peoples any interest at all in their traditional lands."[14] Assertion of sovereignty alone was not sufficient. Acquisition of land required reaching an agreement through a treaty or passing a law that clearly and plainly extinguished those interests.

> Sovereignty of a country is not necessarily the same as owning the land in it ... In technical terms, for those who like to use Latin, the distinction is between *imperium,* or sovereignty over a territory, and *dominium,* ownership of land.

British and Canadian Sovereignty

The arrival of people from Britain did not necessarily coincide with the assertion of British sovereignty. For example, British explorers and traders visited what is now British Columbia in the 1770s, but British sovereignty was not established until the Treaty of Oregon between the United States and Britain in 1846.[15] There are different dates for contact and British sovereignty – and for effective control, which generally occurred later – in different parts of Canada.[16] Specific dates have been established for each area, although a general assertion of sovereignty was made in the Royal Proclamation of 1763, which referred to "our Sovereignty, Protection and Dominion."[17] The dates of contact, assertion of sovereignty, and effective control are important legally since Aboriginal rights (except for the Métis) are based on the date of contact, Aboriginal title is based on the date of sovereignty, and Métis rights are based on the date of effective control by Britain.[18]

The assertion of sovereignty is a political act and not in itself a matter for the courts to determine, although that assertion has fundamental legal consequences. In a case involving the legal status of Quebec, the SCC agreed that "sovereignty is a political fact for which no purely legal authority can be constituted."[19] The Courts of Appeal for BC and Alberta have dismissed challenges to the sovereignty of the Crown and the jurisdiction of the Canadian courts over Aboriginal people.[20] At the trial of the *Delgamuukw* case, for example, the trial judge said that no court had "the jurisdiction to undo the establishment of the Colony, Confederation or the constitutional arrangements which are now in place."[21] When the case got to the SCC, Bruce

Clark, a lawyer for one of the appellants, filed a motion to oppose the jurisdiction of the Canadian courts over the claim as contrary to the *Mohegan* case (discussed in Chapter 2), which, he argued, required an independent court. The Court rejected the motion on the grounds that the argument had not been raised earlier.[22] In the *Mabo* case, Justice Brennan of the High Court of Australia stated, "The Crown's acquisition of sovereignty over the several parts of Australia cannot be challenged in an Australian municipal court."[23]

Legally, this refusal to accept challenges to Crown sovereignty can be seen as applying the act of state doctrine, which was described by Justice Hall in the *Calder* case as meaning that a court has "no jurisdiction to review the manner in which the Sovereign acquires new territory."[24] Canadian courts are one of "the principal organs" of the Canadian state (together with the legislatures and the executive branch – the prime minister and cabinet),[25] so they are not able to question the sovereignty of that state or, by extension, their own authority. They can and do question the exercise of powers by state officials, but only under the rules recognized by the Canadian legal system. Note that the SCC usually refers to the *assertion* of "Crown sovereignty" rather than its *acquisition*. Some writers have suggested that this indicates doubt on the part of the Court about the legitimacy of Canadian sovereignty. In my view, this is not the case. So far as the Canadian courts are concerned, the assertion of British and Canadian sovereignty must be accepted as a political fact and legally valid; no more justification is required. Of course, this does not resolve moral and political questions about Crown sovereignty.

Canadian sovereignty derives from earlier British sovereignty, but Canada is now independent. How and when this occurred is not clear. There was no

Sovereignty as Political Fact

So far as the Canadian courts are concerned, the assertion of British and Canadian sovereignty must be accepted as a political fact and legally valid; no more justification is required. A court has "no jurisdiction to review the manner in which the Sovereign acquires new territory." Of course, this fact does not resolve moral and political questions about Crown sovereignty.

declaration or war of independence. Canada's Constitution is made up of UK legislation and, in theory, could be unilaterally repealed or amended by the UK Parliament under the doctrine of parliamentary supremacy.[26] The preamble to the *Constitution Act, 1867* refers to promoting "the interests of the British Empire," and Section 132 describes Canada as "part of the British Empire." However, the sovereignty of Canada as a nation independent of Britain is a political fact and cannot be seriously contested, as acknowledged by the SCC: "There can be no doubt now that Canada has become a sovereign state. Its sovereignty was acquired in the period between its separate signature of the Treaty of Versailles in 1919 and the Statute of Westminster, 1931."[27] In the words of Brian Slattery, professor at Osgoode Hall Law School, "Canada attained independence by a process of accretion ... The true position seems to be that our independence is founded on the factual assumption of sovereign powers by Canadian authorities and the accompanying withdrawal of British power in the period after World War I."[28]

So far, I have been using the term "Canadian sovereignty" as if Canada were a unitary and not a federal state. Since it is a federal state, the powers are divided between the federal government and the provinces under Sections 91 to 95 of the *Constitution Act, 1867*. In the case of Aboriginal law, as I have mentioned earlier, the federal government has exclusive power with respect to "Indians, and Lands reserved for the Indians" under Section 91(24) of that act. "Indians" for this purpose includes all the Aboriginal peoples covered by Section 35 of the *Constitution Act, 1982*.[29] Therefore, federal power to pass laws in this area is clear. What is far from clear is the power of a province to do so. This confusion is illustrated by the fact that a 2006 decision of the SCC on the power of a province to regulate Aboriginal and treaty rights was reversed in 2014.[30] The law is evolving in the direction of giving greater powers to the provinces, although it is not entirely clear how this can be reconciled with prior law and, indeed, the exclusive federal jurisdiction in Section 91(24).

The law relating to the powers of a province may be summarized as follows:

(a) A province cannot legislate "in pith and substance" with respect to matters covered by Section 91(24), since these are supposedly within the exclusive powers of the federal government. This means that it cannot aim its legislation at "Indians, and Lands reserved for the Indians" (which includes lands held in Aboriginal title). For example, the SCC held in *Delgamuukw* that provinces could not purport to extinguish Aboriginal rights and title, and in *Sutherland* that provincial hunting laws could not single out Aboriginal people for special treatment.[31]

(b) However, a province can still legislate within its own areas of jurisdiction, including most issues of civil law within the province, so long as it does not single out "Indians, or Lands reserved for the Indians" for special treatment. For example, in *Kitkatla,* the SCC upheld BC legislation that granted permits to cut down culturally modified trees.[32] The legislation was held not to be contrary to Section 91(24) but to fall within the provincial jurisdiction over property and civil rights in the province. This was because it applied to both Aboriginal and non-Aboriginal people and did not single out Aboriginal people, although it had a disproportionate impact on them. If the provincial law were inconsistent with a federal law, the doctrine of paramountcy would give priority to the federal law.[33]

(c) Section 88 of the *Indian Act* makes "Indians" (as defined by that act) subject to provincial laws that apply generally, with some important qualifications. The SCC held that this section was effective to apply a provincial wildlife act to Indians hunting off-reserve.[34]

(d) Until the 2014 *Tsilhqot'in* decision of the SCC, the law applied what is called the principle of interjurisdictional immunity. This meant that provincial laws that were otherwise valid would not apply if they impaired the "core" of federal jurisdiction over Indians or land reserved for Indians. Therefore, for example, it was held that provincial matrimonial laws did not apply to reserve lands.[35]

(e) In *Tsilhqot'in*, the Court reversed its earlier ruling on interjurisdictional immunity and held it did not apply to Aboriginal title and rights. Instead, provinces could pass laws of general application within their areas of jurisdiction, even if they infringed Aboriginal rights, so long as they could justify such infringement under principles derived from the *Sparrow* case, discussed in Chapter 4. This puts provinces in a position similar to that of the federal government for this purpose. It is not clear what this will mean in practice except that it obviously gives the provinces powers to infringe the rights of Aboriginal peoples. It is also a step away from the historical practice since colonial times of reducing the power that the colonial/provincial legislature representing the local settler society holds over Aboriginal peoples, and giving that power to a more independent government body in London or Ottawa.[36]

(f) In *Grassy Narrows,* the Court confirmed the ruling in *Tsilhqot'in* and also held that the Province of Ontario could exercise the power of the Crown under a treaty to "take up" land.[37]

The Impact of Assertion of British Sovereignty on Aboriginal Sovereignty

The SCC has acknowledged the "pre-existence of Aboriginal sovereignty" at the time of the assertion of British sovereignty.[38] This raises the question, What impact did the assertion have on Aboriginal sovereignty and what sovereignty remains? The legal answer is to be found in the doctrine of discovery, as explained by Chief Justice Marshall of the US Supreme Court in decisions quoted at length by the SCC,[39] and in the doctrine of continuity.

The discovery doctrine was a rule used by European nations to determine among themselves who could claim sovereignty over a colony.[40] It has been expressed in different ways and sometimes confused with the idea of *terra nullius* (land not occupied or owned, which has never applied to Canada),[41] suggesting that European claims to have "discovered" an empty North America were the basis of legal entitlement to the land and to sovereignty over Aboriginal peoples. In his decisions, Chief Justice Marshall acknowledged the pre-existence of Aboriginal peoples and was at pains to stress that the doctrine of discovery was only intended to apply among the European nations and not to Aboriginal peoples. In *Johnson v. McIntosh,* he said discovery "gave title to the government by whose subjects, or by whose authority, it was made, against all other European governments."[42] He further explained a few years later, in *Worcester v. Georgia,* that discovery "was an exclusive principle which shut out the rights of competition among those who had agreed to it: not one which could annul the previous rights of those who had not agreed to it. It regulated the right given by discovery among the European discoverers but could not affect the rights of those already in possession."[43] In effect, he saw the discovery doctrine as a principle accepted by European powers on how they were going to regulate among themselves who could deal with the Aboriginal peoples of North America. Of course, it necessarily limited the power of those peoples to deal with whomever they wished and, thus, "their right to complete sovereignty, as independent nations,"[44] but it was not otherwise intended to deprive them of their rights, including their now limited sovereignty. That sovereignty was vulnerable (like their interest in land) to further limitation by the Crown following the assertion of its sovereignty.

In fact, far from taking away their powers of governance, British imperial law (made applicable by the assertion of Crown sovereignty) recognized Aboriginal laws and customs under another related doctrine – the doctrine of continuity – unless and until they were abolished or replaced by law made in exercise of British sovereignty. The doctrine of continuity goes back hundreds of years to the period when the sovereignty of the English king was extended to Wales, Ireland, and Scotland.[45] In 1722, the English Privy Council held that, "where the King of England conquers a country ... he may impose ... what laws ... he pleases. But, [u]ntil such laws given by the conquering prince, the laws and customs of the conquered country shall hold place."[46] This principle was adopted by Justice Hall of the SCC in the *Calder* case, and he held that it must be applicable to lands which became subject to British sovereignty by means other than conquest.[47]

The doctrine of continuity has been accepted in other SCC cases.[48] In the *Van der Peet* case, Justice McLachlin said that running through the long history of the interface of Europeans and the Aboriginal peoples "from its earliest beginnings to the present time is a golden thread – the recognition by the common law of the ancestral laws and customs of the aboriginal peoples who occupied the land prior to European settlement."[49] In the absence of a law validly passed by the British or Canadian sovereign, the existing laws and customs of the Aboriginal peoples (including those relating to government) continued under the doctrine of continuity unless found to be incompatible with the assertion of British sovereignty.[50] In short, Aboriginal sovereignty was limited but not abolished. We will see that the doctrine was applied restrictively in *Pamajewon* to recognize only those rights of self-government that existed at the time of contact with Europeans.[51]

Legislation and Agreements regarding Self-Government Powers

The *Indian Act,* with its delegation of municipal-style government powers, including the power to levy property taxes, continues to apply to most First Nations.[52] More recently, legislation has been passed to delegate additional powers to those First Nations that wish to exercise them.[53] This has included greater powers over management of reserve lands,[54] election of band councils,[55] and matrimonial property legislation.[56]

In 1995, the federal government issued a policy statement recognizing the inherent right of self-government as an existing Aboriginal right within Section 35.[57] This recognition is based on the view that the Aboriginal peoples of Canada have the right to govern themselves when it comes to internal concerns of their communities; matters related to their special relationship

Aboriginal Peoples and the Law

to their lands and their resources; and subjects integral to their unique cultures, identities, traditions, languages, and institutions. However, although described as "inherent," self-government will be implemented through the negotiation of agreements between First Nations and federal and provincial governments. As Tony Penikett, former premier of Yukon, observed, "almost every aspect of this 'right' must be negotiated."[58] Further, the negotiations have to satisfy some conditions, including the paramountcy of federal and provincial law in some situations. In the words of anthropologist Michael Asch, "In sum, while it was presented as an opportunity to negotiate, the policy introduced in 1995 dictated the conditions for government participation in the process to such a degree that it amounted to a final offer, made on a take-it-or leave-it basis."[59] In his view, "the negotiations process is one in which Indigenous peoples confirm that they are reconciling their political rights with Crown sovereignty."[60] Political scientist Kiera Ladner argues that the federal vision expects Aboriginal peoples "to negotiate their inferiority by accepting the responsibility for jurisdictions over which the federal and provincial governments maintain sovereignty."[61]

Some First Nations have negotiated either modern treaties that give them greater government powers or self-government agreements with the federal and provincial governments.[62] In one case, the provisions in the Nisga'a Treaty giving powers to the Nisga'a were interpreted as valid delegations by federal and provincial governments of their powers.[63] First Nations have also negotiated agreements to deliver federal and provincial programs (such as social welfare and housing programs) on reserves, funded by the respective government. Noting that "more than 80 percent of the money spent by Aboriginal Affairs and Northern Development Canada is now disbursed through band and regional offices," Greg Poelzer and Ken Coates comment in *From Treaty Peoples to Treaty Nation* that "the transition to self-administration if not full self-government has been quite remarkable."[64]

Cases on Canadian and Aboriginal Sovereignty
In addition to early decisions dealing with the doctrines of discovery and continuity, *Mohegan Indians v. Connecticut*, which lasted from 1704 to 1773, was an early case (also discussed in Chapter 2) that concerned a land dispute and touched on some issues of Aboriginal sovereignty. It is a complicated case, and there is disagreement on its significance, especially on the question whether it recognized the Mohegans as sovereign. "However, the case does confirm that British law recognized that such nations were, in certain circumstances at least, governed internally by systems of Aboriginal customary

law and government which were independent from the local legal systems of the colonies in which they were located."[65]

After these early cases, there was silence from senior courts until the *Calder* case was heard by the SCC in 1973. A lower court held in 1929 that the "uncivilized" Mi'kmaq lacked sovereignty and had no capacity to enter into a treaty.[66] In his dissenting opinion in *Calder*, Justice Hall considered the act of state doctrine noted above and concluded that it had no application because the Nisga'a were not disputing the jurisdiction of the British or Canadian governments to extinguish their title: "They do not deny the right of the Crown to dispossess them but say the Crown has not done so."[67] He accepted the discovery doctrine as explained by Chief Justice Marshall, as did the Court in *Guerin*.[68] In commenting on the continuance of Aboriginal title, the Court referred to a "change of sovereignty," thus recognizing without discussion that paramount British sovereignty had replaced Aboriginal sovereignty.[69] The 1990 *Sparrow* decision contains a key passage in response to the argument that Aboriginal rights included the power to regulate the fisheries: "there was from the outset never any doubt that sovereignty and legislative power, and indeed the underlying title to such lands, vested in the Crown."[70] Again, there is no discussion of this fundamental issue. It is baldly stated as something that goes almost without saying, which is, indeed, the case so far as Canadian courts are concerned. The sovereignty of the British and Canadian governments is simply a political fact that they must accept as an organ of the Canadian state.

According to Justice La Forest of the SCC in another 1990 case, "The historical record leaves no doubt that native peoples acknowledged the ultimate sovereignty of the British Crown."[71] In other cases primarily concerned with Aboriginal fishing rights decided in 1996, the Court stressed that "distinctive aboriginal societies exist within, and are part of, a broader social, political and economic community, over which the Crown is sovereign," and that the role of Section 35 is to "reconcile the existence of distinctive aboriginal societies prior to the arrival of Europeans in North America with the assertion of Crown sovereignty over that territory."[72] The SCC has thus clearly upheld the sovereignty of the Canadian government as a bedrock principle and subordinated "aboriginal societies" to it. Indeed, this version of reconciliation sees the role of the constitutional protection for Aboriginal and treaty rights as ensuring that the pre-existence of

> The SCC has thus clearly upheld the sovereignty of the Canadian government as a bedrock principle and subordinated "aboriginal societies" to it.

Aboriginal societies is "reconciled" with Crown sovereignty at the cost of those rights.[73]

In contrast to its repeated references to the Crown's sovereignty, the Court has not said much about Aboriginal sovereignty or self-government.[74] The only clear guidance is contained in the following passage from the *Pamajewon* decision of 1996, in which Chief Justice Lamer states:

> The appellants' claim involves the assertion that s. 35(1) encompasses the right of self-government, and that this right includes the right to regulate gambling activities on the reservation ... Assuming s. 35(1) encompasses claims to aboriginal self-government, such claims must be considered in light of the purposes underlying that provision and must, therefore, be considered against the test derived from consideration of those purposes. This is the test laid out in *Van der Peet*. In so far as they can be made under s. 35(1), claims to self-government are no different from other claims to the enjoyment of aboriginal rights and must, as such, be measured against the same standard.[75]

He then explained the test in *Van der Peet*: "In order to be an aboriginal right an activity must be an element of a practice, custom or tradition integral to the distinctive culture of the aboriginal group claiming the right."[76] A general claim of a right to self-government or to manage the use of lands was not sufficiently specific. Applied to this case, the test required evidence of participation in and regulation of gambling, especially large-scale gambling at the time of contact with Europeans. There was no such evidence, and the claim was rejected. The requirement to show this level of specificity to support a right of self-government will make it very difficult for claims to succeed.[77] As with Aboriginal rights generally, it freezes the right at the time of contact and does not allow them to adapt to modern circumstances.[78]

The following year, Chief Justice Lamer handed down his decision in the *Delgamuukw* case, which, until the *Tsilhqot'in* decision in 2014, was the leading case on Aboriginal title. In the lower courts it had been argued primarily on the basis of a right to self-government, and the argument was rejected by those courts. When it reached the SCC, the Court carefully avoided dealing with that issue. In his judgment, the chief justice commented that the broad nature of the claim at trial led to "a failure of the parties to address many of the difficult conceptual issues which surround the recognition of aboriginal self-government." He noted that the Royal Commission on Aboriginal Peoples had devoted 277 pages to the issue.[79]

The Court had another chance to consider Aboriginal self-government in 2001, when the *Mitchell* case came before it, but the majority again decided not to take that opportunity. The case involved a claim that trading across the border is an Aboriginal right. The Court found that the alleged right had not been proven. The claimant based much of the argument on self-government, but the majority of the judges declined to consider it. Two of the judges reviewed some of the issues involved in self-government, including the US law on domestic dependent nations,[80] and the possibility of a "shared" or "merged" sovereignty in which "aboriginal and non-aboriginal Canadians *together* form a sovereign entity with a measure of common purpose and united effort."[81] They reviewed the RCAP report and continued, "What is significant is that the Royal Commission itself sees aboriginal peoples as full participants with non-aboriginal peoples in a shared Canadian sovereignty. Aboriginal people do not stand in opposition to, nor are they subjugated by, Canadian sovereignty. They are part of it."[82] They were clear that self-government must not be incompatible with Crown sovereignty, so that, for example, an Aboriginal group could not claim an Aboriginal right "to engage in military adventures on Canadian territory" since the Crown had a monopoly on the lawful use of military force.[83]

They also referred to "the challenge aboriginal self-government poses to the orthodox view that constitutional powers in Canada are wholly and exhaustively distributed between the federal and provincial governments."[84] They noted without comment that the issue – usually described as "the third order of government" issue – was currently before the courts in British Columbia. This was a reference to the *Campbell* case, brought by the leader of the opposition party (and future premier) to challenge the Nisga'a treaty. In this case it was argued that by recognizing the paramountcy of Nisga'a self-government powers in some areas, the treaty violated "the orthodox view" that the Constitution only recognizes the federal and provincial levels of government, leaving no space for a third Aboriginal order. The BC Supreme Court (the first level of court) had rejected the challenge and upheld a "diminished" power of self-government.[85] This decision was not appealed and remains the most detailed discussion of the issue by a court.[86] In a more recent case, the BC Court of Appeal carefully avoided deciding the issue and said the Nisga'a self-government powers could be upheld on the basis of delegation from the federal and provincial governments.[87] This key constitutional and political issue remains unresolved, but if the orthodox view prevails, self-government powers will be delegated rather than inherent powers. In practice, this means they can be retracted by the federal or provincial government that delegated them, subject only to the duty to justify the retraction if it would result in an infringement of a treaty or Aboriginal right for the purposes of Section 35.[88]

In the 2004 *Haida* and *Taku* cases on the duty to consult, the SCC made some interesting comments about sovereignty. In *Haida*, Chief Justice McLachlin said, "Treaties serve to reconcile pre-existing Aboriginal sovereignty with assumed Crown sovereignty ... sovereignty claims [are] reconciled through the process of honourable negotiation."[89] She also noted, "Many bands reconciled their claims with the sovereignty of the Crown through negotiated treaties. Others, notably in British Columbia, have yet to do so."[90] In *Taku* she said that "the purpose of s. 35(1) of the *Constitution Act, 1982* is to facilitate the ultimate reconciliation of prior Aboriginal occupation with *de facto* Crown sovereignty."[91] Some commentators have seized on the use of "assumed" and "de facto" as suggesting that the Court was saying that, in the absence of a treaty, the Crown's sovereignty "lacked legitimacy" and is "constitutionally illegitimate."[92] "De facto" means something existing in fact that may not be legally valid. For the reasons discussed above, I doubt very much if the Court intended these words to be given such revolutionary meaning. However, the comments do show that Crown sovereignty has not yet been reconciled with "pre-existing Aboriginal sovereignty" where treaties have not been signed.

As noted, the SCC greatly increased provincial powers over Aboriginal title lands in *Tsilhqot'in*. By implication, it also denied a governmental role for Aboriginal governments (as distinct from their management powers as owners) by saying that, in the absence of provincial powers, there would be "no one in charge" and that the lands might be immune from regulation, resulting in "legislative vacuums."[93] Clearly, the Court saw no role for a third level of government – the Aboriginal level – that had been recommended by RCAP.

The Court returned to the concept of a negotiated acceptance of British and Canadian sovereignty by Aboriginal peoples in the 2013 *Manitoba Métis* case, which involved a dispute over land grants to Métis children under the *Manitoba Act, 1870*. It stated that the act "represents the terms under which the Métis people agreed to surrender their claims to govern themselves and their territory and bec[o]me part of the new nation of Canada." The land claim that was in dispute was described as "a collective claim of the Métis people, based on a promise made to them in return for their agreement to recognize Canada's sovereignty over them."[94]

Comments on Aboriginal Sovereignty

The degree of legal recognition given to Aboriginal sovereignty or the lack of recognition is a matter of much discussion by academics.[95] Generally, commentators have seen this as the major area in which Aboriginal law has failed to meet the aspirations of Aboriginal peoples, as expressed during the constitutional talks of the 1980s and by the Royal Commission on Aboriginal Peoples. This failure is often contrasted with the relative success achieved in the other main issue in Aboriginal law: the recognition of property interests.

As we have seen, the SCC has clearly upheld the sovereignty of the Canadian government but not that of Aboriginal groups except in the limited form that it had at the time of contact. This was appropriate to the hunter-gatherer economy of most Aboriginal peoples but does not allow them to adapt to current circumstances. The doctrine of continuity has thus been given only a restricted application. Further, the "orthodox view" of the Constitution (which has not been successfully challenged except in one lower-level decision, and which appears to have been applied in *Tsilhqot'in*) only accepts the federal and provincial levels of government and treats Aboriginal self-government powers as delegated powers rather than an inherent right. Also, it must be kept in mind that any treaty or Aboriginal right to self-government protected by Section 35 is subject to infringement by both federal and provincial governments if this can be justified to the satisfaction of a court.

> Any treaty or Aboriginal right to self-government protected by Section 35 is subject to infringement by both federal and provincial governments if this can be justified to the satisfaction of a court.

This overall approach has been described as a "citizen-state" approach, recognizing limited special rights of Aboriginal peoples but always under the sovereignty of Canada.[96] Any change in this position is unlikely to come from the courts and may require a constitutional amendment, such as that proposed in the Charlottetown Accord of 1992, to overcome the third-order-of-government issue.

One of the practical problems is that many of the over six hundred First Nations and other Aboriginal groups in Canada are small in size and remote from other communities. RCAP concluded "that the right of self-government cannot reasonably be exercised by small, separate communities, whether First Nations, Inuit or Métis. It should be exercised by groups of a certain size – groups with a claim to the term 'nation.'"[97] The small, separate communities would have to be reconstructed into between sixty and eighty such nations with constitutions and membership codes. The Truth and Reconciliation Commission of 2015 endorsed this approach.[98] However, when a similar approach was suggested in British Columbia in 2009 as part of the legislative proposal to recognize Aboriginal rights and title in that province without litigation, it led to opposition from Aboriginal groups and contributed to the defeat of the proposal.[99]

One writer advocating a citizen-state or "citizen plus" approach has pointed out that independent statehood is not an option: "Although [Aboriginal peoples] have been subjected to colonial treatment, its natural resolution by independence is unavailable ... They will exist in the midst of their former colonizers."[100] However, some Aboriginal people strongly feel that the claim of Canadian sovereignty over them is illegitimate and must be challenged: "It is necessary to incorporate a Decolonization Principle to break down the bedrock of the Canadian Constitution that dominates Indigenous Peoples and our lands."[101] The TRC went some way to adopting this approach in 2015 in the following recommendation: "We call upon federal, provincial, territorial, and municipal governments to repudiate concepts used to justify European sovereignty over Indigenous peoples and lands, such as the Doctrine of Discovery and *terra nullius*, and to reform those laws, government policies, and litigation strategies that continue to rely on such concepts."[102] This echoes the recommendation made by RCAP in 1996 that governments recognize that "concepts such as *terra nullius* and the doctrine of discovery are factually, legally and morally wrong."[103] The TRC stated, "We are not suggesting that the repudiation of the Doctrine of Discovery necessarily gives rise to the invalidation of Crown sovereignty," and the commissioners accepted that "there are other means to establish the validity of Crown sovereignty."[104] However, they did not explain what those means were,[105] or how they would be consistent with their call to "repudiate concepts used to justify European sovereignty over Indigenous peoples and lands." Given the implications for the entire legal system of repudiating concepts used to justify Canadian sovereignty (as the successor to "European sovereignty"), this TRC recommendation is not likely to be implemented, despite the Liberal government's acceptance of all the TRC recommendations.

At the other end of the debate, some writers completely reject Aboriginal sovereignty: "All the talk about aboriginal nationhood and sovereignty are merely fallacious legal arguments made for the purpose of obtaining compensation from the government."[106] Tom Flanagan describes inherent sovereignty as "only a rhetorical turn of phrase" and "contrary to the history, jurisprudence and national interests of Canada."[107]

Perhaps because of the difficult issues involved, the national debate of the 1980s and 1990s about Aboriginal sovereignty has largely been put on the back burner except by academics and some Aboriginal leaders.[108] Time will tell if the TRC recommendation or recent proposals by Quebec to amend the Constitution will revive it.[109] In the meantime, it is important to bear in mind that, in practice, the powers of First Nation governments have increased greatly over the last thirty or so years through delegation of powers from the federal and provincial governments or through modern treaties and agreements. The *Indian Act* remains on the books, but its day-to-day application is limited on many reserves.

Duties Owed by the Federal and Provincial Governments

This section considers two types of legal duties owed by the Crown to Aboriginal peoples: fiduciary duties and duties arising from the honour of the Crown, which are closely related to fiduciary duties. Duties more directly related to Aboriginal and treaty rights protected by Section 35, including the duty to justify any infringement and the duty of consultation, are discussed in later chapters. Keep in mind that, depending on the context, the term "the Crown" includes both the federal and provincial governments. As the SCC observed in the *Grassy Narrows* case, "These duties bind the *Crown*. When a *government* – be it the federal or a provincial government – exercises Crown power, the exercise of that power is burdened by the Crown obligations toward the Aboriginal people in question."[110]

Fiduciary Duties Generally

The law relating to fiduciary duties goes back centuries to feudal England. It was developed to deal with abuses by trustees into whose name property had been transferred to be held for another person. The basic fiduciary duties are to be loyal and to act in the best interests of another person, applying care in managing property for them. Over time, the fiduciary duties were extended to other relationships – for example, agents, employees, lawyers, parents, partners, or company directors. The particular duties owed depend on the relationship and the circumstances, but the duties of loyalty and acting in the best interests of another are fundamental. This is unusual in the law, which generally takes a more individualistic approach. It

> The basic fiduciary duties are to be loyal and to act in the best interests of another person.

generally prevents acts that harm others but does not require you to be loyal to other people or to put their interests above your own.

As mentioned, fiduciary duties have spread from the trust relationship to other relationships; they are referred to as "per se" (by or in itself) fiduciary relationships, meaning a presumption is made that obligations owed by the fiduciary party – for example, the partner or company director – are governed by fiduciary principles. Courts have pointed out that not all obligations in such relationships are fiduciary in nature, but this is usually the case. There is a second basis on which to impose fiduciary duties: relationships not ordinarily considered to be fiduciary but in which, based on the particular facts, one person owes fiduciary duties to the other. This is referred to as the "ad hoc" (for this purpose) type of fiduciary relationship.[111] Establishing fiduciary duties in this type of relationship requires proof on a case-by-case basis and is more difficult.

In 1984, in the *Guerin* decision, the SCC first recognized that the Crown has a fiduciary relationship with Aboriginal peoples. In the *Sparrow* decision of 1990, the Court said "the Government has the responsibility to act in a fiduciary capacity with respect to aboriginal peoples."[112] And in the 2016 *Daniels* case, the Court described the fiduciary relationship as "settled law."[113] The following year, the Supreme Court of New Zealand applied *Guerin* and found that the government owed fiduciary duties to the Māori with respect to certain lands.[114] Although some writers have written premature obituaries or suggested that it has been replaced by the related duty of the honour of the Crown,[115] the fiduciary relationship clearly remains a cornerstone of modern Aboriginal law.

Developments in the law by the SCC since the *Guerin* decision have resulted in the Crown automatically owing fiduciary duties so long as

- there is "a specific or cognizable Aboriginal interest"
- there is an undertaking by the Crown of discretionary control over that interest.

This can be seen as an example of a per se or sui generis (unique) fiduciary relationship.

If an Aboriginal group cannot meet these requirements, it may still be able to rely on fiduciary obligations being owed by the Crown under the current test for ad hoc fiduciary duties by showing that the following three conditions have been met:

- There is an undertaking by the Crown to act in the best interests of the group.
- The group is vulnerable to the control of the Crown.
- A legal or substantial practical interest of the group could be adversely affected by the Crown's exercise of discretion or control.

This additional test broadens the scope of fiduciary duties beyond the original facts of cases like *Guerin*, which involve discretionary control of Aboriginal interests such as reserve lands.

Over the last thirty or so years, courts and government officials have applied fiduciary principles in hundreds of cases between the Crown and Aboriginal groups, either as part of litigation or to resolve claims out of court, such as under the specific claims process.[116] These cases often arose out of mismanagement by the Crown of reserve lands or monies. Fiduciary principles were also incorporated by the *Sparrow* case as part of the Section 35 protection for existing Aboriginal and treaty rights as a check on the ability of the Crown to infringe Aboriginal rights. They were then subsequently extended in the *Badger*[117] and *Delgamuukw* cases to protect treaty rights and Aboriginal title.[118] Space does not permit anything more than a summary here of the leading decisions of the SCC to show the development of the law and to give some examples of how the Court has applied fiduciary principles to the Crown-Aboriginal relationship.[119]

Leading Decisions on Fiduciary Duty
The facts of the *Guerin* case are shocking. An exclusive golf club in Vancouver was compelled by the termination of its lease to find another location and fixed its sights on the Musqueam Indian Reserve. The golf club officials met and negotiated a lease with representatives of the Department of Indian Affairs. Band members were not present at these meetings or fully informed of the proposed terms. In 1957, members voted to surrender one-third of the reserve lands, consisting of the highest and best land, to enable a lease to be granted by the government to the golf club on the terms to which members had agreed. Only in 1970 did the determined efforts of Chief Delbert Guerin enable them to get a copy of the lease and so discover the real terms. Instead of being able to freely negotiate rent during the seventy-five-year duration of the lease, future rent increases were limited by the terms of the lease. The existing law did not offer much hope for them to get compensation. There were two main problems: the government might be able to

successfully answer the band's claim for compensation because too much time had passed before the Musqueam went to court ("limitation of actions" and related defences) and, more fundamentally, on the grounds that it did not owe a legal duty to Aboriginal peoples but only a political obligation. The band was successful in a breach of trust action at trial and awarded $10 million as compensation. The trial judge said the conduct of the government officials was unconscionable, and he rejected the defence based on passage of time on the grounds of "concealed fraud," because the government officials did not reveal the true lease terms to the band. For technical reasons, he also refused to consider the government's defence that any trust was "a political trust" and not enforceable in court as it imposed only political and not legal obligations on the government. On appeal, the Federal Court of Appeal found for the government on the political trust grounds.

On further appeal to the SCC, the band was successful, and the defence of political trust was rejected. All the judges found in favour of the band. However, they differed in their reasons for reaching this result. The majority declined to find that the federal government acted as a trustee but still found it to be a fiduciary. The other judges found the government to be either a trustee or an agent of the band. They all agreed that the government owed fiduciary obligations to the band. Since the government had taken upon itself the power to manage the lands without involving the band, it owed them a duty to act in their best interests – a fiduciary duty. Specifically, it should have gone back to the band to consult with members when it was not able to get the lease terms that the members thought they were getting when they voted to surrender the lands. This was the origin of the duty to consult as part of Aboriginal law, which will be discussed in Chapter 6.

In its 1990 *Sparrow* decision, also involving the Musqueam, the Court embedded the fiduciary relationship into the constitutional protection for Aboriginal and treaty rights, stating:

> In our opinion, *Guerin*, together with *R. v. Taylor and Williams* [a decision saying that treaties were to be interpreted in accordance with the honour of the Crown],[120] ground a general guiding principle for s. 35(1). That is, the Government has the responsibility to act in a fiduciary capacity with respect to aboriginal peoples. The relationship between the Government and aboriginals is trust-like, rather than adversarial, and contemporary recognition and affirmation of aboriginal rights must be defined in light of this historic relationship.[121]

In the *Blueberry River* case,[122] decided in 1995, the SCC applied *Guerin* in finding the government liable for breach of its fiduciary duty in the management of reserve lands. An Indian band surrendered its reserve to the Crown. The Department of Indian Affairs transferred the lands to the director of the Veterans' Land but did not reserve the mineral rights. The land was then sold to veterans. Oil and gas were discovered on the lands, and the revenues went to the veterans and not the band. The successor bands sued the government, claiming several breaches of fiduciary duty. The Court rejected most of the claims based on the facts but held that the transfer of the mineral rights constituted a breach of fiduciary duty.

The question before the SCC in the *Osoyoos Indian Band* case,[123] decided in 2001, was whether a strip of land located on a reserve and used by a municipality as an irrigation canal remained part of the reserve for the purposes of the band's power of property taxation after a federal order-in-council consented to the province's expropriating the land. A majority of judges decided that it maintained its reserve status. All agreed with an approach that dealt with a key issue relating to fiduciary law and, indeed, Aboriginal law generally: how to reconcile the interests of Aboriginal peoples with those of the public. They adopted a two-stage approach. In the first stage, the Crown acts in the public interest in determining that an expropriation involving Indian lands is required in order to fulfill some public purpose. At this stage, no fiduciary duty exists. However, once the general decision to expropriate has been made, the fiduciary obligations of the Crown arise, requiring that it expropriate only the minimum amount necessary to fulfill that purpose while preserving the Aboriginal group's interest in the land to the greatest extent practicable.[124]

A key issue relating to fiduciary law and, indeed, Aboriginal law generally is how to reconcile the interests of Aboriginal peoples with those of the public.

The following year, the Court decided the *Wewaykum* case,[125] in which it sought to place some limits on the number of "fiduciary duty" cases. *Wewaykum* involved actions by two Indian bands against the federal government for alleged breach of fiduciary duty arising out of the creation of two reserves. The actions were unsuccessful. In the course of the judgment, the Court stated that, since *Guerin*, Canadian courts had "experienced a flood of 'fiduciary duty' claims by Indian bands across a whole spectrum of possible complaints," ranging from provision of social services to elections.[126] After noting the positive aspects of the fiduciary relationship, the judgment continued, "But there are limits. The appellants seemed at times to invoke

Aboriginal Peoples and the Law

the 'fiduciary duty' as a source of plenary Crown liability covering all aspects of the Crown-Indian band relationship. This overshoots the mark. The fiduciary duty imposed on the Crown does not exist at large but in relation to specific Indian interests."[127] The Aboriginal interest in land was an example of such an interest. In the course of the judgment, the Court stated, "The Crown can be no ordinary fiduciary; it wears many hats and represents many interests, some of which cannot help but be conflicting."[128]

In the *Haida* decision of 2004, the Court held that in the case of asserted but not yet proven Aboriginal rights, the duty to consult was based on "the honour of the Crown" rather than a fiduciary duty because the Aboriginal interest had not been proven to exist and was insufficiently defined. It summarized the law on fiduciary obligations as follows:

> Where the Crown has assumed discretionary control over specific
> Aboriginal interests, the honour of the Crown gives rise to a fiduciary
> duty ... The content of the fiduciary duty may vary to take into account
> the Crown's broader obligations. However, the duty's fulfillment requires
> that the Crown act with reference to the Aboriginal group's best interests
> in exercising discretionary control over the specific Aboriginal interest
> at stake ... The term "fiduciary duty" does not connote a universal trust
> relationship encompassing all aspects of the relationship between the
> Crown and Aboriginal peoples.[129]

The 2009 decision of the Court in the *Ermineskin* case dealt with statutory limits on the powers of governments.[130] The Ermineskin and Samson Nations of Alberta sued the federal government for failure to invest the income from oil wells on reserve lands in the way a prudent investor would have invested such a large amount of money. Instead, the funds were kept in the government's general bank account – the consolidated revenue fund – and the rate of return was based on government bonds. The Court acknowledged that it was undeniable that a fiduciary obligation was owed with regard to the funds. However, the content of the obligation depended on the source of the obligation and had to take into account any valid statutory limits on the government. If the obligation was based on a treaty, as argued by the two nations, then Section 35 of the *Constitution Act, 1982* protecting treaty rights would render unconstitutional any statutory limits. The Court found that the source of the fiduciary obligation was not the treaty but the surrender of the oil rights and so limited by statutory provisions requiring that the funds be deposited in the consolidated revenue fund thus earning only a low rate of interest. In the words of the Court, "A fiduciary that acts in accordance with legislation cannot be said to be breaching its fiduciary duty."[131]

The next decision of note is that in *Manitoba Métis*, which also addressed the honour of the Crown. This case involved claims that the federal government had failed to carry out its obligations, enshrined in the *Manitoba Act*, to allocate land to Métis children. The Court held that the act did not impose a fiduciary duty on the government after applying the two tests noted above.

Although the Crown undertook discretionary control of the administration of the land grants under the *Manitoba Act*, and although the Métis are Aboriginal and had an interest in the land, the first test for fiduciary duty was not made because neither the legislation nor the evidence established a pre-existing communal Aboriginal interest held by the Métis. Nor was a fiduciary duty established on the basis of the second test. There was no undertaking to act in the best interests of the Métis children that took priority over other legitimate concerns.

Williams Lake,[132] decided by the SCC in 2018, concerned the alleged failures of the imperial and Canadian governments to prevent an Aboriginal group's village lands from being acquired by settlers in the early history of British Columbia. A majority of the Court upheld a ruling of the Specific Claims Tribunal that both governments owed and breached their fiduciary obligations by not acting in the group's best interests and by failing to use ordinary prudence. Those obligations arose from the Crown's discretionary control over the lands. Such control did not have to be complete or exclusive, and the fact that other lands were set aside as a reserve did not undo the breach, although it was relevant to the compensation payable. The majority upheld the potential liability of the federal government for the breach by the imperial government prior to Confederation under the relevant legislation.

The Honour of the Crown

The honour of the Crown is a principle that can be traced back centuries in the general law and to early cases in Aboriginal law, but it has been given new application in a few recent SCC decisions. References to the honour of the Crown can be found as early as 1608 in cases that held that the honour of the king prevented courts from interpreting grants of land or other favours from him in a manner that invalidated the grant – in other words, the courts assume that the King or the Crown will always act honourably and would never make an invalid grant.[133] The concept has been referenced in Aboriginal law from at least 1895 in the context of the performance of treaty obligations in accordance with "a trust graciously assumed by the Crown to the fulfillment of which with the Indians the faith and honour of the Crown is pledged."[134] This link between the Crown's trust or fiduciary obligations and the honour of the Crown has remained consistent, and until the *Haida* case in 2004, the honour of the Crown was often used synonymously with the Crown's fiduciary obligations to Aboriginal peoples. For example, in *Mitchell* it was said, "With this assertion of [sovereignty by the Crown] arose an obligation to treat aboriginal peoples fairly and honourably, and to protect them from exploitation, a duty characterized as 'fiduciary' in *Guerin*."[135] The Court has often repeated that "the honour of the Crown is always at stake in its dealings with Indian people."[136] The honour of the Crown has not been regarded as a distinct legal doctrine or body of law but a fundamental, overarching principle to be applied to the Crown in all its dealings with Aboriginal peoples. It might be viewed as "upstream" of, or the common foundation for, such distinct doctrines and should not be seen as replacing or competing with them.

The first case in which the Court discussed the honour of the Crown as being distinct from the Crown's trust-like or fiduciary relationship with Aboriginal peoples was *Haida* in 2004. We have seen that the Court rejected a duty to consult based on fiduciary obligations because the asserted interest was unproven and not specific enough to trigger such obligations. However, a duty was upheld based on the honour of the Crown: "The government's duty to consult with Aboriginal peoples and accommodate their interests is grounded in the honour of the Crown. The honour of the Crown is always at stake in its dealings with Aboriginal peoples ... It is not a mere incantation, but rather a core precept that finds its application in concrete practices."[137] The Court went on to observe that the honour of the Crown gives rise to different duties in different circumstances. Where the Crown has assumed discretionary control over specific Aboriginal interests, it gives rise to a fiduciary duty. It also infuses the processes of treaty making and treaty interpretation. Where treaties remain to be concluded, it requires negotiations leading to a just settlement of Aboriginal claims. It also requires that Aboriginal rights be "determined, recognized and respected."[138]

The *Little Salmon* case dealt with the application of the duty to consult to modern treaties and will be considered in Chapter 6. Here, it may be observed that the Court stated that the obligation of honourable dealing was recognized from the outset by the Crown itself in the Royal Proclamation of 1763, in which the British Crown pledged its honour to the protection of Aboriginal peoples from exploitation by non-Aboriginal people. The honour of the Crown has since become an important anchor in this area of the law and has been confirmed in its status as a constitutional principle. The Court commented that "the Crown cannot contract out of its duty of honourable dealing with Aboriginal people."[139]

In the 2013 *Manitoba Métis* case, as in the *Haida* case, the Court found against a fiduciary duty being owed by the Crown but went on to find a breach of the honour of the Crown. What is curious about the decision is the following passage:

> The honour of the Crown imposes a heavy obligation, and not all inter-
> actions between the Crown and Aboriginal people engage it. In the past,
> it has been found to be engaged in situations involving reconciliation of
> Aboriginal rights with Crown sovereignty. As stated in *Badger* ... "the
> honour of the Crown is always at stake in its dealing with Indian
> people."[140]

The statement that the honour of the Crown is always at stake in its dealing with "Indian" people was also made by the Court in *Haida,* as quoted above. It is difficult to reconcile this statement with the earlier statement that "not all interactions between the Crown and Aboriginal people engage it." This inconsistency creates uncertainty.

As mentioned above, *Manitoba Métis* dealt with the performance by the federal government of its constitutional obligation to allot land to Métis children under the *Manitoba Act.* The Court found that it had failed to do so in a purposive and diligent fashion as required by the principle of the honour of the Crown. In making this ruling, the Court created another concrete application for the principle: a duty on the part of the Crown to take a broad purposive approach to interpreting its constitutional obligations to Aboriginal peoples, and to act diligently to fulfill those obligations. Not every mistake or negligent act in implementing a constitutional obligation to an Aboriginal people brings dishonour to the Crown. However, a persistent pattern of errors and indifference that substantially frustrates the purposes of a solemn promise may amount to a betrayal of the Crown's duty to act honourably in fulfilling its promise. Nor does the honour of the Crown constitute a guarantee that the purposes of the promise will be achieved, as circumstances and events may prevent fulfillment despite the Crown's diligent efforts.

One of the judges, Justice Rothstein, wrote a strongly worded dissent. He stated: "The new duty derived from the honour of the Crown that my colleagues have created has the potential to expand Crown liability in un-predictable ways."[141] In his view, a duty of diligent fulfillment of solemn obligations may well prove to be an appropriate expansion of Crown obliga-tions. However, the duty crafted in the majority reasons was problematic. The threshold test for what constitutes a solemn obligation was unclear.[142] "Reducing honour of the Crown to a test about whether or not an obligation is owed simply to an Aboriginal group [risked] making claims under the honour of the Crown into 'fiduciary duty-light.'" This new duty, with a broader scope of application and a lower threshold for breach, was a significant ex-pansion of Crown liability.[143]

Comments on Fiduciary Duties and the Honour of the Crown

The law relating to fiduciary duties and the honour of the Crown has pro-voked strong passion on the part of some legal commentators. In a recent book, Jamie Dickson goes so far to describe the fiduciary relationship as "one of the disasters of Canada's colonial history" because it reinforces "a paternalistic and constitutionally immoral power structure."[144] He sees recent developments in the law relating to the honour of the Crown as very positive and close to totally eclipsing the fiduciary obligation developed by the SCC in the Crown-Aboriginal context, which he thinks is "a good thing."[145] With respect, this misconceives the nature of fiduciary obligations. Inequality between the parties is not a requirement for a fiduciary relationship, and not all fiduciaries are in a superior position to the beneficiary. Equal partners owe fiduciary duties to each other. A very wealthy employer is still owed a fiduciary duty of loyalty by his low-paid employees. So far as the charge of paternalism is concerned, this seems more justified with regard to the honour of the Crown, with its association of *noblesse oblige*. However, the SCC has denied that either the fiduciary relationship or the honour of the Crown principle is paternalistic, pointing out that they derive from the period when the Crown needed alliances with Aboriginal groups that still had consider-able military capacities.[146] This view also misunderstands the connection between the honour of the Crown principle and the Crown's fiduciary obli-gations. As we have seen, the SCC has been very clear that the latter is an application of the former and not in competition with it. So far as an "eclipse" is concerned, the Court reaffirmed in 2016 that the fiduciary relationship is "settled law."[147]

On the other hand, P.G. McHugh, an academic lawyer from New Zealand, is critical of developments relating to the honour of the Crown. He complains that it is "not an exacting or principled standard. It is a means by which the

Court can characterize Crown conduct as inadequate or falling short of contemporary standards set by judges."[148] We have seen that, in the *Manitoba Métis* case, Justice Rothstein was also very critical of the uncertainty surrounding the application of the principle in specific situations.

In my view, these concerns about the uncertainty of the honour of the Crown principle are justified. The concrete application of the principle is far from clear. For example, in *Kokopenace,* the SCC reversed a ruling of the majority of the Ontario Court of Appeal that a provision aimed at increasing Aboriginal representation on juries engaged the honour of the Crown.[149] The principle harkens back to an earlier period in our legal history when the part of law known as equity was being developed by the judges in the courts of the Lord Chancellor, separate from the general law known as the common law. One famous criticism stated: "Equity is a roguish thing: for law we have a measure, know what to trust to; equity is according to the conscience of him that is Chancellor, and as that is larger or narrower, so is equity."[150] Time will tell if this criticism fairly applies to the honour of the Crown principle as it is now being developed by the SCC.

The honour of the Crown principle is valuable so far as it is the source of more clearly defined legally enforceable obligations such as fiduciary obligations, the duty to consult, and honourable implementation of treaties and constitutional obligations, but it cannot, and should not, replace them.

TO SUM UP

- There are several variations of sovereignty, self-determination, and self-government.
- The sovereignty of a country is not necessarily the same as owning land in it.
- The question of sovereignty is not really a legal question but a political one, and Canadian courts will not accept challenges to Canadian sovereignty or their own powers as part of the Canadian state.
- The courts have clearly recognized Canadian sovereignty.
- The federal power to pass laws with respect to Aboriginal peoples and lands reserved for them is clear, but the power of the provinces is far from clear. The law is evolving in the direction of giving greater power to the provinces.
- The discovery doctrine was a principle accepted by European powers on how they were going to regulate among themselves who could deal with the Aboriginal peoples of North America. It necessarily limited the power of those peoples to deal with whomever they wished.
- The doctrine of continuity meant that Aboriginal laws and customs were recognized by the British and Canadian governments until they passed a law that was incompatible.
- The *Indian Act* and other federal legislation delegated limited self-government powers to Aboriginal groups.
- In 1995, the federal government issued a policy statement on the "inherent" right of self-government, recognizing some self-government powers, subject to conditions and negotiations.
- Cases on Canadian and Aboriginal sovereignty clearly have recognized the former but not the latter.

- The courts have generally avoided dealing with claims of Aboriginal self-government. In *Pamajewon*, the Supreme Court of Canada froze the right at the time of contact with Europeans and required evidence of the specific claimed right rather than of a general power of self-government.

- The orthodox view of the Constitution recognizes federal and provincial powers but does not allow for Aboriginal governments as a third order of government.

- RCAP and the TRC recommended broad powers of self-government for Aboriginal groups large enough to claim the right and said smaller communities would have to be reconstituted into between sixty and eighty nations across Canada. They also recommended the repudiation of concepts, such as the doctrine of discovery used to justify European sovereignty over Indigenous peoples.

- The federal and provincial governments owe fiduciary obligations to Aboriginal groups if certain conditions are satisfied and, in particular, if the government has discretionary control of an Aboriginal interest.

- The honour of the Crown, which has been given new application in recent SCC decisions, can give rise to a duty to consult Aboriginal groups regarding adverse impacts on their asserted Aboriginal rights and to fiduciary obligations. It applies to the processes of treaty making and implementation and may impose a duty to diligently meet constitutional obligations to Aboriginal peoples.

Aboriginal Rights and Title

4

Section 35 of the *Constitution Act, 1982* protects existing Aboriginal and treaty rights. It does not specifically reference Aboriginal title, which is included within Aboriginal rights generally. The Supreme Court of Canada has described a spectrum of Aboriginal rights, and Aboriginal title forms part of this spectrum. When it was drafted, however, Section 35 did not define the rights being protected or how to identify them. This was to be done at constitutional conferences. When they failed, the task then fell to the Court, which addressed key questions: How would "Aboriginal rights" be defined? At what time (or times) did they have to exist to be recognized? Could these rights change to reflect current circumstances and the impact of colonialism, or were they frozen in the form they were in prior to colonization? Were they generic and able to be exercised by all Aboriginal peoples, or were they dependent on the distinctive culture of a particular Aboriginal group? Would Aboriginal title be treated like other Aboriginal rights, or would special rules apply? What would be the content of the rights? Could they be limited? If so, what would be the test to justify a limitation? Finally, who would apply the test, and what would be the participation of Aboriginal peoples?

Source and Continuance of Aboriginal Rights

The Constitution recognizes and affirms Aboriginal rights, but it is not their source. Rather, to be recognized as Aboriginal rights, they must have pre-existed the arrival of Europeans (except in the case of the Métis, where a different test applies). The legal basis for Aboriginal rights is the doctrine of continuity, which was acknowledged by the SCC in *Mitchell*:

> English law, which ultimately came to govern aboriginal rights, accepted that the aboriginal peoples possessed pre-existing laws and interests, and recognized their continuance in the absence of extinguishment, by cession [transfer of territory], conquest, or legislation ... [A]boriginal interests and customary laws were presumed to survive the assertion of sovereignty, and were absorbed into the common law as rights, unless (1) they were incompatible with the Crown's assertion of sovereignty, (2) they were surrendered voluntarily via the treaty process, or (3) the government extinguished them.[1]

Unlike treaty rights, Aboriginal rights are not based on any agreement but on the facts and the law as applied by judges.

The burden of showing that a right has been extinguished is on the Crown, and the Court held in *Sparrow* that "the Sovereign's intention must be clear and plain if it is to extinguish an aboriginal right."[2] However, "the intent need not be express and therefore aboriginal rights may also be extinguished implicitly."[3] *Sparrow* established that regulation of a right does not result in its extinguishment and that "existing" in Section 35 meant unextinguished at the time the section was passed in 1982. Since then, the power to extinguish no longer exists.[4] In view of the general denial of the existence of Aboriginal rights and title prior to the *Calder* case in 1973,[5] it is unlikely that governments intended to extinguish them.

Proving an Aboriginal Right

The 1990 decision in *Sparrow* was the first case in which the SCC considered Section 35 and the protection for existing Aboriginal rights. Its main findings of law were that regulation prior to 1982 did not extinguish a right or prevent it from being an "existing right" (as already noted) and that the government could infringe the right if it could satisfy the justification test. It dealt with a charge of fishing with a net longer than the limit permitted by regulations. The question of whether Ron Sparrow was exercising an Aboriginal right to fish was not discussed in detail as "the existence of the right was not the subject of serious dispute."[6] The Court noted, in words that assumed great importance in the subsequent development of the law, that the anthropological evidence suggested that "for the Musqueam, the salmon fishery has always constituted an integral part of their distinctive culture."[7] This involved not only consumption for subsistence but also consumption on ceremonial and social occasions. The Court declined to consider if the right extended to commercial fishing as this had not been argued in the lower courts.

A few years later, the Court decided three cases together (called the *Van der Peet* trilogy after the case in which the Court set out its views in detail) and developed what is referred to as the "integral to a distinctive culture" test. The other cases were *Gladstone* and *N.T.C. Smokehouse*.[8] All the cases dealt with claims by BC First Nations that they had an Aboriginal right to barter or sell fish, thus raising the issue of a right to fish commercially. The claims were rejected by the majority of the Court except in *Gladstone,* where a right to sell herring spawn on kelp was upheld based on the evidence and the test for finding an Aboriginal right that had been set out in *Van der Peet.* There were separate dissenting judgments written by Justices L'Heureux-Dubé and McLachlin.

Writing for the majority, Chief Justice Lamer said that the first step was to identify the precise nature of the claim of Aboriginal right.[9] Examples would be a right to fish for food, for social and ceremonial purposes, to barter for subsistence purposes, or to sell commercially. The next step was to see if the evidence showed that the activity so identified was "an element of a practice, custom or tradition integral to the distinctive culture of the aboriginal group claiming the right."[10] The critical time was first contact with Europeans. The chief justice elaborated on the test by setting out ten factors to be considered in deciding whether the test has been satisfied,[11] including the following:

- the practice must be of central significance to the Aboriginal society in question
- "distinctive" did not mean "distinct" but rather "characteristic" of the culture, such as fishing by the Musqueam
- courts must approach the rules of evidence conscious of the difficulties in proving a right that originates in times when there were no written records
- claims must be decided on a specific rather than a general basis, with a focus on the practices of the particular Aboriginal group claiming the right

- "where the practice, custom or tradition arose solely as a response to European influences then that practice, custom or tradition will not meet the standard for recognition of an aboriginal right."[12]

The dissenting judges were very critical of the test and proposed their own (which have not been adopted). In the view of Justice L'Heureux-Dubé, "s. 35(1) should be viewed as protecting, not a catalogue of individualized practices, traditions or customs, as the Chief Justice does, but the 'distinctive culture' of which aboriginal activities are manifestations."[13] Using a specific date meant that a "frozen rights" approach was being adopted, contrary to the warning in *Sparrow* to reject such an approach.[14] It imposed a heavy and unfair burden, embodied "inappropriate and unprovable assumptions about aboriginal culture and society," and forced the claimant to search "for a pristine aboriginal society."[15] Justice McLachlin was equally critical of the majority decision. She stated that "aboriginal rights find their source not in a magic moment of European contact, but in the traditional laws and customs of the aboriginal people in question,"[16] and she noted the difficulties of an inquiry into the precise moment of European contact. Her test would include as an Aboriginal right "the right to be sustained from the land or waters upon which an aboriginal people have traditionally relied for sustenance. Trade in the resource to the extent necessary to maintain traditional levels of sustenance is a permitted exercise of this right."[17] This would

Integral to a Distinctive Culture

Developed in *Van der Peet,* the first step of this test of Aboriginal rights is to identify the precise nature of the right claimed (e.g., a right to fish for food, to barter for subsistence purposes, or to sell commercially). The next step is to see if the evidence shows that the activity so identified was "an element of a practice, custom or tradition integral to the distinctive culture of the aboriginal group claiming the right" at the time of contact with European people and not arising because of their influence. This test has been modified for the Métis so that the relevant time is the date of effective control by European laws rather than contact.

Aboriginal Peoples and the Law

enable them to obtain the modern equivalent to the amenities which they would have traditionally obtained from the resource.

In a later case, *Sappier*, the Court said that flexibility is important when engaging in the *Van der Peet* analysis because the object is to provide cultural security and continuity for the Aboriginal society.[18] Regarding the meaning of "culture" in the integral-to-a-distinctive-culture test, it elaborated that what is meant by "culture" is "really an inquiry into the pre-contact way of life of a particular aboriginal community, including their means of survival, their socialization methods, their legal systems, and potentially their trading habits ... The notion of aboriginality must not be reduced to 'racialized stereotypes of Aboriginal peoples.'"[19] In an even later case, *Lax Kw'alaams*, the Court expanded upon this clarification by stating that "the reference in *Sappier* to a pre-contact 'way of life' should not be read as departing from the 'distinctive culture' test set out in *Van der Peet*."[20] The result is some confusion as to what is required.

Sappier confirmed that an Aboriginal right is a communal right, stating that Section 35 recognized and affirmed existing Aboriginal and treaty rights in order to help ensure the continued existence of Aboriginal societies and to help maintain the distinctive character of those societies. Such rights are to be exercised for these purposes only, and are not to be exercised by any member of the Aboriginal community independently of the Aboriginal society they are meant to preserve.[21] The rights may be restricted to specific sites if the evidence requires this. However, Aboriginal rights are not always based in Aboriginal title to land, and Aboriginal title is simply one manifestation of a broader-based conception of Aboriginal rights.[22]

Examples of Aboriginal Rights

Aboriginal rights are specific to each Aboriginal group and "vary in accordance with the variety of aboriginal cultures and traditions which exist in this country."[23] We have seen that the Court has upheld rights to fish for food, social, and ceremonial purposes in *Sparrow*,[24] and to sell herring spawn on kelp in *Gladstone*. It found a right to harvest wood on Crown land for domestic purposes, such as constructing houses and making furniture for domestic use, in *Sappier*. The Court stated the nature of the right cannot be frozen in its pre-contact form but rather must be determined in light of present-day circumstances. The right to harvest wood for the construction of temporary shelters must be allowed to evolve into the right to harvest wood by modern means to be used in the construction of a modern dwelling. "If aboriginal rights are not permitted to evolve and take modern forms, then they will become utterly useless."[25] However, the right had no commercial dimension. The harvested wood could not be sold, traded, or bartered to produce assets or raise money, even if the object of such trade or barter was to finance the building of a dwelling.

In the *Tsilhqot'in* case, which also addressed Aboriginal title,[26] the BC Court of Appeal granted a declaration that the Aboriginal group had hunting and trapping rights (including the right to catch wild horses) and a right to earn a moderate livelihood from those rights over an area of approximately 4,000 square miles.[27] An Aboriginal right will normally include an incidental right to teach the practices, customs, or traditions to the next generation.[28] Finally, a controversial lower court decision in Ontario held that the practice of traditional medicine was an Aboriginal right that permitted a mother to oppose chemotherapy treatment for her child.[29]

Based on the lack of supporting evidence, the Court rejected claims of Aboriginal rights to the following:

- to participate in and regulate gambling[30]
- to bring goods across the Canada–United States boundary at the St. Lawrence River for purposes of trade[31]
- to harvest and sell on a commercial scale all species of fisheries resources from the claimed territories.[32]

The Court held that allowance for natural evolution does not justify the award of a quantitatively and qualitatively different right. A full-blown twenty-first-century commercial fishery could not be built on the narrow support of an ancestral trade in eulachon grease.[33]

The Métis

In *Powley*, the SCC applied the *Van der Peet* test to a Métis claim to hunt for food in the Sault Ste. Marie area.[34] However, it modified certain elements of the contact test to reflect the distinctive history and post-contact origins of the Métis, and the resulting differences between "Indian" claims and Métis claims. The Court held that "the focus should be on the period after a particular Métis community arose and before it came under the effective control of European laws and customs. This pre-control test enables us to identify those practices, customs and traditions that predate the imposition of European laws and customs on the Métis."[35] The applicable date in that case was 1850. The Court also held that, for the purposes of Section 35, claimants

Aboriginal Peoples and the Law

had to self-identify as members of a Métis community, present evidence of an ancestral connection to a historical Métis community, and demonstrate that they are accepted by the modern community whose continuity with the historical community provides the legal foundation for the right being claimed. In practice, lower courts have generally rejected claims of Métis Aboriginal rights because of the inability of claimants to show an ancestral connection to a historical Métis community situated where the claimed right was exercised.[36]

There is an anomaly between the rights of Métis and "Indian" descendants of their common "Indian" ancestors. For example, a Métis community that traces its ancestry to an "Indian" group might claim an Aboriginal right to trade furs that arose after contact but before effective control, while the "Indian" descendants of that group could not claim such a right.

Criticism of the Test for Aboriginal Rights

Commentators have generally supported the criticism of the dissenting judges in *Van der Peet*.[37] The integral-to-a-distinctive-culture test requires judges to look to the remote past and try to determine if the alleged right was of central significance to the society. This means going back as far as 1550 in Newfoundland[38] and 1603 in Quebec.[39] Proving the critical facts may be difficult and expensive, since the burden is on the Aboriginal group to show facts specific to their ancestral group at the time of contact (or control in the case of the Métis). It may be a matter of luck. For example, the ancestors of the Ahousaht people had the foresight to take an English sailor captive, and his account of their fishing was critical to their success.[40] As noted, the majority of the judges in *Van der Peet* acknowledged the difficulties of proof. In the *Delgamuukw* case on Aboriginal title,[41] decided the following year, the Court went further, permitting oral history to be given greater weight and put on an "equal footing" with other historical evidence, such as documents. A few years later, in *Mitchell,* however, the Court said that "a consciousness of the special nature of aboriginal claims does not negate the operation of general evidentiary principles."[42]

The test also excludes activities that may have been central to the Aboriginal society since contact, such as the fur trade (except in the case of the Métis, as discussed above). Of most importance, it ignores the current needs of Aboriginal societies. In particular, the Court has been very reluctant to allow any commercial benefit. Douglas Lambert, a former judge of the BC Court of Appeal and author of some very significant judgments in

Aboriginal law, has commented that reconciliation is unlikely with Aboriginal rights (as distinct from Aboriginal title), since they "simply preserve the opportunity to keep on doing the characteristic Indigenous activities that were being done at the time of first meaningful contact. In short, with rare exceptions, Aboriginal rights simply preserve the past."[43] As expressed by the SCC in one case, "they embody the right of native people to continue living as their forefathers lived."[44] They do not give Aboriginal societies what they need today to resolve their socio-economic problems and to meet the challenges posed by colonization.

It should be noted, however, that the potential to establish Aboriginal rights (or Aboriginal title or treaty rights) has been the stimulus for much negotiation in recent years that has led to benefits for Aboriginal peoples. The Crown has a duty of consultation and, if appropriate, accommodation if its actions will infringe Aboriginal interests even prior to those interests being proven in court. To avoid the delay and expense of litigation, governments and industry will often enter into agreements to ameliorate infringement, and some government programs have been the result, such as the Aboriginal Fisheries Strategy, introduced in response to the *Sparrow* decision, which gives the First Nations involved limited opportunities to catch fish for sale as well as food fishing.

Title versus Rights

Aboriginal title is part of the Aboriginal rights spectrum. However, it has some special features that require separate treatment. Some of these features may have arisen out of the strong reaction to the majority decision in *Van der Peet,* as they appeared in the *Delgamuukw* decision the following year. One difference relates to the source of Aboriginal title in the prior exclusive occupation of the land rather than in specific practices integral to a distinctive culture, although title, like other rights, is based on the pre-existence of Aboriginal peoples.[45] This difference has relevance for what needs to be proven. Another difference is that the relevant date for proof of Aboriginal title is the date of British sovereignty rather than contact (or effective control, as in the case of the Métis). Also, the content of Aboriginal title is largely generic, applying to all Aboriginal groups rather than based on the distinct culture of a specific group. There are, however, some common features shared by Aboriginal title with other Aboriginal rights, such as the communal nature of the right, the possibility of extinguishment prior to 1982, and the power of governments to infringe if justification can be shown.

Looking at the source of Aboriginal title, it is now clear that title does not derive from the Royal Proclamation of 1763, as thought earlier.[46] Instead it "arises from the prior occupation of Canada by aboriginal peoples."[47] This distinguishes it from "normal" property interests, like fee simple (freehold) title, that derive from the Crown. This pre-sovereignty source suggests a second source in "the relationship between common law and pre-existing systems of aboriginal law."[48]

> Aboriginal title does not derive from the Royal Proclamation of 1763, as thought earlier ... It "arises from the prior occupation of Canada by aboriginal peoples." This distinguishes it from "normal" property interests, like fee simple (freehold) title, that derive from the Crown.

Another major issue in *Calder* that has since been resolved in favour of Aboriginal peoples (at least in British Columbia) is extinguishment.[49] The test is the existence of "clear and plain" intention, as noted above in *Sparrow*.[50] In view of the constitutional division of powers established in 1867, which gave jurisdiction over "lands reserved for the Indians" to the federal government, only the federal government, not provincial governments, could have extinguished Aboriginal title. After 1982, neither government can do so.[51]

Crown Title and Sovereignty

Before considering the details of Aboriginal title, we must note the continued existence of Crown title to Aboriginal title lands, just as it exists over other lands.[52] This situation has been severely criticized by some writers,[53] who claim that it is due to the doctrine of discovery. However, it should be kept in mind that "discovery," or contact, usually pre-dated assertion of sovereignty, which is when Crown title arises.[54] In my view, this nominal ownership of the Crown is more a legal technicality or fiction, arising out of the doctrine of tenure (a principle of English feudal land law requiring the Crown to have underlying title to all land),[55] than a matter of real significance. The situation was explained in *Tsilhqot'in:* "At the time of assertion of European sovereignty, the Crown acquired radical or underlying title to all the land in the province. This Crown title, however, was burdened by the pre-existing legal rights of Aboriginal people who occupied and used the land prior to European arrival."[56] The Court remarked in *Guerin* on the "principle that a change in sovereignty over a particular territory does not in general affect the presumptive title of the inhabitants."[57]

Crown title is what is left when Aboriginal title is subtracted from the overall title, and, as we shall see, Aboriginal title confers "ownership rights similar to those associated with fee simple,"[58] which is the highest form of ownership. What is left for the Crown does not include enjoyment of the lands but only a nominal ownership. As stated in *Tsilhqot'in,* "the Crown does not retain a beneficial interest in Aboriginal title land."[59]

Of greater significance than nominal ownership is the sovereignty of the federal and provincial governments, which means that they can infringe Aboriginal title if they can justify the infringement. The Crown has the power to "encroach subject to justification."[60] This, in my view, is better seen as part of Crown sovereignty or jurisdiction rather than ownership.[61] As noted in Chapter 3, these two concepts should be kept distinct. The Court explained in *Delgamuukw* that "ownership of lands held pursuant to aboriginal title" was different from "jurisdiction over those lands," meaning the ability to make laws for them.[62] This was graphically illustrated by Felix Cohen, the lead author of the classic text on the US law, who noted that "after paying Napoleon 15 million dollars for the cession of political authority over the Louisiana Territory, we proceeded to pay the Indian tribes of the ceded territory more than twenty times this sum for such land in their possession as they were willing to sell."[63] Whatever the technical basis, the power of non-Aboriginal governments to have the last word is deeply offensive to many Aboriginal people. John Borrows writes, "More work is necessary to expunge all discriminatory vestiges of underlying Crown title that have submerged Indigenous sovereignty. Until that day occurs, Canada remains a deeply colonial state built on the vilest of discriminatory tenets."[64]

History of the Law of Aboriginal Title

Aboriginal title in Canada has a long history. Taking British Columbia as an example, especially given that the leading cases come from that province, we note the evidence of anthropologist Wilson Duff, quoted in *Calder:* "The patterns of ownership and utilization which [Aboriginal peoples] imposed

The Two Fundamental Principles of Aboriginal Title

1. The Crown's interest in the land is subject to existing Aboriginal interests in the land.
2. Those interests are to be removed only by solemn treaty.

Aboriginal Peoples and the Law

upon the lands and waters were different from those recognized by our system of law, but were nonetheless clearly defined and mutually respected." He explained, "Except for barren and inaccessible areas which are not utilized even today, every part of the Province was formerly within the owned and recognized territory of one or other of the Indian tribes."[65] This ownership was recognized by the doctrine of continuity, by specific laws such as the Royal Proclamation of 1763, and by cases decided in the early 1800s by the US Supreme Court. In *Cherokee Nation*, for example, the Court affirmed that "the Indians are acknowledged to have an unquestionable, and heretofore unquestioned, right to the land they occupy until that right shall be extinguished by a voluntary cession to our government."[66] This was also the "fundamental understanding – the *Grundnorm* of settlement in Canada," as confirmed by Justice McLachlin in *Van der Peet*. The common law recognized two fundamental principles: "the Crown took subject to existing aboriginal interests in the lands," and those interests "were to be removed only by solemn treaty."[67]

It is a breach of these fundamental principles that gives rise to Aboriginal title cases. Such breaches are most common in British Columbia and the Maritime provinces, where land surrender treaties were not generally signed. However, Aboriginal title cases may arise in other provinces, as shown by the December 2016 action commenced on behalf of the Algonquin Nation, which includes lands used for the Parliament Buildings, the SCC, and the National Library in Ottawa.[68] Much of southern Quebec is also without treaties.

Justice McLachlin noted that the fundamental principles held sway in British Columbia prior to the union with Canada in 1871, and that Governor Douglas negotiated a few treaties there. However, his requests for funding from both the colonial legislature in Victoria and the imperial government in London were rebuffed. Both agreed that treaties ought to be negotiated, but the former said that the latter should pay and the latter said it was the responsibility of the former. The amount involved was relatively small – £3,000 in 1861. Rarely can such penny-pinching have resulted in such enormous expense for future generations. Apart from the extension into the province of Treaty 8, treaty making came to an end for over a century. In the words of Justice McLachlin:

Tragically, [the early] policy was overtaken by the less generous views that accompanied the rapid settlement of British Columbia. The policy of negotiating treaties with the aboriginals was never formally abandoned.

It was simply overridden, as the settlers, aided by administrations more concerned for short-term solutions than the duty of the Crown towards the first peoples of the colony settled where they wished and allocated to the aboriginals what they deemed appropriate.[69]

It is worth noting that, unlike settlers, Aboriginal people were not permitted to acquire land under colonial and subsequent provincial law until 1953.[70]

The Nisga'a of northern British Columbia attempted to get a judicial determination of their claim to Aboriginal title but could not do so without the consent of the federal government.[71] It presented them in 1914 with a no-win alternative: if title were upheld, they had to surrender it completely in return for the same sort of treaty benefits awarded elsewhere, without compensation for the past and, furthermore, they had to use a lawyer appointed by the government.[72] In 1927, a Special Committee of Parliament said that since the Nisga'a had not accepted the opportunity to put their case to the court, "the matter should now be regarded as finally closed."[73] Legislation was also passed to make it an offence to raise funds to pursue land claims. This law remained in force until 1951 and effectively prevented a judicial determination for decades.[74]

The first Aboriginal title cases in Canada, dating from the 1800s, had involved the question of whether the federal or the provincial government owned lands in which the Aboriginal title had been surrendered. The Aboriginal group was not a party to the case and not represented. However, the courts made some vague and confusing comments that formed the legal background during the displacement and assimilation stage of Canada's history. These comments threw doubt on the fundamental principles summarized above by Justice McLachlin and appeared to uphold the denial of Aboriginal title that had become the policy of some governments, especially in BC. The Privy Council in London, England, then the final court of appeal for Canada, described Aboriginal title in the 1888 St. Catherine's Milling case as "a personal and usufructuary right dependent upon the good will of the Sovereign."[75] The "usufruct" is part of Roman and not English law, and is the right to use property belonging to another.

These confusing judicial statements, and the lack of any decision clearly deciding the issue, left much uncertainty about the legal status of Aboriginal title. In 1916, a leading text on the Canadian Constitution said the subject did "not seem to call for extended treatment" and expressed doubt that any action would be available to vindicate "the Indian 'title.'"[76] Aboriginal title then disappeared from Canadian textbooks for several decades. The 1969

White Paper of the federal government dismissed "aboriginal claims to land" in a couple of sentences "as too general and undefined to be capable of a specific remedy." In 1970, the first Canadian text on Aboriginal law stated:

> The claims of half of Canada's Indians were dealt with [in treaties] in an orderly way and on the basis that they had legal possessory rights to surrender. This raises significant questions about the legal correctness of dealings with land in the remaining areas. If a legal remedy exists for non-treaty areas now in non-Indian ownership, it could only be a claim for compensation. Such a claim has not, to date, been pursued in our courts.[77]

In fact, a pioneering case on Aboriginal title was being pursued and would be argued before the SCC and decided in 1973. This case, *Calder*,[78] was brought by the Nisga'a to finally obtain a judicial determination. The remedy they sought was not compensation or return of land but a declaration of title that could then be used to negotiate with the governments. There was some opposition to the case from other First Nations, who were concerned that a loss in court would mean a loss for all claims.[79]

Remarkably, given the heavy burden of proof currently placed on Aboriginal groups, the lawyer for the province conceded that the Nisga'a had inhabited the Nass Valley since time immemorial and had obtained a living from the lands and waters. Tom Berger, the lawyer for the Nisga'a, has commented: "These were vital concessions. To concede them was no more than common sense, but today no such concessions would be made. Instead, the courts would have to sit for weeks, months or years while elders of the tribe, together with anthropologists and other experts in disciplines unknown in 1969, struggle to advance extensive and tedious proof of the obvious."[80] The issue in *Calder* was whether colonial laws had extinguished the rights and title of the Nisga'a. There was little discussion of the nature of any title that still existed,[81] and it should be noted that no claim was made to land in which third parties had an interest: the Nisga'a were "prepared to accept things as they are."[82]

The decision was four to three against the Nisga'a. Technically, the case only decided that the litigation should not have been brought because a fiat (consent to sue the Crown) had not been obtained as was then required.[83] (We will see that technical rules having nothing to do with the merits have confused other cases.) The six judges who considered the issue split evenly on the issue of extinguishment. Justice Judson, speaking for three judges, ruled that the "sovereign authority" exercised "complete dominion over the lands in question adverse to any right of occupancy which [the Nisga'a] might have had when, by legislation, it opened up such lands for settlement."[84] Justice Hall gave reasons for the other three judges. In his seventy-seven-page judgment he examined the history and law of Aboriginal title, including the Royal Proclamation of 1763 and treaties. On the issue of extinguishment, he concluded after a review of cases from the US and British colonies that a "clear and plain" intention to extinguish title had to be shown, and the province had failed to do so.[85]

It is somewhat ironic, since he rejected the claim, that the following statement by Justice Judson has become the most quoted passage from *Calder* and, in its reference to the pre-existence of Aboriginal peoples, forms the basis of the modern law on Aboriginal rights and title: "The fact is that when the settlers came the Indians were there, organized in societies and occupying their land as their forefathers had done for centuries. This is what Indian title means."[86] This passage has been quoted as showing that all the judges who considered the issue recognized Aboriginal title unless it had been extinguished.[87] It is not entirely clear that Justice Judson intended this interpretation.[88] In any event, to quote Chief Justice McLachlin, in this case "the Supreme Court of Canada ushered in the modern era of Aboriginal land law."[89]

> "The fact is that when the settlers came the Indians were there, organized in societies and occupying their land as their forefathers had done for centuries. This is what Indian title means."
>
> Justice Judson in *Calder*

The decision caused the federal government in 1973 to implement a new policy on comprehensive land claims. In Berger's words, it "catapulted the question of aboriginal title into the political arena."[90] The first modern treaty, the James Bay Treaty, was signed two years later. One prominent critic and adviser to the BC government complained that "*Calder* is no support whatsoever for a land claims policy that sees vast areas of public land transferred in fee simple to native people."[91] Despite the change of policy at the federal level, the BC government's position of denial was to remain unaltered for another eighteen years. In 1978, Premier Bennett confirmed the provincial view that "if any aboriginal title or interest may once have existed, that title or interest was extinguished prior to the union of British Columbia with Canada in 1871."[92] In 1991, following the report of a Claims Task Force, the newly elected NDP government in BC agreed to set up a process to negotiate "land claims."

Aboriginal Peoples and the Law

The next stepping stone on the path to judicial recognition of Aboriginal title by the SCC was *Guerin*.[93] Chief Justice McLachlin noted in *Tsilhqot'in*, "The starting point in characterizing the legal nature of Aboriginal title is Dickson J.'s concurring judgment in *Guerin*."[94] This case concerned reserve lands, but the SCC held that the Indian interest in such lands was the same as that in Aboriginal title lands. Justice Dickson noted that "the reserve in question here was created out of the ancient tribal territory of the Musqueam Band."[95] As explained by Chief Justice McLachlin in *Tsilhqot'in*, "the Court confirmed the potential for Aboriginal title in ancestral lands."[96] In his opinion, Justice Dickson addressed the theory behind Aboriginal title as part of his analysis of the government's fiduciary duty. He held that the Crown had underlying and ultimate title. However, this title was burdened by the "preexisting legal right" of Aboriginal people based on their use and occupation of the land prior to European arrival.[97] He characterized this Aboriginal interest in the land as "an independent legal interest."[98] The recognition by the Court that Aboriginal title was a legal interest that pre-dated British sovereignty and was not dependent on a grant by the Crown was important to the future development of the law. It resolved the uncertainty left by *St. Catherine's Milling* and the divided opinions in *Calder* on whether Aboriginal title was a legal property right in the land.[99]

We have seen that the *Sparrow* decision in 1990 dealt with the issues of extinguishment and justification for infringement in the context of Aboriginal rights. On the first issue, it agreed with the minority opinion of Justice Hall in *Calder* that a clear and plain intention had to be proven.[100] This was a major development that also applied to Aboriginal title. In looking at the background to Section 35, the Court commented, "For many years, the rights of the Indians to their aboriginal lands – certainly as *legal* rights – were virtually ignored."[101]

The first Canadian case to give a comprehensive account of Aboriginal title was *Delgamuukw*, decided in 1997. In her account of the jurisprudential backdrop to the 2014 *Tsilhqot'in* decision, Chief Justice McLachlin observed that "the principles developed in *Calder*, *Guerin* and *Sparrow* were consolidated and applied in the context of a claim for Aboriginal title in *Delgamuukw*."[102] This was another case from British Columbia, and it shows how the approach to Aboriginal title litigation had changed. The trial lasted 374 days, compared with 5 days for *Calder*. The trial decision was 394 pages long compared with 35 pages. There were sixty-one witnesses giving very detailed evidence on genealogy, anthropology, and history as no admissions were made by the Crown on occupancy. This complexity and associated expense is typical of modern cases and is a major factor inhibiting them. What had not changed was the attitude of some judges. In *Calder*, Justice Hall rebuked the then chief justice of BC for describing the Nisga'a as "a very primitive people."[103] The trial judge in *Delgamuukw* was Chief Justice McEachern, who offended many Aboriginal people by stating that "aboriginal life in the territory was, at best, 'nasty, brutish and short,'" and the claimants were "a primitive people."[104] He dismissed the claims of Aboriginal title and self-government and found that the actions of the colonial government showed a clear and plain intention to extinguish Aboriginal title and rights except for fishing and hunting rights on unoccupied Crown lands. On appeal, the majority of the BC court essentially upheld the judgment except on the extinguishment issue.

On further appeal, the SCC said the failure of Chief Justice McEachern to give any independent weight to oral history evidence, as well as problems with how the case was pleaded, meant that a new trial was necessary (which has not taken place). Technically, the fact that the Court did not decide the outcome of the appeal might mean that, although authoritative, its statements on the law are not strictly binding on other courts (they are *obiter dicta* – said in passing). However, the Court's decision in *Tsilhqot'in* restated the principles in a way that is clearly binding. The main decision of Chief Justice Lamer in *Delgamuukw* is long (ninety-eight pages) and somewhat rambling and repetitive. The restatement is much easier to follow. The decision is striking for being decided on first principles rather than on the basis of other cases, which is the usual approach of the common law. This was understandable in view of the lack of Canadian cases dealing with Aboriginal title. Considerable reliance was placed on the views of legal academics.

The next time the SCC considered Aboriginal title was in *Marshall/ Bernard*,[105] two cases heard jointly in 2005, which involved a defence to a criminal charge of illegal logging from the Maritimes. Since peace and friendship treaties, not land treaties, were common in that part of Canada, the Court proceeded on the basis that there had been no surrender of title. The case created some uncertainty over the state of the law and whether the Court was pulling back from *Delgamuukw*. In particular, the majority reasons written by Chief Justice McLachlin in *Marshall/Bernard* took a restrictive view on what evidence would establish title and raised doubt "whether nomadic and semi-nomadic people can ever claim title to land."[106] She noted that, although sufficiently regular and exclusive exploitation of resources may translate into aboriginal title, "more typically, seasonal hunting and fishing rights exercised in a particular area will translate into a hunting or fishing right."[107] In reaching the decision, the Court overturned the decision of Justice Cromwell, then sitting in the Nova Scotia Court of Appeal. The requirement for proof of physical occupation was stressed, and the possibility of using Indigenous law to prove title (suggested in *Delgamuukw*) was left out. The decision was greeted with dismay by commentators sympathetic to Aboriginal peoples and welcomed by lawyers acting for governments.[108] Fortunately, it has been overtaken by the subsequent decision in *Tsilhqot'in*, which resolved the uncertainty.

Tsilhqot'in, decided in 2014, is now the leading case on Aboriginal title and sets out the current law, which will be summarized below. The case took twenty-five years from commencement to the SCC decision, including a trial of 339 days over five years. Not counting appendices, the decision of Justice Vickers, the trial judge and a former candidate for leadership of the BC New Democratic Party with a record of advancing social justice issues and especially the rights of those with disabilities, was 248 pages long. About thirty lawyers participated in the trial. The case started as a reaction to the devastation of clear-cut logging in the traditional territory of the Tsilhqot'in in central British Columbia. They claimed a declaration of title to approximately 4,380 square kilometres, and hunting and trapping rights. They were successful at trial and in the BC Court of Appeal with regard to the Aboriginal right to hunt and trap, and no appeal was taken to the SCC on this point. Justice Vickers declined to grant the declaration of title for technical reasons involving the pleadings (the formal documents setting out the legal claim and intended to give the other side an opportunity to reply). However, he considered the facts and the law and prepared "an expression of opinion ... to assist the parties in the negotiations that lie ahead."[109] His opinion was that Aboriginal title could be proven over 2,000 square kilometres.

The BC Court of Appeal reversed the trial judge on the pleadings point and disagreed with his opinion. The court expressed its view on the key issue of the area potentially covered by Aboriginal title. Giving the decision, Justice Groberman wrote: "I do not see a broad territorial claim as fitting within the purposes behind Section 35 of the *Constitution Act, 1982* or the rationale for the common law's recognition of Aboriginal title. Finally, I see broad territorial claims to title as antithetical to the goal of reconciliation, which demands that, so far as possible, the traditional rights of First Nations be fully respected without placing unnecessary limitations on the sovereignty of the Crown or on the aspirations of all Canadians, Aboriginal and non-Aboriginal."[110] Instead, title was limited to specific sites that were regularly and intensively used: "Examples might include salt licks, narrow defiles between mountains and cliffs, particular rocks or promontories used for netting salmon, or, in other areas of the country, buffalo jumps."[111] This restrictive view was referred to by critics as the "small spot" or "postage stamp" theory.

The SCC forcefully rejected this restrictive view and, for the first time in Canada, declared that an Aboriginal group had Aboriginal title – a historic ruling. The area involved was essentially the same as that covered in the opinion of the trial judge. In its ruling, the Court effectively reversed its position on sufficiency of occupation as set out in *Marshall/Bernard* without admitting that it was doing so. As noted above, in that case, it had rejected the decision of Justice Cromwell. In contrast, in *Tsilhqot'in,* it adopted several passages from his judgment. It may be relevant that he had since joined the SCC. We shall consider what the Court said on this issue and other legal issues below. Before doing so, it is important to observe how favourable the facts were to the Tsilhqot'in. It is unlikely that many other cases will enjoy these advantages. To summarize some of them: the Tsilhqot'in had a well-preserved oral history showing occupation of the lands; a Jesuit priest ventured into the territory in 1845 (the date of British sovereignty in British Columbia is 1846, which is the critical date in that province to prove title) and recorded information that helped at trial; there were no private lands, so no impact on fee simple owners; there were also no overlapping claims of other Aboriginal groups; and the area was remote and undeveloped.[112] The court also ordered that the Tsilhqot'in receive test-case funding so they could bring their case to trial.

> In *Tsilhqot'in,* for the first time in Canada, the Supreme Court of Canada declared that an Aboriginal group had Aboriginal title – a historic ruling.

Proof of Title

The burden of proving Aboriginal title is on the Aboriginal group.[113] This is a major cause of criticism given the obvious occupancy by most Aboriginal groups before assertion of European sovereignty. As noted by Justice Judson in *Calder,* "the fact is that when the settlers came, the Indians were there ... occupying the land."[114] Courts have not given an explanation for placing the onus on Aboriginal groups. Kent McNeil, of Osgoode Hall Law School, has reviewed some possible explanations but considers none of them entirely satisfactory.[115] The Truth and Reconciliation Commission said that the existing law was "manifestly unjust" and recommended reform.[116]

We have seen that the SCC has said that oral history must be put on "an equal footing" with documentary evidence. The Court recognized in *Delgamuukw* that "oral histories ... for many aboriginal nations are the only record of their past."[117] However, the Court also recognized the difficulties of such evidence and noted that accepting it is an exception to the usual hearsay rule, which requires statements be made in court in the presence of the judge and are subject to cross-examination. In practice, this will mean members of the Aboriginal group will give evidence explaining the "genealogy" of the evidence, setting out where the information came from. Some critics have complained that "trial courts remain suspicious of the reliability or value of Indigenous oral traditions,"[118] while others share the concerns of trial judges who suggest oral histories may be too general or biased and "do not reflect the western concept of objective fact tested by evidence."[119] Extensive reports from anthropologists and historians will also be submitted. Relevant evidence would include traditional place names, legends associated with geographical landmarks, trail networks, and use of the land for dwelling, hunting, and trapping.[120]

The relevant time for proof of Aboriginal title is assertion of British sovereignty.[121] This is different from the relevant time for other Aboriginal rights, which, as we have seen, is the date of contact or, in the case of the Métis, the date of effective European control. The distinction is based on Aboriginal title being a burden on Crown title, which only came into existence with sovereignty. The relevant date for British Columbia is 1846, when the Treaty of Oregon was signed with the United States, settling the border. It is not necessary to satisfy the test, applied to other Aboriginal rights, of being "integral to a distinctive culture" and not influenced by contact with Europeans.

A key issue in some cases will be to identify the correct descendant or successor group to the Aboriginal group at the time of sovereignty – the proper title holder.[122] There is a requirement to show continuity, as "claimants must establish they are rights holders."[123] This is an issue common to other forms of Aboriginal rights, but so far it seems to have only been contested in *Tsilhqot'in*, where the trial judge and the Court of Appeal held that the Tsilhqot'in Nation, not *Indian Act* bands, was the correct group. The Court of Appeal agreed that "the definition of the proper rights holder is a matter to be determined primarily from the viewpoint of the Aboriginal collective itself."[124] (This may be far from easy if there are competing groups claiming to represent the collective.)

The current test for proving Aboriginal title was summarized in *Tsilhqot'in*:

> [50] The claimant group bears the onus of establishing Aboriginal title.
> The task is to identify how pre-sovereignty rights and interests can
> properly find expression in modern common law terms. In asking
> whether Aboriginal title is established, the general requirements are:
> (1) "sufficient occupation" of the land claimed to establish title at the
> time of assertion of European sovereignty; (2) continuity of occupa-
> tion where present occupation is relied on; and (3) exclusive historic
> occupation. In determining what constitutes sufficient occupation,
> one looks to the Aboriginal culture and practices, and compares
> them in a culturally sensitive way with what was required at com-
> mon law to establish title on the basis of occupation. Occupation
> sufficient to ground Aboriginal title is not confined to specific sites
> of settlement but extends to tracts of land that were regularly used
> for hunting, fishing or otherwise exploiting resources and over
> which the group exercised effective control at the time of assertion
> of European sovereignty.

The major decision in *Tsilhqot'in* (together with the recognition of provincial powers to infringe Aboriginal rights and title) was acceptance of the
"territorial" approach and rejection of the "postage stamp" theory – an issue
the Court said was "at the heart of this appeal."[125] The Court held sufficient
occupation required "evidence of a strong presence" demonstrating that the
land "belonged to, or was controlled by, or was under the exclusive stewardship of the claimant group."[126] Exclusivity "should be understood in the sense
of intention and capacity to control the land," including granting or refusing
permission to enter.[127] In *Marshall/Bernard*, the Court confirmed the view
expressed in *Delgamuukw* that "shared exclusivity may result in joint title."[128]
To date, there have been no cases of joint title.

Since the legal test for Aboriginal title is based on exclusive, pre-
sovereignty occupation, it may be difficult for a Métis group to satisfy this
test unless, like the test for other Aboriginal rights, it is modified for them.[129]

The Content of Aboriginal Title

What rights are conferred by Aboriginal title? The law was established in
Delgamuukw and summarized in *Tsilhqot'in*. Before considering the content
of Aboriginal title, it is important to note that, unlike other Aboriginal rights,
which are specific to the Aboriginal group involved (although they may

share common characteristics), Aboriginal title rights are largely uniform or generic and do not vary from group to group. Subject to exceptions flowing from the inherent limit and compensation for infringement mentioned below, the law treats all groups the same. They have the exclusive right to use the land for a range of purposes and are not limited to those inherent to their distinctive culture. "These uses are not confined to the uses and customs of pre-sovereignty times; like other landowners, Aboriginal title holders of modern times can use their land in modern ways, if that is their choice."[130] Therefore, a group that traditionally used its land for hunting is not limited to that use and can use it for other purposes, provided they do not ruin the land or prevent it from being used for its original purpose – strip-mining land originally used for hunting is an example of an activity that could be prevented by the inherent limit.[131]

> Unlike other Aboriginal rights, which are specific to the Aboriginal group involved (although they may share common characteristics), Aboriginal title rights are largely uniform or generic and do not vary from group to group.

The rights were summarized in *Tsilhqot'in:*

[73] Aboriginal title confers ownership rights similar to those associated
with fee simple, including: the right to decide how the land will be
used; the right of enjoyment and occupancy of the land; the right to
possess the land; the right to the economic benefits of the land; and
the right to pro-actively use and manage the land.

"Fee simple" is generally described as the highest possible ownership interest that the common law recognizes and is the usual form of ownership. However, the Court went on to note an important restriction:

[74] Aboriginal title, however, comes with an important restriction – it
is collective title held not only for the present generation but for all
succeeding generations. This means it cannot be alienated except to
the Crown or encumbered in ways that would prevent future generations of the group from using and enjoying it. Nor can the land
be developed or misused in a way that would substantially deprive
future generations of the benefit of the land.

We can see some significant distinctions from other property interests. Aboriginal title, like other Aboriginal rights and treaty rights, is a collective and not an individual interest: "Aboriginal title cannot be held by individual aboriginal persons; it is a collective right to land held by all members of an aboriginal nation. Decisions with respect to that land are also made by that community."[132] It cannot be "alienated" (sold or transferred) except to "the Crown." (This term is not explained and might refer either to the federal or provincial government or both. Usually, the province would obtain title to land following a surrender of Aboriginal title.[133]) Another distinction is the source of Aboriginal title as "the unique product of the historic relationship between the Crown and the Aboriginal group in question"; it is a right that "arises from possession before the assertion of British sovereignty whereas normal estates like fee simple arise afterward."[134] In *Delgamuukw* it was said that these three "key dimensions" (collective right, inalienability except to the Crown, and source) could only be understood "by reference to both common law and aboriginal perspectives," which makes Aboriginal title unique or "*sui generis*."[135] Another difference is the inherent limit on use so that future generations may benefit. A further difference is that Aboriginal property rights, unlike other property rights, have constitutional protection under Section 35. It has also been held in British Columbia that, unlike other interests in land, Aboriginal title lands cannot be registered in the provincial land title system.[136] Brian Slattery, a leading authority on Aboriginal title, has suggested that Aboriginal title should be considered "a concept of *public law*," not private law, and is similar to provincial title, "its close relative."[137]

Aboriginal Title versus Other Property Interests

- Aboriginal title is a collective rather than an individual interest.
- Aboriginal title cannot be sold or transferred except to "the Crown."
- Aboriginal title "arises from possession before the assertion of British sovereignty."
- Aboriginal title land cannot be used in a way that would substantially deprive future generations of its benefits.
- Aboriginal property rights have constitutional protection under Section 35.
- Provincial law may not permit Aboriginal title lands to be registered in the provincial land title system.

Commentators have been critical of the contents of Aboriginal title. Thomas Flanagan, a conservative/libertarian political scientist, thinks the SCC has defined Aboriginal title "in a way that will make its use impossible in a modern economy."[138] According to Flanagan, the *Delgamuukw* judgment "lacks empirical reference points ... The Court laid down a set of principles, but it is hard to say what they mean in practice."[139] He writes that "communal ownership is an awkward instrument in a dynamic market economy," and inalienability will limit its usefulness. The "inherent limit" will result in "potential restrictions on use that in particular cases can be articulated only by the courts," which "cannot help but detract from economic value by introducing uncertainty."[140] It is this uncertainty that is the biggest problem: "in spite of its attempts at conceptual sophistication, the [judgment] leaves most of the pressing practical issues unsettled. As [Melvin Smith] has said, *Delgamuukw* 'undermined everything but settled nothing.'"[141] Flanagan concludes that the judgment "is a lawyer's dream but an entrepreneur's nightmare."

Other commentators have soundly condemned the imposition of the inherent limit as lacking any basis in law and for being paternalistic. In contrast, in *Johnson v. McIntosh,* the US Supreme Court said tribes could "use [the land] according to their own discretion."[142] In the view of Brian Slattery, the Court "appears to have created the inherent limit out of whole cloth."[143] Several writers have said the inherent limit should not be imposed if the Aboriginal group does not want restrictions.

There is also uncertainty as to the current scope of the limit. This is how it is described in *Tsilhqot'in:* "Nor can the land be developed or misused in a way that would substantially deprive future generations of the benefit of the land."[144] This is a bit different from *Delgamuukw,* which included the additional restriction that "lands subject to aboriginal title cannot be put to such uses as may be irreconcilable with the nature of the occupation of that land and the relationship that the particular group has had with the land."[145] It is not clear what this restriction was intended to cover, since the Court was also at pains to point out that "[t]his is not ... a limitation that restricts the use of the land to those activities that have traditionally been carried out on it."[146] It seems that lands traditionally used for hunting might be used for tourism, as this might be reconcilable with hunting, but they could not be used for farming, ranching, or residential development, as this would not be reconcilable with hunting. Kent McNeil, another leading authority, has suggested that "present uses are not restricted to, but they are restricted by, past practices and traditions," and "Aboriginal peoples may be prisoners of the past."[147] The absence of a reference to this additional restriction in *Tsilhqot'in* may or may not be significant, and the scope of the limit described in that case is also uncertain. If lands are leased under a long-term lease with all rent paid up-front (a common type of development), will this "substantially deprive future generations of the benefit of the land"?

Aboriginal title holders enjoy the usual remedies for any breaches, adapted as may be necessary to reflect the special nature of Aboriginal title and the Crown's fiduciary obligation.[148]

Justification for Infringing Aboriginal Rights and Title

In *Tsilhqot'in* the Court noted, "The right to control the land conferred by Aboriginal title means that governments and others seeking to use the land must obtain the consent of the Aboriginal title holders. If the Aboriginal group does not consent to the use, the government's only recourse is to establish that the proposed incursion on the land is justified under Section 35 of the *Constitution Act, 1982*."[149]

A fundamental feature of Aboriginal law is the ability of the federal and provincial governments to infringe constitutionally protected Aboriginal and treaty rights (including title) if they can satisfy the justification test. This test is another creation of the judges and is not mentioned in Section 35 of the *Constitution Act, 1982* or elsewhere in the Constitution. In fact, a review of Parts 1 and 2 of the act indicates that no such ability was intended by Parliament. Section 35 is contained in Part 2, "Rights of the Aboriginal Peoples of Canada." Part 1 is the "Canadian Charter of Rights and Freedoms," which deals with the rights of individuals such as the right to vote and freedom of expression. Charter rights are subject to Section 1, which permits "such reasonable limits prescribed by law as can be demonstrably justified in a free and democratic society." Some Charter rights are also subject to the notwithstanding clause in Section 33 that permits Parliament or the legislature of a province to override them. Neither Section 1 nor Section 33 applies to Aboriginal and treaty rights. In effect, the SCC rewrote the Constitution to impose equivalent limits to those found in Section 1, despite the clear intention of Parliament that no such limits should apply.[150] In the words of Justice McLachlin in a dissenting judgment, "to read judicially the equivalent of s. 1 into s. 35 [is] contrary to the intention of the framers of the Constitution."[151]

In *Sparrow* and later cases, the Court is at pains to always balance the existence of the right with the ability of the governments to infringe it, as if infringement somehow formed part of the right instead of an exceptional action. It is as if the right and the infringement are opposite sides of the coin and we should not think of the right without contemplating its infringement. What the Court gives with one hand it allows non-Aboriginal governments to take away with the other without any meaningful participation by the Aboriginal group beyond a right to be consulted. This is a peculiar way to look at rights, especially constitutionally protected rights. McNeil has suggested that the Court's approach had little to do with the actual words of Section 35 and a great deal to do with policy considerations and a colonial attitude.[152]

Aboriginal rights and title are not absolute and can be overridden by the federal and provincial governments for the broader public good if the test of justification is satisfied.

The justification test was summarized in *Tsilh-qot'in* as follows:

[77] To justify overriding the Aboriginal title-holding group's wishes on the basis of the broader public good, the government must show: (1) that it discharged its procedural duty to consult and accommodate; (2) that its actions were backed by a compelling and substantial objective; and (3) that the governmental action is consistent with the Crown's fiduciary obligation to the group: *Sparrow*.

We shall review the "procedural duty to consult and accommodate" in Chapter 6, but here we can note that, based on the facts of the case in *Tsilhqot'in*, the Court found a breach of the duty to consult, so this element of justification was not satisfied. The requirement to show "a compelling and substantial objective" was explained as part of the process of reconciling Aboriginal interests with the broader interests of society as a whole. This is the *raison d'être* of the principle of justification. To constitute a compelling and substantial objective, the broader public goal asserted by the government must further the goal of reconciliation, having regard to both the Aboriginal interest and the broader public interest.[153]

The Court illustrated the types of interests that are potentially capable of justifying an incursion on Aboriginal title by quoting the following passage from *Delgamuukw*:

The range of legislative objectives that can justify the infringement of aboriginal title is fairly broad ... In my opinion, the development of agriculture, forestry, mining, and hydroelectric power, the general economic development of the interior of British Columbia, protection of the environment or endangered species, the building of infrastructure and the settlement of foreign populations to support those aims, are the kinds of objectives that are consistent with this purpose and, in principle, can justify the infringement of aboriginal title.[154]

One writer has suggested that "it is difficult to see in these objectives much difference from the early justification of dispossession in terms of the superiority of European derived societies and their development imperatives."[155] Another writer has said that the list "effectively defines the continuation of the colonial project."[156]

The Court has also given the "pursuit of economic and regional fairness" and participation in the fishery by non-Aboriginal groups as examples of objectives that justify infringement.[157] In *Sparrow*, the Court said that the public interest was too vague to be used as justification,[158] but these examples show that the Court is now using public interest arguments despite their vagueness and the political choices that must be made in applying them. In *Tsilhqot'in*, the Court expressly referred to the "broader public interest."[159] Clearly, the interests of non-Aboriginal people are very much in the Court's mind. However, in *Tsilhqot'in* the Court agreed that no compelling and substantial objective existed based on the evidence. The trial judge found that the two objectives put forward by the province – the economic benefits that would be realized as a result of logging in the claim area and the need to prevent the spread of a mountain pine beetle infestation – were not supported by the evidence.[160]

As noted by Justice McLachlin in her dissenting judgment in *Van der Peet*:

> The extension of the concept of compelling objective to matters like economic and regional fairness and the interests of non-aboriginal fishers ... would negate the very aboriginal right to fish itself, on the ground that this is required for the reconciliation of aboriginal rights and other interests and the consequent good of the community as a whole. This is not limitation required for the responsible exercise of the right, but rather limitation on the basis of the economic demands of non-aboriginals.[161]

She saw this extension as appearing to permit the constitutional Aboriginal right to be conveyed to non-Aboriginal people in the interests of community

Aboriginal Peoples and the Law

harmony and reconciliation. However, by not including an express limit, the framers of Section 35(1) deliberately chose not to subordinate the exercise of Aboriginal rights to the good of society as a whole. This concept of justification was "ultimately more political than legal,"[162] and in her view it was unconstitutional, since it authorized the Crown to convey a portion of the Aboriginal right to non-Aboriginal people and so cut down the right without the consent of the Aboriginal group: "To reallocate the benefit of the right from aboriginal to non-aboriginals, would be to diminish the substance of the right that s. 35(1) ... guarantees to the aboriginal people. This no court can do."[163]

Justice Vickers, the trial judge in *Tsilhqot'in*, echoed these concerns, saying, "The result is that the interests of the broader Canadian community, as opposed to the constitutionally entrenched rights of Aboriginal peoples, are to be foremost in the consideration of the Court. In that type of analysis, reconciliation does not focus on the historical injustices suffered by Aboriginal peoples. It is reconciliation on terms imposed by the needs of the colonizer."[164] In the view of Aboriginal legal scholar John Borrows, "Courts have read Aboriginal rights to lands and resources as requiring a reconciliation that asks more of Aboriginal peoples than it does of Canadians. Reconciliation should not be a front for assimilation."[165] Kent Roach argues that "[i]n its efforts to recognize the impact of Aboriginal rights on the non-Aboriginal majority of British Columbia, the Court has run the risk of making Aboriginal rights hostage to the interests of the majority."[166]

In the third part of the test, the Crown must satisfy its fiduciary obligation to the Aboriginal group. This can be seen as a check on the power of the Crown. In the words of *Sparrow*, "the words 'recognition' and 'affirmation' [in Section 35] incorporate the fiduciary relationship ... and so import some restraint on the exercise of sovereign power ... federal power must be reconciled with federal duty."[167] This was the source and original meaning of "reconciliation," which plays such a large part in modern Aboriginal law. The Court later stated, "The way in which a legislative objective is to be attained must uphold the honour of the Crown."[168] The first question to be asked on this part of the test is whether the legislation in question has the effect of interfering with an existing Aboriginal right. The burden is on the Aboriginal group to show "a *prima facie*" (first impressions) infringement, meaning an infringement that is more than trivial. Examples include an unreasonable limitation or one that imposes undue hardship or that denies to the Aboriginal group their preferred means of exercising the right.[169] In *Nikal* it was held that requiring a licence without a fee to exercise the right is not necessarily an infringement, but in *Badger* the requirement for a fee was held to be an infringement. An overly broad discretion on the part of a decision maker is also an infringement.[170] In *Tsilhqot'in*, the Court said that general regulatory forest legislation will not usually be an infringement but the issue of timber licences would be a serious infringement that would not lightly be justified.[171]

Once a *prima facie* infringement has been shown, the burden passes to the government to show it has satisfied its fiduciary obligation. This will obviously depend on the specific facts. If resource allocation is an issue, as with the right to fish, *Sparrow* held that, although conservation needs must be respected, the Aboriginal group is entitled to priority over other user groups. For example, in *Adams,* the government could not infringe the Aboriginal right to fish in order to benefit recreational fishers. The Court relaxed priority in *Gladstone* in the case of an Aboriginal right to fish commercially to avoid an exclusive fishery, but it was still necessary for the government to take steps to enable Aboriginal participation and involvement through measures such as reduced licence fees.[172] The Court stated in *Tsilhqot'in* that the fiduciary duty

> infuses an obligation of proportionality into the justification process.
> Implicit in the Crown's fiduciary duty to the Aboriginal group is the requirement that the incursion is necessary to achieve the government's goal (rational connection); that the government go no further than necessary to achieve it (minimal impairment); and that the benefits that may be expected to flow from that goal are not outweighed by adverse effects on the Aboriginal interest (proportionality of impact).[173]

In the case of Aboriginal title, the Crown cannot justify incursions "if they would substantially deprive future generations of the benefit of the land,"[174] thus applying the internal limit to the Crown.

One important issue that remains unexplored in any detail is the payment of compensation for an infringement. Giving the majority judgment, Chief Justice Lamer was clear in *Delgamuukw* that fair compensation is "ordinarily" payable but was vague on the principles to be used, stating only that "the amount of the compensation payable will vary with the nature of the particular aboriginal title affected and with the nature and severity of the infringement and the extent to which aboriginal interests were accommodated."[175] Justice La Forest was equally vague:

It must be emphasized, nonetheless, that fair compensation in the present context is not equated with the price of a fee simple. Rather, compensation must be viewed in terms of the right and in keeping with the honour of the Crown. Thus, generally speaking, compensation may be greater where the expropriation relates to a village area as opposed to a remotely visited area. I add that account must be taken of the interdependence of traditional uses to which the land was put.[176]

One writer has suggested melding fiduciary principles with expropriation principles.[177] The former would generally result in higher compensation than the latter. Another writer has referred to the uncertainty over the time to be used when calculating compensation – i.e., modern values versus traditional land values.[178]

TO SUM UP

- The legal basis for Aboriginal rights and title is the doctrine of continuity.

- The Supreme Court of Canada has created different tests for Aboriginal title and for other Aboriginal rights.

- Aboriginal title requires proof of exclusive occupation of the land at the time of assertion of Crown sovereignty.

- Other Aboriginal rights require proof that the Aboriginal group exercised the practice at the time of contact with non-Aboriginal people (or at the time of control by the Crown in the case of the Métis) and that the practice was integral to their distinctive culture (the *Van der Peet* test). This test has been criticized for freezing Aboriginal rights to practices at the time of contact.

- Governments could extinguish Aboriginal rights and title prior to their constitutional recognition in 1982, but extinguishment required a clear and plain intention. The SCC split evenly on this question in *Calder* in 1973.

- The first case to give a comprehensive account of Aboriginal title was *Delgamuukw* (1996), and the first case to find Aboriginal title was *Tsilhqot'in* (2014), which accepted a territorial approach to finding title and rejected the "postage stamp" approach.

- Aboriginal title confers ownership rights similar to those associated with fee simple or freehold private ownership of land, including the rights to decide how the land will be used and to the economic benefit of the land.

- Aboriginal title comes with important restrictions to reflect its collective nature and the interests of future generations. It can only be transferred to the government and cannot be developed or used in a way that would substantially deprive future generations of the benefit of the land (the inherent limit).

- The inherent limit has been criticised for being paternalistic and uncertain and for limiting the value of the land.

- All Aboriginal rights, including title, can be infringed upon by governments if they can satisfy the requirements of the justification test first set out in the *Sparrow* case. The justification test requires the government to show (a) it has consulted with the Aboriginal group, (b) its actions were backed by a compelling and substantial objective, and (c) the actions are consistent with its fiduciary obligation to the group.

- The range of governmental objectives that can justify infringement are very broad and include economic development and "the settlement of foreign populations." Critics have said this effectively continues colonialism and allows the interests of non-Aboriginal people to trump constitutionally protected Aboriginal rights.

- The law has developed greatly in the last few decades, but there are several questions that remain to be answered about Aboriginal rights and title, including fundamental issues such as whether Aboriginal title prevails over the ownership of land by other people, the extent of the inherent limit on uses of Aboriginal title lands, and compensation for infringement of title.

5

Treaties

The major legal significance of treaties is that they terminated Aboriginal rights and title to most of Canada, leaving relatively small parcels of lands for Aboriginal peoples ("reserves" for historical treaties and "settlement lands" for modern treaties) and some remaining hunting and fishing rights to undeveloped parts of the traditional territory. In doing so, they opened land for non-Aboriginal settlement during the colonial settlement era (historical treaties), or regularized the failure to satisfy legal requirements for terminating such rights and title prior to the dispossession of Aboriginal peoples (modern treaties). We saw in Chapter 4 that the "fundamental understanding ... of settlement in Canada" (however much it is ignored in practice) was that "the Crown took subject to existing aboriginal interests in the lands," and those interests "were to be removed only by solemn treaty."[1]

When it comes to treaties, there are a number of key questions to consider: What parts of Canada are covered by treaties? How do treaties differ? What is their role and legal nature? What principles govern treaty interpretation? What legal issues arise from historical treaties given the circumstances under which they were entered into, the differing understandings of the parties, and the inequality of bargaining power? What progress is being made with modern treaties?

Treaties versus Aboriginal Rights

From the perspective of Aboriginal peoples, there are advantages to concluding a treaty if they are doubtful of their ability to successfully prove Aboriginal
rights or title, or if the benefits to be gained with a treaty exceed those of
Aboriginal rights and title and the costs of proving them.[2] The treaty process
does not require Aboriginal groups to prove Aboriginal rights and title. In
addition to land, treaties can cover such matters as

- trading rights[3]
- political and social rights[4]
- medical, educational, and financial benefits[5]
- the cessation of hostilities.[6]

Treaties also enable the parties to agree and therefore provide greater certainty
on the scope of their rights and obligations.

Although treaties arose in response to Aboriginal rights, the SCC has
explained the differences:

> There is no doubt that aboriginal and treaty rights differ in both origin
> and structure. Aboriginal rights flow from the customs and traditions of
> the native people ... they embody the right of native people to continue
> living as their forefathers lived. Treaty rights, on the other hand, are
> those contained in official agreements between the Crown and the native
> peoples ... They create enforceable obligations based on the mutual con-
> sent of the parties.[7]

We shall see that, in the case of the historical treaties, there is much doubt
as to the extent of that mutual consent.

Aboriginal rights and treaties share some common legal characteristics:

- They are included within the protection of Section 35.
- They are collective rights.[8]
- They are in a class of their own ("*sui generis*" to use legal jargon).[9]
- They may be infringed by federal and provincial governments if the
  infringement can be justified under the test described in Chapter 4.[10]

But, as pointed out by Kent Roach, "The judicial invention of a general gov-ernmental power to limit all treaty rights has no textual foundation in the text of the treaties or in the *Constitution Act, 1982.*"[11]

In some cases, treaties expressly confirmed that Aboriginal rights like hunting and fishing could continue to be exercised "as formerly" with modi-fication, such as excluding hunting from occupied lands.[12] Some treaties allow governments to curtail such rights by "taking up" the lands to permit development.[13] Modern treaties may also modify the attributes and geo-graphical extent of Aboriginal rights and title, and the modified rights and title continue for the purposes of Section 35.[14]

Treaties can vary in length from a simple one-paragraph document written in 1760, considered by the SCC in *Sioui*,[15] to almost incomprehensible multi-volume modern treaties.[16] Although much of Canada is covered by the Robinson treaties and the numbered treaties completed between 1850 and the 1920s, which share many common terms, there are hundreds of treaties, and their legal consequences must be considered individually. "Treaty rights, like aboriginal rights, are specific and may be exercised ex-clusively by the First Nation that signed the treaty. The interpretation of each treaty must take into account the First Nation signatory and the circumstances that surrounded the signing of the treaty."[17] In one case, Justice Binnie referred to "the anomalies of an on-again off-again treaty making process with a dodgy record that stretches back more than 250 years" and to "serendipitous differences in the wording of the treaties," contrasting the "medicine chest" clause in Treaty No. 6 with the absence of the clause in Treaty No. 5.[18]

The SCC has urged governments and Aboriginal peoples to negotiate treaties in preference to litigation over the existence and extent of Aboriginal rights and title,[19] and has seen treaties as serving "to reconcile pre-existing Aboriginal sovereignty with assumed Crown sovereignty."[20] It has held that "where treaties remain to be concluded, the honour of the Crown requires negotiations leading to a just settlement of Aboriginal claims."[21] To enable such negotiations to take place, and in an attempt to avoid significant impacts on asserted Aboriginal rights during the negotiation period, the Court has recognized a duty on the part of the Crown to consult and, as appropriate, accommodate potential, but yet unproven, Aboriginal interests.[22] We shall consider this duty, which flows from the honour of the Crown principle, in the next chapter. It may be noted here that the duty to consult also applies to the exercise of rights by the Crown under existing treaties, such as the above-mentioned clause in some treaties permitting the Crown to "take up" land for development.[23]

The Court has described the modern treaty process as an "attempt to further the objectives of reconciliation [of Aboriginal and non-Aboriginal Canadians] not only by addressing grievances over the land claims but by creating the legal basis to foster a positive long-term relationship between Aboriginal and non-Aboriginal communities."[24] In *Nacho Nyak Dun*, the Court stated:

> As expressions of partnership between nations, modern treaties play a critical role in fostering reconciliation. Through s. 35 of the *Constitution Act, 1982*, they have assumed a vital place in our constitutional fabric. Negotiating modern treaties, and living by the mutual rights and responsibilities they set out, has the potential to forge a renewed relationship between the Crown and Indigenous peoples.[25]

In its 1996 report, the Royal Commission on Aboriginal Peoples gave central importance to treaty making. This meant treaty making for Aboriginal nations without treaties, but it also meant renewal of existing treaties and a new relationship with non-Aboriginal governments based on treaties. "It is within the treaty processes we propose that our substantive recommendations on matters such as governance, lands and resources, and economic issues will ultimately be addressed."[26]

The Truth and Reconciliation Commission's 2015 report said that "without Treaties, Canada would have no legitimacy as a nation. Treaties between Indigenous nations and the Crown established the legal and constitutional foundation of this country."[27] This is the "treaty federalism" theory.[28] The TRC refers to the Royal Proclamation of 1763 and its relationship to the Treaty of Niagara of 1764. Recall that the Royal Proclamation asserted Crown sovereignty and said that Aboriginal lands could only be acquired by the Crown, and only with the consent of the Aboriginal group. This proclamation was approved, as a treaty would be, by over two thousand Aboriginal leaders who had gathered at Niagara in the summer of 1764. The TRC states, "The Royal Proclamation of 1763, in conjunction with the Treaty of Niagara of 1764, established the legal and political foundation of Canada and the principles of Treaty making based on mutual recognition and respect."[29] Michael Asch argues that failing to honour treaties calls into question the legitimacy of non-Aboriginal settlement, "for they are the foundation that legitimizes our settlement on these lands."[30] The treaty federalism theory raises the question of the legitimacy of settlement in non-treaty areas.

History of Treaties

The history of treaties is reflective of the three stages of post-contact history in Canada described in Chapter 2.[31] The stage of contact and co-operation is reflected in the peace and friendship treaties in parts of Quebec and the Maritime provinces; the stage of displacement and assimilation in the land treaties formally dispossessing Aboriginal peoples, as in the Robinson and numbered treaties; and the stage of negotiation and renewal in the modern treaties.

The stage of contact and co-operation is reflected in the peace and friendship treaties in parts of Quebec and the Maritime provinces; the stage of displacement and assimilation in the land treaties formally dispossessing Aboriginal peoples, as in the Robinson and numbered treaties; and the stage of negotiation and renewal in the modern treaties.

Some agreements that are now recognized as treaties pre-date the Royal Proclamation. In 1615, Champlain entered into alliances with the Huron in what is now Quebec, and the Huron signed agreements with the French in 1624, 1645, and 1655. The Great Peace of Montreal was signed with the Iroquois in 1701 to end hostilities between them and the French. Sébastian Grammond, former professor of civil law at the University of Ottawa and now a federal court judge, notes that these agreements have never been considered by the courts.[32] Treaties of peace and friendship were signed between the British Crown and Aboriginal groups in Nova Scotia as early as 1725.[33] Essentially, these were agreements to cease hostility and live in peace. Like the early Quebec agreements, they did not generally deal with ownership of land, but some contained provisions such as the following in the 1725 treaty: "Saving unto the Penoscot, Narridgewalk And other Tribes within His Majesties Province aforesaid and their Natural descendants respectively All their Lands liberties & properties not by them Conveyed or sold to, or possess'd by any of the English." Justice Binnie commented in one case, "In the maritime provinces ... nothing is said in at least some of the treaties about cession of lands. The Indians say these treaties were treaties of peace and friendship. Nevertheless, as the waves of non-aboriginal settlement arrived, the Indian bands still wound up being dispossessed of their traditional territories (except reserves) regardless of consent."[34]

Between 1780 and 1850 a number of treaties were signed in Ontario with differing terms but generally including surrenders of relatively small areas for one-time payments. The first large-scale land treaties were the Robinson treaties of 1850, which covered the north shore of Lakes Huron and Superior north to the southern boundary of the Hudson's Bay Company territories.[35] They set the pattern for the numbered treaties, which covered much of southern Canada as far west as British Columbia's eastern border. A policy of denial of Aboriginal title (described in Chapter 4) meant that most of BC is not subject to any historical treaty, except for relatively small areas of Vancouver Island, where Governor Douglas concluded fourteen treaties between 1850 and 1853,[36] and parts of the northeast covered by Treaty 8. The Douglas treaties recorded the surrender to the Hudson's Bay Company of land that was to become "the entire property of the white people for ever" for a one-time payment, with "small exceptions" of village sites and enclosed fields, and hunting and fishing rights over unoccupied areas. The treaties cover about 350 square miles. Each was written in longhand by a Hudson's Bay clerk. In some cases the document was blank, and the "Indians" signed "Xs," with the standard wording inserted later.[37]

The numbered treaties were concluded between 1871 and 1921 and followed the westward expansion of settlement of non-Aboriginal people.[38] Treaties 1 to 4, made between 1871 and 1874, included territory that extended from the land covered by the Robinson treaties in Ontario to the southeastern corner of Alberta. Treaties 5 to 11, made between 1875 and 1921, included a small area of Quebec, parts of Ontario, the Prairie provinces, and part of the Northwest Territories. Alexander Morris, who negotiated Treaties 3 to 6, wrote a record of the treaty-making process and included the following summary of their content:

1. A relinquishment ... of all their right and title to the land covered by the treaties saving certain reservations for their own use.
2. In return for such relinquishment, permission to the Indians to hunt over the ceded territory and to fish in the waters thereof, excepting such portions of the territory as pass from the Crown into the occupation of individuals or otherwise.
3. The perpetual payment of annuities of five dollars per head to each Indian – man, woman and child. The payment of an annual salary of twenty-five dollars to each Chief, and of fifteen dollars to each Councillor, or head man, of a Chief (thus making them in a sense officers of the Crown), and in addition, suits of official clothing for the Chiefs and head men, British flags for the Chiefs, and silver medals ...
4. The allotment of lands to the Indians, to be set aside as reserves for them for homes and agricultural purposes, and which cannot be sold or alienated without their consent, and then only for their

benefit; the extent of lands thus set apart being generally one section for each family of five ...

5. A very important feature of all the treaties is the giving to the Indian bands, agricultural implements, oxen, cattle (to form the nuclei of herds) and seed grain ...

6. The treaties provide for the establishment of schools on the reserves for the instruction of Indian children ...

7. The treaties all provide for the exclusion of the sale of spirits or "firewater" on the reserves.

... Such are the main features of the treaties between Canada and the Indians, and few as they are, they comprehend the whole future of the Indians and of their relations to the Dominion.[39]

It should be noted that in the case of Alberta, Saskatchewan, and Manitoba, the Natural Resources Transfer Agreements signed in 1929 and 1930 have been held by the SCC to "merge and consolidate" rights under the numbered treaties. The agreements transferred ownership of natural resources and Crown lands from the federal government to the provinces and received constitutional effect by the *Constitution Act, 1930*. They contain the following provision: "The said Indians shall have the right which the Province hereby assures to them of hunting, trapping and fishing game for food at all seasons of the year on all unoccupied Crown lands and on any other lands to which the said Indians may have a right of access." There have been a number of decisions by the SCC on this provision. In one case, the Court said that it had modified treaty rights, which had been "merged and consolidated" into the rights recognized by the provision.[40] This meant that any treaty right to hunt commercially has been extinguished and replaced by a right to hunt only for food. Therefore, a hunter was rightly convicted for selling a grizzly bear hide. The decision also confirmed that the right given by the provision was not confined to the treaty area. A subsequent decision held that hunting for food was not permitted if the land was being put to visible incompatible use.[41] The Court has also held that the Métis are not considered "Indians" for the purposes of the provision, so they derive no rights under it.[42]

The Williams treaties were signed in 1923 and cover 28,000 square kilometres in southern and central Ontario. No hunting or fishing rights were retained outside of the reserves.[43] Following the Williams treaties, no treaties were signed for about fifty years. For a time it looked as if no more treaties would be signed and even that existing treaties might be terminated. In a

1969 speech, Prime Minister Pierre Trudeau suggested, "Perhaps the treaties shouldn't go on forever. It's inconceivable, I think, that in a given society one section of the society have a treaty with the other section of the society. We must be all equal under the laws and we must not sign treaties amongst ourselves."[44] However, although a majority of the SCC in *Calder* rejected the Nisga'a's claim of Aboriginal title in 1973,[45] it led to a reversal of the federal policy denying such title and a revival of treaty making that is likely to continue for many decades.

The James Bay and Northern Quebec Agreement was signed in 1975, marking the commencement of the modern treaties and setting the pattern for subsequent treaties. There are now over twenty modern treaties, which are usually described as comprehensive land claims agreements or final agreements. There are also self-government agreements that may qualify as treaties, although they may also expressly state that they are not treaties for the purposes of Section 35.[46]

The modern treaties are comprehensive, complex documents that defy a short summary, and the terms of each agreement are specific to the group involved. To take one example, the Tsawwassen Final Agreement from British Columbia, signed in 2007, has twenty-five chapters that comprehensively define the rights of Tsawwassen First Nation (TFN); the responsibilities of the parties; applicable procedures relating to Tsawwassen lands; land and environmental management; forest resources; wildlife harvesting and fisheries allocations; taxation; dispute resolution and numerous other issues. There are also side-agreements on taxation and harvesting that do not form part of the treaty and are outside Section 35. The *Indian Act* no longer applies to TFN, with some limited exceptions. Federal and provincial laws generally apply to TFN, but TFN does have self-government and law-making authority within certain areas. If the Tsawwassen government makes laws in those areas, some of them will have priority over federal and provincial laws (e.g., laws regarding membership, TFN assets, and child adoption and protection) while others will be subject to any contrary federal or provincial laws (e.g., laws regarding post-secondary education, health and social services, and regulation of business). There are provisions to negotiate financing agreements every five years or as agreed. With some modifications, TFN land becomes fee simple land, which is the usual form of ownership and can be registered in the provincial land title system.

A key provision is the one that modifies TFN's Aboriginal rights and title so that they are exhaustively set out and modified by the agreement and continue only as modified. TFN releases all past claims relating to Aboriginal rights and title, and the Final Agreement is a full and final settlement of all such claims. This "certainty" language is used in place of the "cede, release and surrender" language of the numbered treaties and early modern treaties. The governments' insistence on requiring the extinguishment of Aboriginal rights and title was strongly criticized by the Royal Commission on Aboriginal Peoples in 1995,[47] and it remains a source of strong criticism.[48]

In October 2016 the federal and Ontario governments signed a non-binding agreement-in-principle with the Algonquins of Ontario, which covers about 36,000 square kilometres in eastern Ontario. If successfully negotiated, the resulting treaty will be the first modern treaty and the largest land claim in the province. The proposed terms include the transfer of 47,550 hectares of Crown lands to the Algonquin as settlement lands, payment of $300 million to them, and defined harvesting rights. Competing claims by other Aboriginal groups, including those in Quebec, led to litigation commencing within a few weeks of the signing that sought a declaration of Aboriginal title to lands that included the sites of the Parliament and Supreme Court Buildings in Ottawa. Such overlaps are common and greatly complicate the negotiation of treaties as well as litigation over Aboriginal title.

Legal Nature of a Treaty

In 1970, the author of *Native Rights in Canada* stated, "It is remarkable that we cannot say with certainty what rules our courts will apply when dealing with treaties. It reflects the fact that treaties are rarely before our courts."[49]

As with other aspects of Aboriginal law, there has been much greater development of the law relating to treaties in the last thirty or so years than in the preceding centuries.

In view of the ability of the federal government to extinguish or modify treaty rights before Section 35 took effect in 1982,[50] the 1966 Hawthorn Report referred to "rights" in quotation marks and said they were "moral, if not necessarily legally enforceable, obligations."[51] Writing in 1969, Harold Cardinal concluded, "Together, actions of the government and decisions of the courts of Canada have demoted the Indian treaties to the status of mere ancient promises or agreements between the Indians and the dominion, promises that may be forgotten or abrogated at any time by the federal government."[52] As with other aspects of Aboriginal law, there has been much greater development of the law relating to treaties in the last thirty or so years than in the preceding centuries. However, some commentators have pointed out that

Aboriginal Peoples and the Law

there still remains some doubt about the detailed principles applying to treaty implementation and the remedies available.[53]

In *Simon,* the 1985 case that marked the beginning of this development, the SCC soundly rejected a 1929 decision that had found that the Mi'kmaq, as an "uncivilized" people, did not have the capacity to enter into a 1752 treaty. The Court said such language "reflects the biases and prejudices of another era" and "is no longer acceptable in Canadian law and indeed is inconsistent with a growing sensitivity to native rights in Canada."[54] In *Badger,* Justice Cory said that "a treaty represents an exchange of solemn promises between the Crown and the various Indian nations. It is an agreement whose nature is sacred."[55] He went on to say that the honour of the Crown was at stake, and its integrity had to be maintained. It was to be presumed that the Crown intended to fulfill its promises and no appearance of sharp dealing would be sanctioned. As with Aboriginal rights, the burden of showing an extinguishment of treaty rights was on the Crown, and the intention had to be clear and plain.

In *Sioui* in 1990, the following 1760 document from Quebec was held to be a treaty and not merely a surrender and safe conduct pass:

> THESE are to certify that the CHIEF of the HURON tribe of Indians, having come to me in the name of His Nation, to submit to His BRITANNICK MAJESTY, and make Peace, has been received under my Protection, with his whole Tribe; and henceforth no English Officer or party is to molest, or interrupt them in returning to their Settlement at LORETTE; and they are received upon the same terms with the Canadians, being allowed the free Exercise of their Religion, their Customs, and Liberty of trading with the English: – recommending it to the Officers commanding the Posts, to treat them kindly.

The Court reviewed extrinsic evidence (evidence outside the document) to conclude that the general historical context of the time and events surrounding the issue of the document meant it was intended to be a treaty. One of these events was the presentation of a belt that was part of the treaty-making ceremony at the time. The decision permits the present-day descendants of the Huron to camp, cut trees, and make fires for ceremonial purposes in provincial parks in Quebec. Likewise, in *White and Bob,* the Court accepted that the agreements made by Governor Douglas on Vancouver Island were legally treaties.

Some of the rules that apply to normal contracts between private parties may also apply to treaties, such as implying terms to implement the intent of the parties.[56] If the honour of the Crown requires, the Court will more liberally apply the usual rules so as, for example, to imply a right of access to things to trade (e.g., furs, fish) in order to implement a treaty right to trade.[57] The solemn, sacred, and public nature of treaties puts them in a special class of agreement that is distinguished, above all, by the honour of the Crown principle, which requires them to be interpreted and implemented using special rules.

> In addition to the rights expressly set out in the treaty, treaty rights include things reasonably incidental to those rights in today's context and a logical evolution of the right.

In addition to the rights expressly set out in the treaty, treaty rights include things reasonably incidental to those rights in today's context and a logical evolution of the right. For example, in *Simon*, carrying of guns was included in the right to hunt contained in a 1752 treaty. As noted in *Sundown*, "in the past it was reasonably incidental to hunting rights to carry a quiver of arrows. Today it is reasonably incidental to hunting rights to carry the appropriate box of shotgun shells or rifle cartridges."[58] The Court explained, "That which is reasonably incidental is something which allows the claimant to exercise the right in the manner that his or her ancestors did, taking into account acceptable modern developments or unforeseen alterations in the right."[59] Applying this test, it found that building a small log cabin was reasonably incidental to the right to hunt under Treaty 6. The Court stated in *Marshall/Bernard*:

> Of course, treaty rights are not frozen in time. Modern peoples do
> traditional things in modern ways. The question is whether the modern
> trading activity in question represents a logical evolution from the trad-
> itional trading activity at the time the treaty was made ... Logical evolu-
> tion means the same sort of activity, carried on in the modern economy
> by modern means. This prevents aboriginal rights from being unfairly
> confined simply by changes in the economy and technology. But the
> activity must be essentially the same. "While treaty rights are capable
> of evolution within limits ... their subject matter ... cannot be wholly
> transformed."[60]

The early peace and friendship treaties were entered into at a time when the British government "felt that the Indian nations had sufficient independence and played a large enough role in North America for it to be good policy

Aboriginal Peoples and the Law

to maintain relations with them very close to those maintained between sovereign nations."[61] However, treaties with Aboriginal groups are not regarded as forms of international treaties. The SCC has noted that while it may be helpful in some instances to draw analogies with principles of international treaty law, these principles do not determine the meaning of the treaty. The Court has stated, "An Indian treaty is unique; it is an agreement *sui generis* which is neither created nor terminated according to the rules of international law."[62]

Principles of Treaty Interpretation

In *Marshall I,* Justice McLachlin noted that the SCC had set out the principles governing treaty interpretation on many occasions.[63] They include the following principles:

1. Aboriginal treaties constitute a unique type of agreement and attract special principles of interpretation.
2. Treaties should be liberally construed, and ambiguities or doubtful expressions should be resolved in favour of the aboriginal signatories.
3. The goal of treaty interpretation is to choose from among the various possible interpretations of common intention the one which best reconciles the interests of both parties at the time the treaty was signed.
4. In searching for the common intention of the parties, the integrity and honour of the Crown is presumed.
5. In determining the signatories' respective understanding and intentions, the court must be sensitive to the unique cultural and linguistic differences between the parties.
6. The words of the treaty must be given the sense which they would naturally have held for the parties at the time.[64]
7. A technical or contractual interpretation of treaty wording should be avoided.
8. While construing the language generously, courts cannot alter the terms of the treaty by exceeding what "is possible on the language" or realistic.
9. Treaty rights of aboriginal peoples must not be interpreted in a static or rigid way. They are not frozen at the date of signature. The interpreting court must update treaty rights to provide for their modern exercise. This involves determining what modern practices are reasonably incidental to the core treaty right in its modern context.

In order to interpret a treaty, especially the older ones, which were often vaguely written, evidence may be given of the circumstances surrounding the treaty, including any oral promises. It has been held that it would be unconscionable for the Crown to ignore oral terms and rely simply on the written words of a treaty. "Extrinsic evidence can be used to give the proper effect to the terms of the treaty as they were understood by all signatories."[65]

> It would be unconscionable for the Crown to ignore oral terms and rely simply on the written words of a treaty.

We have seen one example of the application of these principles in the *Sioui* case. Another important illustration was the decision in *Marshall I*.[66] A 1760 treaty contained a promise by the Mi'kmaq not to "Traffick, Barter or Exchange any Commodities in any manner but with such persons, or the Manager of such Truckhouses as shall be appointed or established by His majesty's Governor." The majority of the Court held that the surviving treaty right was not the literal promise of a truckhouse (a trading post) but a right to obtain a moderate livelihood by trading the products of fishing and hunting and (less clearly) gathering. This was based on evidence of a British promise that the Mi'kmaq would have access to "necessaries" through a trade in wildlife they had harvested.

The ruling was vaguely worded and capable of a very broad interpretation, which led to a dramatic increase in lobster fishing and claims that the promise extended to natural resources, including offshore natural gas.[67] An ugly backlash from non-Aboriginal people resulted, with serious violence, road blocks, and boats being sunk.[68] In a very unusual development, further reasons were issued two months later, and the Court "clarified" its decision, stressing the limited rights being recognized, the absence of any commercial priority, and the ability of the government to impose regulations, including catch limits.[69] These further reasons, and protracted negotiations, have failed to resolve the dispute; as recently as October 2017, boats were burned in acts of arson linked to claims of illegal sales of lobsters.[70] In yet another ruling on the same treaty in 2005, the Court decided that trade in forest products was not contemplated by the parties and that logging was not a logical evolution of the activities traditionally engaged in by the Mi'kmaq at the time of the treaties.[71]

The above principles of interpretation have less application to modern treaties for the reasons explained by Justice Binnie in the *Little Salmon*

Aboriginal Peoples and the Law

case. Having noted that, "unlike their historical counterparts, the modern comprehensive treaty is the product of lengthy negotiations between well-resourced and sophisticated parties,"[72] he continued:

> [12] The increased detail and sophistication of modern treaties represents a quantum leap beyond the ... historical treaties ... The historical treaties were typically expressed in lofty terms of high generality and were often ambiguous. The courts were obliged to resort to general principles (such as the honour of the Crown) to fill the gaps and achieve a fair outcome. Modern comprehensive land claim agreements, on the other hand ... while still to be interpreted and applied in a manner that upholds the honour of the Crown, were nevertheless intended to create some precision around property and governance rights and obligations ... [T]he modern treaties are designed to place Aboriginal and non-Aboriginal relations in the mainstream legal system with its advantages of continuity, transparency, and predictability. It is up to the parties, when treaty issues arise, to act diligently to advance their respective interests.

The Court echoed these views in its 2017 *Nacho Nyak Dun* decision, noting the role of judicial forbearance: "In resolving disputes that arise under modern treaties, courts should generally leave space for the parties to govern together and work out their differences. Indeed, reconciliation often demands judicial forbearance."[73] However, the Court went on to say that "modern treaties are constitutional documents, and courts play a critical role in safeguarding the rights they enshrine. Therefore, judicial forbearance should not come at the expense of adequate scrutiny of Crown conduct to ensure constitutional compliance,"[74] including compliance with Section 35 and the honour of the Crown. A treaty should be interpreted as a whole and in the light of its objectives.

Modern treaties may expressly exclude the application of the principles of treaty interpretation.[75] Although the legal status of historical treaties has been questioned and arguments for their invalidity or renewal have been put forward, in practice the courts have upheld them, and governments are reluctant to renegotiate them. The primary legal protection for Aboriginal groups that have signed treaties will likely be the application of the principles of treaty interpretation discussed above.

Historical Land Treaties: Legal Issues

The Royal Commission on Aboriginal Peoples considered in some detail the topic of "historical treaties: the need for justice and reconciliation," and the vulnerability of these treaties to legal challenge. The commission reported:

> Each treaty is a unique compact, but there is remarkable consistence
> in the principles of the treaties as expressed by the treaty nations them-
> selves. They maintain with virtual unanimity that they did not give up
> either their relationship to the land (or as Europeans called it, their title)
> or their sovereignty as nations by entering into treaties with the Crown.
> Instead, they regard the act of treaty making as an affirmation of those
> fundamental rights.[76]

Representatives of Aboriginal groups told the commissioners that there was no concept of extinguishment in their cultures and that the Aboriginal groups did not intend to transfer complete ownership but only share the land.[77] One Aboriginal writer recently summed up their approach: "Treaties aren't legal instruments; they're frameworks for right relationships."[78] The trial judge found in the recent *Grassy Narrows* case that the Ojibway agreed in Treaty 3 to share the land so long as it would not significantly interfere with their harvesting rights. They did not agree to increasing erosion of their right by way of the "taking up" clause (which was not explained to them) permitting incompatible development.[79] These findings were ignored by the SCC, which accepted the validity of the clause and considered only whether the province could exercise it.

Critics of the historical treaties have referred to the transcripts of the negotiations to support these claims and to point out the absence of discussion about the treaty clause surrendering Aboriginal rights.[80] They also refer to the inability of the Aboriginal groups to understand English and legal technicalities and note that they were dependent on translators, who were usually appointed by the colonial authorities and lacked independent advice. This led to a gross inequality of bargaining power, as did the desperate plight of Aboriginal groups on the prairies following the spread of diseases and the disappearance of the buffalo; the federal government used the resulting starvation to obtain treaties.[81] Treaties were written in advance, and the Aboriginal "signatories" held the pen while the government officials made their marks. Oral promises were not put in writing: "They promised every-thing. They wrote bloody little" according to Harold Cardinal.[82]

The gross unfairness of the terms has also been criticized.[83] In return for the surrender of rights to vast areas, the Aboriginal group received such benefits as small annual payments, agricultural implements, and schools. The provisions dealing with reserves and hunting and fishing cannot be regarded as benefits since they were simply exceptions to the surrender. In 1968, the president of the Manitoba Indian Brotherhood accused government officials of having "committed a legal fraud in a very sophisticated manner upon unsophisticated, unsuspecting, illiterate, uninformed natives."[84]

There was also the hard fact that "it was clear that white settlement would come whether the Indians consented or not ... By the treaties, the Indians were essentially giving consent to what was inevitable. It is this fact which gives the sense of unreality to the treaty-making procedure more, really, than the culturally weaker position of the Indians in negotiating legal documents."[85] When the first of the numbered treaties was being made, Lieutenant-Governor Archibald explained that "whether they wished it or not, immigrants would come in and fill up the country ... If they thought it better to have no treaty at all, they might do without one, but they must make up their minds; if there was to be a treaty, it must be on a basis like that offered."[86] In short, it was a take-it-or-leave-it offer. It was noted by Justice Binnie in *Mikisew Cree* that the treaty commissioner had told one Aboriginal group as Treaty 8 negotiations commenced: "The white man is bound to come in and open up the country, and we come before him to explain the relations that must exist between you, and thus prevent any trouble."[87] The references to "the relations that must exist" and preventing trouble show what little freedom existed for the Aboriginal groups to genuinely negotiate terms.

The Royal Commission on Aboriginal Peoples concluded the historical land treaties were vulnerable to legal challenge:

> The Commission believes that if the treaty nations were to choose to
> use all legal means at their disposal to challenge the orthodox legal inter-
> pretation of the written text of their treaties, some key provisions of the
> treaties might well be vulnerable in light of legal doctrines such as duress,
> *non est factum* [document signed in error], fundamental breach, and
> breach of the Crown's fiduciary duty. Such proceedings might result in
> grave legal and financial uncertainty across Canada as long-held rights
> were called into question.[88]

In the view of the commission, "notwithstanding clear words calling for extinguishment in many historical treaties, it is highly probable that no consent was ever given by Aboriginal parties to that result."[89] It considered that the legal doctrines listed above might invalidate the treaties, and if they did, "Aboriginal title ... may well continue to exist over the large portion of the Canadian land mass dealt with in the numbered treaties," as well as in the areas where no treaties were concluded.[90] The commission noted that in one case the Northwest Territories Supreme Court had held that there was enough doubt about the way Treaties 8 and 11 had been negotiated to enable sixteen Indian bands to register a caveat (a notice) in the land registry office claiming that they still possessed Aboriginal title.[91]

RCAP stressed that challenging the legal texts of the treaties did not represent the position of the treaty nations. They had waited steadfastly for implementation of their treaty rights as they understood them. It was the Crown that had marginalized the treaties to the point where questioning their validity – clearly as a last resort – might become an option. The commission recommended that negotiations commence to implement and renew the treaties and help restore the relationship to a true partnership. This would involve

- a broad and liberal interpretation of the treaty promises and agreements as understood by both parties without giving undue weight to the treaty text, and
- a negotiated compromise on issues where a thorough examination of the evidence led to a conclusion that the treaty parties themselves had failed to reach consensus.

Specific recommendations included a new proclamation to supplement that of 1763, which would contain a commitment to implement and renew existing treaties and make new treaties as well as a number of other commitments. Companion legislation would set out the guiding principles of the treaty process, provide for the establishment of the institutions to implement them (such as treaty commissions and land and treaty tribunals), and introduce certain reforms of the law in relation to the interpretation of treaties. The spirit and intent of the historical treaties should be implemented in accordance with certain fundamental principles, including a presumption that treaty nations did not intend to consent to a blanket extinguishment of their Aboriginal rights and title but to share the territory and jurisdiction and management over it.[92] These recommendations have not been implemented.

On the other hand, other writers, including prominent supporters of Aboriginal rights, have defended land treaties. In answer to the question of whether the "Indians" received anything like a fair price for what they sold, Felix Cohen, a leading authority on American Indian law and a passionate advocate for tribes, said:

> The only fair answer to that question is that except in a very few cases where military duress was present the price paid for the land was one that satisfied the Indians. Whether the Indians should have been satisfied and what the land would be worth now if it had never been sold are questions that lead us to ethereal realms of speculation.[93]

The Royal Commission on Aboriginal Peoples recommended that the historical treaties be implemented and renewed in accordance with their spirit and intent with a presumption that treaty nations did not intend to consent to a blanket extinguishment of their Aboriginal rights and title but to share the territory and jurisdiction and management over it.

He pointed out that European goods and land might have very different values to the different parties.

John Borrows, a writer on Aboriginal law with Indigenous ancestry, has offered this general view of Canadian treaties without necessarily endorsing specific treaties:

> Treaties recognize Indigenous peoples' right to make decisions in accordance with their laws to share or give land to others. They recognize non-Indigenous peoples' right to do the same thing ... Treaties between the Indigenous peoples and the Crown promote peace and order across cultures and are the basis of the country's formation and continued reformation.[94]

Tom Flanagan severely criticized the recommendations of the commission and its view that the treaties should not be seen as extinguishing Aboriginal title but rather that Aboriginal peoples should be regarded as co-owners,

> even though they signed agreements extinguishing their land rights, have received substantial benefits for doing so, and continue to seek

punctilious fulfilment of those treaty clauses from which they draw benefits. The Commission's call for the "implementation and renewal of treaties" comes down in the end to a one-sided reading of the treaties. Implementation means that any clause conferring benefits must be fulfilled to the letter, while renewal means that any clause by which the Indians gave up something must be ignored, reinterpreted or replaced.[95]

His conclusion was that "the treaties mean what they say. Their reinterpretation ... has the potential to be both expensive and mischievous for the economies of all provinces in which treaties have been signed."[96]

The SCC has acknowledged some of the concerns related to the numbered treaties. In *Badger* it noted:

> The treaties, as written documents, recorded an agreement that had already been reached orally and they did not always record the full extent of the oral agreement ... The treaties were drafted in English by representatives of the Canadian government who, it should be assumed, were familiar with common law doctrines. Yet the treaties were not translated in written form into the languages ... of the various Indian nations who were signatories. Even if they had been, it is unlikely that the Indians, who had a history of communicating only orally, would have understood them any differently.[97]

In the Court's view, the 1923 treaty at issue in *Howard* did not "raise the same concerns as treaties signed in the more distant past or in more remote territories where one can legitimately question the understanding of the Indian parties."[98] Likewise, in *Little Salmon*, the Court contrasted "the fairness in the procedure" that led to the modern treaty in that case with Treaty 8.[99] In *Manitoba Métis Federation*, the Court commented that "historical treaties were framed in that unfamiliar legal system, and negotiated and drafted in a foreign language."[100] Chief Justice McLachlin wrote in an article, "Where treaties were made, they sometimes were grounded in deception and misunderstanding."[101]

The Court has never considered the arguments advanced by RCAP regarding legal validity. Despite the concerns noted above, it has held that the land treaties were effective to surrender Aboriginal rights and title. This was the clear finding in the 1991 *Bear Island* case, a major land claim to four thousand square miles in northern Ontario. After stating that an Aboriginal right had existed pre-treaty, the Court said, "It is unnecessary, however, to examine the specific nature of the aboriginal right because, in our view, whatever may have been the situation upon the signing of the Robinson-Huron Treaty, that right was in any event surrendered by arrangements subsequent to that treaty by which the Indians adhered to the treaty in exchange for treaty annuities and a reserve."[102] Kent McNeil has been critical of the lack of analysis by the Court, including its assumptions about the extent of the understanding of the Aboriginal group and whether the facts showed that they agreed to become parties to the treaty.[103] The Court said the reasoning was equally applicable in *Howard* a few years later, where the conviction of a member of the Hiawatha Band of Ontario for unlawful fishing was upheld because a 1923 treaty surrendered fishing rights. The Court noted that the Aboriginal signatories were businessmen and a civil servant, and literate. It concluded that "the terms of the Treaty ... are entirely clear and would have been understood by the seven signatories."[104]

The Court has repeatedly described the numbered treaties as land surrenders. In *Horse* it stated, "In the period of 1871–1877 seven treaties were entered into by the Dominion Government with the Indians inhabiting the northwestern part of Canada. Generally, the Indians ceded land to the Government of Canada which in return undertook to set aside particular areas known as Indian reserves and to grant annuities and various supplies to the Indians."[105] Of Treaty 6 the Court said in *Ermineskin*: "All rights were relinquished to the Crown, and the Crown then agreed to set aside certain lands for use by the Indian signatories."[106] In *Cunningham* it commented that "most Indians on the prairies are Treaty Indians. In exchange for surrendering their traditional lands to the Crown, they were granted reservations and other benefits, such as the right to hunt and trap on Crown lands."[107] (The use of "granted" is curious and perhaps revealing since, of course, reserve lands and the right to hunt and trap were reserved out of the grant of land by the Aboriginal groups and not "granted" by the Crown.) According to the Court in *Mikisew Cree,* the Treaty 8 First Nations paid a hefty price for their entitlement to honourable conduct on the part of the Crown: "surrender of the aboriginal interest in an area larger than France."[108] Likewise, in *Grassy Narrows,* the Court said of Treaty 3, "The Ojibway yielded ownership of their territory except for certain lands reserved to them,"[109] ignoring the finding of fact of the trial judge noted above that they had only agreed to share the land and only if their harvesting rights were not significantly affected.

Rather than expressing doubts similar to those of the RCAP regarding the effectiveness of the historical treaties to surrender Aboriginal rights and title, the Court has addressed its concerns by adopting the principles of interpretation described above.[110] These may moderate some of the strict terms of the treaties by, for example, permitting reasonable incidental use and allowing for changes in circumstances since signature. But in the final analysis, the surrender has been acknowledged based on the language of the written terms. This raises fundamental questions about the justice of decisions supporting the interpretation of the numbered treaties as surrenders of Aboriginal rights and title to much of Canada, as well as the consequences for the current owners and occupiers of any decision that failed to uphold the surrender provisions of the treaties and the resulting injustice to them.

The specific provision in the numbered treaties allowing the Crown to "take up" land for development, and so reduce the exercise of Aboriginal rights, has also been contentious. In *Horse* the question was whether Treaty 6 included a hunting right over lands that had been "taken up" for settlement and were occupied by private owners. The Aboriginal defendant referred to passages of the Morris transcripts of treaty negotiations in support of the asserted treaty right to joint use so long as crops were not damaged. The Court reluctantly reviewed the passages but concluded:

> When the passages from the negotiations sought to be introduced by the appellants are viewed in the context of the various treaties covered in the Morris text it becomes clear that while the Indians were entitled to continue their mode of life by hunting, the preservation of that right did not include the grant of access to lands privately owned and occupied by settlers.[111]

In *Badger,* the Court established the "visible, incompatible land use" test for determining whether land had been "taken up" and so was no longer available for hunting, trapping, or fishing.

The "taken up" clause has also been considered in a couple of other cases at the SCC, which have moderated some of the clause's severity. *Mikisew Cree* dealt with a winter road the federal government had constructed in lands within Treaty 8 without consulting the Aboriginal group whose ability to hunt was affected by the road. The Federal Court of Appeal held this was a proper exercise of the right to "take up" land under the treaty and not an infringement of it. Reversing this decision, the SCC held that the signing of the treaty was only a stage in the "long process of reconciliation" and "was not the complete discharge of the duty arising from the honour of the Crown but a rededication of it."[112] Although the Crown has a treaty right to "take up" surrendered lands for regional transportation purposes without infringing the treaty, it was "nevertheless under an obligation to inform itself of the impact its project will have on the exercise by the Mikisew of their hunting and trapping rights, and to communicate its findings to the Mikisew. The Crown must then attempt to deal with the Mikisew 'in good faith, and with the intention of substantially addressing Mikisew concerns.'"[113] Treaty 8 gave rise to procedural rights, such as consultation, as well as substantive rights such as hunting, fishing, and trapping rights.[114] (In a subsequent decision, the duty to consult was applied to a modern treaty, although the Court stressed that the parties were free to negotiate a different mechanism in their treaty to uphold the honour of the Crown.)[115]

In *Grassy Narrows*, decided in 2014, the Court held that Ontario, not the federal government, had the right to "take up" land under Treaty 3. The province has a duty of prior consultation and "is subject to the fiduciary duties that lie on the Crown in dealing with Aboriginal interests."[116] Further, "if the taking up leaves the Ojibway with no meaningful right to hunt, fish or trap in relation to the territories over which they traditionally hunted, fished, and trapped, a potential action for treaty infringement will arise."[117] This raises the issue (that we will explore further in the next chapter on the duty to consult) of the cumulative impacts of multiple unrelated activities on Aboriginal and treaty rights, and how they are to be determined.

Litigation has failed to provide any legal remedy for the concerns expressed over the historical land treaties.[118] Negotiation has been more successful. There have been agreements to supplement treaties, such as the Dene and Métis comprehensive land claim settlements in the Northwest Territories. Some of the groups subject to the Douglas treaties are participating in the BC treaty process to obtain modern treaties. Also, treaty land entitlement agreements have been negotiated, primarily in Manitoba and Saskatchewan, to provide additional land under the terms of the numbered treaties in order to resolve disputes over the method of calculation. However, attention has been drawn to the lack of progress in treaty renewal for most Aboriginal groups in those provinces, as well as Ontario and Alberta, which are all covered by the historical treaties. Critics point to the growing gap in community well-being statistics (based on income, education, housing, and labour-force activity) that have been created, at least in part, by legal developments in other parts of the country arising from court decisions and the negotiation of modern treaties. Between 1981 and 2006 the well-being of modern treaty First Nations improved twice as fast as the condition of those First Nations with historical treaties, with the numbered treaty First Nations having the lowest well-being scores of all treaty First Nations.[119]

Some observers say that the provincial and federal governments have shown little interest in revisiting the treaties to create new benefits, such as sharing revenue from resource projects.[120]

Another fundamental problem, even assuming their validity and fairness when signed and the possibility of some modification to reflect changing times, is that the historical treaties are the products of another era. In 1966, the Hawthorn Report said that the benefits provided were "insignificant in relation to both Indian needs and the positive role played by modern governments. The economic base of Indian existence will continue to diverge from the traditional dependence on game, fish and fur, and reserve-centred activities."[121] It concluded that "the rights to which Indians are entitled under treaty provisions bear little relation to their contemporary needs for massive programs of socio-economic change."[122] Also, continued development of traditional lands has rendered the right to hunt and fish of decreasing value. The proposed alternative of agriculture on reserve lands has proven of limited value. Farming was never part of the traditional way of life for most Aboriginal groups. As well, changes in the economy and promotion of government policy to protect settlers hindered farming by Aboriginal groups.

> Between 1981 and 2006 the well-being of modern treaty First Nations improved twice as fast as the condition of those First Nations with historical treaties, with the numbered treaty First Nations having the lowest well-being scores of all treaty First Nations.

In 1969, Prime Minister Pierre Trudeau referred to the decreasing significance of the historical treaties as one reason to terminate them: "I don't think we should encourage Indians to feel that their treaties should last forever within Canada so that they [will] be able to receive their twine or their gun powder."[123] But the Hawthorn Report noted that "although the substantive effects of the treaties are minimal, they are symbolically very important to many Indians."[124] For example, the historic document *Citizens Plus,* prepared by the Indian Chiefs of Alberta in response to the 1969 White Paper that proposed the end of the special status of Indians, began: "To us who are Treaty Indians there is nothing more important than our Treaties, our lands and the well being of our future generation." Harold Cardinal wrote, "While we find much to quarrel with in the treaties as they were signed, they are, we contend, important, not so much for their content as for the principles they imply in their existence."[125] From personal experience with some treaty nations, I can confirm that this has remained the case. Looking only at the written terms, it is difficult to understand the obvious attachment that most nations have to their treaty. However, the entire agreement – written and oral – is still seen as reflecting a nation-to-nation arrangement negotiated with representatives of the British monarchy, containing oral terms based on the original spirit and intent, which reflected a sharing of the land rather than a land surrender. This disconnect between the terms of the written document and the understanding of the Aboriginal groups is likely to remain a source of friction and misunderstanding, especially as historical treaty rights have received less attention than unsurrendered Aboriginal rights and title, and as modern treaties are negotiated to resolve claims of such rights and title.

> The entire agreement – written and oral – is still seen by treaty nations as reflecting a nation-to-nation arrangement negotiated with representatives of the British monarchy, containing oral terms based on the original spirit and intent, which reflected a sharing of the land rather than a land surrender.

Criticism of Modern Treaties

The insistence of governments that modern treaties contain "certainty" language that either expressly or in practice extinguishes Aboriginal rights and title has been the main criticism of modern treaties.[126] In its report on this topic, the Royal Commission on Aboriginal Peoples said that this policy was out of step with the spirit and purpose of the Royal Proclamation of 1763, Section 35, and the Crown's fiduciary responsibilities. The commissioners stated:

> We believe that a policy that recognizes and affirms Aboriginal rights
> and emphasizes co-existence, mutual recognition and shared ownership
> and jurisdiction is to be preferred over current federal extinguishment
> policy. Federal, provincial and territorial governments can achieve a
> sufficient degree of clarity and certainty without requiring Aboriginal
> nations to agree to extinguish existing Aboriginal rights in exchange for
> treaty-based rights.[127]

There are severe critics of the substance of the modern treaties who maintain that "the financial and economic benefits of these land claim settlements to a relatively few native peoples are enormous"; the complexity of negotiating the agreements results in millions of dollars paid to lawyers, consultants, and bureaucrats; and implementation will result in still more governments and bureaucracy.[128] Also, it is argued that the economic logic behind modern treaties is flawed: the infusion of money and other benefits into Aboriginal communities will not create viable economies in remote areas. Instead, there must be intensive social services so that they can acquire the skills and attitudes to participate in a productive economy and so bridge "the developmental gap."[129]

There has been a great deal of criticism of the slow pace and the process around the negotiation of modern treaties. Across Canada there were approximately one hundred comprehensive claim negotiating tables in 2015, but only six treaties have been signed since 2006, including four in British Columbia.[130] The BC process is generally regarded as a failure, with only those four treaties being implemented since it began in 1992.[131] Only about half of the two hundred *Indian Act* bands in the province are formally participating; of those, about a third are not in active negotiations. There are many defects in the modern process:

> There has been a great deal of criticism of the slow pace and the process around the negotiation of modern treaties.

- considerable costs
- overly complex procedures
- the large number of parties, with dozens of separate negotiations taking place, resulting, in part, from the fragmentation of the Aboriginal groups into many separate sub-groups
- delays
- the breadth of the issues
- the limited mandates of government negotiators
- the requirement that government negotiators check with several levels within their own governments before making decisions
- the dependence of Aboriginal groups on the non-Aboriginal governments for funding
- the involvement of professional negotiators who may have an interest in prolonging the process
- the lack of teeth of the BC Treaty Commission, which has no powers to force the parties to negotiate.[132]

Clearly, it will take several more decades for most First Nations in the province to sign treaties, assuming that they ever do. In his book on the process, Tony Penikett quotes a First Nation lawyer who likens it to a fish farm: "We're all penned up and fed our little pellets. We can look up at the sky and dream our small fry dreams, but most of us are going nowhere. Someday, someone may escape towards a treaty, but most of us can only dream."[133]

Following signature comes implementation of treaties, and concerns have been expressed about what will happen at this stage, including questions about whether government funding will be available to ensure terms are carried out.[134]

Despite its encouragement of treaty negotiations, the Supreme Court of Canada is partly responsible for the failure to conclude treaties in British Columbia and some other regions. The *Delgamuukw* and *Tsilhqot'in* decisions are widely perceived to have discouraged treaty making by offering a better alternative in the form of litigation and settlement agreements that do not require surrender of rights and title on such a large scale. Also, the *Haida* decision on consultation and accommodation, discussed in the next chapter, has resulted in limited resources being devoted to consultations and negotiating impact/benefit and accommodation agreements.

TO SUM UP

- Treaties are the preferred method to resolve claims of Aboriginal rights and title and to give certainty to the current ownership of land by other people.

- Much of Canada is covered by historical treaties, which were concluded by the 1920s.

- There have been several modern treaties since treaty making was resumed following the *Calder* decision on Aboriginal title in 1973.

- Large parts of the country, such as British Columbia, are not generally subject to treaties, and recent progress on completing treaties has been slow.

- Treaties vary greatly, ranging from one-paragraph historical treaties to comprehensive modern treaties.

- Treaties serve an important role in reconciliation and legitimizing non-Aboriginal settlement.

- Treaties are considered solemn and sacred agreements in a special class of their own. Distinguished by the honour of the Crown principle, they require special rules for their interpretation and implementation, which should be favourable to the Aboriginal group.

- Historical treaties pose significant legal issues because of the circumstances in which they were entered into, the different understandings of the parties, and the inequality of bargaining power. These issues have not been considered in detail by the Supreme Court of Canada, which has consistently held that the treaties were effective to surrender Aboriginal rights and title.

- First Nations with historical treaties appear to be falling behind those with modern treaties with respect to community well-being, and there have been calls for treaty renewal.

- The provision in some treaties allowing governments to "take up" land for development is contentious.
- Modern treaties are subject to criticism from those who consider them too generous to Aboriginal groups as well as those who are critical of the slow pace and process of their negotiation.

Consultation, Accommodation, and Consent

6

The duty to consult has attracted a great deal of attention, often over-shadowing other areas of consideration and debate. What is the duty? How is it connected to the related duty of accommodation and to the duty to obtain consent? Who owes the duty? Why was it extended from established rights to asserted rights? When does it arise? What is its scope and content? Must Aboriginal groups participate in the process? How does it fit into existing administrative procedures? How is it working in practice? And, finally, what changes are required?

The Duty to Consult

The duty to consult is often misunderstood.[1] Part of the problem is that there are many sources for the duty depending on the circumstances and whether an Aboriginal right has been established (through litigation or agreement with the Crown). There is also the question of whether there is a claim of an infringement of an established Aboriginal or treaty right that the Crown is seeking to justify. As discussed in Chapter 4, consultation is one of the requirements for justifying infringement. There is an additional duty to consult when the Crown is taking steps to exercise its powers under a treaty in a way that will affect the rights of an Aboriginal group. There may also be a duty to consult based on

- administrative law principles
- legislation
- government policy
- a condition of a government approval.

These different sources may result in different triggers for the duty as well as differing content. To avoid confusion, it's necessary to keep the many situations leading to a duty to consult in mind.

In practice, the duty to consult based on asserted rights occupies an intermediate position between non-recognition of asserted rights and full recognition of established rights. The duty was created by the Supreme Court of Canada in *Haida* as a protection for asserted rights, pending negotiation of treaties or litigation to establish their validity. It is, in theory, a form of interim relief, like an interim court order to preserve something of the status quo and prevent harm that cannot be remediated if a right is ultimately established. In practice, for some Aboriginal groups, the duty to consult has effectively replaced both treaty negotiation and litigation to establish rights. It is a more cost-effective alternative that can provide negotiated benefits without a surrender by treaty of whatever rights may exist. It also has advantages for governments, as claims of Aboriginal rights and title can be settled, avoided, or deferred by negotiating agreements outside the treaty process.

In *Haida*, the Supreme Court of Canada created the duty to consult as a protection for asserted rights, pending negotiation of treaties or litigation to establish their validity.

The Court has stressed that, in the case of unproven rights, the duty to consult is a procedural and not a substantive obligation.[2] As one writer has pointed out, the duty to consult "resembles the administrative law duty of fairness imposed upon the Crown's dealings with all its subjects."[3] It is not an Aboriginal right. It is much more about how the Crown must do something rather than what it can do. If the Crown follows the correct procedure in a manner that it can defend as reasonable, then a court will allow it to go ahead despite the adverse impact on the asserted Aboriginal right.[4] As the Court noted in *Haida*, "the focus ... is not on the outcome, but on the process of consultation and accommodation."[5] It confirmed in *Ktunaxa* that "[t]he s. 35 right to consultation and accommodation is a right to a process, not a right to a particular outcome," and that a court reviewing an administrative decision under Section 35 does not decide if the administrative decision maker's finding was correct but if it was reasonable.[6] We shall consider some of the practical results of this judicial deference to governments later.

The Development of the Law on the Duty to Consult

In *Little Salmon,* Justice Deschamps referred to the way in which the duty to consult has developed over the last thirty years:

> The Crown's constitutional duty to specifically consult Aboriginal peoples was initially recognized as a factor going to the determination of whether an Aboriginal right was infringed (*Guerin*), and was later established as one component of the test for determining whether infringements of Aboriginal rights by the Crown were justified: *R. v. Sparrow.* The Court was subsequently asked in *Haida,* and *Taku,* whether such a duty to consult could apply even before an Aboriginal or treaty right is proven to exist.[7]

The *Mikisew Cree* decision, which deals with consultation in the context of the exercise of powers under a treaty, should be added to this summary.

Guerin was the 1984 case that established that the Crown owed fiduciary duties to Aboriginal peoples in certain circumstances. It involved the lease of reserve lands (which the Court equated with Aboriginal title lands) to a golf course. The Court found that after the Crown's agents had induced the Musqueam Band to surrender its land on the understanding that the land would be leased on certain terms, it would be unconscionable to permit the Crown to ignore those terms. "When the promised lease proved impossible to obtain, the Crown, instead of proceeding to lease the land on different, unfavourable terms, should have returned to the Band to explain what had occurred and seek the Band's counsel on how to proceed."[8] The failure to do so constituted a breach of fiduciary obligation. Therefore, in some situations, the duty to consult is part of a broader fiduciary obligation.

The duty to consult made a reappearance six years later in the *Sparrow* case, also involving the Musqueam, which was the first decision of the Court to consider Section 35. In *Sparrow,* the Court upheld an Aboriginal right to fish. In setting out the test that the Crown must satisfy if it is to justify infringing an established Aboriginal right, the Court stated, "Within the analysis of justification, there are further questions to be addressed, depending on the circumstances of the inquiry. These include the questions ... whether the aboriginal group in question has been consulted with respect to the conservation measures being implemented."[9] The Court expanded on the requirement for consultation in *Nikal,* decided in 1996: "In the aspects of information and consultation the concept of reasonableness must come into play. For example, the need for the dissemination of information and a request for consultations cannot simply be denied. So long as every reasonable effort is made to inform and to consult, such efforts would suffice to meet the justification requirement."[10]

In *Delgamuukw*, which dealt with Aboriginal title and was decided the following year, Chief Justice Lamer said:

> There is always a duty of consultation. Whether the aboriginal group
> has been consulted is relevant to determining whether the infringement
> of aboriginal title is justified, in the same way that the Crown's failure to
> consult an aboriginal group with respect to the terms by which reserve
> land is leased may breach its fiduciary duty at common law: *Guerin*. The
> nature and scope of the duty of consultation will vary with the
> circumstances.

He divided the duty of consultations into three general categories:

1. "Rare" or "occasional cases" when the breach is less serious or relatively minor – in such cases there will be a minimum acceptable standard of discussing important decisions, but this "mere consultation" must still be in good faith, with the intention of substantially addressing the concerns of the aboriginal peoples whose lands are at issue.
2. "Most cases" – in which the duty "will be significantly deeper than mere consultation."
3. "Some cases may even require the full consent of an aboriginal nation, particularly when provinces enact hunting and fishing regulations in relation to aboriginal lands."[11]

The extension of the duty to consult from established or proven Aboriginal rights to asserted but unproven rights took place in 2004 in *Haida* (which was heard together with its companion case of *Taku*). The central issue was whether the provincial government could transfer forestry licences without prior consultation in spite of assertions of Aboriginal rights that had not yet been established by treaty or litigation. Aboriginal people were very upset at seeing resource development and depletion of their traditional lands that might irretrievably lessen the value of those lands to them. The Court noted:

> The stakes are huge. The Haida argue that absent consultation and ac-
> commodation, they will win their title but find themselves deprived of

forests that are vital to their economy and their culture. Forests take generations to mature, they point out, and old-growth forests can never be replaced. The Haida's claim to title to Haida Gwaii is strong, as found by the chambers judge. But it is also complex and will take many years to prove. In the meantime, the Haida argue, their heritage will be irretrievably despoiled.[12]

The Court held that the province should have consulted the Haida before transferring the forestry licences, and it created more judge-made law by doing so. As noted in *Taku*, "The obligation to consult does not arise only upon proof of an Aboriginal claim, in order to justify infringement."[13] It might also arise prior to proof of the claim.

The Court first considered and rejected the argument of the province that the remedy of the Haida was to seek an interlocutory injunction (a court order preventing the government from transferring the permits until their claim of Aboriginal title had been determined). For several reasons, it concluded that such injunctions offer only partial imperfect relief and fail to adequately take account of Aboriginal interests prior to their final determination.[14] In *Rio Tinto*, the Court observed that, absent a duty of consultation, Aboriginal groups seeking to protect their interests pending a final settlement would need to commence litigation and seek interlocutory injunctions to halt the threatening activity.[15] These remedies have proven time-consuming, expensive, and often ineffective. Moreover, with a few exceptions, many Aboriginal groups have enjoyed limited success in obtaining injunctions to halt development or activities on the land in order to protect contested Aboriginal or treaty rights.[16] Rather than pitting Aboriginal peoples against the Crown in the litigation process, the duty to consult recognizes that both must work together to reconcile their interests. It also accommodates the reality that Aboriginal peoples are often involved in exploiting the resource. "Shutting down development by court injunction may serve the interest of no one."[17]

> Rather than pitting Aboriginal peoples against the Crown in the litigation process, the duty to consult recognizes that both must work together to reconcile their interests.

After dealing with interlocutory injunctions in *Haida,* the Court went on to see whether the special relationship with the Crown that the Haida relied on gave rise to a duty to consult and, if appropriate, accommodate. It discussed

Aboriginal Peoples and the Law

- the source of the duty to consult
- when the duty arises
- the scope and content of the duty
- whether the duty extends to third parties
- whether it applies to the provincial government and not exclusively the federal government.

In the case of the asserted but not yet established rights at issue in *Haida,* the source of the duty was found in the doctrine of the honour of the Crown rather than in the Crown's fiduciary obligations, as held by the BC Court of Appeal. Since Aboriginal rights and title had been asserted but not defined or proven, the Aboriginal interest in question was insufficiently specific for the honour of the Crown to mandate that the Crown act in the Aboriginal group's best interest, as a fiduciary, in exercising discretionary control over the subject of the right or title. According to the Court, where treaties remain to be concluded, the honour of the Crown requires negotiations leading to a just settlement of Aboriginal claims. This, in turn, implies a duty to consult and, if appropriate, accommodate. To unilaterally exploit a claimed resource during the process of proving and resolving the Aboriginal claim to that resource may deprive the Aboriginal claimants of some or all of the benefit of the resource. "When the distant goal of proof is finally reached, the Aboriginal peoples may find their land and resources changed and denuded. This is not reconciliation. Nor is it honourable."[18]

The Court concluded with regard to the source of the duty: "The honour of the Crown requires that [the rights protected by Section 35] be determined, recognized and respected. This, in turn, requires the Crown, acting honourably, to participate in processes of negotiation. While this process continues, the honour of the Crown may require it to consult and, where indicated, accommodate Aboriginal interests."[19] The Court rejected the argument of the province that any duty of consultation was owed only by the federal government.

The relationship between *Sparrow* and *Haida* was explained by the Court in the *Little Salmon* case:

> *Haida Nation* represented a shift in focus from *Sparrow.* Whereas the Court in *Sparrow* had been concerned about sorting out the consequences of infringement, *Haida Nation* attempted to head off such confrontations by imposing on the parties a duty to consult and (if

appropriate) accommodate in circumstances where development
might have a significant impact on Aboriginal rights when and if
established.[20]

The distinction between unproven and established Aboriginal rights and
title was further explained in *Tsilhqot'in*:

> Where Aboriginal title is unproven, the Crown owes a procedural duty
> imposed by the honour of the Crown to consult and, if appropriate, ac-
> commodate the unproven Aboriginal interest. By contrast, where title
> has been established, the Crown must not only comply with its proced-
> ural duties, but must also ensure that the proposed government action is
> substantively consistent with the requirements of s. 35 of the *Constitu-
> tion Act, 1982*. This requires both a compelling and substantial govern-
> mental objective and that the government action is consistent with the
> fiduciary duty owed by the Crown to the Aboriginal group.[21]

Turning to treaty rights, we saw that the justification test (which includes
consultations as an element of that test) applies to infringements of such
rights. In *Mikisew Cree*, decided in 2005 shortly after *Haida*, the Court distinguished between the duty to consult as part of the duty to justify treaty
infringements and a stand-alone duty to consult if there is to be a proper
exercise of powers under the treaty. The federal government had approved
a winter road through a reserve created under Treaty 8. This interfered,
directly and indirectly, with the Mikisew Cree's ability to hunt and trap. There
was no prior consultation with the Aboriginal group. The trial judge found
that this was an infringement of the treaty that could not be justified under
the *Sparrow* test. The Federal Court of Appeal reversed the decision on the
grounds that the road was a "taking up" of land within the treaty and there
was no infringement that required justification. In its view, there was no legal
requirement for consultation, although it would have been "good practice."
The Supreme Court of Canada agreed that the road was a "taking up" permitted by the treaty, so there was no infringement requiring justification.
However, it held that the Crown should still have consulted with the Mikisew
Cree prior to approving the road. This conclusion was based on the application of the honour of the Crown principle and the *Haida* decision to treaty
implementation. As we've seen, the application of the honour of the Crown
principle to treaty implementation is well established, but this was the first
decision of the Court to apply the duty to consult. The Court commented

Aboriginal Peoples and the Law

on the broad general importance of the principle of consultation before interference with existing treaty rights to relations between Aboriginal and non-Aboriginal people. "It goes to the heart of the relationship and concerns not only the Mikisew but other First Nations and non-aboriginal governments as well."[22]

Most modern treaties contain detailed provisions dealing with the Crown's duty of consultation and set up elaborate procedures and agencies for this purpose. The question in the 2010 *Little Salmon* decision was whether the detailed provisions in a modern Yukon treaty excluded any implied duty to consult regarding a land grant to a third party based on the honour of the Crown as applied to the implementation of historical treaties in *Mikisew Cree*. The majority held that a continuing duty to consult existed. Members of the Aboriginal group possessed an express treaty right to hunt and fish for subsistence on their traditional lands, which had been surrendered and were now classified as Crown lands. Although the treaty did not prevent the government from making land grants – and, indeed, it contemplated such an eventuality – it was obvious that such grants might adversely affect the traditional economic and cultural activities of the group. Therefore, the Yukon government was required to consult with them to determine the nature and extent of such adverse effects. The honour of the Crown operated independently of the intentions of the parties as expressed in the treaty, and the Crown could not contract out of this duty. "However, the honour of the Crown may not *always require consultation*. The parties may, in their treaty, negotiate a different mechanism which, nevertheless, in the result, upholds the honour of the Crown."[23] In this case, there was a duty to consult (although not to accommodate), which the government had satisfied. The Court stated: "Whether or not a court would have reached a different conclusion on the facts is not relevant. The decision to approve or not to approve the grant was given by the Legislature to the Minister who, in the usual way, delegated the authority to the Director. His disposition was not unreasonable."[24]

Two of the judges dissented vigorously. Writing for them, Justice Deschamps said:

> To allow one party to renege unilaterally on its constitutional undertaking by superimposing further rights and obligations relating to matters already provided for in the treaty could result in a paternalistic legal contempt, compromise the national treaty negotiation process and frustrate the ultimate objective of reconciliation. This is the danger of what seems to me to be an unfortunate attempt to take the constitutional principle of

the honour of the Crown hostage together with the principle of the duty
to consult Aboriginal peoples that flows from it.[25]

In their view, the treaty did provide for consultation in the circumstances
of this case, and that duty was satisfied. In the course of their judgment, they
noted that

> the constitutional duty to consult Aboriginal peoples involves three
> objectives: in the short term, to provide "interim" or "interlocutory"
> protection for the constitutional rights of those peoples; in the medium
> term, to favour negotiation of the framework for exercising such rights
> over having that framework defined by the courts; and, in the longer
> term, to assist in reconciling the interests of Aboriginal peoples with
> those of other stakeholders.[26]

The Court made another decision on the duty to consult in 2010 in *Rio
Tinto,* which highlighted a significant limitation to the effectiveness of the
duty, especially in areas where developments have already seriously impacted
Aboriginal rights. The main issue was whether the duty applied to past conduct or decisions of the Crown, or only to proposed ones. It was decided that
the duty did not apply to the past but only to the future. The foundation of
consultation articulated in *Haida* has the potential for state-authorized developments to have adverse impacts on Aboriginal interests: "Consultation
centres on how the resource is to be developed in a way that prevents irreversible harm to existing Aboriginal interests."[27] The parties must meet in
good faith to discuss the development with a view
to accommodate the conflicting interests. "Such a
conversation is impossible where the resource has
long since been altered and the present government conduct or decision does not have any further
impact on the resource. The issue then is not consultation about the further development of the resource, but negotiation about compensation for its
alteration without having properly consulted in the past."[28] The question in
pre-proof consultation cases is whether there is a claim or right that potentially may be adversely impacted by the *current* government conduct or decision in question.

The 2014 decision of the Court in *Behn* confirmed that the duty to consult is owed to the Aboriginal group that holds the Aboriginal or treaty rights

Consultation centres on how the
resource is to be developed in a way
that prevents irreversible harm to
existing Aboriginal interests.

Supreme Court of Canada in *Rio Tinto*

and not to individuals. "The duty to consult exists to protect the collective rights of Aboriginal peoples. For this reason, it is owed to the Aboriginal group that holds the s. 35 rights, which are collective in nature ... But an Aboriginal group can authorize an individual or an organization to represent it for the purpose of asserting its s. 35 rights."[29] Therefore, there was no duty to consult an individual member of the group, even though his trapline was directly impacted by a timber sale licence issued by the BC government. For this and other reasons, his blockade of the area was unlawful.

Two SCC decisions in 2017 – *Clyde River*[30] and *Chippewas of the Thames*[31] – dealt with the role of regulatory bodies in discharging the Crown's duty to consult; they are considered below. Also in 2017, the Court decided in *Ktunaxa* that a provincial minister had adequately consulted an Aboriginal group that opposed a proposed ski resort on the grounds that it would drive the Grizzly Bear Spirit from its sacred site. The decision provided a useful summary of the current law.[32]

When Does the Duty to Consult Arise?

Whether a duty to consult exists in the case of a fiduciary obligation (or other obligation) will depend on the facts and law relevant to that obligation, as in *Guerin*. In the case of an established Aboriginal or treaty right, the duty to consult is always present as part of the fiduciary duty of the Crown to justify any infringement of the right under the *Sparrow* test. As we have seen from *Mikisew Cree* and *Little Salmon*, it is also present as part of the honour of the Crown in the case of any implementation of a treaty unless, in the case of a modern treaty, the parties have agreed on some other manner of satisfying the Crown's honour.

In the case of unproven Aboriginal rights, the situation was restated in *Rio Tinto*. According to the Court, there are three elements that give rise to a duty to consult:

- the Crown's knowledge of a claim or right
- Crown conduct or decision
- the adverse effect of the proposed Crown conduct on an Aboriginal claim or right.

As to the first requirement of knowledge, the Court said:

To trigger the duty to consult, the Crown must have real or constructive knowledge of a claim to the resource or land to which it attaches. The threshold, informed by the need to maintain the honour of the Crown, is not high. Actual knowledge arises when a claim has been filed in court or advanced in the context of negotiations, or when a treaty right may be impacted. Constructive knowledge arises when lands are known or reasonably suspected to have been traditionally occupied by an Aboriginal community or an impact on rights may reasonably be anticipated. While the existence of a potential claim is essential, proof that the claim will succeed is not. What is required is a credible claim. Tenuous claims, for which a strong *prima facie* case is absent, may attract a mere duty of notice.[33]

In *Haida* the trial judge found that, based on first impressions (a *prima facie* case), the Haida had shown they had a credible claim to Aboriginal title, and the province had knowledge of it. Likewise, in *Taku*, the province had knowledge of the claim through the treaty process.

The Court confirmed in *Rio Tinto* that the second requirement of Crown conduct or decision is not confined to government exercise of statutory powers nor to decisions or conduct that have an immediate impact on lands

When Does the Duty to Consult Arise?

In the case of an established Aboriginal or treaty right, the duty to consult is always present as part of the Crown's fiduciary duty to justify any infringement of the right. It is also present as part of the honour of the Crown in the case of any implementation of a treaty unless, in the case of a modern treaty, the parties have agreed on some other manner of satisfying the Crown's honour.

In the case of unproven Aboriginal rights, there is a duty to consult if

(a) the Crown knows of an Aboriginal group's claim or right to land or resources

(b) an actual or potential action or decision of the Crown may have an impact on the lands or resources

(c) the action or decision could adversely affect the potential claim or right.

and resources. A potential for adverse impact is sufficient. Thus, the duty to consult extends to "strategic, higher-level decisions" that may have an impact on Aboriginal claims and rights, such as

- the transfer of tree licences that would permit the cutting of old-growth forest
- the approval of a multi-year forest management plan for a large geographic area
- the establishment of a review process for a major gas pipeline
- the conduct of a comprehensive inquiry to determine a province's infrastructure and capacity needs for electricity transmission.

However, the Court left "for another day the question of whether government conduct includes legislative action."[34]

The third element of a duty to consult is the possibility that the Crown conduct may adversely affect the Aboriginal claim or right. The claimant must show a causal relationship between the proposed government conduct or decision and a potential for adverse impacts on pending Aboriginal claims or rights. Past wrongs (including previous breaches of the duty to consult), mere speculative impacts, or adverse effect on a First Nation's future negotiating position do not suffice. Adverse impacts extend to any effect that may prejudice a pending Aboriginal claim or right.

As seen above, in *Mikisew Cree* the Court applied the *Haida* test for triggering the duty to consult to implementation of treaties. In the case of a treaty, the Crown, as a party, will always have notice of its contents. The question in each case will therefore be to determine the degree to which conduct contemplated by the Crown would adversely affect those rights so as to trigger the duty to consult. The Court observed that *Haida* and *Taku* set a low threshold to trigger the duty.[35]

It should be noted that the duty is required at all stages of a project. The Court stated in *Taku* that it was expected that, throughout the permitting, approval, and licensing process, as well as in the development of a land-use strategy, the Crown would continue to fulfill its honourable duty to consult and, if indicated, accommodate the Aboriginal group.[36]

The Scope and Content of the Duty

Dealing first with established rights, the Supreme Court of Canada made it clear in *Tsilhqot'in* that in such cases "the required level of consultation and accommodation is greatest," using the spectrum of consultation described in *Haida* in the context of pre-proof claims.[37] The Court confirmed in *Clyde River* that a duty of deep consultation is owed in the case of established treaty rights.[38]

In *Haida*, the Court held that the content of the duty to consult and accommodate in the context of pre-proof claims varies with the circumstances, and it developed a consultation spectrum. In general terms, the scope of the duty is proportionate to a preliminary assessment of the strength of the case supporting the existence of the right or title, and to the seriousness of the potentially adverse effect on the right or title claimed.[39] Writing for the Court, Chief Justice McLachlin quoted the passage from *Delgamuukw* summarized above, in which Chief Justice Lamer divided the duty of consultation into three general categories in the context of established claims.[40] She transposed this passage to pre-proof consultations. As stated in the passage from *Delgamuukw*, the common thread on the Crown's part must be "the intention of substantially addressing [Aboriginal] concerns" as they are raised through a meaningful process of consultation. "At all stages, good faith on both sides is required ... Sharp dealing is not permitted. However, there is no duty to agree; rather, the commitment is to a meaningful process of consultation."[41]

> Generally, the scope of the duty to consult is proportionate to a preliminary assessment of the strength of the case supporting the existence of the right or title, and to the seriousness of the potentially adverse effect on the right or title claimed.

Against this background, Chief Justice McLachlin turned to the kind of duties that may arise in different situations. She noted that the concept of a spectrum may be helpful, not to suggest watertight legal compartments, but rather to indicate what the honour of the Crown may require in particular circumstances. "At one end of the spectrum lie cases where the claim to title is weak, the Aboriginal right limited, or the potential for infringement minor. In such cases, the only duty on the Crown may be to give notice, disclose information, and discuss any issues raised in response to the notice." She then turned to the other end of the spectrum, where a strong *prima facie* case for the claim is established, the right and potential infringement is of high significance to Aboriginal peoples, and the risk of non-compensable damage is high. She held that in such cases deep consultation, aimed at finding a satisfactory interim solution, may be required. She continued, "While precise requirements will vary with the circumstances, the consultation required at this stage may entail the opportunity to make submissions for consideration, formal participation in the decision-making process, and

156   Aboriginal Peoples and the Law

provision of written reasons to show that Aboriginal concerns were considered and to reveal the impact they had on the decision."[42]

Other situations will lie between these two extremes. Every case must be approached individually and flexibly, since the level of consultation required may change as the process goes on and new information comes to light. The controlling question in all situations is, What is required to maintain the honour of the Crown and to effect reconciliation between the Crown and Aboriginal peoples with respect to the interests at stake? Pending settlement, the Crown is bound by its honour to balance societal and Aboriginal interests when it makes decisions that may affect Aboriginal claims. It may be required to make decisions in the face of disagreement as to the adequacy of its response to Aboriginal concerns. "Balance and compromise will then be necessary."[43]

In *Mikisew Cree*, dealing with the duty to consult in the context of implementation of a treaty, the Court added:

> One variable will be the specificity of the promises made ... If the respective obligations are clear the parties should get on with performance. Another contextual factor will be the seriousness of the impact on the aboriginal people of the Crown's proposed course of action. The more serious the impact the more important will be the role of consultation ... The history of dealings between the Crown and a particular First Nation may also be significant.[44]

The Court also said:

> The duty here has both informational and response components ... The Crown was required to provide notice to the Mikisew and to engage directly with them (and not, as seems to have been the case here, as an afterthought to a general public consultation with Park users) ... The Crown was required to solicit and to listen carefully to the Mikisew concerns, and to attempt to minimize adverse impacts on the Mikisew hunting, fishing and trapping rights.[45]

This process ought to have included the provision of information about the project, addressing what the Crown knew to be the interests of the Aboriginal group and what the Crown anticipated might be the potential adverse impact on those interests. The Court quoted with approval a decision of the BC Court of Appeal that said that the Crown should ensure that the representations of the group are seriously considered and, wherever possible, demonstrably integrated into the proposed plan of action.

In *Haida,* the Court noted that the BC government had a provincial policy for consultation with First Nations to direct the terms of provincial ministries' and agencies' operational guidelines. It commented that "such a policy, while falling short of a regulatory scheme, may guard against unstructured discretion and provide a guide for decision-makers."[46] A report of the Fraser Institute in 2016 reviewed provincial policies and found "discrepancies around duty-to-consult policies and guidelines across the country."[47] It recommended greater consistency because this "patchwork of requirements ... creates different expectations from First Nations communities across the country and makes it more difficult to navigate the consultation process for proponents who are trying to advance projects that cross provincial boundaries."[48] Of course, such policies are not law and are subordinate to the legal requirements for meaningful consultation as established by the courts.[49] Some are unlikely to survive legal challenge, such as the arbitrary timelines for Aboriginal groups to respond or "engagement matrices" setting out the obligations of governments that do not take into account specific circumstances.

The Duty to Accommodate

The duty to accommodate, described by the Court in *Haida,* is a potential outcome of the duty to consult:

> When the consultation process suggests amendment of Crown policy, we arrive at the stage of accommodation. Thus the effect of good faith consultation may be to reveal a duty to accommodate. Where a strong *prima facie* case exists for the claim, and the consequences of the government's proposed decision may adversely affect it in a significant way, addressing the Aboriginal concerns may require taking steps to avoid irreparable harm or to minimize the effects of infringement, pending final resolution of the underlying claim. Accommodation is achieved through consultation.[50]

The Court described accommodation in the context of pre-proof consultation as a process of compromise: "What is required is a process of balancing interests, of give and take ... The accommodation that may result from pre-proof consultation is just this – seeking compromise in an attempt to

Aboriginal Peoples and the Law

harmonize conflicting interests and move further down the path of reconciliation."[51] This means "the Crown must balance Aboriginal concerns reasonably with the potential impact of the decision on the asserted right or
title and with other societal interests."[52] In *Chippewas of the Thames,* the
Court commented that the Aboriginal group was "not entitled to a one-sided
process, but rather a cooperative one with a view towards reconciliation.
Balance and compromise are inherent in that process."[53]

The Court was unable to determine in *Haida* if accommodation was
required because the government had failed to consult, but the strength of
claim and the adverse impact of logging suggested that significant accommodation was required to preserve the Aboriginal interest pending resolution of the claim. In *Taku,* the Court found that the strength of the claim was
relatively strong and the adverse impact of the decision to approve a road
was high. Therefore, the Aboriginal group was entitled "to a level of respon-
siveness to its concerns that can be characterized as accommodation."[54] The
facts presented in court showed that the duty to accommodate was satisfied
as the government included mitigation strategies to address the claims of
the group. In *Mikisew Cree,* the Court held that "consultation that excludes
from the outset any form of accommodation would be meaningless. The
contemplated process is not simply one of giving the Mikisew an opportunity
to blow off steam before the Minister proceeds to do what she intended to
do all along."[55] The Court commented that "accommodation may or may not
result in an agreement."[56] In this case, the Crown had failed to consult, so
the Court could not determine if accommodation was required, although it
indicated that changes in the road alignment or construction would go a
long way toward satisfying the Mikisew objections. In *Little Salmon,* the
Court observed that accommodation is not required "to the point of undue
hardship for the non-Aboriginal population" and held that there was no
requirement for accommodation in the circumstances.[57]

The references to compromise and mitigation indicate what the Court
has in mind when it refers to the duty to accommodate. However, the cases
lack detailed discussion equivalent to that available for the duty to consult.
In particular, it is not clear if there is a legal entitlement to compensation
where there has been a failure to consult on asserted rights. Justice La Forest
commented in *Delgamuukw* that consultation was one aspect of accommodation for infringement of Aboriginal title, and "another aspect of accommodation is fair compensation."[58] In practice, both governments and industry
proponents may be willing to enter into accommodation agreements or
impact benefit agreements (IBAs) to compensate Aboriginal groups for the

adverse consequences of a proposed project in return for not bringing, or for settling, proceedings challenging the project.

No Veto – Consent

It is a mantra of governments and industry proponents that the duty to consult does not give Aboriginal groups a veto.[59] This reflects the position of the Court, although *Haida* was inconsistent on this key issue. In one paragraph the Court said the "full consent of [the] aboriginal nation" was required on "very serious issues," quoting from the decision of Chief Justice Lamer in *Delgamuukw* and adding, "These words apply as much to unresolved claims as to intrusions on settled claims."[60] Later, however, it said, "This process does not give Aboriginal groups a veto over what can be done with land pending final proof of the claim. The Aboriginal 'consent' spoken of in *Delgamuukw* is appropriate only in cases of established rights, and then by no means in every case."[61] Subsequent statements of the Court have clarified the inconsistency in *Haida* in favour of the "no veto" passage. In *Mikisew Cree,* Justice Binnie, speaking for the Court, stated, "Had the consultation process gone ahead, it would not have given the Mikisew a veto over the alignment of the road. As emphasized in *Haida,* consultation will not always lead to accommodation, and accommodation may or may not result in an agreement."[62] In *Little Salmon,* he said:

> The First Nation protests that its concerns were not taken seriously – if they had been, it contends, the [land transfer] application would have been denied. This overstates the scope of the duty to consult in this case. The First Nation does not have a veto over the approval process. No such substantive right is found in the treaty or in the general law, constitutional or otherwise.[63]

The Court added in *Ktunaxa,* dealing with an unproven claim, that "s. 35 does not give unsatisfied claimants a veto over development. Where adequate consultation has occurred, a development may proceed without the consent of an Indigenous group."[64]

> The Supreme Court of Canada said in *Ktunaxa,* dealing with an unproven claim, that "s. 35 does not give unsatisfied claimants a veto over development. Where adequate consultation has occurred, a development may proceed without the consent of an Indigenous group."

In the case of established Aboriginal title, the consent of the Aboriginal group is required for any use of the land unless the Crown can justify an infringement. In *Tsilhqot'in,* the Court held that "the right to control the land conferred by Aboriginal title means that governments and others seeking to use the land must obtain the consent of the Aboriginal title holders." If the Aboriginal group does not consent to the use, the government must establish that the proposed incursion on the land is justified under Section 35 of the *Constitution Act, 1982.*[65]

> In the case of established Aboriginal title, the consent of the Aboriginal group is required for any use of the land unless the Crown can justify an infringement under Section 35 of the *Constitution Act, 1982.*

As we'll see when we discuss international law, the United Nations Declaration on the Rights of Indigenous Peoples requires governments to "consult and cooperate in good faith with the Indigenous peoples ... to obtain their free and informed consent prior to the approval of any project affecting their lands or territories and other resources." Although the current federal government has expressed its "full support" for the declaration, it has, arguably, diluted that duty so that consultations "aim" to secure such consent rather than being required to obtain it.[66]

The Duty on Aboriginal Groups to Participate

In *Haida,* the Court decided that there was a reciprocal obligation on Aboriginal groups to participate in the consultation process. First, they should help the Crown reach an understanding of their asserted rights, and the strength of those rights, in order to trigger the duty: "To facilitate this determination, claimants should outline their claims with clarity, focussing on the scope and nature of the Aboriginal rights they assert and on the alleged infringements."[67] During the process, "they must not frustrate the Crown's reasonable good faith attempts, nor should they take unreasonable positions to thwart government from making decisions or acting in cases where, despite meaningful consultation, agreement is not reached. Mere hard bargaining, however, will not offend an Aboriginal people's right to be consulted."[68] In *Mikisew Cree,* the Court observed, "It is true, as the Minister argues, that there is some reciprocal onus on the Mikisew to carry their end of the consultation, to make their concerns known, to respond to the government's attempt to meet their concerns and suggestions, and to try to reach some mutually satisfactory solution."[69]

An important issue that was raised in *Haida* but not answered is whether there is an obligation on the part of Aboriginal groups to seriously pursue their claims by negotiating treaties with the Crown or by litigation.

The Court held that the Crown was under a duty to negotiate treaties, and the rationale for the duty to consult was to facilitate such negotiation by providing a measure of protection to Aboriginal interests during negotiations so their lands and resources would not be changed and denuded during the long process of negotiation.[70] "The Crown, acting honourably, cannot cavalierly run roughshod over Aboriginal interests where claims affecting these interests are being seriously pursued in the process of treaty negotiation and proof."[71] This statement suggests that there may be an obligation on an Aboriginal group to make serious efforts to pursue claims if the Crown is to be obligated to consult with it on unproven claims.

A couple of cases illustrate the issue of Aboriginal participation. In *Long Plain,* which involved the transfer of a large parcel of land in Winnipeg by the federal government, the Federal Court of Appeal found the government in breach of its duty to consult and ordered new consultations, but also found that some of the First Nations were partially at fault for not being responsive to the Crown's efforts. It warned, "A continuation of this sort of conduct in the future by any of the four respondents exposes them to risk. If they behave uncooperatively or recalcitrantly, they may be foreclosed in the future from complaining that they were not sufficiently consulted."[72] However, an Aboriginal group cannot be faulted for refusing to participate in a fundamentally flawed process, as held by the BC Court of Appeal in *Chartrand:* "It cannot be said that offering the [Aboriginal group] an opportunity to participate in fundamentally inadequate consultations preserves the honour of the Crown."[73]

Third Parties

The BC Court of Appeal held in *Haida* that the duty to consult extended to the forestry company to which the licence had been transferred, as well as to the provincial government. The Supreme Court of Canada ordered that this part of the decision be reversed, finding no duty on third parties. The legal reason for the different conclusions resulted from the different basis found for the duty to consult in cases of pre-proof claims. The Court of Appeal had found the basis for the duty in the Crown's fiduciary obligations and applied the principle that third parties who knowingly receive a benefit from a breach of those obligations are equally obligated. As we have seen, the SCC based liability on the honour of the Crown, which it said "cannot be delegated," thereby letting third parties off the hook.[74] However, it also said that "the Crown may delegate procedural aspects of consultation to industry proponents seeking a particular development; this is not infrequently done in environmental assessments."[75] There was no further elaboration, and the extent to which third parties can validly discharge the Crown's obligations is far from clear. The decision seems contradictory on this point. Since the Court has said that the duty to consult in the case of pre-proof claims is procedural and not substantive,[76] every aspect of consultation may be seen as procedural and so can be delegated, despite the bald statements that "the ultimate legal responsibility for consultation and accommodation rests with the Crown. The honour of the Crown cannot be delegated."[77] The Court's objective does not seem to have been to exclude third parties from the process but to provide them with immunity: "They cannot be held liable for failing to discharge the Crown's duty to consult and accommodate."[78]

In practice, third-party proponents and their consultants will often take the lead in consultations to the exclusion of governments. Agreements are often negotiated with Aboriginal groups to allow major projects to proceed without opposition or with only limited opposition from Aboriginal groups. These agreements will usually include benefits such as cash payments, employment, and business opportunities, and they may include an equity (ownership) position. There may be a role for the Aboriginal group in preventing, mitigating, or remediating adverse environmental effects of a project, which will enable it to carry out stewardship of its lands. The negotiation of such agreements may be a condition of regulatory approval.

Administrative Procedures

The Court made it clear in *Taku* that the duty to consult does not require a separate consultation process if meaningful consultation can take place within an existing administrative process: "The Province was not required to develop special consultation measures to address [the Aboriginal group's] concerns, outside of the process provided for by the *Environmental Assessment Act*, which specifically set out a scheme that required consultation with affected Aboriginal peoples."[79] In *Little Salmon*, the Court said, "Participation in a forum created for other purposes may nevertheless satisfy the duty to consult if *in substance* an appropriate level of consultation is provided."[80] It is necessary in each case to consider if the administrative process satisfies the requirements of the duty for meaningful consultation. The decisions in *Clyde*

River and *Chippewas of the Thames* illustrate this point: in the former, the National Energy Board's process was held to be inadequate, while it sufficed in the latter. Relevant factors were the availability of oral hearings, the availability of funding to enable participation, and the provision of written reasons. Sometimes governments take the view that the administrative process partially satisfies the requirements and add a supplementary direct consultation phase to fill in the gaps, as was done with the Northern Gateway and Trans Mountain pipeline projects in western Canada in 2014 to 2016. If a government is relying on an administrative process, it must advise Aboriginal groups and permit them to raise any concerns.[81]

In *Rio Tinto,* the Court considered the role of administrative tribunals, such as the BC Utilities Commission, which was involved in that case. It held that the duty of a tribunal to consider adequacy of consultation by the Crown and to undertake consultation depended on the mandate conferred by the legislation that created the tribunal. Sometimes, the legislation delegates the Crown's duty to consult. In other cases, the legislation may confine the tribunal's role to determining if adequate consultations have taken place. "Tribunals considering resource issues touching on Aboriginal interests may have neither of these duties, one of these duties, or both depending on what responsibilities the legislature has conferred on them."[82]

Remedies

The Court said in *Rio Tinto,* "The remedy for a breach of the duty to consult also varies with the situation. The Crown's failure to consult can lead to a number of remedies ranging from injunctive relief against the threatening activity altogether, to damages, to an order to carry out the consultation prior to proceeding further with the proposed government conduct."[83] It held in *Clyde River* that a decision based on inadequate consultation should be quashed on judicial review.[84] Usually an Aboriginal group would pursue a claim for breach of the duty by applying for judicial review of the decision made by the government. Compared with bringing an action for breach of a treaty or Aboriginal right, this is a much less complex and expensive process, without the necessity for a trial and extensive pre-trial procedures. Evidence is usually given by sworn statements rather than witnesses appearing in court. However, time limits may be very tight. For example, Section 18 of the *Federal Court Act* requires that an application be brought within thirty days of the applicant receiving the decision, although this period can be extended by

Aboriginal Peoples and the Law

a judge. In *Ktunaxa*, the SCC made it clear that judicial review proceedings are not a suitable process by which to seek a judicial declaration on the validity of Aboriginal rights. Such a declaration should only be given following a trial and not as an incident of administrative law proceedings that centre on the adequacy of consultation and accommodation.[85]

Discussion of the Duty to Consult

Tom Isaac, a lawyer who advises governments and industry on Aboriginal issues, and a prominent writer on the topic, has summarized the practical importance of the duty to consult:

> From a practical perspective, the Crown's duty to consult has been, and
> will likely continue to be, an important component to Crown-Aboriginal
> and business-Aboriginal relations across Canada. It has dominated
> Aboriginal litigation in recent years, has provided Aboriginal peoples
> with a powerful tool to influence governmental decision-making pro-
> cesses and has had a profound effect on industry and businesses that
> are dependent upon governmental approvals and regulation.[86]

Dwight Newman, professor of law at the University of Saskatchewan, has described the duty as establishing "a new realm of Aboriginal law."[87] Sébastian Grammond stated previously that, "with its seminal *Haida Nation* decision concerning the duty to consult and accommodate, the Supreme Court seems to shift the emphasis from the allocation of rights to the sharing of decision making power over land as the dominant paradigm of indigenous peoples' law."[88]

The significant development in Aboriginal law resulting from *Haida* has been warmly welcomed by many commentators. Writing soon after the decision was given, Calvin Helin, an Aboriginal lawyer and businessman, said, "With growing resource development in their traditional territories ... and legal decisions requiring genuine consultations, Aboriginal Canadians for the first time have real leverage over a substantial area of the Canadian economy. This results in an unprecedented opportunity to forge a new era of self-reliance."[89] Experience has not always borne out these optimistic forecasts. Natan Obed, the president of the Inuit Tapiriit Kanatami, the national organization representing Canada's 65,000 Inuit, has stated that their experience "has shown us that consultations tend to have predetermined outcomes, are rarely collaborative in nature, and by their orientation situate final decision-making powers with non-Indigenous governments."[90]

There can be no doubt that the *Haida* decision provided an incentive for negotiations that may not have happened without it. It has provided the legal basis for negotiations that have led to agreements with Aboriginal groups to obtain their support for (or lack of active opposition to) proposed projects. We shall see that, as a result of litigation to establish their rights and enforce the duty to consult, combined with negotiations to resolve actual or threatened litigation, some Aboriginal groups, such as the Musqueam in Vancouver, have signed agreements that have resulted in the transfer/return to them of valuable land and the payment of many millions of dollars.

On the other hand, although the duty to consult was intended to provide an interim solution to claims of unproven rights and so facilitate their resolution, it may instead have delayed or frustrated fundamental resolution through treaties (the preference of the Court) or litigation, as short-term objectives prevailed. In the meantime, Aboriginal peoples are deprived of the full benefits of their rights and title or, if the claims lack legal merit, non-Aboriginal Canadians may be providing accommodation for unmerited claims. In the case of unproven claims, the duty to consult and accommodate is a valuable interim remedy. The SCC commented in *Ktunaxa* that "in the difficult period between claim assertion and claim resolution, consultation and accommodation, imperfect as they may be, are the best available legal tools in the reconciliation basket."[91] But, in my view, they should not be regarded as the focus of Aboriginal law or divorced from the resolution of claims of Aboriginal rights and title.[92] As the Court noted in *Chippewas of the Thames,* the duty to consult "is not the vehicle to address historical grievances" and "is limited in scope."[93] Dwight Newman has suggested that there is a danger that the duty to consult may discourage the development of other areas of Aboriginal law.[94] In addition to this general comment, there are a number of more detailed concerns.

> Although the duty to consult was intended to provide an interim solution to claims of unproven rights and so facilitate their resolution, it may instead have delayed or frustrated fundamental resolution through treaties ... or litigation.

Since the duty to consult in the context of pre-proof claims is procedural and not substantive, it gives the Aboriginal group only limited powers to challenge a proposed decision. As the Court stated in *Haida,* "The focus [of the court] ... is not on the outcome, but on the process of consultation and accommodation."[95] Once consultations are undertaken at the correct level on the spectrum extending from minimal to deep consultation, the obligation of the government is essentially the usual administrative law duty to be reasonable. As noted, for example, in *Little Salmon*, "Within the limits established by the law and the Constitution ... the Director's decision should be reviewed on a standard of reasonableness ... In other words, if there was adequate consultation, did the Director's decision to approve the Paulsen grant, having regard to all the relevant considerations, fall within the range of reasonable outcomes?"[96] Whether a court would have reached a different conclusion on the facts was not relevant. Courts will usually defer to the government on questions of fact or mixed fact and law.[97]

In practice, it is often difficult for an Aboriginal group to persuade a judge that a decision falls outside the range of reasonable outcomes. Given their greater resources and familiarity with paperwork and procedures, government officials can usually produce enough evidence that "they ticked all the boxes" and, on paper, reached a reasonable conclusion. Even if an application to overturn a decision for failure to adequately consult is successful, the remedy is often an order that the Crown should redo the consultations to improve the deficient process. For example, in a decision overturning the federal government's approval of the Northern Gateway project, the Federal Court of Appeal described the new consultations as "a matter that, if well-organized and well-executed, need not take long," estimating a timeline in the neighbourhood of four months.[98] The practical result may be that a project is merely delayed for a short period, although in this case, a change of government meant the end of the project. On the other hand, one critic has expressed concern that *Haida* contains open-ended language that "is an invitation to second-guessing [of government decisions] by the various levels of the judiciary."[99]

Some critics complain that consultation is an apparently endless process that delays or frustrates the ability to reach agreement, or is a delaying or avoidance tactic used by governments. These concerns are increased by language such as the following in *Rio Tinto*: "Consultation is concerned with an ethic of ongoing relationships and seeks to further an ongoing process of reconciliation by articulating a preference for remedies that promote ongoing negotiations."[100] One critic states that "the ever increasing 'duty to consult' process becomes the one that all parties can obsess over because consultation requires no tough decisions, only endless disclosures, analysis, over-analysis, procedural wrangling, and then more discussion."[101] In his view, "unintentionally, the Court has established process as the Holy Grail, rather than the methodology." Certainly, in my experience, process can overtake issues of substance with endless meetings that may comprise little more than PowerPoint presentations full of simplistic diagrams or glossy photographs, which are then portrayed as "consultation." Sometimes government officials are little more than note takers, keeping records of questions and concerns expressed by the Aboriginal group, never responding to specific issues, but only giving generic, noncommittal responses.[102] The process is then brought to an end by the imposition of an apparently arbitrary deadline or one effectively imposed by the industry proponent. Aboriginal concerns are left unaddressed, and Aboriginal groups must consider costly and uncertain litigation.

The obligation on an Aboriginal group to participate may place a heavy burden on them. Most lack the resources to handle the large volume of "referrals" they receive, which may range from minor roadwork to major pipeline proposals in their territories. They are usually no match for the well-oiled bureaucratic machine available to governments and proponents, or the consultants retained by them, who keep meticulous records of every contact or attempted "engagement" with the group and then use the sheer volume as evidence of consultations, however meaningless the actual contents of the "engagement." Nor can Aboriginal groups reasonably be expected to provide comments or concerns on proposed projects as described in voluminous technical reports that have been compiled by governments or proponents, sometimes over many years prior to the consultation process. Aboriginal groups lack the technical expertise, finances, and time to fully understand or provide comments on how the proposal will affect their rights. There is no clear authority requiring governments and proponents to make funding available to the Aboriginal groups, although it was mentioned as a factor in determining the adequacy of consultations in *Clyde River*.[103] In practice, when funding is provided, the amount is often a fraction of the true cost needed to prepare comments on a proposal. It would be fairer to place the burden on governments and proponents to show that the proposed project does not unreasonably affect established or asserted rights before approval is given.

Despite the sometimes unfair nature of the process, Aboriginal groups run a risk if they do not participate. Their failure to participate may be taken as frustrating the Crown's good faith attempts at consultation. They are also under great pressure to accept whatever "accommodation" the Crown may propose. If they fail to do so, they run the risk that a court may say the Crown acted reasonably and so discharged its obligation to consult. Since there is no obligation to agree, they may end up with nothing, even as the project goes ahead despite their concerns. The vagueness about when the duty to accommodate arises and the deference of courts to governments mean that an Aboriginal group may deplete its limited resources trying unsuccessfully to protect its interests from threats posed by a major project such as a pipeline, perhaps promoted by a multinational proponent with enormous resources, and end up with no reduction in the threat and no benefits as compensation.

In many cases, there is a gross inequality in bargaining power between Aboriginal peoples and governments/proponents, which may render illusory the benefits of consultation as described by the Court. The "process of balancing interests, of give and take," spoken of in *Haida*,[104] and the process of working together to reconcile interests, spoken of in *Rio Tinto*,[105] require greater equality of bargaining power than the impoverished position of most Aboriginal peoples will permit.

Despite the sometimes unfair nature of the process, Aboriginal groups run a risk if they do not participate. Their failure to participate may be taken as frustrating the Crown's good faith attempts at consultation.

Another concern is that the consultation process may not deal adequately with the cumulative impacts of development. In the context of consultations over the implementation of a treaty, Justice Binnie noted that "the severity of the impact of land grants, whether taken individually or cumulatively, properly constituted an important element of the consultation."[106] In *Chippewas of the Thames*, the Court noted that "cumulative effects of an on-going project, and historical context, may ... inform the scope of the duty to consult.[107] However, the decision in *Rio Tinto* that excluded consultation about past decisions or conduct may effectively rule out consultation over cumulative impacts in pre-proof consultations. Also, the nature of the duty to consult, which focuses on discrete Crown conduct and decisions, makes it difficult to analyze the cumulative impacts, especially if there are several Crown agencies involved and a lack of central planning for the resource.

When the government uses administrative proceedings to discharge completely or partially the duty to consult, there is a risk that the government will rely on the administrative body to fulfill the duty and the administrative body will rely on the government to do so. In some cases, such as those involving the National Energy Board, administrative processes are based on legislation and procedures that pre-date *Haida* and fall short of the requirements for meaningful consultations. As well, members of the administrative body may lack familiarity with Aboriginal law and those requirements. In *Haida*, the Court said, "It is open to governments to set up regulatory schemes to address the procedural requirements appropriate to different problems at different stages, thereby strengthening the reconciliation process and reducing recourse to the courts."[108] Such specialized schemes, with qualified administrative bodies, including effective Aboriginal representation, would be a better route than using administrative schemes set up for other purposes.

Despite the legal inability to delegate the honour of the Crown, the delegation in practice of much consultation by governments to third-party proponents means that Aboriginal groups may be required to deal with representatives who have a vested interest in seeing the project proceed – a clear conflict of interest that may colour the information provided to governments and their response to the concerns of the Aboriginal group. This privatization of the honour of the Crown is also troubling in principle. Historically, going back to the Royal Proclamation of 1763, the practice has been to interpose the Crown between Aboriginal peoples and those who wish to use their lands.[109]

On balance, the *Haida* duty to consult has been a welcome development, but its contribution to Aboriginal law should not be overstated, nor should the benefits it confers on most Aboriginal groups. It has undoubtedly provided major benefits to some groups since it may trigger negotiations that provide substantive benefits. However, it is a procedural requirement, similar to the administrative duty of fairness, that is intended to preserve rights not implement them. It does not confer decision-making powers on Aboriginal groups. Also, as discussed above, there are significant issues to be resolved, such as the role of accommodation and consent, cumulative impacts, administrative bodies, and interested third parties, especially industry.

Reform is required to make consultations fairer and more meaningful for Aboriginal groups. Adequate funding should be a precondition of any obligation on an Aboriginal group to participate in consultations carried out for a project advanced by government or industry. Consultation policies should be developed jointly by government and Aboriginal groups and made mandatory. Unless the Aboriginal group agrees to it, the Crown should not be permitted to delegate its duties. A specialized body with effective Aboriginal representation should supervise major consultations. The burden should be on governments and proponents to show that the proposed action will not unreasonably impact established or asserted Aboriginal and treaty rights.

An example to be considered is the Australian *Native Title Act*.[110] This act contains provisions that seek to bring about agreements over proposed

Aboriginal Peoples and the Law

"future acts," such as mining and other leases, that will affect Native title rights and interests. There are two types of agreements involved:

- Indigenous land use agreements (ILUAs)
- right-to-negotiate agreements.

ILUAs can be registered with the Native Title Registrar to make them binding. They cover benefits similar to those found in Impact Benefit Agreements in Canada, such as employment and training, agreements for development, and compensation. The right-to-negotiate provisions provide a greater degree of supervision, mediation, and arbitration. The key provision is Section 31(1)(b), which requires all parties to "negotiate in good faith with a view to obtaining the agreement of each of the native title parties" to the future act. If successfully negotiated, the terms of the agreement may again be similar to those of an IBA. The government must be a party to the agreement, and the proposed grantee of an interest under the "future act" will usually be a party as well. If no agreement is reached within six months, any party can make an application to the National Native Title Tribunal for a binding determination on whether the "future act" can be done, done subject to conditions, or not done.

The Australian model may or may not be a good example for Canada, but for all the advantages of the duty to consult, there remain a number of questions and concerns as it has developed since the *Haida* decision. Given its practical importance, it would be better if these were addressed collaboratively by Aboriginal and non-Aboriginal governments rather than left to the courts – for reasons that will become clear when the limits of litigation are discussed.

TO SUM UP

- There are many sources for the duty to consult, and they should be kept in mind as they influence the scope of the duty and when it arises.

- In the case of unproven rights, the duty is a procedural and not a substantive obligation. It deals with how a government must do something rather than what it must do – the process and not the outcome.

- In *Guerin,* the court ruled that the duty to consult may be part of a government's fiduciary obligation to an Aboriginal group with respect to an established right.

- *Sparrow* and *Badger* established that the duty to consult is also part of the duty of a government to justify infringements of an established Aboriginal or treaty right.

- To protect the Aboriginal interest pending proof during litigation or agreement by government, *Haida* extended the duty to consult to asserted rights. The basis was the honour of the Crown principle.

- The duty was applied to the exercise of powers under a treaty in *Mikisew Cree* (historical treaty) and *Little Salmon* (modern treaty).

- In *Rio Tinto,* the court established that the duty to consult in pre-proof situations does not apply to past decisions or actions of the government.

- *Behn* established that the duty is owed to the Aboriginal group and not individuals.

- The *Haida* duty arises if (a) a government knows of a potential claim or right, (b) an actual or potential action or decision of the government may have an impact on lands or resources, and (c) the action or decision could adversely affect the claim or right.

- In the case of established rights, the required level of consultation is the greatest.

- In the case of pre-proof claims, the content of the duty varies with the circumstances and, in general terms, is proportionate to a preliminary assessment of the strength of the case supporting the existence of the asserted right and the seriousness of the potentially adverse effect on the claim.

- The duty to accommodate has received less consideration by the SCC and is somewhat vague. It refers to steps taken by a government to avoid harm or to minimize the impact of a decision on the Aboriginal interest.

- In the case of unproven claims, the Aboriginal group does not have a veto and, where adequate consultation has occurred, a development may proceed without consent. In the case of established Aboriginal title, the consent of the Aboriginal group is required for any use of the land, unless the government can justify an infringement.

- The Aboriginal group is under a duty to participate in the consultation process.

- Third parties are not obligated to consult Aboriginal groups, although "procedural aspects" can be delegated to them by a government. In practice, they will often take the lead in order to avoid or minimize opposition to their project.

- The duty to consult does not require a separate process if meaningful consultation can take place within an existing administrative process.

- The *Haida* duty to consult has been a major and welcome development in Aboriginal law, but it should not overshadow other areas, and there are significant issues to be resolved to make it fairer and more meaningful to Aboriginal peoples.

Indigenous and International Law

7

There are bodies of law – Indigenous and international – that are not directly part of Canadian Aboriginal law but that may influence and be adopted into it.[1] They also provide differing perspectives from which to consider Canadian Aboriginal law. To understand Aboriginal law, it's important to consider a number of issues and questions, including how it differs from Indigenous law. Regarding the latter, what are its sources and content, how does it compare with Canadian common law, and to what extent does the Canadian legal system recognize it? Relatedly, what role does international law play in the legal affairs of Canadian Aboriginal peoples? In particular, what are the key provisions of the United Nations Declaration on the Rights of Indigenous Peoples (UNDRIP), how does it compare with the American Declaration on the Rights of Indigenous Peoples, and what changes would be required if the former were to be adopted into Canadian law?

Indigenous Laws versus Aboriginal Law

In its 2015 report, the Truth and Reconciliation Commission wrote: "All Canadians need to understand the difference between Indigenous laws and Aboriginal law ... Each Indigenous nation across the country has its own laws and legal traditions. Aboriginal law is the body of law that exists within the Canadian legal system."[2] The TRC defined "reconciliation" as an ongoing process of establishing and maintaining respectful relationships, which requires the revitalization of Indigenous laws and legal traditions.[3] Indigenous laws should "receive heightened attention, encouragement and support,"[4] because they "have great relevance for Aboriginal peoples and all Canadians today. They should be regarded as the laws of the land and applied to the broader reconciliation process."[5] The TRC called for the Crown to issue a Royal Proclamation of Reconciliation that would include a commitment to "reconcile Aboriginal and Crown constitutional and legal orders to ensure that Aboriginal peoples are full partners in Confederation, including the recognition and integration of Indigenous laws and legal traditions in negotiation and implementation processes involving Treaties, land claims and other constructive agreements."[6]

The Truth and Reconciliation Commission defined "reconciliation" as an ongoing process of establishing and maintaining respectful relationships, which requires the revitalization of Indigenous laws and legal traditions.

Indigenous laws, then, refer to a continuation of the laws and legal traditions that governed Indigenous or Aboriginal groups before the arrival of Europeans. Apart from an overview, drawn from publications by Indigenous scholars, to give a sense of their content, this book does not purport to describe Indigenous laws. Since its scope is limited to Aboriginal law as described by the TRC, it will concentrate on the recognition of Indigenous laws by the Canadian legal system. It does so from the perspective of the Canadian legal system and not that of any Indigenous legal system, although I note the concern of some Aboriginal legal scholars that recognition by the dominant system may "ensnare" Indigenous law,[7] or distort it.[8]

Like international law, Indigenous laws exist on a separate plane from the Canadian legal system and do not form part of the Canadian law except to the extent that they have been incorporated into Canadian common law.[9] The situation was described by Justice Mandamin of the Federal Court (who formerly presided in the Tsuu Tina and Siksika Courts) in a 2014 decision: "I should think that Aboriginal customary laws, while they exist on their own independent footing, are not an effectual part of Canadian common law or Canadian domestic law until there is some means or process by which the independent Aboriginal customary law is recognized as being part of Canadian domestic law."[10]

The recognition of Indigenous laws as part of the Canadian legal system may be regarded as an application in the Canadian context of a fundamental rule found in all legal systems – the rule of recognition.[11] In its recent decision on the exit of the United Kingdom from the European Union, the Supreme Court of the UK described the rule as "the fundamental rule by reference to which all other rules are validated."[12] It is "the rule which identifies the sources of law in our legal system and imposes a duty to give effect to laws emanating from those sources."[13] The recognition of Indigenous laws within the Canadian legal system is also an example of legal pluralism, which for our purposes we can define as the presence of different legal traditions within the same legal system.[14] At the provincial level, Canada has a pluralist system, with the civil law derived from French law in effect in Quebec, and the common law derived from English law in the rest of the country. Advocates for greater recognition of Indigenous laws, such as John Borrows, have relied on this analogy.[15]

Overview of Indigenous Laws

The TRC report provides some representative examples of Indigenous laws.[16] Further examples are given by John Borrows in his publications.[17] He describes the sources of Indigenous laws and gives examples. There are many, sometimes overlapping, sources, including some that would not usually be regarded as sources of Canadian common or civil law – the "two major legal traditions" in Canada.[18] It is important to note that there is no pan-Indigenous law that applies across Canada any more than there is only one Indigenous language. This diversity should be kept in mind while reading the comments below regarding recognition of Indigenous laws by the Canadian legal system. Each Indigenous law would have to be considered separately. However, there are similarities among the Indigenous laws compared with laws in the European tradition, such as the absence of state institutions and written laws.

The Rule of Recognition and Legal Pluralism

The Supreme Court of the UK described the rule of recognition as "the fundamental rule by reference to which all other rules are validated." It is "the rule which identifies the sources of law in our legal system and imposes a duty to give effect to laws emanating from those sources."

"Legal pluralism" can be defined as the presence of different legal traditions within the same legal system.

According to Borrows, some Indigenous laws have sacred sources, such as creation stories, which contain guidance on how to live with the world and overcome conflict.[19] Another source is observation of the natural world, and legends and stories regarding events that have shaped the natural environment. For example, "For the Gitksan, as with many Indigenous peoples, the law is read from the land," illustrated by a story about how a landslide was created by the Giant Grizzly Bear to punish people for not giving proper respect to fish.[20] "An especially broad source of Indigenous legal tradition is formed through the processes of persuasion, deliberation, council and discussion."[21] This may mean the use of circles to invite participation in developing legal standards. Feasts and other large public assemblies are also used, especially in British Columbia. At these gatherings, land disputes and boundaries may be resolved. Band council meetings are modern examples of this, as are sentencing circles used as part of some criminal procedures. "Another source of Indigenous laws can be found in the proclamations, rules, regulations, codes, teachings, and axioms that are regarded as binding or regulating people's behaviour."[22] These laws may be made by chiefs or clan mothers. A final type of law is custom, which Borrows defines as "those

Sources of Indigenous Law

- sacred sources, such as creation stories, which contain guidance on how to live with the world and overcome conflict
- observation of the natural world
- legends and stories regarding events that have shaped the natural environment
- processes of persuasion, deliberation, council and discussion (for example, the use of circles to invite participation in developing legal standards, feasts and other large public assemblies, Band council meetings)
- proclamations, rules, regulations, codes, teachings, and axioms made by chiefs or clan mothers
- custom (for example, marriages and adoptions)
- dances and songs.

practices developed through repetitive patterns of social interaction that are accepted as binding on those who participate in them."[23] Examples would include marriages and adoptions. Ojibway writer Kah-Ge-Ga-Gah-Bowh said in 1850, "Customs handed down from generation to generation have been the only laws to guide them.[24]

Some indication of the nature and scope of Indigenous laws as practised in particular communities can be gathered from evidence given in litigation. For example, in *Tsilhqot'in,* evidence was given on some Tsilhqot'in laws, such as those related to killing, stealing, and creating a disturbance.[25] And Valerie Napoleon's PhD thesis is partially a review of the evidence given in *Delgamuukw* on Gitksan law.[26] A number of legends concern proper treatment of animals and the serious consequences for mistreatment, such as famine. "In this example, it is obvious that the larger legal principles are about maintaining the reciprocal relationships with animals so that they will continue to feed the people."[27] She comments that "a useful way to think about the various proceedings – the practices, rituals and conventions – is that in their entirety, they contain an ongoing record of Gitksan law,"[28] and she includes a number of cases that illustrate the application of Gitksan law, such as the legitimacy of the chief, compensation relating to intentional and accidental death, disputes about names, and adoptions. Compared with Canadian common law, the emphasis is on remedies, including various types of compensation, rather than guilt.[29]

Some writers have commented generally that Indigenous laws are made up of community values rather than specific rules or norms established by a central authority, as is the case with European-based legal systems.

Indigenous Laws and Canadian Common Law

Some writers have commented generally that Indigenous laws are made up of community values rather than specific rules or norms established by a central authority, as is the case with European-based legal systems. Values such as respect and consensus are conveyed through stories, legends, ceremonies, dances, and songs. These values are then used to determine what action should be taken to avoid or resolve conflicts.[30] Borrows states: "In my experience, Indigenous laws are those procedures and substantive values, principles, practices, and teachings that reflect, create, respect, enhance, and protect the world and our relationships within it."[31] Another Aboriginal scholar, Aaron Mills, states, "law isn't the formal obligation to respect rules (i.e. rights and correlative duties). Rather, law consists in the informal responsibility to coordinate mutual aid (i.e. gifts and needs)" within a particular relationship.[32] This goes far beyond the usual understanding of the role of law for those trained in European-based legal systems, and suggests that not all types of Indigenous laws are likely to be recognized by Canadian common law. Common law consists of rules, not values or teachings, although they may be the basis for the rules. Also, Canadian common law is generally individualistic and concentrates on avoiding harm to other people rather than aiding them or protecting relationships and the world.

Another key distinction between Indigenous laws and legal systems derived from Europe is the absence of a state and legal institutions – such as a legislature, courts, and legal officials – that are separate from other social institutions. Instead, "law is embedded in social, political and spiritual institutions."[33] Some legal theorists (positivists) identify state institutions as essential to a legal system and describe societies without them as pre-legal, relying on morality or voluntary acceptance of custom rather than on laws.[34] Proponents of Indigenous laws have responded to such views by arguing that state institutions are not a requirement for a functioning legal system. For example, Val Napoleon finds all the required elements in the Gitksan law, including the fundamental rule of recognition.[35]

In *Van der Peet*, the Supreme Court of Canada referred to "the meeting of two vastly dissimilar legal cultures."[36] As we have seen, there was acceptance by the British of Indigenous laws during the era of contact and co-operation, but this turned to attempts to assimilate during the era of displacement and assimilation, and steps were taken to eradicate some Indigenous laws, such as ceremonies like the potlatch. There were also clashes of values. An example that figures prominently in the literature was the punishment by the colonial legal system of those who followed traditional Cree and Anishinabek laws on how to deal with the *wetiko* or *windigo,* a term used to describe people who are harmful or destructive to others, perhaps as the result of a mental disorder, and often believed to be cannibal spirits.[37] If all other measures failed, the individual might be killed to protect the community, and steps taken to compensate those who were dependent on them.[38] We saw a modern example of a clash of values in our discussion in Chapter 1 of *Thomas v. Norris,*[39] which applied contemporary Canadian protection for the individual over traditional laws that allegedly permitted involuntary confinement as part of spirit dancing.[40]

It is also important to acknowledge that some misunderstanding results from "surface views of deep Indigenous concepts without the context of how Indigenous knowledge systems operate," which is very different from how Western knowledge systems operate and may require fluency in the Indigenous language.[41]

Recognition of Indigenous Laws by the Canadian Legal System

In its comprehensive 1986 report *The Recognition of Aboriginal Customary Law*, the Australian Law Reform Commission concluded that "the recognition of Aboriginal customary laws by the general law has continued to be erratic, uncoordinated and incomplete."[42] This conclusion applies equally to the current state of Canadian law. (In fact, Australian law now attaches greater weight to traditional or Indigenous laws as they are a part of the statutory definition of Native title, unlike Canadian law, which relies more on physical possession at the time of Crown sovereignty to prove Aboriginal title.)[43]

Some recognition of Indigenous laws in Canada has occurred in case law based on the common law recognition of customs, which has a long history.[44] Some recognition has occurred by statute in specific situations.[45] Sébastian Grammond has summarized the situation: "In practice ... courts have recognized only indigenous marriages and adoptions. The practice has not been uniform across the various provinces and territories. Legislation, on its part, has focused on specific aspects of indigenous laws."[46] The *Indian Act* recognizes band councils "chosen according to the custom of a band,"[47] and customary election systems apply to the majority of bands.[48] The act also defines a "child" to include "a child adopted in accordance with Indian custom." In 2008, an amendment to the *Canadian Human Rights Act* said it was to be interpreted "in a manner that gives due regard to First Nations legal traditions and customary law ... to the extent they are consistent with the principles of gender equality."[49] It may be noted that Indigenous laws are very present on most reserves in the customary land-holding practices, which have been described as "the most common system of property rights on Canadian Indian reserves."[50] However, they are not recognized by the Canadian legal system.[51]

As we have seen, the Supreme Court of Canada has endorsed the doctrine of continuity – "the recognition by the common law of the ancestral laws and customs of the aboriginal peoples" – described by Justice McLachlin as "a golden thread" running through the long history of the interface between Europeans and Aboriginal peoples.[52] However, in practice, this does not mean that the Indigenous law is recognized in its original form – rather, there is a process of translation into common law concepts. The Indigenous law must be "cognizable to the non-aboriginal legal system."[53] A process of translation is required to convert it into "a modern legal right."[54] It is only in this translated fashion that Indigenous laws form part of "the intersocietal law" referenced in *Van der Peet*.[55] This process of translation of Indigenous laws into common law rights is contrary to earlier cases that warned against trying to apply "traditional real property rules" to Aboriginal interests.[56] The SCC attempted (in my view, unsuccessfully) to square the circle in *Tsilhqot'in* by saying that "the court must be careful not to lose or distort the Aboriginal perspective by forcing ancestral practices into the square boxes of common law concepts, thus frustrating the goal of faithfully translating pre-sovereignty Aboriginal interests into equivalent modern legal rights."[57]

In practice, the Court has not defined Aboriginal rights in terms of Indigenous laws. In *Sappier*, the Court said, "The aboriginal rights doctrine, which has been constitutionalized by s. 35, arises from the simple fact of prior occupation of lands now forming part of Canada."[58] This statement confirmed that the "simple fact" of prior occupation, not Indigenous law, is the basis of rights recognized by the Canadian common law. Kent McNeil has reviewed the leading decisions in *Delgamuukw, Marshall/Bernard,* and *Tsilhqot'in*. He concludes that "Indigenous law relates to Aboriginal title in two ways: it is part of the evidence that can be relied upon to establish the exclusive occupation necessary for title at the time of Crown assertion of sovereignty, and it continues thereafter to govern the communal land rights of the Aboriginal titleholders."[59] It should be noted that the first conclusion is based on express statements in the decisions.[60] The second is more a matter of argument given the absence of decided cases. What is significant is that the Court does not apply any Indigenous law in its decisions in either *Delgamuukw* or *Tsilhqot'in*, which both concern the content of Aboriginal title. If the Court had done so, it would have looked to Gitksan and Wet'-suwet'en law in *Delgamuukw* and Tsilhqot'in law in *Tsilhqot'in* to find the content of their respective titles. Instead, it described a generic type of Aboriginal title that applies to all Aboriginal groups and is based on the Court's own views reflecting common law concepts such as exclusive occupation. This was in spite of references in *Delgamuukw* to the characteristics of Aboriginal title being derived, in part, from "the rules of property found in aboriginal legal systems" and references to "the relationship between the common law and pre-existing systems of aboriginal law."[61]

> The Supreme Court of Canada does not apply any Indigenous law in its decisions in either *Delgamuukw* or *Tsilhqot'in,* which both concern the content of Aboriginal title.

As noted by John Borrows, "Despite attempts to incorporate Indigenous perspectives and laws, Section 35(1) remains securely tied to its non-Aboriginal foundations. There is no real Indigenous law cited in arriving at appropriate decisions."[62] The Court appears to be paying lip-service only.

Proposals for Greater Recognition of Indigenous Laws

To date, the most detailed review of the issues involved in recognition of Indigenous laws in a common law system was conducted by the Australian Law Reform Commission in the report mentioned above. This was a monumental work and very relevant to Canadian proposals. The commission reviewed the existing law and proposals for reform. It considered and rejected various objections, including

- unacceptable rules
- the secrecy of some laws
- the loss of Aboriginal control over their laws
- the need to protect women
- the fact that the laws had changed in many respects and no longer existed in pristine form
- their declining importance
- difficulties of definition.

It concluded that these objections were not persuasive and that they were not objections to recognition as such (as distinct from considerations when framing proposals for recognition).[63] A particularly important concern was that recognition of Indigenous laws would be discriminatory and violate the principle of equality before the law. The commission's conclusion was that appropriate safeguards could be created to avoid this concern. It found that there were good arguments for recognizing Aboriginal customary law, including

- the need to acknowledge the relevance and validity of the laws for many Aboriginal people
- their desire for recognition
- their right to live in accordance with their customs and traditions
- the injustice of non-recognition.

The commission's general recommendation (not implemented) was that Aboriginal customary law should be recognized in appropriate ways by the

Australian legal system through a draft *Aboriginal Customary Law (Recognition) Bill.*[64]

By comparison, the former Law Commission of Canada gave a relatively cursory review in its 2006 discussion paper *Justice Within: Indigenous Legal Traditions* (issued just before the commission was killed by the Conservative government).[65] The paper discusses the following subjects in general terms:

- the nature of Indigenous laws
- their limited recognition to date
- the need to support their revitalization as part of the regeneration of Indigenous cultures
- the issues and challenges associated with revitalization, including:

  - identifying and interpreting Indigenous legal traditions
  - intelligibility and accessibility
  - equality
  - applicability
  - accountability.

Justice Within concludes with suggestions on how the place of Indigenous legal traditions might be enhanced in Canada by, for example, working within Indigenous communities to identify and rekindle their legal traditions; lobbying for more judicial appointments of people conversant with Indigenous legal traditions at all levels, including the Supreme Court of Canada; implementing more Indigenous justice initiatives, such as special courts; and offering courses in Indigenous laws. The paper mentions the possibility of formal legislative recognition of Indigenous legal traditions to remove any ambiguity about their status in the courts, but it does not provide a detailed discussion.[66]

The discussion paper was, in fact, a summary of a more detailed report on Indigenous legal traditions in Canada, prepared for the Law Commission by John Borrows.[67] Anyone wishing more particulars should refer to that report and to his book *Canada's Indigenous Constitution,* published in 2010, which is an expanded version of the report and goes into much more detail on the issues. Borrows provides detailed outlines for courses on aspects of Indigenous laws and makes specific recommendations for legislation by Indigenous and Canadian governments that would recognize and harmonize Indigenous legal traditions with the common and civil law.[68]

Recognition and a Few Reservations

There is a momentum toward greater recognition of Indigenous laws and adoption of them into the Canadian common and civil law, which is to be greatly welcomed. In the words of two writers involved in promoting Indigenous laws: "We are on the cusp of a new era: The renaissance or resurgence of Indigenous laws, claimed, recognized and engaged with seriously as *law*."[69] This momentum is reflected in publications on Indigenous laws, especially by writers of Indigenous ancestry, and initiatives to re-establish control over justice systems in Indigenous communities.[70] It is also reflected in the mainstream legal and academic communities. In 2013, the Canadian Bar Association passed a resolution to recognize and advance Indigenous legal traditions in Canada, and courses on Indigenous laws have been offered by professional legal bodies.[71] Law journals have devoted whole issues to the topic.[72] The former chief justice of British Columbia has called on non-Aboriginal lawyers to become familiar with Indigenous laws.[73] The TRC's recommendation for greater funding for the development, use, and understanding of Indigenous laws has been accepted by the federal government in its acceptance of all their recommendations. Universities are offering courses on Indigenous laws, and the University of Victoria has announced a joint Indigenous-Canadian common law degree.[74] The Nunavut government announced in 2016 that it would revive funding to train Inuit lawyers in conjunction with the University of Saskatchewan, following a course that incorporates Inuit legal traditions.[75] Courts in some provinces are setting up special processes for Aboriginal offenders, such as the Cree circuit court in northern Saskatchewan, the First Nations Court in BC, and the Tsuu T'ina Peacemaking Court in southern Alberta, which may incorporate Indigenous laws.[76] In 2016, the Akwesasne Court was set up by the Mohawk to apply Indigenous law to civil matters.[77]

Despite my support for greater awareness and use of Indigenous laws as part of both Canada's legal heritage and that of Indigenous cultures, I have misgivings that, on occasion, they may be exclusionary and violate the fundamental principle of equal treatment by the law. Separate (and sometimes more lenient) sentencing procedures are available only to Aboriginal offenders, based not on specific disadvantages (which may be shared by others) but on Aboriginal status alone.[78] Defences to criminal prosecutions based on traditional beliefs in, for example, *windigos* or spirit dancing may become available to Aboriginal defendants, despite being contrary to fundamental Canadian values by denying the rights of victims. There may be claims of cultural appropriation if someone outside the community writes on Indigenous laws using traditional stories.[79] One practical limitation is the impairment of Indigenous legal traditions through colonization, and the need for "intentional acts of recovery and revitalization" and "gathering up the threads" before Indigenous laws can be applied.[80]

There is also a risk that Indigenous laws may lead to the type of pluralism that existed in British and Dutch Asian colonies, as described by J.S. Furnivall:

> The first thing that strikes the visitor is the medley of peoples – European, Chinese, Indian and native. It is in the strictest sense a medley, for they mix but do not combine. Each group holds by its own religion, its own culture and language, its own ideas and ways ... There is a plural society, with different sections of community living side by side, but separately, within the same political unit.[81]

This passage brings to mind the two-row wampum or parallel-paths model advanced by some writers. It is based on Haudenosaunee tradition and is symbolized by two groups, one in a canoe and one in a boat (one representing the Aboriginal group and the other the rest of Canadian society), travelling down a river separately but side by side in peaceful co-existence and co-operation, each with separate laws and neither party interfering in the affairs of the other. The challenge is to ensure that we do travel together in a way that does not emphasize separateness at the cost of the benefits for all parties of closer co-operation and joint effort. How do we ensure that "the revitalization and application of Indigenous laws will benefit First Nations, Inuit, and Métis communities, Aboriginal-Crown relations, and the nation as a whole,"[82] to quote the TRC? It would be ironic if the process of "decolonization" in Canada should result in replicating an outdated colonial model.

Recognition of Indigenous laws by the Canadian legal system requires much more discussion than has taken place in Canada so far.

Key to this question is how and to what extent Indigenous laws would interact with applicable federal and provincial law. For example, one Indigenous writer has suggested that agreements should be signed, "recognizing the right of Indigenous peoples to use their own criminal law within their territory."[83] Who would be affected and how? Would the law only apply within reserves or settlement lands in the case of modern treaties, or to Aboriginal title lands where they exist? Would non-members of the Aboriginal group be affected? What say would they have in developing the law? Would members be affected in all areas of the traditional territory and, perhaps, beyond? What rules would regulate conflicts between Indigenous, federal, and provincial law and between different Indigenous laws? These issues require much more discussion than has taken place in Canada so far.[84] Aboriginal and other legal writers should be commended for having commenced that discussion, but more needs to be done – along the lines of the work done by the Australian Law Reform Commission – before a fundamental change is made to the Canadian legal system by incorporating Indigenous laws within that system to become "the laws of the land," as recommended by the TRC. If, however, the TRC was recommending only that Indigenous laws should continue to operate within Indigenous legal systems in Canada, this does not raise issues for the Canadian legal system but is a matter for each Aboriginal group.

International Law

International law has had a marginal role to play in the legal affairs of Canadian Aboriginal peoples.[85] In the 1920s, the Haudenosaunee applied unsuccessfully for membership in the League of Nations,[86] and on occasion Aboriginal individuals and groups have sought to use international law to challenge government action or lack of action.[87] The most famous case was *Lovelace v. Canada,* in which the UN Human Rights Committee ruled in 1981 that Canada was in breach of the *International Convention on Civil and Political Rights.* Lovelace had petitioned the UN Human Rights Committee with respect to the former *Indian Act,* which denied Indian status to a woman who married a non-Indian man. Without status, the woman lost the legal right to live on a reserve and enjoy her culture.[88] The UN ruling led to changes to the act that restored status to such women.

It is important to note that, as recently stated by the Supreme Court of the United Kingdom in the case involving the departure of the UK from the European Community, there is a "so-called dualist theory which is based on the proposition that international law and domestic law operate in independent spheres."[89] Generally speaking, international law does not have direct effect in Canadian law and must be expressly adopted into the law. As the UK Supreme Court also stated in that case, "Although they are binding on the United Kingdom in international law, [international] treaties are not part of the UK law and give rise to no legal rights or obligations in domestic law."[90] This is equally true of Canada.[91] The most important international law document that might affect Aboriginal peoples in Canada is the

United Nations Declaration on the Rights of Indigenous Peoples, adopted by the General Assembly of the United Nations in 2007.[92] The recent adoption of the American Declaration on the Rights of Indigenous Peoples (ADRIP) by the General Assembly of the Organization of American States is also worthy of mention.[93] These documents are declarations rather than treaties, and under international law principles are not direct sources of international law and lack binding force – they are considered "soft law."[94] However, they represent international consensus on minimum rights to be enjoyed by Indigenous peoples and, arguably, some provisions may be enforceable in international law as part of customary international law.[95]

The United Nations Declaration on the Rights of Indigenous Peoples (UNDRIP)

UNDRIP contains some potentially far-reaching provisions recognizing the right to self-determination and requiring Aboriginal consent to legislation and proposed development of their lands, as well as compensation for past taking of their land without consent. However, despite the Truth and Reconciliation Commission's recommendation in 2015 "to fully adopt and implement" UNDRIP,[96] and promises by the current federal government, the declaration currently has no legal effect in Canada except as a possible aid to interpretation of legislation or, arguably, under the honour of the Crown principle as the result of such promises. Statements by the ministers of Indigenous affairs and justice indicate that it is unlikely to have full legal effect in Canada for some time.

> Despite the Truth and Reconciliation Commission's recommendation in 2015 "to fully adopt and implement" the United Nations Declaration on the Rights of Indigenous Peoples, and promises by the current federal government, the declaration currently has no legal effect in Canada except as a possible aid to interpretation of legislation or, arguably, under the honour of the Crown principle as the result of such promises.

Significant provisions of UNDRIP include Articles 3 and 4, which recognize the right to self-determination and self-government in internal affairs, and Article 19, which requires states to "consult and cooperate in good faith with the indigenous peoples concerned ... in order to obtain their free, prior and informed consent" before "adopting and implementing legislative or administrative measures that may affect them." Article 26 provides that "Indigenous peoples have the right to own, use and develop and control the lands, territories and resources that they possess by reason of traditional ownership or other traditional occupation or use, as well as those which they have otherwise acquired." Article 27 requires states to establish, "in conjunction with indigenous peoples concerned, a fair, independent, impartial, open and transparent process, giving due recognition to indigenous peoples' laws, traditions, customs and land tenure systems, to recognize and adjudicate the rights of indigenous peoples pertaining to their lands, territories and resources." Article 28 gives a right to "redress, by means that can include resti-

tution, or when this is not possible, just, fair and equitable compensation for the lands, territories and resources which they have traditionally owned, or otherwise occupied or used, and which have been confiscated, taken, occupied, used or damaged without their free, prior and informed consent." Under Article 32, the state has a duty to consult with Indigenous peoples "in order to obtain their free and informed consent prior to the approval of any project affecting their lands or territories and other resources, particularly in connection with the development ... of ... resources." Under Article 37, Indigenous peoples have the right to the recognition, observance, and enforcement of treaties.

If UNDRIP were adopted into Canadian law, with the interpretations given below applied to these provisions, it would mean major changes to the Canadian legal system. John Borrows has suggested that the broad framing of rights in UNDRIP may be used to challenge the narrow interpretation currently given to Aboriginal rights, discussed in Chapter 4.[97] We have seen that Canadian law has not yet recognized a right of self-determination, as provided in Articles 3 and 4. We have also seen that, far from requiring consent, as stated in Article 19, the Supreme Court of Canada left "for another day the question of whether government conduct [triggering the duty to consult] includes legislative action."[98] With regard to the requirement in Article 27 for "fair, independent, impartial" adjudication of Aboriginal land rights, it is debatable whether the Canadian legal system satisfies this requirement, given that courts are part of the Canadian state and judges are non-Aboriginal – with very few exceptions.

So far as Article 32 is concerned, the SCC has said the Crown's duty to consult and accommodate in the case of unproven rights does not give a veto to Aboriginal peoples.[99] In the case of established rights, the refusal of the Aboriginal group to provide consent can be overcome if the infringement can be justified under the test that the Court established.[100] The requirement for consultation and co-operation "in order to obtain" the "free, prior and informed consent" in Articles 19 and 32 would seem to indicate (subject to Article 46, discussed below) that if such consent is not obtained, the state cannot proceed with the proposed legislation or development, although the wording is not entirely free from doubt.[101] If this interpretation is correct, this would be a major change in the law and effectively would give Aboriginal peoples a qualified veto over legislative and administrative measures that might affect them, and over developments on their traditional lands and resources. Even if this interpretation is not correct and there is no veto, Article 28 clearly gives a right to restitution (that is, restoration to the original situation) if possible or, if not, compensation if consent has not been obtained for the taking or use of land. Further, Article 28 provides a legal basis to challenge the historical treaties on the grounds that the lands were taken without free, prior, and informed consent. The SCC has expressed concerns about the ability of the Aboriginal parties to understand treaties drawn up in a foreign language containing unfamiliar legal concepts, and about the fairness of the process in the case of some of those treaties.[102]

To defend breaches of these articles in UNDRIP, the government would be forced to rely on Article 46, which states that the declaration is not to be interpreted as encouraging any action "to impair, totally or in part ... the political unity of sovereign and independent states," and goes on to say that the exercise of rights under the declaration is subject "only to such limitations as are determined by law and in accordance with international human rights obligations." These limitations "determined by law" must be "non-discriminatory and strictly necessary solely for the purpose of securing due recognition and respect for the rights and freedoms of others and for meeting the just and most compelling requirements of a democratic society." Clearly, Article 46 sets out a different basis for limiting rights than the justification test for infringing Section 35 rights under Canadian law. Article 46 is vague, and we don't know how it might be applied in practice.

Chief Justice Hinkson of the BC Supreme Court has expressed the view that the declaration "is too general in nature to provide real guidance to courts."[103] (This is a fair comment on some articles, but others, such as Article 28, leave little room for doubt as to their intent, although the details are vague.) In other cases, courts have noted that UNDRIP may help to correctly interpret the Constitution or a statutory provision so that the principles of the declaration are implemented rather than a contrary interpretation.[104]

Canada, together with Australia, New Zealand, and the United States, voted against adopting UNDRIP when it was presented as a resolution of the UN General Assembly on September 13, 2007. All four countries have subsequently dropped their objections. In 2010, the former Conservative government of Canada endorsed the declaration, but only as an aspirational, non-binding document. The government was especially concerned about the provisions requiring the "free, prior and informed consent" of Aboriginal peoples in some situations mentioned above, as it would give them a veto. An NDP member of Parliament, Romeo Saganash, has repeatedly introduced draft legislation affirming UNDRIP "as a universal international human rights instrument with application in Canadian law" and requiring the federal government, "in consultation and cooperation with indigenous peoples in Canada, [to] take all measures necessary to ensure that the laws of Canada are consistent with" UNDRIP.[105] However, the bills failed to proceed due to lack of support from the Conservative government. In 2015, Carolyn Bennett, speaking for the then Liberal opposition, indicated that they would support the bill.[106] There was some uncertainty if this remained their position once they formed the government but, in November 2017, Jody Wilson-Raybould, the minister of justice, confirmed their support, although she noted that implementation would "require other appropriate measures."[107] The bill received second reading in the House of Commons on February 7, 2018.

Since its election, the Trudeau government has indicated that its "full support without qualifications" for UNDRIP does not mean any immediate changes for Canadian domestic law, and it remains unclear what the promised "adoption" and "implementation" of the declaration will mean, or how and when it will be achieved. In a speech to the United Nations on May 10, 2016, Bennett declared that Canada was "a full supporter without qualifications of UNDRIP." She stated, without any detailed explanation, "We intend nothing less than to adopt and implement the Declaration *in accordance with the Canadian Constitution*."[108] In her speech to the Assembly of First Nations' thirty-seventh annual general assembly on July 12, 2016, the justice minister said that the new government did not intend to adopt the declaration as Canadian law, which it regarded as a "simplistic" approach:

> Simplistic approaches such as adopting the UNDRIP as being Canadian law are unworkable and, respectfully, a political distraction to undertaking

Since its election, the Trudeau government has indicated that its "full support" for UNDRIP does not mean any immediate changes for Canadian domestic law, and it remains unclear what the promised "adoption" and "implementation" of the declaration will mean, or how and when it will be achieved.

the hard work required to actually implement it ... Accordingly, the way the UNDRIP will get implemented in Canada will be through a mixture of legislative policy and action initiated and taken by Indigenous Nations themselves. Ultimately, the UNDRIP will be articulated through the constitutional framework of section 35.[109]

The reference to Section 35 has raised concerns that the federal government intends to use the justification test developed under Section 35 to justify infringements of UNDRIP.[110] In August 2017, the federal government released a document setting out ten principles for its relationship with Aboriginal peoples. One of the principles stated that "the Government of Canada recognizes that meaningful engagement with Indigenous peoples aims to secure their free, prior, and informed consent when Canada proposes to take actions which impact them and their rights, including their lands, territories and resources."[111] Arguably, this principle restates and weakens Article 32 of UNDRIP by substituting an "aim" to secure consent rather than an obligation to actually obtain it.

If UNDRIP, as it is written (including the requirements to consult in order to obtain the free, prior, and informed consent of Aboriginal peoples and without incorporation of the justification test), is not made part of Canadian law, there may be legal challenges on the grounds of an alleged breach of the honour of the Crown. In *Badger*, the Supreme Court of Canada said, "The honour of the Crown is always at stake in its dealing with Indian people ... It is always assumed that the Crown intends to fulfil its promises. No appearance of 'sharp dealing' will be sanctioned."[112] In the words of one commentator, "How can the Crown, in keeping with the assumption that it intends to fulfil its promises and the principle that no sharp dealing will be sanctioned, be heard to say in court or elsewhere that Canada's endorsement of the Declaration is an act without domestic legal significance?"[113]

One prominent Aboriginal leader, the late Arthur Manuel, described the position of the government as a "sleight of hand" and a tossing aside of the most important advance in Indigenous rights in the past five hundred years of history. In his view, "The Liberals had not in fact adopted UNDRIP, the one passed by the UN General Assembly in 2007, it had adopted some undefined Canadian version of UNDRIP whose actual content they would decide behind closed doors and, finally, the declaration would apparently change nothing in Canada because it was designed to confirm to existing Canadian laws and policies."[114]

The American Declaration on the Rights of Indigenous Peoples

In June 2016, the General Assembly of the Organization of American States adopted the American Declaration on the Rights of Indigenous Peoples (ADRIP).[115] Canada added a footnote to say that it reiterated its commitment to a renewed relationship with Indigenous peoples and was engaged in full partnership with them to move forward with the implementation of UNDRIP in accordance with Canada's Constitution. However, "as Canada has not participated substantively in recent years in negotiations on the American Declaration on the Rights of Indigenous Peoples, it is not able at this time to take a position on the proposed text of this Declaration."[116]

The two declarations are similar in many respects,[117] and the same wording is used in some of the key provisions, such as those equivalent to Articles 3, 4, 19, 26, 32, and 46 of UNDRIP.[118] However, there are some differences in wording that may be significant, such as the wording of Article XXIX.5 (equivalent to Article 28), dealing with developments that affect Indigenous rights, and the addition in Article XXIV.1 (equivalent to Article 37), dealing with treaties, of a requirement to observe "their true spirit and intent in good faith" and to "give due consideration of the understanding of the indigenous peoples." Article XXII of ADRIP contains a more explicit requirement for recognition of Indigenous laws than UNDRIP.

TO SUM UP

- Indigenous laws are the laws of an Aboriginal group, whereas Aboriginal law exists within the Canadian legal system.
- The TRC called for revitalization of Indigenous laws as part of reconciliation and said they should be regarded as the laws of the land.
- Indigenous laws are not part of Canadian law except to the extent that they have been incorporated into it.
- There are many sources of Indigenous laws, and some would not be recognized by Canadian law.
- Generally speaking, Indigenous laws are made up of community values rather than specific laws established by a central state authority, as is the case with European-based legal systems.
- There has been limited recognition by Canadian law of Indigenous laws in areas such as marriage, adoption, and band councils chosen by custom.
- The SCC has said that Indigenous laws should be translated into equivalent modern legal rights "cognizable to the non-aboriginal legal system."
- In practice, the Court has not defined Aboriginal rights in terms of Indigenous laws.
- There have been proposals for greater recognition of Indigenous laws, and there is a momentum towards their recognition and adoption into Canadian law. Several questions must be answered before this can occur.
- International law has played a marginal role in the legal affairs of Aboriginal peoples in Canada.
- International law does not have direct effect in Canadian law and must be adopted into the law.

- The most important international law that might affect Aboriginal peoples in Canada is UNDRIP. ADRIP is similar in most respects.

- The TRC recommended implementation of UNDRIP, and the Trudeau government said it will fully adopt and implement the declaration.

- These declarations are not binding and have no legal effect in Canada except as a possible aid to the interpretation of legislation. Arguably, UNDRIP is binding under the honour of the Crown principle as the result of the promises of the federal government.

- If UNDRIP is adopted into Canadian law, it will mean major changes to the Canadian legal system and law, including the requirement of free, prior, and informed consent of Aboriginal peoples to legislation and developments affecting them and their land and compensation for land taken or used without such consent.

- It is not yet clear how and when the federal government will keep its promises.

A Just Society?

8

Developments that led to an explosive growth in Aboriginal law were, in large part, triggered by the "just society" program of Pierre Trudeau, including the 1969 White Paper's proposal to terminate the special rights of Aboriginal peoples. A central question is whether that growth (so different from what Pierre Trudeau had in mind) has led to a just society for Aboriginal peoples. Have these legal developments benefitted Aboriginal peoples? What role can the law play in improving their lives and closing the gap between their living standards and that of other Canadians? What are the limits of litigation and negotiation? Should judges play such a large role in making the law? Can political measures bring better results? Should politicians make the kind of fundamental changes proposed over twenty years ago by the Royal Commission on Aboriginal Peoples, or should they continue to leave things to the judges to sort out?

Major Questions for the Future

As we look to the future, the following questions remain:

(a) Will there be greater recognition for Aboriginal sovereignty and self-determination? An inherent right of self-government was a major goal of Aboriginal leaders during the constitutional talks of the 1980s and, in 1996, the Royal Commission on Aboriginal Peoples concluded that it already existed. It remains a concern for many Aboriginal people but has not yet been recognized in Canadian law. My view is that *realpolitik* will prevent recognition by either the SCC or non-Aboriginal governments regardless of the merits, although more powers will be delegated by non-Aboriginal governments through legislation or agreements. A related question is whether Canadian Aboriginal law will provide greater recognition to Indigenous laws.

(b) Will Aboriginal rights and title be further extended and clarified? Despite the criticisms, it seems unlikely that the integral-to-a-distinctive-culture test for Aboriginal rights will change to make Aboriginal rights more relevant to today's circumstances, or that the ability of governments to infringe will be further restricted.

(c) Will the historical treaties be enforced if the concerns over duress, lack of understanding, and lack of any true consent of the Aboriginal groups, raised by RCAP and others, are squarely brought before the Supreme Court of Canada? The Court itself has expressed some concern but has also described the treaties as being effective surrenders of Aboriginal rights. Again, in view of the fundamental consequences (including those for owners of private properties across much of Canada) of not upholding the surrender wording of the written treaties, it seems that any legal challenge will likely fail and the status quo will be upheld. Negotiation to improve living conditions is more likely to succeed, but this requires greater political will.

(d) Will courts give greater weight to cumulative impacts of development in determining the scope of the government's duty to consult? What support will be ordered to ensure that Aboriginal groups are better able to participate meaningfully in the process? Will there be greater clarification of the relationship between consultation, accommodation, and consent? Does the duty to consult for unproven Aboriginal rights apply if the Aboriginal group is not pursuing litigation or treaty negotiations to determine the validity of those rights? What are the limits on the ability of the governments to privatize their obligations? A related question is the extent to which the UN Declaration on the Rights of Indigenous Peoples will be given effect in practice, including its requirement for "free, prior and informed consent."

(e) Will Aboriginal and treaty rights be privatized?

(f) How will "Métis" be defined for the purposes of Section 91(24) of the *Constitution Act, 1867* regarding federal jurisdiction? The SCC declined to give such a definition in *Daniels* when its interpretation included the Métis in that section.[1] On the division of powers question, what will the trend to increase provincial powers over Aboriginal peoples mean in practice?

(g) How will the interests of Aboriginal groups and those of non-Aboriginal people be balanced? A related question is what compensation will be payable for infringements of rights and title to achieve this balance?

Privatization of Aboriginal and Treaty Rights?

One issue that is likely to emerge is that of replacing or supplementing collective rights to Aboriginal lands and resource with individual rights. Granting individual interests in reserve lands has been a feature of the *Indian Act* since the earliest days.[2] However, we have seen that the SCC has been consistent to date in its rulings that Aboriginal and treaty rights are collective and not individual rights. For example, it held in the *Manitoba Métis* case that the rights claimed in that case could not be an Aboriginal interest because the trial judge had found that the Métis used and held land individually rather than communally and permitted alienation.[3] The Court explained in *Sappier* that, since Section 35 recognized Aboriginal rights in order to assist in ensuring the continued existence of Aboriginal societies, the Aboriginal right could not be exercised by a member of the community independently of the Aboriginal society it was meant to preserve.[4] In *Tsilhqot'in*, the Court described Aboriginal title as "collective title held not only for the present generation but for all succeeding generations."[5] The Court arrived at this conclusion based on general principles rather than a consideration of the Indigenous laws of particular Aboriginal societies. (Collective rights do appear to be generally consistent with traditional laws and practices, with some exceptions that gave certain families or sub-groups user rights to particular resource areas, such as beaches to collect shellfish.)[6]

> The Supreme Court of Canada has been consistent to date in its rulings that Aboriginal and treaty rights are collective and not individual rights.

In *Behn*, however, the Court referred to an argument that Aboriginal and treaty rights could be divided into collective and individual rights, and commented that the suggestion bore witness to the diversity of such rights. The Court declined to make any classification at this stage of development in the law and commented:

It will suffice to acknowledge that, despite the critical importance of the collective aspect of Aboriginal and treaty rights, rights may sometimes be assigned to or exercised by individual members of Aboriginal communities, and entitlements may sometimes be created in their favour. In a broad sense, it could be said that these rights might belong to them or that they have an individual aspect regardless of their collective nature. Nothing more need be said at this time.[7]

To date, there has been relatively little discussion in the legal literature on the issue of collective versus individual Aboriginal and treaty rights,[8] but it has a long political history in North America, especially south of the border.

As might be expected, views on the collective nature of Aboriginal society tend to depend on where the observer is located on the political spectrum. The founders of modern communism saw North American Aboriginal societies as examples of "primitive communism" and were fascinated by them.[9] The Marxist martyr Rosa Luxemburg wrote that "the noble survivals of the dim past offered a hand to the revolutionary efforts of the future."[10] Those of a more conservative persuasion are critical and seek to terminate collective ownership. For example, Tom Flanagan (a libertarian and former adviser to Conservative prime minister Stephen Harper) considers that "the treaties and the Indian Act have conspired to imprison [Aboriginal people] within a regime of collective rights that fit badly with the needs of a market economy. Now the Supreme Court of Canada, while asserting and redefining aboriginal property rights, has carved their collective and inalienable character in judicial stone."[11] He and others promoted legislation permitting individual ownership and sale of reserve lands. This proposal received support from the former Conservative government, which announced its intention to explore the option of moving forward with this legislation in the 2012 budget and its 2015 election platform.[12] The proposed legislation was overwhelmingly rejected at the 2010 annual general meeting of the Assembly of First Nations by a resolution that stated the proposed legislation would "lead ultimately to the individual privatization of indigenous collective lands and resources and impose the colonizer's model on our Peoples."[13]

Among the Aboriginal opponents of attempts to individualize reserve lands is author Thomas King, who refers to the disasters created by American initiatives such as the General Allotment (or Dawes) Act of 1887, which saw reservations decrease from 138 million acres to around 48 million acres, "much of it desert," and by termination legislation from 1943 to 1961.[14] In response to the proposal from Flanagan, he asks, "But why would we want to repeat the mistakes of the past? Why drag a failed policy such as termination out of its grave when history has shown us that this particular strategy was an utter disaster?"[15] He also refers to the settlement in Alaska under which all Aboriginal rights were surrendered in return for shares in corporations that owned the settlement lands. Under the legislation, the land or the shares could be sold to non-Aboriginal people, resulting in loss of control of the land. King comments, "It makes me uneasy ... makes me suspect that corporations are just the latest fashion in assimilation."[16]

We can expect this issue to reappear both in the courts and in the broader political arena.

Balancing Aboriginal Interests and Those of Non-Aboriginal People

One definition of "reconciliation" is "a principled reconciliation of Aboriginal rights with the interests of all Canadians."[17] This is to be achieved using the test developed by the SCC through its Section 35 jurisprudence to justify infringements of Aboriginal and treaty rights. In the words of one critic, "The mechanisms of reconciliation and justification were created by the Court, in part, to protect third parties *against* the operation of Aboriginal Rights: A legal sword, rather than a shield."[18] The weighing of rights (especially constitutional rights) against interests should be underlined. It has been claimed that the Court has turned the Constitution on its head by allowing interests that are not constitutional to trump rights that are.[19] The passage of Section 35 in 1982 terminated the legal power of governments to extinguish Aboriginal and treaty rights.[20] However, the development of the justification test went a long way to allowing them to effectively negate rights in practice. If we accept that Aboriginal and non-Aboriginal interests are to be balanced and that no right is absolute, then the key questions to discuss are as follow:

- Do Aboriginal peoples have a fair opportunity to participate in the process of balancing interests?
- How will their interests (as well as their rights) be protected?
- Are judges the ones to do the balancing?

A significant criticism of judicial law making is that the development of the justification test has intruded into the political arena in order to protect the interests of non-Aboriginal people and without any significant participation by Aboriginal people.

> One definition of "reconciliation" is "a principled reconciliation of Aboriginal rights with the interests of all Canadians."

It is the Court's treatment of the test's requirement for a "compelling and substantial objective" to justify infringement that has generated most criticism, as it has been defined broadly to include economic development and "the settlement of foreign populations."[21] The Court has held that these objectives are of sufficient importance to the broader community as a whole that limits might be placed on Aboriginal rights as a necessary part of reconciliation.[22]

This weighing of Aboriginal rights and interests against the interests of other Canadians occurs in different areas of Aboriginal law. The SCC noted in *Wewaykum*, "When exercising ordinary government powers in matters involving disputes between Indians and non-Indians, the Crown was (and is) obliged to have regard to the interest of all affected parties, not just the Indian interest. The Crown can be no ordinary fiduciary; it wears many hats and represents many interests, some of which cannot help but be conflicting."[23] The Court has narrowed the definition of Aboriginal rights to avoid any commercial preference and said the historical participation of non-Aboriginal groups in resource use was a factor in applying the justification analysis to limit Aboriginal rights. This was extended by *Delgamuukw* in the context of Aboriginal title to permit a wide range of objectives to justify infringement. In the context of treaties, the Court has allowed governments to limit treaty rights using the justification test despite the absence of any wording in the treaties to permit such limitation. It has also applied the test of "visible, incompatible use" to regulate the exercise of the treaty right to hunt over private lands.[24]

A fundamental and, as yet, unanswered question (and probably the most important question for non-Aboriginal people in areas such as British Columbia, where treaties have not been signed and Aboriginal title still exists) is, What does Aboriginal title mean for private property rights? As stated by Justice Southin in 2001, "Sooner or later, the question of whether those who hold certificates of title, whether to ranch lands on Kamloops Lake ... or an office tower on Georgia Street in the City of Vancouver, are subject to claims of Aboriginal title must be decided."[25] She said this cloud on title had grown over the previous twenty years "to lower over the whole of the Province, save that part encompassed in the Nisga'a Treaty, Treaty No. 8, and the so-called Douglas Treaties."[26] Since then, the cloud has only grown larger with the declaration of Aboriginal title in *Tsilhqot'in* and the few additional treaties being signed under the BC treaty process. *Tsilhqot'in* did not discuss this key question, since the Tsilhqot'in requested the Court to exclude "privately owned or underwater lands" from their claim.[27] As we've seen, the Court compared and contrasted Aboriginal title with fee simple title. What is important is that both confer exclusive use and possession. It is difficult to see how these "battling exclusivities" can both exist in the same land.[28] In the words of recent commentators, "Aboriginal title, as currently set out by [the SCC], is inherently at odds with fee simple interests." In their view, "without an evolution of the law, Aboriginal title, where claimed, will threaten the fee simple interests of individual Canadians and pose a significant threat to reconciliation."[29] The High Court of Australia has answered the question with the following statement: "Native title is extinguished by a grant in fee simple."[30]

To date, the Supreme Court of Canada has made no ruling. A decision of the Ontario Court of Appeal, *Chippewas of Sarnia*,[31] considered some of the issues and found against the Aboriginal group, but its facts were very different from those likely to be presented in British Columbia.[32] In *Saik'uz*,[33] the BC Court of Appeal held that an Aboriginal group could pursue a claim for nuisance against a private company based, in part, on claims of Aboriginal rights and title. It was not necessary to first obtain a court determination on the validity of the claims. The Court stated that Aboriginal rights and title "do exist prior to declaration or recognition. All that a court declaration or Crown acceptance does is to identify the exact nature and extent of the title or other rights."[34]

Some legal writers have expressed their views on the question. John Borrows points out that Aboriginal title enjoys constitutional protection under Section 35, but there is no such protection for private property rights. He states that "Aboriginal title in British Columbia is a prior and senior right to land"[35] and that "constitutionalized Aboriginal title rights should obviously trump non-constitutionalized property interests."[36] However, "the holders of the Crown's flawed grant would not be without remedies and protection. Their presence on Aboriginal title land can be protected by Indigenous law, future treaties and Canada's broader constitutional framework."[37] Gordon Christie, another Aboriginal law professor, observes that it remains to be seen exactly how the SCC will deal with the potential intersection of Aboriginal title and private property, but "[t]here seems little doubt ... that acting as an arm of the Canadian state it will find a way to protect private property owners."[38]

Thomas Isaac, a lawyer who represents industry and government, and a prominent writer on Aboriginal law, refers to the passage from *Delgamuukw*, stating that "the settlement of foreign populations" was an example of an objective that could justify infringement[39] and says that this indicates the grant of fee simple interests is likely to be a justifiable infringement.[40] Isaac also comments, "While compensation will not always be the remedy of choice for an Aboriginal group, it is likely to be a widely used remedy" for such infringements.[41]

I share the view that, when the question comes before the SCC, it will give priority to fee simple interests over Aboriginal title, probably on the basis of the passage from *Delgamuukw* where Chief Justice Lamer wrote that "settlement of foreign populations" to further economic development is the type of objective that can justify infringements of Aboriginal title, as well as the concluding statement in his judgment: "Let us face it, we are all here to stay."[42] This passage was quoted in *Tsilhqot'in*.[43] But that decision presents a new issue since the Court stated, "The beneficial interest in the land held by the Aboriginal group vests communally in the title-holding group. This means that incursions on Aboriginal title cannot be justified if they would substantially deprive future generations of the benefit of the land."[44] It is difficult to see how validating fee simple interests as they currently exist would not have the effect of depriving future generations of that benefit. The Court will likely clarify this statement to make it consistent with the passage from *Delgamuukw*. In doing so, it should also clarify the vague state of the law on the inherent limit to Aboriginal title and compensation for infringement, past and future, in a way that seeks to do justice for both Aboriginal peoples and non-Aboriginal people.[45]

A further issue to be clarified is the right of property owners to receive notice of Aboriginal title claims. It has been held by lower courts that no notice need be given as this would frustrate the litigation.[46] This seems unfair. Some means should be found to give third parties a voice without allowing the number of parties to become unmanageable. In one case, the judge suggested the appointment of an amicus curiae (a lawyer appointed to assist the court) to represent the third-party interests.[47]

It may also be noted that private property is not on the table in treaty negotiations except on a "willing seller" basis to acquire land to transfer to the Aboriginal group.

Evaluation of Existing Law

In my view, judicial law making in the area of Aboriginal law has had mixed results, and there is a need for other means to be used to achieve reconciliation in its different meanings, including

- reconciling the powers of governments with their duties,
- providing justice to Aboriginal peoples for past wrongs done to them and so furthering their reconciliation with the rest of Canadian society, and
- reconciling the interests of Aboriginal peoples (and not just their rights) with those of other Canadians for the future.

Among the positive developments in the law have been the following rulings by the SCC:

> Judicial law making in the area of Aboriginal law has had mixed results, and there is a need for other means to be used to achieve reconciliation in its different meanings.

- Holding that governments have legally enforceable and not merely political obligations towards Aboriginal peoples.[48]
- Giving meaning to the vague reference to the recognition and affirmation of "existing aboriginal and treaty rights" in Section 35,[49] when it might have interpreted the section as nothing more than "aspirational,"[50] as a guide to interpretation of other legislation, or as only giving constitutional protection to rights already recognized and actually being exercised when the section came into effect.
- Giving teeth to the section by incorporating the fiduciary duty into Section 35 and demanding that the government's power to regulate rights be reconciled with its duty to recognize them.[51]
- Giving an interpretation to the extinguishment of Aboriginal and treaty rights, which requires that the intention be "clear and plain."[52]
- Giving interim protection to asserted Aboriginal rights pending determination of their validity through the duty to consult and, if appropriate, accommodate the asserted rights.[53]
- Applying the honour of the Crown principle to situations where the fiduciary duty is not available to protect Aboriginal interests, such as in implementation of constitutional obligations.[54]
- Developing liberal rules for the interpretation of treaties and applying the duty to consult to treaty implementation.[55]

On the other hand, there are the following criticisms of the SCC:

- Failing to give meaningful consideration to claims of Aboriginal self-government.[56]

- Limiting Aboriginal rights to those integral to a distinctive culture at the time of contact (or at the time of effective control by the Crown in the case of the Métis).[57] This severely limits the protection provided by Section 35 and effectively freezes rights in their historical form without regard to what is necessary for Aboriginal peoples to cope with modern circumstances forced upon them by colonialism. Aboriginal title protects a much broader range of activities, but there remains uncertainty as to key issues, such as the extent of the inherent limit, the impact on private property rights, and the amount of compensation payable for infringement.
- Applying the test of justification broadly and permitting a wide variety of governmental objectives to justify infringement of Aboriginal rights and treaties without meaningful participation by Aboriginal people in making these decisions.
- Placing too much reliance on the procedural duty to consult and deferring too much to government officials in how the process is done, and failing to adequately develop the related concepts of accommodation and consent. The Court has also assumed a false equivalency in the positions of Aboriginal groups on the one hand and government and industry on the other.
- Being vague in some of its rulings, creating confusion and even chaos, as with *Marshall I.*

Mixed Benefits from Legal Developments

One writer has stated, "The possession of legal rights has not made tribes worse off, but equally it is less clear whether it has significantly – or even marginally – improved their general lot."[58] Based on my own experience acting as a lawyer for First Nations, mainly the Musqueam Indian Band in Vancouver, for almost forty years, I think some Aboriginal groups have benefitted greatly from developments in Aboriginal law, but many have not.

The Musqueam are one Aboriginal group that have reaped the benefits of developments in Aboriginal law and have been leaders in both litigation and negotiation. They were the successful party in the seminal *Guerin* and *Sparrow* decisions on fiduciary duties and Aboriginal rights. They have also successfully litigated the failure of the federal and provincial governments to adequately consult on dispositions of land and grants of licences in their traditional territory,[59] as well as on other matters, such as payment of property taxes on lands acquired under a settlement agreement.[60] (They have been unsuccessful in other litigation, including seeking higher rent from leased lands,[61] an injunction to prevent the proposed sale of federal buildings,[62] and a ruling on property taxes levied on reserve lands.[63]) Using their litigation success, they negotiated the return in fee simple of lands worth hundreds of millions of dollars, including 146 acres leased as the UBC golf course; a 21-acre parcel next to the university, which is being developed; the lands underlying a casino; and a 37-acre parcel that has been added to the Musqueam reserve.[64] They have also negotiated several other agreements. One especially satisfying acquisition was that of a former village site to protect ancestral remains that had been threatened with development. Together with their neighbouring First Nations, they established MST Development Corporation, which is described on its website as a corporation "established to oversee properties owned by the MST Partnership, a historic partnership of the Musqueam Indian Band, Squamish Nation and Tsleil-Waututh Nation. Our three nations are full or co-owners of six prime properties throughout Metro Vancouver. These properties total more than 160 acres of developable land and are currently valued at over $1 billion."[65]

It would have been impossible to imagine the Musqueam's current assets (clearly recognized by the Canadian legal system) before the birth of modern Aboriginal law some forty years ago. Time will tell how successful the band will be in the future. There are obviously risks, and significant socio-economic challenges persist. Despite the occasional setbacks, I think there is no doubt that, due to their determination to protect their Aboriginal rights, the Musqueam have been a major beneficiary of the changes in the law for which they are partially responsible. However, it must also be said that, unlike most other First Nations, they have enjoyed the benefit of their location within a major city, giving easy access to what some judges have called the commercial mainstream. Above all, the Musqueam have a good legal claim to land for which there is enormous demand in the mainstream economy, and this gives them bargaining power.

There may be few other Aboriginal groups in a position to benefit as much as the Musqueam from litigation and negotiation. In the 2006 *God's Lake* case, Justice Binnie described the plight of one isolated community that was party to Treaty 5, under which more than a hundred thousand square kilometres of land was surrendered.[66] The God's Lake Reserve, located 1,037 kilometres northeast of Winnipeg, had no conventional roads or railways linking it to the rest of the province. It was accessible only by air or by winter ice road after freeze-up. Local employment was limited to band government and small entrepreneurs, such as grocery stores. The community consisted of fewer than 1,300 people but accounted for 10 percent of all tuberculosis cases in Manitoba. Only about 10 percent of the homes had basic sewer systems. The band was entirely funded by the federal government through annual comprehensive funding arrangements. Justice Binnie commented that "the prospect of significant participation in the off-reserve economy is likely as remote as their geographic location."[67] In his view, "the trouble was (and is) that dispossession from much of their traditional economic base and subsequent changes in the economy have left most band governments too few resources to be self-sufficient."[68] They have "inadequate resources to achieve financial independence in a market economy."[69] He concluded that "bands, like God's Lake have no access to the commercial mainstream and no realistic prospect of ever obtaining it."[70]

This situation is widespread in Aboriginal communities. The Royal Commission on Aboriginal Peoples found that Aboriginal people in Canada suffer ill health, insufficient and unsafe housing, polluted water supplies, inadequate education, poverty, and family breakdown at levels usually associated with impoverished developing countries.[71] As of December 31, 2017, there were ninety-one drinking water advisories that had been in place for more than a year warning First Nations of the dangers of drinking their water.[72]

The Vagaries of Litigation

In *God's Lake,* Justice Binnie contrasted the terms of different treaties and referred to "the vagaries of the treaty-making process."[73] To this might be added the vagaries of litigation. Some Aboriginal groups are likely to be unsuccessful in litigation for reasons other than the merits of their case. For one thing, there is good reason that litigation is often called a lottery. You have to be able to pay to participate, and in the case of Aboriginal claims, the cost can be considerable. In *Delgamuukw,* Chief Justice Lamer said that litigation was long and expensive in both economic and human terms, and he would "not necessarily encourage the parties to proceed to litigation and settle their disputes through the courts."[74] The SCC noted in *Haida* that claims "can be very complex and require years and even decades to resolve in the courts."[75] For major litigation, the costs are in the tens of millions of dollars. In some rare "special" cases, courts may order the Crown to provide funding.[76] As well, it may be a matter of luck what evidence has been preserved or what witnesses are still alive to support historical claims.

Chief Justice Lamer noted the human as well as economic cost of litigation, and this should not be underestimated. Valerie Napoleon's PhD thesis was partly a study of the impact of the *Delgamuukw* case on the Gitksan community. She observes, "Failure to thoroughly ground the litigation in the over-arching aboriginal political struggle could easily create a situation where the legal action becomes an end in itself, absorbing all the aboriginal group's resources – time, energy and finances. Despite many persons' best efforts, this may have occurred in *Delga-muukw*."[77] Expectations may be raised only to be dashed; deeply held beliefs about historical facts may be challenged by the government and not up-held by the court;[78] elders may be cross-examined in a manner that is considered disrespectful. And the adversarial nature of litigation is another factor. In *Clyde River*, the Court commented that "true reconciliation is rarely, if ever, achieved in courtrooms."[79] Litigation can be a bruising experience.

> Litigation often produces mixed results. It is possible to win the legal battle but lose the political war.

One consideration not to be overlooked is that litigation often produces mixed results. It is possible to win the legal battle but lose the political war. Some Aboriginal commentators have been critical of successes in the SCC. For example, Gordon Christie has noted a common pattern of the Court – what it gave with one hand in *Sparrow, Gladstone, Marshall,* and *Tsilhqot'in,* it took away with the other.[80] And Indigenous lawyers Halie Bruce and Ardith Walkem have commented, "We fight for victories in court or at the negotiating tables, without fully realizing that a victory in these arenas can nonetheless mean an overall loss. *Sparrow,* for example, was hailed as a victory and yet recognized the exclusive government power to regulate Aboriginal Rights and opened up the door for government infringement of those rights."[81]

The technical and often costly rules of court procedure and evidence must be satisfied, although some flexibility may be given for Aboriginal rights litigation. As noted by the Court in *Van der Peet,* "Courts adjudicating aboriginal rights must ... be sensitive to the aboriginal perspective, but they must also be aware that aboriginal rights exist within the general legal system of Canada."[82] The rules of evidence have been relaxed to some extent to permit oral history to be given greater weight, but there are limits. Likewise, the interpretation of treaties employs some special rules, but a court cannot exceed what is possible on the language or realistic. In the *Lax Kw'alaams* case,[83] Justice Binnie stressed the requirement to respect the ordinary rules governing civil litigation, including the rules of pleading (these are rules for formally defining the issues in writing so each side knows what it needs to answer). He commented, "At this point in the evolution of Aboriginal rights litigation, the contending parties are generally well resourced and represented by experienced counsel."[84] (The first part of the statement overlooks the obvious disparity in resources between governments and Aboriginal groups.) Writing a preface to the lawyer's text on Aboriginal and treaty rights practice, he noted that it demonstrated "aboriginal and treaty rights litigation, like much else in the courts, is often won or lost in the trenches of mundane procedure."[85]

In *Lax Kw'alaams*, Justice Binnie rejected the suggestion that a court should act as a commission of inquiry. This rejection reflects the adversarial nature of litigation in Canada, where each side presents its view of the facts, and the judge makes a determination between the two versions rather than being actively involved in investigating the facts, as happens in some legal systems, such as European civil law systems. This adversarial nature was cause for complaint by the trial judge in *Tsilhqot'in*, who wrote, "This case demonstrates how the Court, confined by the issues raised in the pleadings and the jurisprudence on Aboriginal rights and title, is ill equipped to effect a reconciliation ... In an adversarial system, claims are dealt with in order to produce a win/lose result."[86]

One technical issue that may have great consequences in practice is that of defences based on delay in bringing a claim. These defences may be based on limitation legislation (a law that sets the latest time after an event that a legal claim can be brought) or on the principles of "acquiescence" and "laches" (unreasonable delay). The SCC has said that "the policy behind limitation periods is to strike a balance between protecting the defendant's entitlement, after a time, to organize his affairs without fearing a suit, and treating the plaintiff fairly with regard to his circumstances. This policy applies as much to Aboriginal claims as to other claims."[87] The policy may be relaxed in situations where the Aboriginal group could not reasonably have known they had a claim (see the description of the facts in *Guerin* in Chapter 3).[88] Also, the Court has held that limitation legislation cannot prevent the courts from issuing a declaration on the constitutionality of the Crown's conduct.[89] Unless an Aboriginal group is able to successfully argue for an exception, it may find that it is denied a remedy if a judge decides it has slept on its rights. In view of the historical nature of many claims, this is a big concern for Aboriginal litigants.[90] The Truth and Reconciliation Commission called on governments to review and amend their statutes of limitations to prevent reliance on limitation defences to deny legal actions of historical abuse brought by Aboriginal people.[91]

Aboriginal Peoples and the Law

Negotiations

An alternative to litigation is negotiation, which the SCC has repeatedly urged. In *Sparrow*, it said that Section 35, "at the least, provides a solid constitutional basis upon which subsequent negotiations can take place."[92] In *Tsilhqot'in* it stated, "Governments are under a legal duty to negotiate in good faith to resolve claims to ancestral lands.[93] In *Delgamuukw*, Chief Justice Lamer said, "Ultimately, it is through negotiated settlements, with good faith and give and take on all sides, reinforced by the judgments of this Court, that we will achieve [reconciliation]."[94] Justice Deschamps added in *Little Salmon* that reconciliation presupposes "active participation by Aboriginal peoples in the negotiation of treaties, as opposed to a necessarily more passive role and an antagonistic attitude in the context of constitutional litigation."[95] The trial judge in *Tsilhqot'in* commented that "interest negotiations, designed to take opposing interests into account, have the potential to achieve a win/win result."[96] All these points are valid. However, litigation and negotiation should not be seen as existing in watertight compartments. In my experience, it is the prospect of litigation that brings government and industry to the negotiating table and provides Aboriginal groups with their bargaining power and their BATNA – the best alternative to a negotiated agreement.[97] I see litigation and negotiation on a continuum:

> prospect of litigation → attempted negotiations/breakdown
> in negotiations → possible litigation to confirm rights and so
> obtain negotiating power → negotiation of agreement conferring
> benefits → implementation of agreement → possible litigation to
> enforce agreement

Successful negotiations require some reasonable equality of bargaining power, which does not exist between governments and industry on the one side and Aboriginal groups on the other. It also requires a genuine willingness to give and take to reach agreement, which is often missing on the part of government, as in the case of resolving specific claims outside the usual court system,[98] as well as when it comes to negotiating treaties. As RCAP stated in 1996, "Before there can be real negotiations, the power imbalance between Aboriginal governments and federal and provincial governments must be addressed."[99] The Assembly of First Nations has also expressed its concern, "Existing policies assume an equality of bargaining position. They do not take into account in their design or policy framework the actual power

imbalance between the parties and how this affects both process and outcomes. The slow progress of negotiations is a symptom of this fundamental
problem."[100] A revealing study by Christopher Alcantara on the negotiation
of modern treaties confirms that governments are
the dominant actors and benefit from delay, and so

> Successful negotiations require some
> reasonable equality of bargaining
> power ... They also require a genuine
> willingness to give and take to reach
> agreement.

hold most of the power in the negotiations.[101] To
be successful, the Aboriginal group must negotiate
only those issues that the government wants to
negotiate, avoid confrontation, and attempt to con-
vince the government representatives to sign the
agreement. Such one-sided negotiation explains, in
part, why so few treaties have been signed in British
Columbia. As one lawyer who represents Aboriginal groups has written,
"Negotiations can be a frustrating, ruinous, and seemingly unending road
if the power and discretion of the Crown are left unchecked."[102] A variety of
dispute resolution processes exist to assist in negotiations.[103] However, in the
final analysis, the inequality of bargaining power and lack of political will
must be addressed, and this requires a political solution. Judicial calls for
negotiations do not take this inequality and lack of will into account.

Limits of Litigation and Negotiation

One common feature of both litigation and negotiation is that they are
usually limited, at least directly, to the parties involved. A case may set a
precedent, as with the SCC decisions that we have considered, but most are
limited by the facts to the parties. Even in the case of true precedents, the
decisions are not automatically applied to other Aboriginal groups or situations. Government lawyers find ways to "distinguish" decisions so they
have minimal application. In the words of Greg Poelzer and Ken Coates,
"When the court system has found government approaches to be wanting
– as has happened with increasing frequency – those same governments
have moved slowly to translate Supreme Court decisions into practical legislation or regulatory action."[104]

It is also wrong in principle that the welfare of Aboriginal groups depends on their success in having their Aboriginal and treaty rights upheld
and on the differing contents of those rights. This impacts their ability to
negotiate. There is evidence of a growing gap in community well-being between those First Nations subject to the historical treaties, with relatively
low benefits, and those experiencing the benefits of recent developments in
Aboriginal law and modern treaties. A rational policy would seek to alleviate

the plight of those most in need. However, Poelzer and Coates argue that the current policy is as follows: "If rights exist ... they are asserted and protected, whatever the costs and the implications. Conversely, if those rights do not exist under the law, then they are not to be applied or granted, even if empowering Indigenous communities would clearly improve Aboriginal lives."[105] It is unfair to distribute benefits primarily to those Aboriginal peoples fortunate enough to still enjoy Aboriginal rights and title or modern treaty rights.

> It is unfair to distribute benefits primarily to those Aboriginal peoples fortunate enough to still enjoy Aboriginal rights and title or modern treaty rights ... Political measures can bring more general benefits.

Law and Politics

In considering the relative merits of litigation versus political action, it is necessary to have a clear understanding both of what the law is and what, realistically, it could be. I hope this book goes some way to explaining the former. I cannot speak for the understanding of the law that other people, including Aboriginal people, have, but I suspect there is much truth in the following statement by Poelzer and Coates: "The legal rights gained through the courts are not as clear, definitive, or extensive as Aboriginal people believe."[106] The challenge for Aboriginal people and others who wish to see improvement in the lives of Aboriginal people is encapsulated in a second question: What role can the law play, bearing in mind the limitations of litigation and judge-made law and the advantages of political action?

Political measures can bring more general benefits than litigation or negotiation since the necessary financial and other resources are within the control of governments and not courts. For example, the defeated Charlottetown Accord included a constitutional obligation to bargain in good faith to reach agreement, addressing, among other things, "economic and fiscal arrangements." In 1996, RCAP made detailed recommendations to improve the lives of all Aboriginal peoples, including additional government expenditures of up to $2 billion per year for the next twenty years. In the commission's view, in the long run, it would be a good investment, and government expenditures would be significantly lower than under the status quo.[107] These recommendations have not been implemented. The commission gave the following justification, which is as true today as it was when it reported:

> We believe that governments should commit significant additional resources to resolve historical claims, restructure the political relationship,

and improve living conditions and economic opportunities for
Aboriginal people. This expenditure is justified to correct the injustices
of the past and present ... Aboriginal people are entitled to equal social,
educational and health outcomes, to a fair share of the country's assets,
and to a much greater share of opportunity than they have had so far.[108]

Such fundamental changes can happen only through political action and not
through the case-by-case approach of litigation and negotiation. Also, in a
democratic society, they should be made by elected politicians and not unelected judges.

Here, I should clarify that, by "politics," I mean non-judicial politics, as
I have no doubt that judges (especially in the SCC) play a major role in law
making, including deciding what is in the public interest – a political process.
This view used to be controversial and is still denied by some judges.[109] In
the 2003 *Paul* decision, Justice Bastarache made the following sweeping
statement on behalf of the SCC: "First, and most important, any adjudicator,
whether a judge or a tribunal, does not create, amend or extinguish aboriginal
rights. Rather, on the basis of the evidence, a judicial or administrative decision maker may recognize the continued existence of an aboriginal right."[110]
I trust the reader will agree that this is not correct: the law of Aboriginal
rights is very much the creation of the judges. It certainly was not the work
of politicians who created the empty box of Section 35 and failed to give it
any content.

Under the traditional view, law was seen as a search for objective answers, pursued impartially by neutral judges in dusty old books and legal
principles uninfluenced by their own political views. The falseness of that
perspective has been exposed in both the United Kingdom and Canada.[111]
In the words of J.A.G. Griffith, "My thesis is that judges in the United Kingdom cannot be politically neutral because they are placed in positions where
they are required to make political choices ... of where the public interest
lies."[112] This statement applies equally in Canada. Joel Bakan has reviewed
in detail how the SCC has decided cases under the Charter of Rights. He
argues that, "though Charter litigation appears a contest of language and
symbols, ideological processes operate just below the surface to ensure, before
the contest even begins, that liberal discourses of rights will prevail over
others."[113] He identifies certain elements of what he means by "liberal dis-
course," including an approach to equality that ignores, among other things,
disparities in resources, political and social power, and social inequality
generally, including that of Aboriginal peoples. In my view, Bakan's analysis

applies to some of the Court's decisions in Aboriginal law, reflected in the false assumption of equality between Aboriginal peoples and governments in decisions relating to consultations and encouragement of negotiations.

The development of the justification test to enable governments to limit Aboriginal and treaty rights is an example of judicial law making and politics. Although Section 35 is not part of the Charter of Rights, the Court has effectively rewritten the Constitution and applied precedents from Charter cases on individual rights to Aboriginal rights, developing the justification test to impose limits on the collective rights protected by Section 35. As noted by Justice McLachlin in dissent in *Van der Peet,* this test is "ultimately more political than legal."[114] After initially denying that the justification test could rely on vague ideas of the public interest to limit Aboriginal rights, the Court has now incorporated the "broader public interest" as a justification, which, of course, means whatever the judges determine. Such determination can be seen as a political choice and will be based, in part, on their beliefs, preconceptions, and values developed from personal experience and background.[115] As Chief Justice McLachlin stated, "To insist that the judge purge all preconceptions and values from the mind is to place an impossible burden on the judge."[116] Judges are shaped by their experiences and cannot be expected to function as "neutral ciphers."[117] (They should, of course, strive as far as possible to rise above their personal views and prejudices and give decisions that take into account the conflicting views of the parties.)[118]

Some writers are strongly opposed to any legal action by Aboriginal peoples because of a perceived favouritism that works against them. Widdowson and Howard maintain, "The pursuit of legal rights always disadvantages the poor and marginal because the law in liberal democratic states is oriented towards protecting private property and limiting the intrusion of the state into the affairs of its citizens."[119] Thomas King, a leading Aboriginal writer, argues, "The court system favours the powerful and the wealthy and the influential, and [the Canadian and US governments know] that if we buy into the notion of an impartial justice system, tribes and bands can be forced through a long, convoluted, and expensive process designed to wear us down and bankrupt our economies."[120] (He does say later that although he still believes this, Aboriginal people have had moments of success with the legal system).[121] In my view, it is not necessary to be so cynical. Litigation can improve, and has improved, the lives of some Aboriginal people.[122] However, it is important to be realistic and recognize that judges are not agents of social change, as acknowledged by Chief Justice McLachlin: "It is not for judges to set the agendas for social change."[123] The type of fundamental changes recommended by RCAP will not (and should not) come from judges.

The lack of meaningful Aboriginal participation in judicial law making is a matter of concern. In Canada, most judges are part of the non-Aboriginal majority. Although there are now a few judges of Aboriginal ancestry (not yet on the Supreme Court of Canada and only about 1 percent of appeal court judges), Aboriginal peoples are still underrepresented based upon their share of the population.[124] So far as Aboriginal law is concerned, law making at the SCC is done by nine unelected and largely unaccountable judges,[125] without Aboriginal ancestry (indeed, there are no visible minority members of the Court), who are making policy decisions affecting Aboriginal people, seeking reconciliation by balancing their rights against the interests of non-Aboriginal Canadians, and determining what is in the public interest. Note that the Court is not protecting the rights of a minority against majority pressure (often advanced as a key role of the courts) but limiting minority rights to protect the interests of the majority as determined by the Court. Also, unlike the Court's decisions on government legislation where, in theory, there may be an opportunity for a "dialogue" and a response from the government through revised legislation,[126] Aboriginal peoples have no opportunity to respond.

> So far as Aboriginal law is concerned, law making at the Supreme Court of Canada is done by nine unelected and largely unaccountable judges, without Aboriginal ancestry.

In fairness, the judges did not ask to be put in this position – the responsibility rests with the failure of politicians, Aboriginal as well as non-Aboriginal, to reach agreement during the constitutional talks of the 1980s, or to make any fundamental changes despite the overwhelming case for such changes made by RCAP in the 1990s. Having acknowledged this history, political science professor Emmett Macfarlane's statement about the Court's role under the Charter applies equally to Section 35: "Yet, if the justices were ordered to go swimming, they have made important choices along the way that have led them into the deep end of the policy-making pool."[127]

Another limitation of law making through litigation is that the process is not designed to result in good policy.[128] In part this is because of the adversarial, rather than inquisitorial, nature of the UK and Canadian legal systems. As noted by Griffith, "The courts of law are not designed as research centres, and judges in our system are most reluctant to assume an inquisitorial role and to seek to discover all the relevant facts."[129] They are limited to what the lawyers for the parties put before them, which, of course, is what favours their clients rather than what assists in developing good policy.[130] At the SCC, other parties can apply for intervenor status, and that provides some scope for other interests to be represented, but their role is limited as is their ability to present arguments. An intervenor is not permitted to raise new issues unless otherwise ordered by a judge.[131] As a former chief justice commented in one case, "To a large extent, the Court is the prisoner of the case which the parties and the interveners have presented to us, and the arguments that have been raised, and the evidence that we have before us."[132] All parties face strict limits on the length of their written and oral arguments. Most cases are decided on the basis of written arguments,[133] which are usually restricted to forty pages for parties and ten pages for intervenors, with some mandatory material included.[134] Oral argument usually does not exceed one hour for each party, and five minutes for each intervenor, which includes questions from the judges.[135]

Hearings take place in public and, indeed, can be watched live on television or viewed later on video. However, the Court's deliberations are in private. Some months after the hearing, probably about six months or so, the decision is released online and that is the end of the matter so far as the SCC is concerned (apart from the very rare case when further reasons are given, as in *Marshall II*[136] and *Wewaykum No. 2*[137]). No draft opinions are released for scrutiny and comment by those affected or possessing relevant knowledge and experience. There is no opportunity to request clarification or amendment of the law that has been proclaimed. When the federal government intends to pass a statute, it is released in draft form for first reading, giving an opportunity for public debate. When the government proposes to change policy, it may issue a "green paper" to elicit comment. There is no equivalent for judicial law making.

In conclusion, developments in Aboriginal law over the last few decades and, in particular, decisions of the SCC have been important and have improved the circumstances of some Aboriginal people. Indeed, since the failure of the constitutional talks in the 1980s and the failure to implement the recommendations of RCAP in the 1990s, they have arguably been the most important developments affecting the position of Aboriginal peoples in Canada. My evaluation of these developments is mixed. I also have concerns about the process of judicial law making and its limitations.

Comprehensive and long-term solutions to alleviate the disadvantages suffered by Aboriginal peoples, which also protect the interests of non-Aboriginal people, must come primarily from the political and not the legal arena. For too long, there has been drift by governments and an absence of resolve to consider and deal with the very difficult and still pressing issues examined in depth by the Royal Commission on Aboriginal Peoples and, more recently, by the Truth and Reconciliation Commission. To some extent, as pointed out by Michael Ignatieff, former leader of the federal Liberal Party, "Section 35 [has] led to a kind of quiescence on the part of Canadian politicians vis-à-vis Aboriginal affairs. It has allowed them to sit back and let the Supreme Court 'sort it out.'"[138]

Courts do have a role to play. They should hold governments to high standards and reconcile their powers with their duties towards Aboriginal peoples, and in this way level, to some extent, the playing field for negotiations. Major consultations and negotiations should, preferably, be supervised by an adequately funded specialist tribunal with effective Aboriginal representation to ensure fairness and good faith and Aboriginal participation. The tribunal could also resolve many disputes over Aboriginal law issues. Such tribunals were recommended by RCAP[139] and the former UN special rapporteur on the rights of Indigenous peoples,[140] and would satisfy the requirement in Article 27 of UNDRIP for states to implement, in conjunction with the Indigenous peoples concerned, a fair, independent and impartial process to adjudicate their lands rights. But more is required.

It is time for politicians to assume responsibility for issues that are central to Canadian identity and the future of our country. In the words of a former special rapporteur:

> [The] possible overall solution [to the problems of Indigenous people] cannot be approached exclusively on the basis of juridical reasoning. The problems ... are essentially political in essence. Thus considerable political will is required from all parties concerned but in particular from the non-indigenous political leadership ... if these problems are to be resolved through forward-looking new approaches.[141]

A detailed response from the federal government to the recommendations of RCAP would be a logical starting place to display this political will.[142] Many of the problems that the commission examined are, unfortunately, still with us.[143] This has meant that there was no reduction in the substantial gap in the statistics for community well-being (based on income, education, housing, and labour force activity) between First Nation and non-Aboriginal communities between 1981 and 2011, despite the changes in the law.[144] Leaving the challenge to the Court has been only partially successful. There is still a long way to go before Canada can claim to be a just society for Aboriginal peoples.

Notes

Preface

1 Harold Cardinal, *The Unjust Society* (Edmonton: M.G. Hurtig, 1969) at pages 28–30, 36.
2 For a critical approach to the current government from one Aboriginal perspective that draws parallels to 1969, see Arthur Manuel and Ronald Derrickson, *The Reconciliation Manifesto: Recovering the Land Rebuilding the Economy* (Toronto: Lorimer, 2017).
3 See page 124, this book.
4 "Principles Respecting the Government of Canada's Relationship with Indigenous Peoples," Department of Justice website, http://www.justice.gc.ca/eng/csj-sjc/principles-principes.html.
5 Jessica Leeder, "Tensions Boil over Off-Season Lobster Fishing," *Globe and Mail*, October 16, 2017, at page A1.
6 Which mean, respectively, "unique," "person who brings a court case," and "person who is being sued."
7 K.W. Wedderburn, *The Worker and the Law* (Harmondsworth, UK: Penguin, 1965).
8 Tom Flanagan, *First Nations? Second Thoughts*, 2nd ed. (Montreal and Kingston: McGill-Queen's University Press, 2008).
9 Felix Cohen, review of Monroe Berger's *Equality by Statute*, reprinted in *The Legal Conscience: Selected Papers of Felix S. Cohen* (New Haven, CT: Yale University Press, 1960) at page 479.
10 [1984] 2 S.C.R. 335.

Chapter 1: What Is Aboriginal Law?

1 Thomas R. Berger, *A Long and Terrible Shadow: White Values, Native Rights in the Americas* (Vancouver: Douglas and McIntyre, 1991) at page 151.
2 Thomas Berger, *Village Journey: The Report of the Alaska Native Review Commission* (New York: Hill and Wang, 1985) at page 156–57.
3 Patrick Macklem, *Indigenous Difference and the Constitution of Canada* (Toronto: University of Toronto Press, 2001) at page 4.
4 See *A.G. Canada v. Canard*, [1976] 1 S.C.R. 170 at page 207; *R. v. Kapp*, 2008 SCC 41 at para. 114.
5 *R. v. Drybones*, [1970] S.C.R. 282.
6 Flanagan, *First Nations?* at pages 22, 194.
7 *R. v. Van der Peet*, [1996] 2 S.C.R. 507 at paras. 17–18 (underlining deleted).
8 *Kapp*; see also *Lovelace v. Ontario* 2000 SCC 37; *Alberta v. Cunningham*, 2011 SCC 37. The US Supreme Court rejected a claim that employment preference for Indians in the Bureau of Indian Affairs is a form of racial discrimination on the grounds that it was "political, rather than racial, in nature": *Morton v. Manzari*, 417 U.S. 535 (1974) at page 553 note 24.

9 *Norwegijick v. Canada*, [1983] 1 S.C.R. 29 at page 36.

10 *Beckman v. Little Salmon*, 2010 SCC 53 at para. 33.

11 *Manitoba Métis Federation v. Canada*, 2013 SCC 14 at para. 72; see *R. v. Kokopenace*, 2015 SCC 28 at paras. 98–101.

12 *First Nations Child and Family Caring Society of Canada v. Canada*, 2016 CHRT 2.

13 *R. v. Williams*, [1998] 1 S.C.R. 1128 at pages 1135 and 1159.

14 *Corbiere v. Canada*, [1999] 2 S.C.R. 203.

15 *Kahkewistahhaw First Nation v. Taypotat*, 2015 SCC 30.

16 *An Act to Amend the Canadian Human Rights Act*, S.C. 2008 c. 30 s. 1.2.

17 *U.S. v. Winans*, 198 U.S. 371 (1905) at 381.

18 See *Cunningham* at para. 6.

19 See *Mikisew Cree First Nation v. Canada*, 2005 SCC 69 at paras. 33, 63.

20 Schedule B to the *Canada Act, 1982* (UK), 1982, c. 11.

21 *Canada's Residential Schools: Reconciliation*, vol. 6 of *The Final Report of the Truth and Reconciliation Commission of Canada* (hereafter *TRC*) (Montreal and Kingston: McGill-Queen's University Press, 2015) at page 51.

22 *McDiarmid Lumber Ltd v. God's Lake First Nation*, 2006 SCC 58 at para. 106.

23 *An Act to Amend the Indian Act*, S.C. 1926–27, c. 32, s. 6.

24 *Report of the Royal Commission on Aboriginal Peoples* (hereafter *RCAP*), vol. 1, *Looking Forward, Looking Back* (Ottawa: Minister of Supply and Services Canada, 1996) at Chapter 9, section 9.5.

25 *R. v. Sparrow*, [1990] 1 S.C.R. 1075 at page 1103 (emphasis in original).

26 Macklem, *Indigenous Difference* at page 93.

27 *Canada's Residential Schools: Reconciliation*, vol. 6 of *TRC* at pages 90–91.

28 For the different theories used in Canada, see Flanagan, *First Nations?* at Chapters 2–4; Michael Asch, *On Being Here to Stay: Treaties and Aboriginal Rights in Canada* (Toronto: University of Toronto Press, 2014) at Chapter 3; and John Borrows, *Canada's Indigenous Constitution* (Toronto: University of Toronto Press, 2010) at pages 14–22.

29 Conrad Black, *Rise to Greatness: The History of Canada from the Vikings to the Present* (Toronto: McClelland and Stewart, 2014) at page 9.

30 Sir Thomas More, *Utopia*, trans. from Latin by Ralph Robinson (1551) with modern spelling: Early English Books Online image 72. See also John Locke, *The Second Treatise of Government* (1690) at Chapter 5.

31 Emer de Vattel, *The Law of Nations* (Philadelphia: Johnson Law Booksellers, 1844) Book 1, Chapter 7, s. 81; Chapter 18, s. 209.

32 Gilbert Malcolm Sproat, *Scenes and Studies of Savage Life* (London: Smith, Elder, 1868) at pages 3–9.

33 *Haida Nation v. B.C.*, 2004 SCC 73 at para. 25.

34 These questions are summarized in John Borrows, *Drawing Out Law: A Spirit's Guide* (Toronto: University of Toronto Press, 2010) at pages 48–72. See also Arthur Manuel and Ronald Derrickson, *The Reconciliation Manifesto: Recovering the Land, Rebuilding the Economy* (Toronto: Lorimer, 2017) at pages 67–71, 88–93.

35 Bev Sellars, *Price Paid: The Fight for First Nations Survival* (Vancouver: Talonbooks, 2016) at epigraph and page 184.

36 Statistics Canada, "Aboriginal Peoples in Canada: Key Results from the 2016 Census" (October 25, 2017).

37 Bill S-3, *An Act to amend the Indian Act (elimination of sex-based inequities in registration)*, 42nd Parl, 1st Sess., 2017. For an estimate of the numbers and costs involved in

implementation, see Office of the Parliamentary Budget Officer, "Bill S-3, Addressing Sex-Based Inequities in Indian Registration," December 5, 2017.

38 Cardinal, *The Unjust Society* at page 20.

39 Paul Chartrand, "The 'Race' for Recognition," in *Aboriginal Title and Indigenous Peoples: Canada, Australia, and New Zealand,* ed. Louis Knafla and Haijo Westra (Vancouver: UBC Press, 2010) at page 135.

40 *R. v. Powley,* 2003 SCC 43.

41 *In Re Eskimo,* [1939] S.C.R. 104.

42 *Daniels v. Canada,* 2016 SCC 12.

43 *Daniels* at para. 18.

44 *Daniels* at para. 47.

45 Sections 75–76 of the Alberta *Métis Settlement Act,* R.S.A. 2000, M-14, set out membership criteria for Métis settlements in that province.

46 See *Cunningham.*

47 *Labrador Metis Nation v. Newfoundland,* 2007 NLCA 75.

48 Section 4(1).

49 Flanagan, *First Nations?* at page 76.

50 Plans were announced in August 2017 to split this department to create a department of Indigenous Services and a department of Crown–Indigenous Relations and Northern Affairs.

51 Eric Andrew-Gee, "The Making of Joseph Boyden: Indigenous Identity and a Complicated History," *Globe and Mail,* August 4, 2017. The issues are summarized in Borrows, *Drawing Out Law* at pages 153–58, 201–5.

52 *Cunningham* at para. 86.

53 *RCAP,* vol. 2, *Restructuring the Relationship,* section 2.2 at page 167.

54 Nell Jessup Newton, ed., *Cohen's Handbook of Federal Indian Law,* 2012 ed. (Newark, NJ: LexisNexis, 2012) at S. 3.03[2].

55 8 U.S.C. s. 1359. This right is based on the Jay Treaty of 1794. Canada does not recognize a right of entry for U.S. "Indians."

56 *Martin v. Chapman,* [1983] 1 S.C.R. 365 at 371.

57 Compare the International Labour Organization's Indigenous and Tribal Peoples Convention, 1989 (No. 169), June 27, 1989, Article 1 para. 1(b). For definitions of Indigenous peoples in international law generally, see Patrick Thornberry, *Indigenous People and Human Rights* (Manchester: Manchester University Press, 2002) at Chapter 2.

58 F.W. Maitland, *Constitutional History of England* (Cambridge: Cambridge University Press, 1919) at 418.

59 Dirk Meissner, "First Nation Leaders Urge Royal Couple to Push Governments for Reconciliation," *Toronto Sun,* September 28, 2016.

60 For the position of the monarch in Canada, see Kenneth Munro, "The Constitution Act, 1982 and the Crown: Twenty-Five Years Later," *Constitutional Forum* 17 (2008): at page 49. Statutes and agreements may make the federal or provincial governments liable for the Imperial Crown: *Williams Lake Indian Band v. Canada,* 2018 SCC 4.

61 *Calvin's Case,* (1608) 77 E.R. 377 (Court of King's Bench) at page 388. The theological and political issues are considered in detail in Ernst H. Kantorowicz, *The King's Two Bodies* (Princeton, NJ: Princeton University Press, 1997).

62 *Miller v. Secretary of State for Exiting the European Community,* 2017 UKSC 5 at para 45.

63 *Grassy Narrows First Nation v. Ontario,* 2014 SCC 48 at para. 33.

64 *Tsilhqot'in Nation v. B.C.,* 2014 SCC 44 at para. 151; and see Chapter 4, this book.

65 *Grassy Narrows* at para. 50.

66 *Grassy Narrows* at para. 35.

67 *Coastal First Nations v. B.C.,* 2016 BCSC 34.

68 See, for example, *Rio Tinto v. Carrier Sekani Tribal Council,* 2010 SCC 43 at para. 81; *Neskonlith Indian Band v. Salmon Arm,* 2012 BCCA 379.

69 *Clyde River (Hamlet) v. Petroleum Geo. Services Inc.,* 2017 SCC 40 at paras. 25–29.

70 See Grace Li Xiu Woo, *Ghost Dancing with Colonialism: Decolonization and Indigenous Rights at the Supreme Court of Canada* (Vancouver: UBC Press, 2011) at pages 169–70 for statistical review of cases.

71 *Sparrow* at page 1108.

72 See Steven J. Heine, *Cultural Psychology,* 2nd ed. (Norton: New York, 2012) at pages 88–92, 205–8, 378.

73 *Delgamuukw v. B.C.,* [1997] 3 S.C.R. 1010 at para. 115; *Tsilhqot'in* at para. 74; *R. v. Sundown,* [1999] 1 S.C.R. 393 at para. 36.

74 *Manitoba Métis* at para. 59.

75 See Chapter 7 for a discussion of the declaration.

76 For different political and philosophical views on group rights and their relationship to liberal-democratic ideology, see P.G. McHugh, *Aboriginal Title: The Modern Jurisprudence of Tribal Land Rights* (Oxford: Oxford University Press, 2011) at pages 311–27; for a discussion of the liberal versus social democratic perspectives on *Charter* litigation, see Andrew Petter, *The Politics of the Charter: The Illusive Promise of Constitutional Rights* (Toronto: University of Toronto Press, 2010).

77 Gordon Christie, "Law, Theory and Aboriginal Peoples," *Indigenous Law Journal* 2 (2003) at page 67.

78 *Employment Equity Act,* S.C. 1996 c. 44 ss. 2, 7; and *Criminal Code,* R.S.C. 1985 c. 46 s. 718.2(e), and *R. v. Gladue,* [1999] 1 S.C.R. 688, respectively.

79 R.S.C. 1985, c. I-5.

80 S.C. 2003, c. 20.

81 *Thomas v. Norris,* 1992 CanLII 354 (BCSC).

82 *Thomas v. Norris* at page 52.

83 See Justice Bastarache in *Kapp* at para. 99.

84 H.B. Hawthorn, ed., *A Survey of the Contemporary Indians of Canada* (Ottawa: Indian Affairs Branch, 1966) at page 211.

85 Ronald St. John Macdonald (chair of research committee), *Native Rights in Canada* (Toronto: Indian-Eskimo Association, 1970) at page 201.

86 Peter A. Cumming and Neil H. Mickenberg, eds., *Native Rights in Canada* (Toronto: Indian-Eskimo Association of Canada, 1972) at page 275.

87 *Sparrow* at page 1103.

88 Thomas Berger, *One Man's Justice: A Life in the Law* (Vancouver: Douglas and McIntyre, 2002) at page 113.

89 McHugh, *Aboriginal Title* at Chapter 2.

90 See, for example, Kent McNeil, *Common Law Aboriginal Title* (Oxford: Clarendon Press, 1989).

91 Alan Cairns, *Citizens Plus: Aboriginal Peoples and the Canadian State* (Vancouver: UBC Press, 2000) at page 175; see also P.G. McHugh, "A Common Law Biography of Section 35," in *From Recognition to Reconciliation: Essays on the Constitutional Entrenchment of Aboriginal and Treaty Rights,* ed. Patrick Macklem and Douglas Sanderson (Toronto: University of Toronto Press, 2016) at pages 144–45.

92 Berger, *One Man's Justice* at page 113.

93 Borrows, *Drawing Out Law* at page 195.

94 *Tsilhqot'in* at para. 23.

95 *R. v. Ipeelee*, 2012 SCC13 at para. 60.

96 *Daniels* at para. 1.

97 Statistics Canada, "Aboriginal Statistics at a Glance," on the Statistics Canada website, http://www.statcan.gc.ca/pub/89-645-x/89-645-x2010001-eng.htm; Aboriginal Affairs and Northern Development Canada, The Community Well-Being Index: Well-Being in First Nations Communities, 1981–2011 (Ottawa: AANDC, 2015).

98 Michael Ignatieff, "Afterword: The Indigenous International and a Jurisprudence of Jurisdictions," in Macklem and Sanderson, *From Recognition to Reconciliation* at page 508.

99 See Chapter 3.

100 *Mikisew Cree* at para. 1.

101 *Little Salmon* at para. 10.

102 Beverley McLachlin C.J.C., "Defining Moments: The Canadian Constitution" (Dickson Lecture, Ottawa, ON, February 13, 2014).

103 *Sparrow* at page 1109; and see *Tsilhqot'in* at para. 119.

104 *Van der Peet* at para. 31. See also *Delgamuukw* at para. 186.

105 Manuel and Derrickson, *Reconciliation Manifesto*.

106 John Borrows, "Canada's Colonial Constitution," in *The Right Relationship: Reimagining the Implementation of Historical Treaties,* ed. John Borrows and Michael Coyle (Toronto: University of Toronto Press, 2017) at page 20.

107 *R. v. Gladstone*, [1996] 2 S.C.R. 723 at para. 75.

108 *R. v. Marshall/R. v. Bernard*, 2005 SCC 43 at para. 51.

109 *Marshall/Bernard* at para. 39.

110 *Mikisew Cree* at para. 1.

111 *Kapp* at para. 65.

112 *Little Salmon* at para. 10.

113 *Lax Kw'alaams Indian Band v. Canada*, 2011 SCC 56 at para. 12.

114 *Cunningham* at para. 86.

115 *Tsilhqot'in* at para. 23.

116 *Tsilhqot'in* at para. 125.

117 *Haida* at para. 32.

118 *Mikisew Cree* at para. 54.

119 *Little Salmon* at para. 52.

120 *Van der Peet* at para. 42.

121 *Paul v. B.C.*, 2003 SCC 55 at para. 24.

122 *Manitoba Métis* at para. 70 (references omitted).

123 *Manitoba Métis* at para. 140.

124 S.C. 1999, c. 24.

125 S.C. 2014, c. 5.

126 For a full discussion correcting misunderstandings see Allan Beever, "The Declaratory Theory of Law," *Oxford Journal of Legal Studies* 33 (2013) at page 421; Kent McNeil, "Indigenous Rights Litigation, Legal History and the Role of Experts," in Borrows and Coyle, *The Right Relationship*.

127 Beverley McLachlin C.J.C., "Judicial Power and Democracy" (annual lecture, Singapore Academy of Law, September 14, 2000). See, generally, Sanjeev Anand, "The Truth about Canadian Judicial Activism," *Constitutional Forum* 15 (2006) at page 87.

128 Beverley McLachlin C.J.C., "The Role of Judges in Modern Society" (presentation, Fourth Worldwide Common Law Judiciary Conference, Vancouver, BC, May 5, 2001).

129 See discussion in Chapter 4 on the test to justify infringements of Aboriginal and treaty rights.

130 John Bowring, ed., *The Works of Jeremy Bentham*, vol. 5 (New York: Russell and Brown, 1962) at page 235.

131 See McNeil, "Indigenous Rights"; P.G. McHugh, "Aboriginal Title: Travelling from (or to?) an Antique Land?" *UBC Law Review* 48 (2015) at page 793.

132 See Beverley McLachlin C.J.C., "The Supreme Court of Canada" (speech given at the Mayor's Breakfast Series, Ottawa, ON, November 25, 2014); Emmett Macfarlane, *Governing from the Bench: The Supreme Court of Canada and the Judicial Role* (Vancouver: UBC Press, 2012). For a summary of the Court's decision-making process, see *Wewaykum Indian Band v. Canada [No. 2]*, 2003 SCC 45 at para. 92.

133 Woo, *Ghost Dancing* at pages 139–44.

134 "The Honourable Sheilah Martin's Questionnaire," on Officer of the Commissioner for Federal Judicial Affairs website.

135 "The Honourable Malcolm Rowe's Questionnaire," on the Officer of the Commissioner for Federal Judicial Affairs website.

136 Gordon Christie, "Who Makes Decisions over Aboriginal Title Lands?" *UBC Law Review* 48, no. 3 (2015) at pages 783–84.

137 *Canada v Craig*, 2012 SCC 43 at paras. 25 and 27.

138 *Tsilhqot'in* at para. 150.

139 See page 102, this book, regarding *Marshall/Bernard*.

140 *Carter v. Canada*, 2015 SCC 5 at para. 44.

141 *R. v. Henry*, 2005 SCC 76 at paras. 52–59.

142 *R. v. Côté*, [1996] 3 S.C.R. 139 at para. 49 quoting Prof. Brian Slattery.

143 *Côté* at para. 53.

144 See Robert Mainville, *An Overview of Aboriginal and Treaty Rights and Compensation for Their Breach* (Saskatoon: Purich, 2001) at pages 62–64.

Chapter 2: Historical Background

1 For a more detailed account of the period prior to 1972, see Peter A. Cumming and Neil H. Mickenberg, eds., *Native Rights in Canada* (Toronto: Indian-Eskimo Association of Canada, 1972) at pages 65–204.

2 Thomas King, *The Inconvenient Indian: A Curious Account of Native People in North America* (Toronto: Anchor Canada, 2012) at page 216. For a history told from a personal and Aboriginal perspective, see Bev Sellars, *Price Paid: The Fight for First Nations Survival* (Vancouver: Talonbooks, 2016).

3 *Report of the Royal Commission on Aboriginal Peoples* (hereafter *RCAP*), vol. 1, *Looking Forward, Looking Back* (Ottawa: Minister of Supply and Services Canada, 1996) at page 36.

4 Ibid. at page 37.

5 Ibid. at page 38.

6 Ibid.

7 Ibid.

8 Quoted in Alan Cairns, *Citizens Plus: Aboriginal Peoples and the Canadian State* (Vancouver: UBC Press, 2000) at page 17.

9 Ibid.

10 Sean Fine, "Chief Justice Says Canada Attempted 'Cultural Genocide' on Aboriginals," *Globe and Mail,* May 28, 2015.

11 Diamond Jenness, *The Indians of Canada* (Ottawa: National Museum of Canada, 1935) at page 350.

12 Stephen Leacock, *Canada: The Foundations of Its Future* (Montreal: House of Seagram, 1941) at page 19.

13 *RCAP,* vol. 1, *Looking Forward, Looking Back* at pages 38–39.

14 *R. v. Marshall,* [1999] 3 S.C.R. 456; *R. v. Marshall/R. v. Bernard,* 2005 SCC 43.

15 See, for example, *Mitchell v. M.N.R.,* 2001 SCC 33 at para. 127. For a discussion of the contemporary significance of the covenant chain, see Mark Walters, "Rights and Remedies within Common Law and Indigenous Legal Traditions: Can the Covenant Chain Be Judicially Enforced Today?" in *The Right Relationship: Reimagining the Implementation of Historical Treaties,* ed. John Borrows and Michael Coyle, 187–207 (Toronto: University of Toronto Press, 2017).

16 *Mississauga of Scugog First Nation v. NAATGWU,* 2007 ONCA 814 at para. 52.

17 Bruce Clark, *Native Liberty, Crown Sovereignty: The Existing Aboriginal Right of Self-Government in Canada* (Montreal and Kingston: McGill-Queen's University Press, 1990) at pages 39–45; Mark D. Walters, "Mohegan Indians v. Connecticut: (1705–1773) and the Legal Status of Aboriginal Customary Laws and Government in British North America," *Osgoode Hall Law Journal* 33 (1995) at page 785; Bruce Clark, *Justice in Paradise* (Montreal and Kingston: McGill-Queen's University Press, 1999) at pages 89–93.

18 *R. v. Marshall/R. v. Bernard* at para. 86.

19 *Calder v. B.C.,* [1973] S.C.R. 313 at page 395.

20 *R. v. Sioui,* [1990] 1 S.C.R. 1025 at page 1064.

21 Cumming and Mickenberg, *Native Rights in Canada* at page 70.

22 *St. Catherine's Milling and Lumber Co. v. The Queen,* (1888), 14 A.C. 46 (P.C.) at page 54.

23 *Guerin v. The Queen,* [1984] 2 S.C.R. 335 at page 377–79.

24 John Borrows, "Wampum at Niagara: The Royal Proclamation, Canadian Legal History, and Self-Government," in *Aboriginal and Treaty Rights in Canada,* ed. Michael Asch, 155–72 (Vancouver: UBC Press, 1997); see also John Borrows, "Constitutional Law from a First Nation Perspective: Self-Government and the Royal Proclamation," *UBC Law Review* 28 (1994) at page 1.

25 *McDiarmid Lumber Ltd v. God's Lake First Nation,* 2006 SCC 58 at para. 116.

26 Tom Flanagan, *First Nations? Second Thoughts,* 2nd ed. (Montreal and Kingston: McGill-Queen's University Press, 2008) at page 120.

27 Thomas Berger, *Village Journey: The Report of the Alaska Native Review Commission* (New York: Hill and Wang, 1985) at page 84.

28 Thomas Isaac, *Aboriginal Law* (Saskatoon: Purich, 1995) at page 349.

29 Bill Gallagher, *Resource Rulers: Fortune and Folly on Canada's Road to Resources* (Waterloo, ON: Gallagher, 2011) at pages 28–30.

30 See, generally, Shin Imai, *Annotated Aboriginal Law: The Constitution, Legislation and Treaties* (Toronto: Thomson Reuters, 2017).

31 See also *Blackwater v. Plint,* 2005 SCC 58.

32 *Manitoba Métis Federation v. Canada,* 2013 SCC 14.

33 *Report of the Special Joint Committee on the Claims of the Allied Tribes of British Columbia,* Journal of the Senate of Canada, 1926–27.

34 S.C. 1926–27, c. 32, s. 6.
35 H.B. Hawthorn, ed., *A Survey of the Contemporary Indians of Canada* (Ottawa: Indian Affairs Branch, 1966).
36 *Statement of the Government of Canada on Indian Policy* (Ottawa: Indian Affairs Branch, 1969).
37 Quoted in Ronald St. John Maconald, *Native Rights in Canada* (Toronto: Indian-Eskimo Association, 1970), Appendix 8.
38 Harold Cardinal, *The Unjust Society* (Edmonton: M.G. Hurtig, 1969) at pages 1, 17.
39 *Citizens Plus* (Edmonton: Indian Association of Alberta, 1970), Preamble.
40 See Ken Coates, *#IdleNoMore and the Remaking of Canada* (Regina: University of Regina Press, 2015).
41 For accounts of civil disobedience and Aboriginal peoples see John Borrows, *Freedom and Indigenous Constitutionalism* (Toronto: University of Toronto Press, 2016), Chapter 2; P.G. McHugh, *Aboriginal Title: The Modern Jurisprudence of Tribal Land Rights* (Oxford: Oxford University Press, 2011) at pages 60–68.
42 Clark, *Justice in Paradise* at pages 160, 210–52; *R. v. Clark*, 1999 CanLII 13543 (ON. LST).
43 Melvin H. Smith, *Our Home or Native Land? What Governments' Aboriginal Policy Is Doing to Canada* (Victoria: Crown Western, 1995) at page 143.
44 Ian Waddell, "The Laboured Birth of Section 35," *The Advocate* 66 (2008), at page 891.
45 Thomas Berger, *One Man's Justice* (Vancouver: Douglas and McIntyre, 2002) at pages 140–64.
46 *Re the Queen v. The Secretary of State for Foreign and Commonwealth Affairs, ex parte The Indian Association of Alberta*, [1982] 3 C.N.L.R. 195 (H. of L.).
47 *R. v. Sparrow*, [1990] 1 SCR 1075 at page 1105.
48 Smith, *Our Home* at page 146.
49 David Hawkes, *Aboriginal Peoples and Constitutional Reform: What Have We Learned?* (Kingston, ON: Queen's University Institute of Intergovernmental Relations, 1989) at pages 9–10.
50 This question was answered by an amendment to Section 35 in 1983 that extended the constitutional protection to future treaties and land claim agreements.
51 See, for example, papers by Roy Romanow, Richard Dalon, and Brian Slattery in *The Quest for Justice: Aboriginal Peoples and Aboriginal Rights*, ed. Menno Boldt and J. Anthony Long (Toronto: University of Toronto Press, 1985).
52 See Maurice Bulbulian, dir., *Dancing around the Table*, Parts 1 and 2 (Ottawa: National Film Board of Canada, 1987).
53 James Miller, *Skyscrapers Hide the Heavens: A History of Indian-White Relations in Canada* (Toronto: University of Toronto Press, 1991) at page 292.
54 The new Government of Newfoundland, which had revoked the previous government's approval of the accord, refused to allow the deadline for approval to be extended.
55 For a discussion of the Charlottetown Accord, see Kent McNeil, *Emerging Justice? Essays on Indigenous Rights in Canada and Australia* (Saskatoon: Native Law Centre, 2001) at pages 161–83.
56 Joel Bakan, *Just Words: Constitutional Rights and Social Wrongs* (Toronto: University of Toronto Press, 1997) at pages 117–33; *Native Women's Assoc. v. Canada*, (1992) 57 F.T.R. 115, aff'd (1992) 145 N.R. 253 (FCA).
57 Pierre Trudeau, *A Mess That Deserves a Big No* (Toronto: Robert Davies Publishing, 1992) at page 72.

58 *RCAP*, vol. 1, *Looking Forward, Looking Back* at page 216.

59 In June 2017, the premier of Quebec announced his desire to have new constitutional talks. Some Aboriginal leaders supported this initiative but the prime minister rejected it: Les Perreaux, "Some Indigenous Groups Embrace Quebec's Proposal to Reopen Constitution," *Globe and Mail*, June 5, 2017.

60 *Reference re Secession of Quebec,* [1998] 2 S.C.R. 217 at para. 82.

61 *R. v. Côté,* [1996] 3 S.C.R. 139 at para. 51.

62 *RCAP*, vol. 1, *Looking Forward, Looking Back* at page 215.

63 For a detailed and critical review, see Cairns, *Citizens Plus,* Chapter 4.

64 "A Word from Commissioners," in *Highlights from the Report of the Royal Commission on Aboriginal Peoples* on the Indigenous and Northern Affairs website, http://www.aadnc-aandc.gc.ca/eng/1100100014597/1100100014637.

65 *RCAP*, vol. 5, *Renewal: A Twenty-Year Commitment,* Appendix A.

66 King, *The Inconvenient Indian* at page 170.

67 See Flanagan, *First Nations?* at page 4.

68 See Flanagan, *First Nations?* and Cairns, *Citizens Plus.*

69 Smith, *Our Home* at page 173.

70 King, *Inconvenient Indian* at page 171.

71 Bill Gallagher, *Resource Rulers: Fortune and Folly on Canada's Road to Resources* (Waterloo, ON: Gallagher, 2011) at pages 15–16.

72 See, for example, *Delgamuukw v. B.C.,* [1997] 3 S.C.R. 1010 at paras. 85 and 171; *Corbiere v. Canada,* [1999] 2 S.C.R. 203 at paras. 17, 71, 82, and 83; *R. v. Powley,* 2003 SCC 43 at para. 10; *Daniels v. Canada,* 2016 SCC 12 at paras. 36–37.

73 Lisa L. Patterson, "Aboriginal Roundtable to Kelowna Accord: Aboriginal Policy Negotiations, 2004–2005" (Ottawa: Library of Parliament, 2006).

74 Tony Penikett, *Reconciliation: First Nations Treaty Making in British Columbia* (Vancouver: Douglas and McIntyre, 2006) at pages 98–110.

75 For a summary, see *Canada v. Fontaine,* 2017 SCC 47 at paras. 5–11.

76 Maura Forrest, "You Just Have to Do Some Simple Math," *National Post,* August 26, 2017.

77 *Final Report of the Truth and Reconciliation Commission of Canada,* 6 vols. (Montreal and Kingston: McGill-Queen's University Press, 2015).

78 In *Honouring the Truth, Reconciling for the Future: Summary of the Final Report of the TRC* at page 16.

79 *Canada's Residential Schools: Reconciliation,* vol. 6 of *TRC* at page 51.

80 *Daniels* at paras. 36–37.

81 See, for example, letter of October 8, 2015, from the Liberal Party of Canada to the First Nations Leadership Council of British Columbia.

82 For a trenchant criticism from two prominent Aboriginal leaders, see Arthur Manuel and Ronald Derrickson, *The Reconciliation Manifesto: Recovering the Land, Rebuilding the Economy* (Toronto: Lorimer, 2017).

83 McHugh, *Aboriginal Title* at pages 240–85. For a discussion of the role of historians as expert witnesses in litigation, in stinging response to McHugh, see Kent McNeil "Indigenous Rights Litigation, Legal History, and the Role of Experts," in Borrows and Coyle, *The Right Relationship,* at pages 70–104.

84 Frances Widdowson and Albert Howard, *Disrobing the Aboriginal Industry: The Deception behind Indigenous Cultural Preservation* (Montreal and Kingston: McGill-Queen's University Press, 2008).

85 McHugh, *Aboriginal Title* at page 329.

86 Gallagher, *Resource Rulers*; and see his blog at http://billgallagher.ca/blog/.

87 Gallagher, *Resource Rulers* at page 1.

88 *Gitxaala Nation v. Canada*, 2016 FCA 187.

Chapter 3: Sovereignty and Aboriginal-Crown Relations

1 Grace Li Xiu Woo, *Ghost Dancing with Colonialism: Decolonization and Indigenous Rights at the Supreme Court of Canada* (Vancouver: UBC Press, 2011) at page 134.

2 Gerald R. Alfred, *Heeding the Voices of Our Ancestors: Kahnawake Mohawk Politics and the Rise of Native Nationalism* (Toronto: Oxford University Press, 1995) at page 104.

3 See page 33, this book.

4 Kiera L. Ladner, "Treaty Federalism: An Indigenous View of Canadian Federalism," in *New Trends in Canadian Federalism,* ed. François Rocher and Miriam Smith, 167–96 (Toronto: University of Toronto Press, 2003).

5 Special Committee on Indian Self-Government, *Indian Self-Government in Canada,* (Ottawa: Queen's Printer for Canada, 1983).

6 *Report of the Royal Commission on Aboriginal Peoples* (hereafter *RCAP*), vol. 2, *Restructuring the Relationship* (Ottawa: Minister of Supply and Services Canada, 1996) Recommendation 2.3.12 at Appendix A page 1039.

7 Note that the Alberta *Métis Settlement Act,* R.S.A. 2000 c.M-14, s. 187.1 states that the Appeal Tribunal shall exercise its power "with a view to ... furthering the attainment of self-governance by Métis settlements *under the laws of Alberta*" (emphasis added).

8 Internal Tax Interpretation 2016–064503117 – 149(1)(c) – Indian Act Bands, July 27, 2016.

9 *RCAP,* vol. 5, *Renewal: A Twenty-Year Commitment* at Appendix A, page 156.

10 *U.S. v. Jicarilla Apache Tribe,* 564 U.S. 162 (2011).

11 Michael Ignatieff, "Afterword: The Indigenous International and a Jurisprudence of Jurisdictions," in *From Recognition to Reconciliation: Essays on the Constitutional Entrenchment of Aboriginal and Treaty Rights,* ed. Patrick Macklem and Douglas Sanderson (Toronto: University of Toronto Press, 2016) at page 510.

12 Tony Penikett, *Reconciliation: First Nations Treaty Making in British Columbia* (Vancouver: Douglas and McIntyre, 2006) at pages 124–36.

13 John Salmond, *Jurisprudence,* 8th ed. (London: Sweet and Maxwell, 1930) at page 554.

14 *Mitchell v. M.N.R.,* 2001 SCC 33 at para. 151.

15 *Delgamuukw v. B.C.,* [1997] 3 S.C.R. 1010 at para. 145.

16 In *R. v. Marshall/R. v. Bernard,* 2005 SCC 43, the dates of sovereignty for mainland Nova Scotia, New Brunswick, and Cape Breton were 1713, 1759, and 1763: see para. 71.

17 See *R. v. Sparrow,* [1990] 1 S.C.R. 1075 at page 1103.

18 See pages 87–88, 90, 92, and 103, this book.

19 *Reference re Secession of Quebec,* [1998] 2 S.C.R. 217 at para. 142.

20 *Delgamuukw v. The Queen,* (1993), 5 WWR 97 (BCCA) at pages 151–52; *R. v. Williams,* [1995] 2 C.N.L.R. 229 (BCCA); *R. v. Ignace,* (1998) 156 D.L.R. (4th) 713 (BCCA); *R. v. Day Chief,* 2007 ABCA 22 at para. 7.

21 *Delgamuukw v. B.C.,* (1991) 79 D.L.R. (4th) 185 (BCSC) at page 285.

22 Bruce Clark, *Justice in Paradise* (Montreal and Kingston: McGill-Queen's University Press, 1999) at pages 366–67.

23 *Mabo v. Queensland (No. 2),* [1992] HCA 23 at para. 83.

24 *Calder v. B.C.,* [1973] 3 S.C.R. 313 at page 404; see *Mabo* at paras 31–32 (Brennan J.).

25 *Miller v. Secretary of State for Exiting the European Community*, 2017 UKSC 5 at para. 41.
26 *Miller v. Secretary of State for Exiting the European Union*, [2016] EWHC 2768 (Admin.) at paras. 20–23.
27 *Reference Re: Offshore Mineral Rights of B.C.*, [1967] S.C.R. 792 at page 816.
28 B. Slattery, "The Independence of Canada," *Supreme Court Law Review* 5 (1983) at pages 390–91.
29 *Daniels v. Canada*, 2016 SCC 12 at para. 35.
30 *R. v. Morris*, 2006 SCC 59, reversed by *Tsilhqot'in Nation v. B.C.*, 2014 SCC 44 at para. 150 on this point.
31 *Delgamuukw* at para. 178; *R. v. Sutherland*, [1980] 2 S.C.R. 451.
32 *Kitkatla Band v. B.C.*, 2002 SCC 31.
33 *Tsilhqot'in* at para. 130.
34 *R. v. Dick*, [1985] 2 S.C.R. 309.
35 *Derrickson v. Derrickson*, [1986] 1 S.C.R. 285.
36 Peter W. Hogg, *Constitutional Law of Canada*, 5th ed. (Toronto: Carswell, 2007; loose-leaf updated 2016), Chapter 28 at page 2; for a discussion of the relationship between Aboriginal peoples and the provinces, see John Borrows, "Canada's Colonial Constitution," in *The Right Relationship: Reimaging the Implementation of the Historical Treaties*, ed. John Borrows and Michael Coyle, 17–38 (Toronto: University of Toronto Press, 2017).
37 *Grassy Narrows First Nation v. Ontario*, 2014 SCC 48.
38 *Haida Nation v. B.C.*, 2004 SCC 73 at para. 20; *Manitoba Métis Federation v. Canada*, 2013 SCC 14 at para. 67.
39 *Calder* at pages 380–85; *Guerin v. The Queen*, [1984] 2 S.C.R. 335 at pages 377–78.
40 See *Canada's Residential Schools: Reconciliation*, vol. 6 of *TRC* at pages 29–33; Felix Hoehn, *Reconciling Sovereignties: Aboriginal Nations and Canada* (Saskatoon: Native Law Centre, University of Saskatchewan, 2012); John Borrows, "The Durability of *Terra Nullius*," *UBC Law Review* 48 (2015) at page 701; Robert Miller, Jacinta Ruru, Larissa Behrendt, and Tracey Lindberg, *Discovering Indigenous Lands: The Doctrine of Discovery in the English Colonies* (Oxford: Oxford University Press, 2010).
41 *Tsilhqot'in* at para. 69.
42 *Johnson v. McIntosh*, 21 U.S. 543 (1823) at page 573.
43 *Worcester v. Georgia*, 31 U.S. 515 (1832) at pages 516–17.
44 Justice Hall in *Calder* at page 382, quoting C.J. Marshall in *Johnson v. McIntosh*.
45 For more details, see Russel Barsh, "Indigenous Rights and the *Lex Loci* in British Imperial Law," in *Advancing Aboriginal Claims: Visions/Strategies/Directions*, ed. Kerry Wilkins, 91–126 (Saskatoon: Purich, 2004).
46 *Anonymous*, (1722) 24 E.R. 646 (P.C.).
47 *Calder* at page 389.
48 *Delgamuukw* at para. 145; *Mitchell* (2001), at paras. 9–10.
49 *R. v. Van der Peet*, [1996] 2 S.C.R. 507 at para. 263.
50 *Mitchell* (2001) at paras. 9–10.
51 *R. v. Pamajewon*, [1996] 2 S.C.R. 821.
52 See sections 81–86.
53 See, generally, Andrew Benyon, Karl Jaques, Jeremy Bouchard, Tony Chambers, and Andrew Ouchterlong, *Modern First Nations Legislation Annotated, 2018* (Toronto: LexisNexis, 2018).

54 *First Nations Land Management Act,* S.C. 1999, c. 24.

55 *First Nations Elections Act,* S.C. 2014, c. 5.

56 *Family Homes on Reserves and Matrimonial Interests or Rights Act,* S.C. 2013, c. 20.

57 Indian and Northern Affairs Canada, *The Government of Canada's Approach to the Implementation of the Inherent Right and the Negotiation of Aboriginal Self-Government* (Ottawa: Indian and Northern Affairs Canada, 1995).

58 Penikett, *Reconciliation* at page 235.

59 Michael Asch, *On Being Here to Stay: Treaties and Aboriginal Rights in Canada* (Toronto: University of Toronto Press, 2014) at page 25.

60 Ibid. at page 28.

61 Kiera Ladner, "Rethinking Aboriginal Governance," in *Reinventing Canada: Politics of the 21st Century,* ed. Janine Brodie and Linda Trimble (Toronto: Prentice Hall, 2003) at page 54.

62 See, for example, the *Yukon First Nations Self-Government Act,* S.C. 1994 c. 35.

63 *Sga'nism Sim'augt (Chief Mountain) v. Canada,* 2013 BCCA 49.

64 Greg Poelzer and Ken Coates, *From Treaty Peoples to Treaty Nation: A Road Map for All Canadians* (Vancouver: UBC Press, 2015) at page 160.

65 Mark D. Walters, "Mohegan Indians v. Connecticut (1705–1773) and the Legal Status of Aboriginal Customary Laws and Government in British North America," *Osgoode Hall Law Journal* 33 (1995) at page 788.

66 *R. v. Syliboy,* [1929] 1 D.L.R. 307 (N.S. Co. Ct.).

67 *Calder* at page 353.

68 *Calder* at pages 380–85; *Guerin* at pages 377–78.

69 *Guerin* at page 378.

70 *Sparrow* at page 1103.

71 *Mitchell v. Peguis Indian Band,* [1990] 2 S.C.R. 85 at page 130.

72 *R. v. Gladstone,* [1996] 2 S.C.R. 723 at para. 73. See also *Van der Peet* at para. 31.

73 *Gladstone* at para. 73.

74 For a review of the cases to 2007, see Kent McNeil, "Judicial Approaches to Self-Government since *Calder,*" in *Let Right Be Done: Aboriginal Title, the Calder Case, and the Future of Indigenous Rights,* ed. Hamar Foster, Heather Raven, and Jeremy Webber, 129–52 (Vancouver: UBC Press, 2007).

75 *Pamajewon* at para. 24.

76 *Pamajewon* at para. 25.

77 For another example of a failed claim to self-government, see *Mississauga of Scugog First Nation v. NAATGWU,* 2007 ONCA 814.

78 See Chapter 4, this book.

79 *Delgamuukw* at paras. 170–71.

80 *Cherokee Nation v. Georgia,* 30 U.S. 1 (1831) at page 17.

81 *Mitchell* (2001) at para. 129.

82 *Mitchell* (2001) at para. 135.

83 *Mitchell* (2001) at paras. 149–54.

84 *Mitchell* (2001) at para. 134. And see *Jones v. A.G. of New Brunswick,* [1975] 2 S.C.R. 182 at page 195.

85 *Campbell v. British Columbia,* (2000), 189 D.L.R. (4th) 333 (B.C.S.C.).

86 See also *Delgamuukw v. B.C.,* 1993 CanLII 4516 (B.C.C.A.) at paras. 168–74 per Macfarlane J.A.

87 *Sga'nism Sim'augt.*

88 See discussion in Chapter 4 on the test of justification for infringements of Aboriginal and treaty rights.

89 *Haida* at para. 20.

90 *Haida* at para. 25.

91 *Taku River Tlingit First Nation v. B.C.,* 2004 SCC 74 at para. 42.

92 F. Hoehn, "Back to the Future – Reconciliation and Aboriginal Sovereignty after *Tsilhqot'in," University of New Brunswick Law Journal* 67 (2016) at pages 132–34; see generally, Hoehn, *Reconciling Sovereignties.*

93 *Tsilhqot'in* at paras. 113–15, 147.

94 *Manitoba Métis* at paras. 5 and 44.

95 See, for example, John Borrows, "Sovereignty's Alchemy," *Osgoode Hall Law Journal* 37 (1999) at page 537; Macklem and Sanderson, eds., *From Recognition to Reconciliation,* Part 1, "Reconciling Sovereignties."

96 Dimitrios Panagos, *Uncertain Accommodation: Aboriginal Identity and Group Rights in the Supreme Court of Canada* (Vancouver: UBC Press, 2016) at page 83.

97 RCAP, "Rebuilding Aboriginal Nations," in *Highlights from the Report of the Royal Commission on Aboriginal Peoples,* Indigenous and Northern Affairs website, http://www.aadnc-aandc.gc.ca/eng/1100100014597/1100100014637; also Recommendation 2.3.3 in *RCAP,* vol. 2, *Restructuring the Relationship* at page 175.

98 *Canada's Residential Schools: Reconciliation,* vol. 6 of *TRC* at page 52.

99 See Vaughan Palmer, "Campbell's Plan Panned by Lawyers," *Vancouver Sun,* June 3, 2009; see generally on the proposed legislation, Bill Gallagher, *Resource Rulers: Fortune and Folly on Canada's Road to Resources* (Waterloo, ON: Gallagher, 2011) at pages 261–66.

100 Alan Cairns, *Citizens Plus: Aboriginal Peoples and the Canadian State* (Vancouver: UBC Press, 2000) at pages 27–28.

101 June McCue, "Afterword," in *Box of Treasures or Empty Box? Two Decades of Section 35,* ed. Ardith Walkem and Halie Bruce (Penticton, BC: Theytus, 2003) at page 371.

102 Call to Action 47; see also Calls to Action 45, 46 and 49 in *Canada's Residential Schools: Reconciliation,* vol. 6 of *TRC* at pages 230–31.

103 Recommendation 1.16.2, in *RCAP,* vol. 5, *Renewal: A Twenty-Year Commitment* at page 141.

104 *Canada's Residential Schools: Reconciliation,* vol. 6 of *TRC* at page 33.

105 As discussed in Chapter 5, the commission advocated the "treaty federalism" theory as the basis for Canada's legitimacy as a nation. It is difficult to see how this theory applies to those significant areas of the country still without treaties.

106 Frances Widdowson and Albert Howard, *Disrobing the Aboriginal Industry* (Montreal and Kingston: McGill-Queen's University Press, 2008) at page 115.

107 Tom Flanagan, *First Nations? Second Thoughts,* 2nd ed. (Montreal and Kingston: McGill-Queen's University Press, 2008) at pages 61 and 66.

108 See Arthur Manuel and Ronald Derrickson, *The Reconciliation Manifesto* (Toronto: Lorimer, 2017).

109 Les Perreaux, "Some Indigenous Groups Embrace Quebec's Proposal to Reopen Constitution," *Globe and Mail,* June 5, 2017.

110 *Grassy Narrows* at para. 50 (emphasis in original).

111 See *Alberta v. Elder Advocates of Alberta Society,* 2011 SCC 24.

112 *Sparrow* at page 1108.

113 *Daniels v. Canada*, 2016 SCC 12 at para. 53.

114 *Wakatu v. Attorney General*, [2017] NZSC 17.

115 See Jamie Dickson, *The Honour and Dishonour of the Crown* (Saskatoon: Purich, 2015) at page 150.

116 See *Specific Claims Tribunal Act*, S.C. 2008, c. 22, s. 14(1)(b), (c).

117 *R. v. Badger*, [1996] 1 S.C.R. 771.

118 See pages 111–13 and 117–18, this book.

119 For fuller accounts, see Leonard Ian Rotman, *Parallel Paths: Fiduciary Doctrine and the Crown-Native Relationship in Canada* (Toronto: University of Toronto Press, 1996); James I. Reynolds, *A Breach of Duty: Fiduciary Obligations and Aboriginal Peoples* (Saskatoon: Purich, 2005); J. Timothy S. McCabe, *The Honour of the Crown and Its Fiduciary Duties to Aboriginal Peoples* (Markham, ON: LexisNexis, 2008).

120 *R. v. Williams and Taylor*, (1981), 34 O.R. (2d) 360 (ONCA).

121 *Sparrow* at page 1108.

122 *Blueberry River Indian Band v. Canada*, [1995] 4 S.C.R. 344.

123 *Osoyoos Indian Band v. Oliver*, 2001 SCC 85.

124 *Osoyoos* at paras. 52–53.

125 *Wewaykum Indian Band v. Canada*, 2002 SCC 79.

126 *Wewaykum* at para. 82.

127 *Wewaykum* at para. 81.

128 *Wewaykum* at para. 96.

129 *Haida* at para. 18.

130 *Ermineskin Indian Band v. Canada*, 2009 SCC 9.

131 *Ermineskin* at para. 128.

132 *Williams Lake Indian Band v. Canada*, 2018 SCC 4.

133 *Earl of Rutland's* case, (1608) 77 E.R. 555.

134 *Province of Ontario v. Dominion of Canada*, (1895) 25 S.C.R. 434 at 512.

135 *Mitchell* (2001) at para. 9.

136 For example, *Badger* at para. 41.

137 *Haida* at paras. 16–17.

138 *Haida* at para. 25.

139 *Beckman v. Little Salmon*, 2010 SCC 53 at para. 61.

140 *Manitoba Métis* at para. 68.

141 *Manitoba Métis* at para. 161.

142 *Manitoba Métis* at para. 204.

143 *Manitoba Métis* at para. 208.

144 Dickson, *Honour and Dishonour* at page 9.

145 Dickson, *Honour and Dishonour* at page 150.

146 *Manitoba Métis* at para. 66.

147 *Daniels* at para. 53.

148 P.G. McHugh, "A Common Law Biography of Section 35," in Macklem and Sanderson, *From Recognition to Reconciliation* at page 161.

149 *R. v. Kokopenace*, 2015 SCC 28 at paras. 99–102.

150 John Selden, *Table Talk*, ed. Samuel Reynolds (first published in 1689; this edition, Oxford: Clarendon Press, 1892) at page 61.

Chapter 4: Aboriginal Rights and Title

1 *Mitchell v. M.N.R.*, 2001 SCC 33 at paras. 9–10.
2 *R. v. Sparrow*, [1990] 1 S.C.R. 1075, at page 1099.
3 *R. v. Sappier*, 2006 SCC 54 at para. 57.
4 *R. v. Van der Peet*, [1996] 2 S.C.R. 507, at para. 28.
5 *Calder v. B.C.*, [1973] S.C.R. 313.
6 *Sparrow* at page 1095.
7 *Sparrow* at page 1099.
8 *R. v. N.T.C. Smokehouse Ltd*, [1996] 2 S.C.R. 672.
9 *Van der Peet* at para. 76.
10 *Van der Peet* at para. 46.
11 *Van der Peet* at paras. 48–74. For a summary, see *Mitchell* at para. 12.
12 *Van der Peet* at para. 73.
13 *Van der Peet* at para. 157.
14 *Sparrow* at page 1093.
15 *Van der Peet* at para 168.
16 *Van der Peet* at para. 247.
17 *Van der Peet* at para. 227.
18 *Sappier* at para. 33.
19 *Sappier* at para. 45.
20 *Lax Kw'alaams Indian Band v. Canada*, 2011 SCC 56 at para. 54.
21 *Sappier* at para. 26; see *R. v. Powley*, 2003 SCC 43 at para. 24.
22 *R. v. Adams*, [1996] 3 S.C.R. 101, at paras. 25–29.
23 *R. v. Gladstone*, [1996] 2 S.C.R. 723 at para. 65.
24 See also *R. v. Nikal*, [1996] 1 S.C.R. 1013; *Adams;* and *R. v. Côté*, [1996] 3 S.C.R. 139.
25 *Sappier* at para. 49.
26 *Tsilhqot'in Nation v. B.C.*, 2014 SCC 44.
27 *Tsilhqot'in v. B.C.*, 2012 BCCA 285.
28 *Côté* at para. 56.
29 *Hamilton Health Sciences Corp. v. H.(D.)*, 2014 ONCJ 603; revised reasons 2015 ONCJ 229.
30 *R. v. Pamajewon*, [1996] 2 S.C.R. 821.
31 *Mitchell.*
32 *Lax Kw'alaams.*
33 *Lax Kw'alaams* at para. 8.
34 *Powley.*
35 *Powley* at para. 37.
36 See, for example, *Ontario v. Beaudrey*, 2006 ONCJ 59.
37 See, for example, John Borrows, "Frozen Rights in Canada: Constitutional Interpretation and the Trickster," *American Indian Law Review* 22 (1997) at page 37.
38 *Drew v. Newfoundland*, 2006 NLCA 53.
39 *Adams* at page 128; *Côté* at page 177.
40 *Ahousaht Indian Band v. Canada*, 2009 BCSC·1494 at paras. 162–174, aff'd 2011 BCCA 237 at paras. 25, 30, 48; 2013 BCCA 300.
41 *Delgamuukw v. B.C.*, [1997] 3 S.C.R. 1010.
42 *Mitchell* at para. 38.
43 Douglas Lambert, "Where to from Here," in *Aboriginal Law since Delgamuukw*, ed. Maria Morellato (Aurora, ON: Canada Law Book, 2009) at page 53.

44 *R. v. Badger,* [1996] 1 S.C.R. 771 at para. 76.

45 *Van der Peet* at para. 33

46 *St. Catherine's Milling and Lumber Co. v. The Queen,* (1888) 14 A.C. 46 (P.C.) at page 54.

47 *Delgamuukw* at para. 114.

48 *Delgamuukw* at para. 114.

49 *Delgamuukw,* (1993), 104 D.L.R. (4th) 470 at pages 525–31 (BCCA).

50 *Delgamuukw* at paras. 172–76.

51 *Van der Peet* at para. 28.

52 Bruce H. Ziff, *Principles of Property Law,* 5th. ed. (Toronto: Carswell, 2010) at page 69.

53 See, for example, Patrick Macklem, "First Nations Self-Government and the Borders of the Canadian Legal Imagination," *McGill Law Journal* 36 (1991) at page 396–414; John Borrows, "The Durability of *Terra Nullius,*" *UBC Law Review* 48 (2015) at page 701.

54 *Delgamuukw* at para. 145.

55 *Mabo v. Queensland (No. 2),* [1992] HCA 23 at paras. 48–54 (Brennan J.).

56 *Tsilhqot'in* at para. 69.

57 *Guerin v. The Queen,* [1984] 2 S.C.R. 335 at page 378.

58 *Tsilhqot'in* at para. 73; see also para. 116.

59 *Tsilhqot'in* at para. 70.

60 *Tsilhqot'in* at para. 112.

61 *Mabo* at para. 50 (Brennan J.).

62 *Delgamuukw* at para. 175.

63 Felix Cohen, *The Legal Conscience: Selected Papers of Felix S. Cohen* (New Haven, CT: Yale University Press, 1960) at pages 281–82.

64 Borrows, "The Durability of *Terra Nullius*" at 742.

65 *Calder* at page 362.

66 *Cherokee Nation v. Georgia,* 30 U.S. 1 (1831) at page 17.

67 *Van der Peet* at paras. 272, 275.

68 "Kitigan Zibi Files Aboriginal Title Claim over Parliament Hill Lands," APTN National News, December 8, 2016.

69 *Van der Peet* at para. 273.

70 *The Pre-Emption Ordinance,* Ordinance No. 13, March 31, 1866, s. 1. Not repealed until 1953.

71 Hamar Foster, "We Are Not O'Meara's Children," in *Let Right Be Done,* ed. Hamar Foster, Heather Raven, and Jeremy Webber, 61–84 (Vancouver: UBC Press, 2007).

72 Paul Tennant, *Aboriginal Peoples and Politics* (Vancouver: UBC Press, 1990) at page 93.

73 Ronald St. John Macdonald, *Native Rights in Canada* (Toronto: Indian-Eskimo Association, 1970) at pages 128–29.

74 *Indian Act,* R.S.C. 1927, c. 98, s. 149A.

75 *St. Catherine's Milling* at page 54; see also *A.G. Canada v. A.G. Ontario,* [1897] A.C. 199 (P.C.).

76 W.H.P. Clement, *The Law of the Canadian Constitution,* 3rd ed. (Toronto: Carswell, 1916) at pages 635, 637–38.

77 Macdonald, *Native Rights,* at page 204.

78 See Hamar Foster, Heather Raven, and Jeremy Webber, ed., *Let Right Be Done* (Vancouver: UBC Press, 2007).

79 Thomas Berger, *One Man's Justice: A Life in the Law* (Vancouver: Douglas and McIntyre, 2002) at page 112.

80 Ibid. at page 115.

81 *Calder* at page 352.

82 *Calder* at page 416.

83 K. Lysyk, "The Indian Title Question in Canada: An Appraisal in the Light of Calder," *Canadian Bar Review* 51 (1973) at page 452.

84 *Calder* at page 344.

85 *Calder* at page 404.

86 *Calder* at page 328.

87 *Guerin* at page 377.

88 David Elliott, "*Baker Lake* and the Concept of Aboriginal Title," *Osgoode Hall Law Journal* 18 (1980) at page 655.

89 *Tsilhqot'in* at para. 10.

90 Thomas Berger, *A Long and Terrible Shadow* (Vancouver: Douglas and McIntyre, 1991) at page 153.

91 Melvin H. Smith, *Our Home or Native Land?* (Victoria: Crown Western, 1995) at page 10.

92 Quoted in Smith, *Our Home,* at page 82.

93 For an important lower court decision, see *Baker Lake v. Minister of Indian Affairs,* [1980] 1 F.C. 518 (F.C.T.D.).

94 *Tsilhqot'in* at para. 69.

95 *Guerin* at page 379.

96 *Tsilhqot'in* at para. 12.

97 *Guerin* at pages 379–82.

98 *Guerin* at page 385.

99 Brian Slattery, "Understanding Aboriginal Rights," *Canadian Bar Review* 66 (1987) at pages 731, 749.

100 *Sparrow* at page 1099.

101 *Sparrow* at page 1103 (emphasis in original).

102 *Tsilhqot'in* at para. 14.

103 *Calder* at page 347.

104 *Delgamuukw,* [1991] 3 W.W.R. 97 (B.C.S.C.) at pages 126, 141.

105 *R. v. Marshall/R. v. Bernard,* 2005 SCC 43.

106 *Marshall/Bernard* at para. 63.

107 *Marshall/Bernard* at para 58.

108 See John J.L. Hunter, "Disappointed Expectations," in Morellato, *Aboriginal Law since Delgamuukw* at pages 17–30.

109 *Tsilhqot'in v. B.C.,* 2007 BCSC 1700 at para. 961.

110 *Tsilhqot'in v. B.C.,* 2012 BCCA 285 at para. 219.

111 *Tsilhqot'in* (BCCA) at para. 221.

112 See David M. Rosenberg and Jack Woodward, "The *Tsilhqot'in* Case: The Recognition and Affirmation of Aboriginal Title in Canada," *UBC Law Review* 48 (2015) at pages 946, 966–68.

113 *Tsilhqot'in* at para 50.

114 *Calder* at page 328.

115 Kent McNeil, *Emerging Justice? Essays on Indigenous Rights in Canada and Australia* (Saskatoon: Native Law Centre, 2001) at page 138.

116 Call to Action 52 in *Canada's Residential Schools: Reconciliation,* vol. 6 of *TRC* at pages 90–91.

117 *Delgamuukw* at para. 84.

118 Ardith Walkem, "An Unfulfilled Promise," in Morellato, *Aboriginal Law since Delgamuukw* at page 401.

119 Frances Widdowson and Albert Howard, *Disrobing the Aboriginal Industry: The Deception behind Indigenous Cultural Preservation* (Montreal and Kingston: McGill-Queen's University Press, 2008) at pages 43–45; Tom Flanagan, *First Nations? Second Thoughts,* 2nd ed. (Montreal and Kingston: McGill-Queen's University Press, 2008) at pages 156–64.

120 David Robbins, "Proving Aboriginal Title" (presentation at "The SCC Tsilhqot'in Decision," a conference organized by the Affinity Institute, Vancouver, 2014).

121 *Delgamuukw* at paras. 144–45.

122 See Kent McNeil, "Aboriginal Title and Indigenous Governance" (Osgoode Hall Law School Research Paper No. 67, 2016).

123 *Marshall/Bernard* at para 67.

124 *Tsilhqot'in* (BCCA) at para. 149.

125 *Tsilhqot'in* at para. 33.

126 *Tsilhqot'in* at para. 38.

127 *Tsilhqot'in* at para. 48.

128 *Marshall/Bernard* at para. 57; see *Delgamuukw* at para. 158.

129 Thomas Isaac, *Aboriginal Law,* 5th ed. (Toronto: Carswell, Thomson Reuters, 2016) at pages 434–37. See, however, Larry Chartrand, "Métis Aboriginal Title in Canada," in *Advancing Aboriginal Claims,* ed. Kerry Wilkins, 151–88 (Saskatoon: Purich, 2004).

130 *Tsilhqot'in* at para. 75.

131 *Delgamuukw* at para. 128.

132 *Delgamuukw* at para. 115.

133 *Delgamuukw* at para. 175; *Grassy Narrows First Nation v. Ontario,* 2014 SCC 48 at para. 31.

134 *Delgamuukw* at para. 114.

135 *Delgamuukw* at paras. 112–15.

136 *Skeetchestn Indian Band v. B.C.,* 2000 BCCA 525.

137 Brian Slattery, "The Constitutional Dimension of Aboriginal Title," *Supreme Court Law Review* 71 (2015) at pages 46, 66.

138 Flanagan, *First Nations?* at page 7.

139 Ibid. at page 127.

140 Ibid. at page 131.

141 Ibid. at page 132, quoting Melvin Smith at a Fraser Institute seminar, May 27, 1999.

142 *Johnson v. McIntosh,* 21 U.S. 543 (1823) at page 574.

143 Slattery, "The Constitutional Dimension of Aboriginal Title" at page 60.

144 *Tsilhqot'in* at para. 74.

145 *Delgamuukw* at para. 128.

146 *Delgamuukw* at para. 132.

147 Kent McNeil, "Defining Aboriginal Title in the 1990s" (12th Annual Robarts Lecture, York University, March 25, 1998) at pages 9–11.

148 *Tsilhqot'in* at para. 90.

149 *Tsilhqot'in* at para. 76.

150 For the Section 1 limits, see *R. v Oakes,* [1986] 1 S.C.R. 103; and see Peter W. Hogg and Daniel Styler, "Statutory Limitations of Aboriginal or Treaty Rights: What Counts as Justification?" *Lakehead Law Journal* 1 (2015) at pages 11–15.

151 *Van der Peet* at para. 308.

152 McNeil, *Emerging Justice?* at pages 184–214.

153 *Tsilhqot'in* at para. 82.

154 *Delgamuukw* at para. 165.

155 James Tully, "The Struggles of Indigenous Peoples for and of Freedom," in *Box of Treasures or Empty Box?* ed. Ardith Walkem and Halie Bruce (Penticton, BC: Theytus, 2003) at page 287. This justification for the dispossession of Aboriginal peoples is discussed in Chapter 1.

156 Ardith Walkem, "Constructing the Constitutional Box," in Walkem and Bruce, *Box of Treasures* at page 207.

157 *Gladstone* at para. 75.

158 *Sparrow* at page 1113.

159 *Tsilhqot'in* at paras. 1, 71 and 139, see also paras. 23, 77, 81, 82, 84, 118, and 125.

160 *Tsilhqot'in* at para. 126.

161 *Van der Peet* at para. 306.

162 *Van der Peet* at para. 302.

163 *Van der Peet* at para. 315.

164 *Tsilhqot'in* (BCSC) at para. 1350.

165 John Borrows, "Domesticating Doctrines: Aboriginal Peoples after the Royal Commission," *McGill Law Journal* 46 (2001) at pages 660–61.

166 Kent Roach, *The Supreme Court on Trial: Judicial Activism or Democratic Dialogue?* (Toronto: Irwin, 2016) at pages 192–93.

167 *Sparrow* at page 1109.

168 *Sparrow* at page 1110.

169 *Sparrow* at pages 1110–11; *Gladstone* at para. 43.

170 *Adams* at para. 54.

171 *Tsilhqot'in* at paras. 124, 127.

172 *Gladstone* at para. 64.

173 *Tsilhqot'in* at para. 87.

174 *Tsilhqot'in* at para. 86.

175 *Delgamuukw* at para. 169; see also Hall J. in *Calder* at pages 352–53.

176 *Delgamuukw* at para. 203.

177 Robert Mainville, *An Overview of Aboriginal and Treaty Rights and Compensation for Their Breach* (Saskatoon: Purich, 2001).

178 Isaac, *Aboriginal Law* at pages 101–2.

Chapter 5: Treaties

1 *R. v. Van der Peet*, [1996] 2 S.C.R. 507 at paras. 272, 275.

2 See Deloitte, *Socio-economic Benefits of Modern Treaties in BC* (Vancouver: BC Treaty Commission, 2016).

3 *R. v. Marshall*, [1999] 3 S.C.R. 456 (*Marshall I*).

4 *R. v. Sioui*, [1990] 1 S.C.R. at page 1043.

5 See, for example, Treaty No. 6, which included provisions for a "medicine chest," a school, and annuities.

6 *Sioui*.

7 *R. v. Badger*, [1996] 1 S.C.R. 771 at para. 76.

8 *R. v. Sundown*, [1999] 1 S.C.R. 393, at para. 36; *Behn v. Moulton Contracting Ltd*, 2013 SCC 26 at para. 30.

9 *Simon v. The Queen*, [1985] 2 S.C.R. 387 at para. 33.

10 *Badger* at paras. 77–82; *Grassy Narrows First Nation v. Ontario*, 2014 SCC 48 at para. 53.

11 Kent Roach, *The Supreme Court on Trial: Judicial Activism or Democratic Dialogue?* (Toronto: Irwin, 2016) at page 191.

12 For example, the Douglas Treaties of the 1850s, which apply to parts of Vancouver Island.

13 For example, Treaty No. 8; see page 136–37, this book, for this provision.

14 See the Tsawwassen Final Agreement (2007), Chapter 2, paras. 13–15.

15 *Sioui*.

16 Tony Penikett, *Reconciliation: First Nations Treaty Making in British Columbia* (Vancouver: Douglas and McIntyre, 2006) at pages 228–38.

17 *Sundown* at para. 25.

18 *McDiarmid Lumber Ltd v. God's Lake First Nation*, 2006 SCC 58 at paras. 78, 92.

19 *Delgamuukw v. B.C.*, [1997] 3 S.C.R. 1010, at para. 186.

20 *Haida Nation v. B.C.*, 2004 SCC 73 at para. 20.

21 *Haida* at para. 20.

22 *Haida* at para. 27.

23 *Mikisew Cree First Nation v. Canada*, 2005 SCC 69; *Grassy Narrows*.

24 *Beckman v. Little Salmon*, 2010 SCC 53 at para. 10.

25 *First Nation of Nacho Nyak Dun v. Yukon*, 2017 SCC 58 at para. 1.

26 *Report of the Royal Commission on Aboriginal Peoples* (hereafter *RCAP*), vol. 2, *Restructuring the Relationship* (Ottawa: Minister of Supply and Services Canada, 1996) at page 16.

27 *Honouring the Truth, Reconciling for the Future: Summary of the Final Report of the TRC* at page 195.

28 Kiera L. Ladner, "Treaty Federalism: An Indigenous View of Canadian Federalism," in *New Trends in Canadian Federalism*, ed. François Rocher and Miriam Smith, 167–96 (Toronto: University of Toronto Press, 2003).

29 *Honouring the Truth, Reconciling for the Future: Summary of the Final Report of the TRC* at page 199.

30 Michael Asch, *On Being Here to Stay: Treaties and Aboriginal Rights in Canada* (Toronto: University of Toronto Press, 2014) at page 164.

31 See J.R. Miller, *Compact, Contract, Covenant: Aboriginal Treaty-Making in Canada* (Toronto: University of Toronto Press, 2009); detailed reports on the historical treaties can be found on the Indigenous and Northern Affairs Canada website, http://www.aadnc-aandc.gc.ca/eng/1100100028653/1100100028654.

32 Sébastian Grammond, *Terms of Coexistence: Indigenous Peoples and Canadian Law* (Toronto: Carswell, 2013) at page 290; see pages 51–65 for the relationship between Aboriginal peoples and New France.

33 See *Simon*, *Sioui*, *Marshall I*, and *R. v. Marshall*, [1999] 3 S.C.R. 533 (*Marshall II*).

34 *God's Lake* at para. 124.

35 See *Ontario v. Bear Island Foundation*, [1991] 2 S.C.R. 570.

36 See *R. v. White and Bob*, (1965), 50 D.L.R. (2d) 613 (B.C.C.A.) aff'd [1965] S.C.R. vi (note); *R. v. Morris*, 2006 SCC 59.

37 Thomas Berger, *One Man's Justice: A Life in the Law* (Vancouver: Douglas and McIntyre, 2002) at pages 91–92.

38 See *R. v. Horse*, [1988] 1 S.C.R. 187; *R. v. Horseman*, [1990] 1 S.C.R. 901; *Badger*; *Sundown*; *Grassy Narrows*.

39 Alexander Morris, *The Treaties of Canada* (Toronto: Bedford, Clarke, 1880) at pages 285–92.

40 *Horseman.*

41 *Badger.*

42 *R. v. Blais,* 2003 SCC 44.

43 *R. v. Howard,* [1994] 3 S.C.R. 299.

44 Quoted in Ronald St. John Macdonald, *Native Rights in Canada* (Toronto: Indian-Eskimo Association, 1970), Appendix 8.

45 *Calder v. B.C.,* [1973] S.C.R. 313.

46 For a summary of the modern treaties and self-government agreements, see the Indigenous and Northern Affairs website, http://www.aadnc-aandc.gc.ca/eng/137338 5502190/1373385561540#s2.

47 RCAP, *Treaty Making in the Spirit of Co-Existence: An Alternative to Extinguishment* (Ottawa: RCAP, 1995).

48 Arthur Manuel and Ronald Derrickson, *The Reconciliation Manifesto: Recovering the Land, Rebuilding the Economy* (Toronto: Lorimer, 2017) at pages 100–8.

49 Macdonald, *Native Rights* at page 167.

50 *Sikyea v. The Queen* (1964) S.C.R. 642. In contrast, it was held in *White and Bob* that provincial law did not limit treaty rights.

51 H.B. Hawthorn, ed., *A Survey of the Contemporary Indians of Canada* (Ottawa: Indian Affairs Branch, 1966) at page 235.

52 Harold Cardinal, *The Unjust Society* (Edmonton: M.G. Hurtig, 1969) at page 47.

53 See Michael Coyle, "As Long as the Sun Shines: Recognizing That Treaties Were Intended to Last," in *The Right Relationship: Reimagining the Implementation of Historical Treaties,* ed. John Borrows and Michael Coyle (Toronto: University of Toronto Press, 2017) at page 42.

54 *Simon* at para. 21.

55 *Badger* at para. 41.

56 *Marshall I* at para. 43.

57 *Marshall I* at para. 44.

58 *Sundown* at para. 29.

59 *Sundown* at para. 30.

60 *R. v. Marshall/R. v. Bernard,* 2005 SCC 43 at para. 25.

61 *Sioui* at page 1053.

62 *Simon* at page 404.

63 *Marshall I* at para. 78.

64 In *Badger* it was said that words in a treaty "must be interpreted in the sense that they would naturally have been understood by the Indians at the time of signing"; see para. 52. But in *Sioui* the Court said the interpretation must "reflect the intention of both parties and not just that of the [Aboriginal group]"; see page 1069; see also *Mikisew Cree* at paras. 28–29.

65 *Ermineskin Indian Band v. Canada,* 2009 SCC 9 at para. 54.

66 See W.C. Wicken, *Mik'maq Treaties on Trial: History, Land, and Donald Marshall Junior* (Toronto: University of Toronto Press, 2009).

67 Christopher Manfredi, "Fear, Hope and Misunderstanding," in *Advancing Aboriginal Claims: Visions/Strategies/Directions,* ed. Kerry Wilkins, 190–201 (Saskatoon: Purich, 2004).

68 Bill Gallagher, *Resource Rulers* (Waterloo, ON: Gallagher, 2011) at pages 47–55.

69 *Marshall II.*

70 Jessica Leeder, "Tensions Boil over Off-Season Lobster Fishing," *Globe and Mail,* October 16, 2017, at page A1.

71 *Marshall/Bernard.*

72 *Little Salmon* at para. 9; see also *Quebec v. Moses,* 2010 SCC 17 at para. 7.

73 *Nacho Nyak Dun* at para. 33.

74 *Nacho Nyak Dun* at para. 34.

75 See, for example, Chapter 2, section 60, of the Tsawwassen Final Agreement.

76 *RCAP,* vol. 2, *Restructuring the Relationship,* section 3.4 at page 37.

77 See also Cardinal, *The Unjust Society;* Treaty 7 Elders and Tribal Council, *The True Spirit and Original Intent of Treaty 7* (Montreal and Kingston: McGill-Queen's University Press, 1996); Asch, *On Being Here to Stay,* Chapter 5.

78 Aaron Mills, "What Is a Treaty? On Contract and Mutual Aid," in Borrows and Coyle, *The Right Relationship* at page 225.

79 *Keewatin v. Ontario,* 2011 ONSC 4801 at paras. 801–2, 864–65, 912–24.

80 See Patrick Macklem, *Indigenous Difference and the Constitution of Canada* (Toronto: University of Toronto Press, 2001) at pages 132–59; Peter W. Hutchins, "Cede, Release and Surrender," in *Aboriginal Law since Delgamuukw,* ed. Maria Morellato (Aurora: Canada Law Book, 2009) at pages 431–64.

81 James Daschuk, *Clearing the Plains: Disease, Politics of Starvation and the Loss of Aboriginal Life* (Regina: University of Regina Press, 2013) at pages 79–126.

82 Cardinal, *The Unjust Society* at page 42.

83 Peter A. Cumming and Neil H. Mickenberg, eds., *Native Rights in Canada* (Toronto: Indian-Eskimo Association of Canada, 1972) at page 125.

84 Quoted in Cardinal, *The Unjust Society* at page 36.

85 Macdonald, *Native Rights* at page 110.

86 Morris, *Treaties of Canada,* at pages 34–35.

87 *Mikisew Cree* at para. 25.

88 *RCAP,* vol. 2, *Restructuring the Relationship,* chapter 2, section 3.5 at page 38. For a detailed discussion of the possible application of duress and undue influence to treaties, see Michael Coyle, "Marginalized by Sui Generis? Duress, Undue Influence and Crown-Aboriginal Treaties," *Manitoba Law Journal* 32 (2007) at page 34.

89 Ibid., section 3.8 at page 43.

90 Ibid., section 7.4 at page 71.

91 *Paulette v. The Queen,* (1973), 42 D.L.R. (3d) 8 (NWTSC); reversed on other grounds: [1977] 2 S.C.R. 628.

92 *RCAP,* vol. 5, *Renewal: A Twenty-Year Commitment,* Appendix A, at pages 148–54.

93 Felix Cohen, *The Legal Conscience* (New Haven, CT: Yale University Press, 1960) at page 283.

94 John Borrows, *Canada's Indigenous Constitution* (Toronto: University of Toronto Press, 2010) at pages 123–24.

95 Tom Flanagan, *First Nations? Second Thoughts,* 2nd ed. (Montreal and Kingston: McGill-Queen's University Press, 2008) at page 153.

96 Flanagan, *First Nations?* at page 7.

97 *Badger* at para. 52.

98 *Howard* at pages 306–7.

99   *Little Salmon* at para. 52.

100 *Manitoba Métis Federation Inc. v. Canada,* 2013 SCC 14 at para. 67. See also *Sioui* at page 1036.

101 Beverley McLachlin, "Aboriginal Peoples and Reconciliation," *Canterbury Law Review* 9 (2003) at page 240.

102 *Bear Island* at page 575.

103 Kent McNeil, *Emerging Justice?: Essays on Indigenous Rights in Canada and Australia* (Saskatoon: Native Law Centre, 2001) at pages 49–57. See also Bruce Clark, *Justice in Paradise* (Montreal and Kingston: McGill-Queen's University Press, 1999) at pages 65–81.

104 *Howard* at pages 306–7.

105 *Horse* at para. 39.

106 *Ermineskin* at para. 50.

107 *Alberta v. Cunningham,* 2011 SCC 37 at para. 6.

108 *Mikisew Cree* at para. 52; see also para. 31.

109 *Grassy Narrows* at para. 2.

110 *Sioui* at page 1036; *Badger* at para. 52.

111 *Horse* at para. 50.

112 *Mikisew Cree* at para. 54.

113 *Mikisew Cree* at para. 55.

114 *Mikisew Cree* at para. 57.

115 *Little Salmon* at para. 71.

116 *Grassy Narrows* at para. 50.

117 *Grassy Narrows* at para. 52.

118 See *Ermineskin v. Canada,* 2006 FCA 415 at paras. 41, 48.

119 Eric Guimond, Erin O'Sullivan, and Jean-Pierre Morin, *Community Well-Being and Treaties: Trends for First Nation Historic and Modern Treaties* (Ottawa: Aboriginal Affairs and Northern Development Canada, 2012).

120 Bob Rae, "The Gap between Historic Treaty People and Everyone Else" (remarks for the University of Regina, October 30, 2014), http://oktlaw.com/drive/uploads/2016/10/BRRegina.pdf.

121 Hawthorn, *Survey of the Contemporary Indians* at page 247.

122 Ibid. at page 253.

123 Cumming and Mickenberg, *Native Rights,* Appendix 8.

124 Hawthorn, *Survey of the Contemporary Indians* at page 248.

125 Cardinal, *The Unjust Society* at page 36.

126 Manuel and Derrickson, *The Reconciliation Manifesto* at pages 113–17.

127 RCAP, *Treaty Making in the Spirit of Co-Existence: An Alternative to Extinguishment* (Ottawa: RCAP, 1995) at page 68.

128 Melvin H. Smith, *Our Home or Native Land? What Governments' Aboriginal Policy Is Doing to Canada* (Victoria: Crown Western, 1995) at pages 11–74.

129 Frances Widdowson and Albert Howard, *Disrobing the Aboriginal Industry: The Deception behind Indigenous Cultural Preservation* (Montreal and Kingston: McGill-Queen's University Press, 2008) at pages 81–105.

130 "Comprehensive Claims" (July 13, 2015) on the Indigenous and Northern Affairs Canada website, https://www.aadnc-aandc.gc.ca/eng/1100100030577/1100100030578.

131 See BC Treaty Commission Annual Report 2017 at pages 36–39. See generally on the BC treaty process: Christopher McKee, *Treaty Talks in British Columbia: Building a New*

Relationship, 3rd ed. (Vancouver: UBC Press, 2009); Andrew Woolford, *Between Justice and Certainty: Treaty Making in British Columbia* (Vancouver: UBC Press, 2005); Penikett, *Reconciliation.*

132 For a review of some of the issues involved with proposals to improve the process, see Canada, British Columbia, and First Nations Summit, "Multilateral Engagement Process to Improve and Expedite Treaty Negotiations in British Columbia," May 24, 2016, which refers to several earlier reports and reviews.

133 Penikett, *Reconciliation* at page 171.

134 Ibid. at pages 174–84.

Chapter 6: Consultation, Accommodation, and Consent

1 For a fuller discussion, see Dwight Newman, *Revisiting the Duty to Consult Aboriginal Peoples* (Saskatoon: Purich, 2014).

2 See repeated references in *Tsilhqot'in Nation v. B.C.,* 2014 SCC 44 at paras. 77, 78, 80, and 88.

3 Thomas Isaac, *Aboriginal Law,* 5th ed. (Toronto: Carswell, Thomson Reuters, 2016) at page 385.

4 *Haida Nation v. B.C.,* 2004 SCC 73 at paras. 60–63; *Beckman v. Little Salmon,* 2010 SCC 53 at para. 48.

5 *Haida* at para. 63.

6 *Ktunaxa Nation v. B.C.,* 2017 SCC 54 at paras. 77, 83.

7 *Little Salmon* at para. 93 (full citations omitted).

8 *Guerin v. The Queen,* [1984] 2 S.C.R. 335 at page 388.

9 *R. v. Sparrow,* [1990] 1 S.C.R. 1075 at page 1119.

10 *R. v. Nikal,* [1996] 1 S.C.R. 1013 at para. 110.

11 *Delgamuukw v. B.C.,* [1997] 3 S.C.R. 1010 at para. 168.

12 *Haida* at para. 7.

13 *Taku River Tlingit First Nation v. B.C.,* 2004 SCC 74 at para. 25.

14 *Haida* at para. 14.

15 *Rio Tinto Alcan Inc. v. Carrier Sekani Tribal Council,* 2010 SCC 43.

16 *Rio Tinto* at para. 33.

17 *Rio Tinto* at para. 34.

18 *Haida* at para. 33.

19 *Haida* at para. 25.

20 *Little Salmon* at para. 53.

21 *Tsilhqot'in* at para. 80.

22 *Mikisew Cree First Nation v. Canada,* 2005 SCC 69 at para. 3.

23 *Little Salmon* at para. 71 (emphasis in original).

24 *Little Salmon* at para. 88.

25 *Little Salmon* at para. 107.

26 *Little Salmon* at para. 103.

27 *Rio Tinto* at para. 83.

28 Ibid.

29 *Behn v. Moulton Contracting Ltd,* 2013 SCC 26 at para 30.

30 *Clyde River (Hamlet) v. Petroleum Geo. Services Inc.,* 2017 SCC 40.

31 *Chippewas of the Thames First Nation v. Enbridge Pipelines Inc.,* 2017 SCC 41.

32 *Ktunaxa* at paras. 80–81.

33 *Rio Tinto* at para. 40 (citations omitted).

34 *Rio Tinto* at para. 44. The Federal Court of Appeal has held that there is no duty to consult on proposed legislation: *Canada v. Mikisew Cree,* 2016 FCA 311; leave to appeal granted by SCC, No. 37441, May 18, 2017.

35 *Mikisew Cree* at para. 34.

36 *Taku* at para. 46.

37 *Tsilhqot'in* at para. 79.

38 *Clyde River* at para. 43.

39 *Haida* at para. 39.

40 *Haida* at para. 40.

41 *Haida* at para. 42.

42 *Haida* at para. 44.

43 *Haida* at para. 45.

44 *Mikisew Cree* at para. 63.

45 *Mikisew Cree* at para. 64.

46 *Haida* at para. 51.

47 Ravina Bains and Kayla Ishkanian, *The Duty to Consult with Aboriginal Peoples: A Patchwork of Canadian Policies* (Vancouver: Fraser Institute, 2016) at page 13; for consultation policies generally see Newman, *Revisiting the Duty to Consult* at pages 115–41.

48 Bains and Ishkanian, *Duty to Consult with Aboriginal Peoples* at page 15.

49 Compare *Maple Lodge Farms v. Canada,* [1982] 2 S.C.R. 2; *Kanthasamy v. Canada,* 2015 SCC 61 at para. 32.

50 *Haida* at para. 47.

51 *Haida* at paras. 48–49.

52 *Haida* at para. 50; see *Chippewas of the Thames* at para 59.

53 *Chippewas of the Thames* at para. 60.

54 *Taku* at para. 32.

55 *Mikisew Cree* at para. 54.

56 *Mikisew Cree* at para. 66.

57 *Little Salmon* at para. 81.

58 *Delgamuukw* at para. 203.

59 For a discussion of the requirement for consent under Aboriginal law, international law, and industry standards, see Shin Imai, "Consult, Consent, and Veto: International Norms and Canadian Treaties," in *The Right Relationship: Reimagining the Implementation of Historical Treaties,* ed. John Borrows and Michael Coyle, at pages 370–408 (Toronto: University of Toronto Press, 2017).

60 *Haida* at para. 24.

61 *Haida* at para. 48.

62 *Mikisew Cree* at para. 66.

63 *Little Salmon* at para. 14.

64 *Ktunaxa* at para. 83.

65 *Tsilhqot'in* at para. 76.

66 See Chapter 7 at page 191, this book.

67 *Haida* at para. 36.

68 *Haida* at para. 42 (citations omitted).

69 *Mikisew Cree* at para. 65.

70 *Haida* at paras. 20, 25–27.

71 *Haida* at para. 27.
72 *Long Plain First Nation v. Canada,* 2015 FCA 177 at para. 161.
73 *Chartrand v. B.C.,* 2015 BCCA 345 at para. 69.
74 *Haida* at para. 53.
75 *Haida* at para. 53.
76 *Tsilhqot'in* at para. 78.
77 *Haida* at para. 53.
78 *Haida* at para 56.
79 *Taku* at para. 40.
80 *Little Salmon* at para. 39 (emphasis in original).
81 *Clyde River* at para. 23.
82 *Rio Tinto* at para. 58.
83 *Rio Tinto* at para. 37.
84 *Clyde River* at para. 24.
85 *Ktunaxa* at para. 84.
86 Isaac, *Aboriginal Law* at page 331.
87 Newman, *Revisiting the Duty to Consult* at page 19.
88 Sébastien Grammond, *Terms of Coexistence: Indigenous Peoples and Canadian Law* (Toronto: Carswell, 2013) at page 204.
89 Calvin Helin, *Dances with Dependency* (Vancouver: Orca Spirit, 2006) at page 30.
90 Natan Obed, "Free, Prior and Informed Consent and the Future of Inuit Self-Determination," *Northern Public Affairs* 4 (2016) at page 41.
91 *Ktunaxa* at para. 86.
92 See P.G. McHugh, *Aboriginal Title: The Modern Jurisprudence of Tribal Land Rights* (Oxford: Oxford University Press, 2011) at pages 147–58.
93 *Chippewas of the Thames* at paras. 41 and 2.
94 Newman, *Revisiting the Duty to Consult* at page 41.
95 *Haida* at para. 63.
96 *Little Salmon* at para. 48.
97 *Haida* at paras. 60–63.
98 *Gitxaala Nation v. Canada,* 2016 FCA 187 at paras. 329, 335.
99 Tom Flanagan, *First Nations? Second Thoughts,* 2nd ed. (Montreal and Kingston: McGill-Queen's University Press, 2008) at page 217.
100 *Rio Tinto* at para. 38 (citations omitted).
101 Michael J. Bryant, "The State of the Crown-Aboriginal Fiduciary Relationship: The Case for an Aboriginal Veto," in *From Recognition to Reconciliation: Essays on the Constitutional Entrenchment of Aboriginal and Treaty Rights,* ed. Patrick Macklem and Douglas Sanderson (Toronto: University of Toronto Press, 2016) at page 233.
102 See, for an example, *Gitxaala Nation.*
103 *Clyde River* at para. 47.
104 *Haida* at para. 48.
105 *Rio Tinto* at para. 34; see also para. 74.
106 *Little Salmon* at para. 21.
107 *Chippewas of the Thames* at para. 42.
108 *Haida* at para. 51.
109 *Guerin* at page 383.
110 No. 110, 1993, as amended.

Chapter 7: Indigenous and International Law

1 For a collection of papers discussing Aboriginal law, international law, and Indigenous laws, see Centre for International Governance Innovation (CIGI), *UNDRIP Implementation: Braiding International, Domestic and Indigenous Laws* (Waterloo, ON: CIGI, 2017).

2 *Canada's Residential Schools: Reconciliation,* vol. 6 of *TRC* at page 45.

3 *Honouring the Truth, Reconciling for the Future: Summary of the Final Report of the TRC* at page 16.

4 *Canada's Residential Schools: Reconciliation,* vol. 6 of *TRC* at page 76.

5 Ibid. at page 74.

6 Call to Action 45 in *Canada's Residential Schools: Reconciliation,* vol. 6 of *TRC* at page 37.

7 See Gordon Christie, "Culture, Self-Determination and Colonialism," *Indigenous Law Journal* 6 (2007) at page 13.

8 Aaron Mills, "The Lifeworlds of Law: On Understanding Indigenous Legal Orders Today," *McGill Law Journal* 61 (2016) at page 847.

9 It should be noted that this use of "common law" includes Quebec, even though that is a civil law jurisdiction: see Chapter 1, this book, at page 26.

10 *Alderville Indian Band v. Canada,* 2014 FC 747 at para. 40.

11 See generally H.L.A. Hart, *The Concept of Law* (Oxford: Clarendon Press, 1961) at pages 97–107.

12 *Miller v. Secretary of State for Exiting the European Community,* 2017 UKSC 5 at para. 60.

13 *Miller* at para. 173.

14 For a full discussion see Brian Z. Tamanaha, "Understanding Legal Pluralism: Past to Present, Local to Global," *Sydney Law Review* 30 (2008) at page 375.

15 John Borrows, *Canada's Indigenous Constitution* (Toronto: University of Toronto Press, 2010) at pages 107–24.

16 *Canada's Residential Schools: Reconciliation,* vol. 6 of *TRC* at pages 55–74.

17 See especially Borrows, *Canada's Indigenous Constitution* at Chapters 2 and 3; John Borrows, *Drawing Out Law: A Spirit's Guide* (Toronto: University of Toronto Press, 2010); John Borrows, *Recovering Canada: The Resurgence of Indigenous Laws* (Toronto: University of Toronto Press, 2002). For an introduction to Anishinaabe law, see Aaron Mills "Opichi: A Transformation Story, An Invitation to Anishinaabe (Ojibwe) Legal Order," *For the Defence* 34 (2013) at page 40.

18 *Federal Law–Civil Law Harmonization Act,* S.C. 2001, c. 4 Preamble.

19 Borrows, *Canada's Indigenous Constitution* at pages 24–28.

20 Ibid. at pages 33–35.

21 Ibid. at page 35.

22 Ibid. at pages 47–48.

23 Ibid. at page 51.

24 George Copway (Kah-Ge-Ga-Gah-Bowh), *The Traditional History and Characteristic Sketches of the Ojibway Nation* (London: Charles Gilpin, 1850) at page 144.

25 *Tsilhqot'in v. B.C.,* 2007 BCSC 1700 at paras. 426–35.

26 Valerie Napoleon, *Ayook: Gitksan Legal Order, Law and Legal Theory* (PhD dissertation, University of Victoria, 2009), http://dspace.library.uvic.ca. See also Antonio Mills, *Eagle Down Is Our Law: Witsuwit'en Law, Feasts, and Land Claims* (Vancouver: UBC Press, 1994) especially Chapter 5 on Wet'suwet'en law.

27 Napoleon, *Ayook* at page 66.

28 Ibid. at page 71.

29 Ibid. at page 156.

30 See Sébastian Grammond, *Terms of Coexistence: Indigenous Peoples and Canadian Law* (Toronto: Carswell, 2013) at page 369.

31 Borrows, *Canada's Indigenous Constitution* at page 289.

32 Mills, "Lifeworlds of Law" at page 865.

33 Val Napoleon, "Thinking about Indigenous Legal Orders" (research paper for the National Centre for First Nations Governance, June 2007) at page 2.

34 See John Austin, *The Province of Jurisprudence Determined* (1832; London: Weidenfeld and Nicolson, 1955) at pages 30–33; Hart, *The Concept of Law* at pages 89–96.

35 Napoleon, *Ayook*, at pages 240–312.

36 *R. v. Van der Peet*, [1996] 2 S.C.R. 507 at para. 42, quoting Mark Walters.

37 *R. v. Machekequonabe*, (1897) 2 C.C.C. 138, 28 O.R. 309 (Ont. Div. Ct.).

38 Sidney Harring, "The Wendigo Killings," in *Violent Crime in North America,* ed. Louis A. Knafla, 75–103 (Westport, CT: Praeger, 2003); Val Napoleon and Hadley Friedland, "Indigenous Legal Traditions: Roots to Renaissance," in Markus D. Dubber and Tatjana Hörnle, *Oxford Handbook of Criminal Law* (Oxford: Oxford University Press, 2014); Borrows, *Canada's Indigenous Constitution* at pages 81–84; Borrows, *Drawing Out Law* at pages 223–27.

39 *Thomas v. Norris,* 1992 CanLII 354 (B.C.S.C.).

40 See page 17, this book.

41 Christine Zuni Cruz, "Law of the Land – Recognition and Resurgence in Indigenous Law and Justice Systems," in *Indigenous Peoples and the Law: Comparative and Critical Perspectives,* ed. Benjamin Richardson (Oxford: Hart Publishing, 2009) at page 321.

42 Australian Law Reform Commission, *The Recognition of Aboriginal Customary Law,* Report No. 31 (Canberra: Australian Government Publishing Service, 1986) at para. 85.

43 *Native Title Act 1993* (Aust.), Section 223(1), and see *Yorta Yorta v. Victoria,* [2002] HCA 58 at para. 37. For a detailed comparison of Canadian and Australian law on proof of Aboriginal title, see P.G. McHugh, *Aboriginal Title: The Modern Jurisprudence of Tribal Land Rights* (Oxford: Oxford University Press, 2011) at Chapter 3.

44 For custom as a source of the common law, see C.K. Allen, *Law in the Making,* 7th ed. (Oxford: Oxford University Press, 1964) at Chapter 1.

45 John Borrows, "With or Without You: First Nations Law (in Canada)," *McGill Law Journal* 41 (1996) at pages 635–46; Grammond, *Terms of Coexistence*, at pages 374–91.

46 Grammond, *Terms of Coexistence*, at page 376.

47 Section 2(1) definition of "council of the band" para. (d).

48 See Shin Imai, *The 2017 Annotated Indian Act and Aboriginal Constitutional Provisions* (Toronto: Carswell, 2016) at page 19.

49 S.C. 2008, c. 30, section 1.2.

50 Tom Flanagan, Christopher Alcantara, and André Le Dressay, *Beyond the Indian Act: Restoring Aboriginal Property Rights* (Montreal and Kingston: McGill-Queen's University Press, 2010) at page 74; see generally pages 73–90.

51 *Lower Nicola Indian Band v. Trans-Canada Displays Ltd,* 2000 BCSC 1209 at para. 151.

52 *Van der Peet* at para 263; and see this book, Chapter 3, at page 64; Grammond, *Terms of Coexistence* at page 376.

53 *Van der Peet* at para. 49.

54 *R. v. Marshall/R. v. Bernard,* 2005 SCC 43 at para. 48; *Tsilhqot'in* at para. 50.

55 *Van der Peet* at para. 42, quoting Prof. Brian Slattery.

56 *Delgamuukw* at para. 130; see also *R. v. Sparrow,* [1990] 1 S.C.R. 1075 at page 1112.

57 *Tsilhqot'in Nation v. B.C.,* 2014 SCC 44 at para. 32.

58 *R. v. Sappier,* 2006 SCC 54 at para. 45.

59 Kent McNeil, "Indigenous Law and Aboriginal Title" (Osgoode Hall Law School Research Paper Series No. 2, 2017).

60 See *Delgamuukw* at paras. 145, 148, 157; *Marshall/Bernard* at paras. 129, 139; *Tsilhqot'in* at paras. 35, 41.

61 *Delgamuukw* at paras. 112 and 145.

62 Borrows, *Canada's Indigenous Constitution* at page 260.

63 Australian Law Reform Commission, *Recognition,* at para. 221.

64 See Australian Law Reform Commission, *Recognition,* Appendix A for draft bill.

65 Law Commission of Canada, *Justice Within: Indigenous Legal Traditions* (Ottawa: Law Commission of Canada, 2006).

66 Law Commission of Canada, *Justice Within* at page 25.

67 John Borrows, "Indigenous Legal Traditions in Canada," available on Government of Canada website, http://publications.gc.ca/collections/collection_2008/lcc-cdc/JL2-66 -2006E.pdf.

68 See Borrows, *Canada's Indigenous Constitution,* Chapter 7.

69 Napoleon and Friedland, "Indigenous Legal Traditions" at page 240.

70 See the Accessing Justice and Reconciliation Project website at www.indigenousbar.ca/ indigenouslaw. For a study of initiatives in three different Coast Salish communities, see Bruce Miller, *The Problem of Justice: Tradition and Law in the Coast Salish World* (Lincoln: University of Nebraska Press, 2001).

71 Napoleon and Friedland, "Indigenous Legal Traditions" at page 240; the Continuing Legal Education Society of British Columbia offered a two-day professional development session, "Indigenous Legal Orders and the Common Law," in Vancouver on November 15 and 16, 2012.

72 Fraser Harland, "Introduction: Moving from the *Why* to the *How* of Indigenous Law," *McGill Law Journal* 61 (2016) at page 721; John Borrows, "Foreword: Indigenous Law, Lands and Literature," *Windsor Yearbook of Access to Justice* 33 (2016) at page v.

73 Lance Finch, "The Duty to Learn: Taking Account of Indigenous Legal Orders in Practice" (paper delivered at Continuing Legal Education Society of BC, "Indigenous Legal Orders and the Common Law," November 2012).

74 Wendy Stueck, "UVic Proposes Joint Indigenous–Canadian Common Law Degree," *Globe and Mail,* November 28, 2016; for a detailed article on teaching Indigenous laws, see John Borrows, "Heroes, Tricksters, Monsters and Caretakers: Indigenous Law and Legal Education," *McGill Law Journal* 61 (2016) at page 795.

75 Thomas Rohner, "Nunavut to Revive Law School, Quassa Says," *Nunatsiaq Online,* March 15, 2016, http://www.nunatsiaqonline.ca/stories/article/65674nunavut_ lawyer_training_program_to_be_revived/; Geoff Ellwand, "Nunavut Government Pushes for Sask. Law Program," *Canadian Lawyer,* January 2017 at page 11.

76 Napoleon and Friedland, "Indigenous Legal Traditions" at page 236; Justine Hunter, "Traditional Justice," *Globe and Mail,* January 8, 2016. Part 7 of Alberta's *Métis Settlement Act,* R.S.A. 2000 c. M-14, establishes the Métis Settlements Appeal Tribunal to resolve disputes under that legislation "with a view to preserving Métis culture and identity."

77 J. Scofield, "First Nations Start Independent Civil Court," *The Lawyer's Weekly,* November 14, 2016.

78 See Frances Widdowson and Albert Howard, *Disrobing the Aboriginal Industry: The Deception behind Indigenous Cultural Preservation* (Montreal and Kingston: McGill-Queen's University Press, 2008) at Chapter 5.

79 Hadley Friedland, "*Waniska*: Reimagining the Future with Indigenous Legal Traditions," *Windsor Yearbook of Access to Justice* (2016) at pages 90–92; Borrows, *Canada's Indigenous Constitution* at pages 148–49; Marsha Lederman, "Apologies over Cultural Appropriation Debate 'Insufficient'": Indigenous Scholar," *Globe and Mail*, May 16, 2017.

80 Hadley Friedland and Val Napoleon, "Gathering the Threads," *Lakehead Law Journal* 1 (2016–17) at pages 17–18.

81 J.S. Furnivall, *Colonial Policy and Practice: A Comparative Study of Burma and Netherlands India* (Cambridge: Cambridge University Press, 1948) at page 304.

82 *Canada's Residential Schools: Reconciliation,* vol. 6 of *TRC* at page 51.

83 Brenda Gunn, "Beyond Van der Peet," in CIGI, *UNDRIP Implementation* at page 36.

84 For a discussion of the issues raised by the jurisdiction of US Indian tribal courts, see William Canby, *American Indian Law in a Nutshell,* 6th ed. (St. Paul, MN: West, 2015) at Chapter 5. The relationship between Aboriginal criminal justice systems and the Canadian Charter of Rights and Freedoms is explored in David Milward, *Aboriginal Justice and the Charter: Realizing a Culturally Sensitive Interpretation of Legal Rights* (Vancouver: UBC Press, 2012).

85 For a comprehensive text on Indigenous peoples and international law, see Patrick Thornberry, *Indigenous People and Human Rights* (Manchester: Manchester University Press, 2002).

86 Grace Li Xiu Woo, *Ghost Dancing with Colonialism: Decolonization and Indigenous Rights at the Supreme Court of Canada* (Vancouver: UBC Press, 2011) at pages 80–82.

87 One current example is the petition of the Hul'qumi'num Treaty Group, submitted in 2007 to the Inter-American Commission on Human Rights, challenging the BC treaty process. The petition was ruled admissible in 2009, but was not decided at the time of writing. See Petition 592–07; Report No. 105/92 (2009).

88 *Lovelace v. Canada,* (1981), U.N. Doc. A/36/40 at 166. A similar action failed in *Canada v. Lavell,* [1974] S.C.R. 1349.

89 *Miller* at para. 55.

90 *Miller* at para. 55.

91 *Capital Cities Comm. v. C.R.T.C.,* [1978] 2 SCR 141 at page 173; *Ordon Estate v. Grail,* [1998] 3 S.C.R. 437 at para. 137.

92 U.N. Doc. A/RES/61/295 (2007).

93 Declaration and Resolutions adopted by the General Assembly, Organization of American States, 46th Regular Session, June 13–15, 2016, Santa Domingo, Res. 2888; available at the OAS website, http://www.oas.org/consejo/GENERAL%20ASSEMBLY/Resoluciones-Declaraciones.asp.

94 M. Barelli, "The Role of Soft Law in the International Legal System: The Case of the United Nations Declaration on the Rights of Indigenous Peoples," *International and Comparative Law Quarterly* 58 (2009) at page 957.

95 See S. James Anaya, *Report of the Special Rapporteur on the Rights of Indigenous People,* UN Doc. A/68/317 (presented to the General Assembly, 68th Sess., 2013) at paras. 60 to 67.

96 Call to Action 43 in *Honouring the Truth, Reconciling for the Future: Summary of the Final Report of the TRC* at page 244.

97 John Borrows "Revitalizing Canada's Indigenous Constitution," in CIGI, *UNDRIP Implementation* at pages 20–27.

98 *Rio Tinto Alcan Inc. v. Carrier Sekani Tribal Council,* 2010 SCC 43 at para. 44.

99 *Haida Nation v. B.C.,* 2004 SCC 73 at para. 48.

100 *Tsilhqot'in* at para. 76.

101 For the contrary view, see S. James Anaya, *Report of the Special Rapporteur on the Situation of Human Rights and Fundamental Freedoms of Indigenous Peoples,* UN Doc A/HRC/12/34 (presented to the Human Rights Committee, 12th. Sess., 2009) at paras. 46–49; Paul Joffe, "'Veto' and 'Consent' – Significant Differences" (paper prepared October 3, 2017), http://quakerservice.ca/wp-content/uploads/2016/03/Veto-and -Consent-Significant-differences-Joffe.pdf.

102 See Chapter 5, this book, at page 134.

103 *Snuneymuxw First Nation v. Board of Education – School District #68,* 2014 BCSC 1173 at para. 59.

104 See, for examples, *Taku River Tlingit v. Canada,* 2016 YKSC 7 at para. 99; *Nunatakavut Community Council v. Canada,* 2015 FC 981 at para. 103. A draft of UNDRIP was referenced by the SCC in *Mitchell v. M.N.R.,* 2001 SCC 33 at para. 81.

105 See Bill C-262, First Reading, April 21, 2016, 42nd Parl., 1st Session.

106 See House of Commons Debates, 41st Parliament, 2nd session, Hansard Number 185 for March 12, 2015, at 1830 (Carolyn Bennett) (http://www.parl.gc.ca/HousePublications/Publication.aspx?Pub=Hansard&Doc=185&Parl=41&Ses=2&Language=E&Mode=1#8614996).

107 John Paul Tasker, "Liberal Government Backs Bill That Demands Full Implementation of UN Indigenous Rights Declaration," CBC News, November 21, 2017, http://www.cbc.ca/news/politics/wilson-raybould-backs-undrip-bill-1.4412037.

108 Tim Fontaine, "Canada Removing Objector Status to UN Declaration on the Rights of Indigenous Peoples," CBC News, May 8, 2016 (emphasis added), http://www.cbc.ca/news/indigenous/canada-position-un-declaration-indigenous-peoples-1.3572777.

109 "Justice Minister Jody Wilson-Raybould Says Adopting UNDRIP into Canadian Law 'Unworkable,'" APTN National News, July 12, 2016, http://aptnnews.ca/2016/07/12/justice-minister-jody-wilson-raybould-says-adopting-undrip-into-canadian-law -unworkable/.

110 Jeffrey Hewitt, "Options for Implementing UNDRIP without Creating Another Empty Box," in CIGI, *UNDRIP Implementation.*

111 "Principles Respecting the Government of Canada's Relationship with Indigenous Peoples," on the Department of Justice website, http://www.justice.gc.ca/eng/csj-sjc/principles-principes.html.

112 *R. v. Badger,* [1996] 1 S.C.R. 771 at para. 41.

113 Gib van Ert, "Three Good Reasons Why UNDRIP Can't Be Law – and One Good Reason Why It Can," *The Advocate* 75 (2017) at page 34.

114 Arthur Manuel and Ronald Derrickson, *The Reconciliation Manifesto: Recovering the Land, Rebuilding the Economy* (Toronto: Lorimer, 2017) at page 55, see also pages 191–99.

115 Declaration and Resolutions adopted by the General Assembly, Organization of American States, 46th Regular Session, June 13–15, 2016, Santa Domingo, Res. 2888; available at the OAS website, http://www.oas.org/consejo/GENERAL%20ASSEMBLY/Resoluciones-Declaraciones.asp.

116 Footnote 2 to the Declaration; University of Ottawa Human Rights Research and Education Centre, "OAS General Assembly Adopts the American Declaration on the

Rights of Indigenous Peoples," available at the centre's website, https://cdp-hrc.uottawa.
ca/en/oas-general-assembly-adopts-american-declaration-rights-indigenous-peoples.
·117 For a detailed comparison, see Indian Law Resource Center, *The American Declaration on the Rights of Indigenous Peoples: Background Materials and Strategies for Implementation* (2017) at pages 3–21, http://indianlaw.org/adrip/adrip-background-materials-strategies-implementation.
118 See Articles III, XXI, XXIII.2, XXV.3, XXIX.4, IV and XXXVI in ADRIP.

Chapter 8: A Just Society?

1 *Daniels v. Canada,* 2016 SCC 12.
2 See *Report of the Royal Commission on Aboriginal Peoples* (hereafter *RCAP*), vol. 1, *Looking Forward, Looking Back* (Ottawa: Minister of Supply and Services Canada, 1996) at chapter 9.
3 *Manitoba Métis Federation v. Canada,* 2013 SCC 14 at paras. 53–59.
4 *R. v. Sappier,* 2006 SCC 54 at para. 26.
5 *Tsilhqot'in Nation v. B.C.,* 2014 SCC 44 at para. 74.
6 See generally Lewis Henry Morgan, *Houses and House-Life of the American Aborigines* (Washington: Government Printing Office, 1881) at pages 63–98; Tom Flanagan, Christopher Alcantara, and André Le Dressay, *Beyond the Indian Act: Restoring Aboriginal Property Rights* (Montreal and Kingston: McGill-Queen's University Press, 2010) at pages 30–41. For one example, see the evidence on the Nisga'a given in *Calder v. British Columbia,* [1973] S.C.R. 313 at pages 359–75.
7 *Behn v. Moulton Contracting Ltd,* 2013 SCC 26 at paras. 34–35.
8 For a discussion of who can advance Aboriginal rights and treaty claims, see Francesca Allodi-Ross, "Who Calls the Shots? Balancing Individual and Collective Interests in the Assertion of Aboriginal and Treaty Harvesting Rights," in *The Right Relationship: Reimagining the Implementation of Historical Treaties,* ed. John Borrows and Michael Coyle, 149–63 (Toronto: University of Toronto Press, 2017).
9 Lawrence Krador, ed. and trans., *The Ethnological Notebooks of Karl Marx,* 2nd ed. (1880–82. Assen, Netherlands: Van Gorcum, 1974) *passim*; Frederick Engels, *The Origin of the Family,* trans. Ernest Unterman (1884. Chicago: Charles Kerr, 1908) at Chapter 3.
10 Rosa Luxemburg, *The Complete Works of Rosa Luxemburg,* ed. Peter Hudis (London: Verso, 2013) vol. 1 at page 162.
11 Tom Flanagan, *First Nations? Second Thoughts,* 2nd ed. (Montreal and Kingston: McGill-Queen's University Press, 2008) at page 133.
12 See Flanagan, Alcantara, and Dressay, *Beyond the Indian Act;* Michael Fabris, *Beyond the New Dawes Act: A Critique of the First Nations Property Ownership Act* (master's thesis, University of BC, 2016) at page 6.
13 Resolution no. 44/2010, Assembly of First Nations Annual General Assembly, July 22, 2010.
14 Thomas King, *The Inconvenient Indian: A Curious Account of Native People in North America* (Toronto: Anchor Canada, 2013) at pages 130–32.
15 Ibid. at pages 199–200.
16 Ibid. at pages 252–58. See also Thomas Berger, *Village Journey: The Report of the Alaska Native Review Commission* (New York: Hill and Wang, 1985) for his report on the original legislation.
17 *Tsilhqot'in* at para. 125.

18 Ardith Walkem, "Constructing the Constitutional Box: The Supreme Court's Section 35(1) Reasoning," in *Box of Treasures or Empty Box? Twenty Years of Section 35*, ed. Ardith Walkem and Halie Bruce (Penticton, BC: Theytus, 2003) at page 204.

19 Kent McNeil, "Defining Aboriginal Title in the 1990s" (12th Annual Robarts Lecture, York University, March 25, 1998) at page 17.

20 *R. v. Van der Peet*, [1996] 2 S.C.R. 507 at para. 28.

21 *Delgamuukw v. The Queen*, [1997] 3 S.C.R. 1010 at para. 165.

22 Ibid.; *R. v. Gladstone*, [1996] 2 S.C.R. 723 at para. 75.

23 *Wewaykum Indian Band v. Canada*, 2002 SCC 79 at para. 96.

24 *R. v. Badger*, [1996] 1 S.C.R. 771 at paras. 54 and 66.

25 *Skeetchestn Indian Band v. B.C.*, 2000 BCCA 525 at para. 5.

26 *Skeetchestn* at para. 6.

27 *Tsilhqot'in* at para. 9.

28 Gordon Christie, "Aboriginal Title and Private Property," in *Aboriginal Law since Delgamuukw*, ed. Maria Morellato, at pages 177–204 (Aurora, ON: Canada Law Book, 2009).

29 Thomas Isaac and Arend Hoekstra, "Uncertainty in Dealing with Private Property Rights and Aboriginal Title," in the Cassels Brock newsletter, September 27, 2017, http://www.casselsbrock.com/CBNewsletter/Uncertainty_in_Dealing_with_Private_Property_Rights_and_Aboriginal_Title.

30 *Fejo v. Northern Territory of Australia*, [1998] HCA 58 at para. 43.

31 *Chippewas of Sarnia Band v. Canada*, (2000), 195 D.L.R. (4th) 135 (Ont. C.A.), leave to appeal to SCC denied, 205 D.L.R. (4th) vii. See also *Skeetchestn*; *Tsilhqot'in*, 2007 BCSC 1700 at paras. 982–1000, 2012 BCCA 285 at para. 219.

32 John Borrows, "Aboriginal Title and Private Property," *Supreme Court Law Review* 71 (2015) at page 124.

33 *Saik'uz First Nation v. Rio Tinto Alcan Inc.*, 2015 BCCA 154.

34 *Saik'uz* at para. 61.

35 Borrows, "Aboriginal Title and Private Property" at page 109.

36 Ibid. at page 117.

37 Ibid. at page 112.

38 Christie, "Aboriginal Title and Private Property" at page 200.

39 *Delgamuukw* at para. 165.

40 Thomas Isaac, *Aboriginal Law*, 5th ed. (Toronto: Carswell, Thomson Reuters, 2016) at page 103.

41 Ibid. at page 105.

42 *Delgamuukw* at para. 186.

43 *Tsilhqot'in* at para. 83.

44 *Tsilhqot'in* at para. 86.

45 See *RCAP*, vol. 2, *Restructuring the Relationship*, Chapter 4, section 6.3 at pages 582–86, recommendations 2.4.15 to 2.4.20; Kent McNeil, "Reconciliation and Third Party Interests," *Indigenous Law Journal* 8 (2010) at page 23; Ronald St. John Macdonald (chair of research committee), *Native Rights in Canada* (Toronto: Indian-Eskimo Association, 1970) at pages 159–60.

46 *William v. Riverside Forest Products Ltd*, 2002 BCSC 1199 at para. 16; *Cowichan Tribes v. Canada*, 2017 BCSC 1575; *Council of the Haida Nation v. B.C.*, 2017 BCSC 1665.

47 *Council of the Haida Nation* at para. 52.

48 *Guerin v. The Queen*, [1984] 2 S.C.R. 335.

49 *R. v. Sparrow*, [1990] 1 S.C.R. 1075.

50 Compare the ineffectiveness of the commitment to promote equal opportunity in Section 36 of the *Constitution Act, 1982,* as exemplified in *Cape Breton v. Nova Scotia,* 2009 NSCA 44 at para. 79; leave to appeal to SCC denied, CanLII 71470, 2009.

51 *Sparrow* at page 1109.

52 *Sparrow* at page 1099.

53 *Haida Nation v. B.C.,* 2004 SCC 73.

54 *Manitoba Métis.*

55 *R. v. Marshall,* [1999] 3 S.C.R. 456 *(Marshall I); Mikisew Cree First Nation v. Canada,* 2005 SCC 69.

56 *R. v. Pamajewon,* [1996] 2 S.C.R. 821.

57 *Van der Peet; R. v. Powley,* 2003 SCC 43.

58 P.G. McHugh, *Aboriginal Title: The Modern Jurisprudence of Tribal Land Rights* (Oxford: Oxford University Press, 2011) at page x.

59 *Musqueam Indian Band v. Canada,* 2004 FC 579 (Garden City lands); *Musqueam Indian Band v. British Columbia,* 2005 BCCA 128 (UBC golf course); *Musqueam Indian Band v. British Columbia,* 2005 BCSC 1069 (relocation of casino).

60 *Musqueam First Nation v. British Columbia,* 2012 BCCA 178.

61 *Musqueam Indian Band v. Glass,* 2000 SCC 52.

62 *Canada v. Musqueam First Nation,* 2008 FCA 214 (401 Burrard Street and Sinclair Centre).

63 *Musqueam Indian Band v. Musqueam Indian Band (Board of Review),* 2016 SCC 36.

64 James I. Reynolds, "'The Beauty of Compromise': The Musqueam Reconciliation Agreement," in *Aboriginal Law Conference 2008* (Vancouver: Continuing Legal Education Society, 2008); the Musqueam Reconciliation Agreement is available on the BC government website, https://www2.gov.bc.ca/gov/content/environment/natural-resource -stewardship/consulting-with-first-nations/first-nations-negotiations/first-nations -a-z-listing/musqueam-indian-band.

65 The MST Development Corporation website is at http://mstdevelopment.ca/.

66 *McDiarmid Lumber Ltd v. God's Lake First Nation,* 2006 SCC 58 at para. 97.

67 *God's Lake* at para. 82.

68 *God's Lake* at para. 95.

69 *God's Lake* at para. 99.

70 *God's Lake* at para. 107.

71 *RCAP,* vol. 3, *Gathering Strength* at page 1.

72 Health Canada, "Drinking Water Advisories: First Nations South of 60," https://www. canada.ca/en/health-canada/topics/health-environment/water-quality-health/drinking -water/advisories-first-nations-south-60.html.

73 *God's Lake* at para. 124.

74 *Delgamuukw* at para. 186.

75 *Haida* at para. 14.

76 *British Columbia v. Okanagan Indian Band,* 2003 SCC 71.

77 Valerie Napoleon, *Ayook: Gitksan Legal Order, Law and Legal Theory* (PhD dissertation, University of Victoria, 2009) at page 236, available at http://dspace.library.uvic.ca.

78 For an example involving the Mi'kmaq, see John Borrows, *Canada's Indigenous Constitution* (Toronto: University of Toronto Press, 2010) at pages 68–69.

79 *Clyde River (Hamlet) v. Petroleum Geo. Services Inc.,* 2017 SCC 40 at para. 24.

80 Gordon Christie, "Who Makes Decisions over Aboriginal Title Lands?" *UBC Law Review* 48 (2015) at page 784.

81 Halie Bruce and Ardith Walkem, "Bringing Our Living Constitutions Home," in Walkem and Bruce, *Box of Treasures* at page 355.

82 *Van der Peet* at para. 49.

83 *Lax Kw'alaams Indian Band v. Canada,* 2011 SCC 56.

84 *Lax Kw'alaams* at para. 12.

85 Mary Locke Macaulay, *Aboriginal and Treaty Rights Practice* (Toronto: Carswell, 2000), Preface.

86 *Tsilhqot'in v. British Columbia,* 2007 BCSC 1700 at paras. 1357, 1360.

87 *Canada v. Lameman,* 2008 SCC 14 at para. 13.

88 *Guerin* at pages 389–90.

89 *Manitoba Métis* at paras. 140–43.

90 See *Buffalo v. Canada,* 2016 FCA 223, leave to appeal to SCC denied, No. 37280, March 9, 2017; reconsideration denied, June 22, 2017; *Peter Ballantyne Cree Nation v. Canada,* 2017 SKCA 5, leave to appeal to SCC denied, No. 37485, June 22, 2017. Limitation defences do not apply to claims made under the *Specific Claims Act,* S.C. 2008, c. 22, s. 19.

91 Call to Action 26 in *Canada's Residential Schools: Reconciliation,* vol. 6 of *TRC* at page 214.

92 *Sparrow* at page 1105.

93 *Tsilhqot'in* at para. 18.

94 *Delgamuukw* at para. 186.

95 *Beckman v. Little Salmon,* 2010 SCC 53 at para. 103.

96 *Tsilhqot'in* (BCSC) at para. 1360.

97 Roger Fisher and William Ury, *Getting to Yes: Negotiating Agreement without Giving In* (New York: Penguin, 1983) at pages 101–11.

98 For an example of the federal government failing to live up to its stated intention to resolve specific claims by negotiation, see Auditor General of Canada, *First Nations Specific Claims,* Report 6 of the *2016 Fall Reports of the Auditor General of Canada* (Ottawa: Office of the Auditor General, November 29, 2016) at paras. 6.39–6.47.

99 *RCAP,* vol. 2, *Restructuring the Relationship,* Chapter 4, section 1 at page 420.

100 Assembly of First Nations, "Negotiations Background Paper" (January 12–13, 2005), quoted by Tony Penikett, *Reconciliation: First Nations Treaty Making in British Columbia* (Vancouver: Douglas and McIntyre, 2006) at page 259.

101 Christopher Alcantara, *Negotiating the Deal: Comprehensive Land Claims Agreements in Canada* (Toronto: University of Toronto Press, 2013).

102 Peter Hutchins, "Conclusion," in *Aboriginal Title and Indigenous Peoples: Canada, Australia, and New Zealand,* ed. Louis Knafla and Haijo Westra (Vancouver: UBC Press, 2010) at page 224.

103 Penikett, *Reconciliation* at pages 218–27; and generally Stephen Goldberg, *Dispute Resolution: Negotiation Mediation and Other Processes,* 6th. ed. (New York: Wolters, Kluwer, 2012).

104 Greg Poelzer and Ken Coates, *From Treaty Peoples to Treaty Nation: A Road Map for All Canadians* (Vancouver: UBC Press, 2015) at page 119.

105 Ibid. at page 96.

106 Ibid. at page 110.

107 *RCAP,* vol. 5, *Renewal: A Twenty-Year Commitment* at pages 54–89.

108 Ibid. at page 55.

109 See statements of Justices Moldaver and Karakatsanis of the SCC that it is not the job of judges to create law, in Oliver Fitgerald, "Distant Echoes: Discussing Judicial Activism

at Canadian and American Supreme Court Nomination Hearings," *Constitutional Forum* 25 (2016) at pages 39–40.

110 *Paul v. B.C.*, 2003 SCC 55 at para. 29.

111 For statements by the former chief justice of Canada on judicial law making, see Beverley McLachlin C.J.C., "Judicial Power and Democracy" (annual lecture, Singapore Academy of Law, September 14, 2000), and "The Role of Judges in Modern Society" (presentation, Fourth Worldwide Common Law Judiciary Conference, Vancouver, BC, May 5, 2001).

112 J.A.G. Griffith, *The Politics of the Judiciary*, 4th ed. (London: Fontana, 1991) at page 319.

113 Joel Bakan, *Just Words: Constitutional Rights and Social Wrongs* (Toronto: University of Toronto Press, 1997) at pages 61–62. For other studies of how judicial attitudes affect SCC decisions, see C.L. Ostberg and Matthew E. Wetstein, *Attitudinal Decision Making in the Supreme Court of Canada* (Vancouver: UBC Press, 2007); Donald R. Songer, Susan Johnson, C.L. Ostberg, and Matthew Wetstein, *Laws, Ideology and Collegiality: Judicial Behaviour in the Supreme Court of Canada* (Montreal and Kingston: McGill-Queen's University Press, 2012); Emmett Macfarlane, *Governing from the Bench: The Supreme Court of Canada and the Judicial Role* (Vancouver: UBC Press, 2012).

114 *Van der Peet* at para. 302.

115 It should be noted that such preconceptions are distinct from bias in the sense of being predisposed to a particular result and not having an open mind: *Wewaykum Indian Band v. Canada [No. 2]*, 2003 SCC 45 at para. 58, although the distinction may be difficult to apply in practice.

116 Beverley McLachlin C.J.C., "Judging in a Democratic State" (Sixth Templeton Lecture on Democracy, June 3, 2004); Macfarlane, *Governing from the Bench* at pages 56–67.

117 *R. v. S. (R.D.)*, [1997] 3 S.C.R. 484 at para. 38.

118 Macfarlane, *Governing from the Bench* at page 58, citing Chief Justice McLachlin.

119 Frances Widdowson and Albert Howard, *Disrobing the Aboriginal Industry: The Deception behind Indigenous Cultural Preservation* (Montreal and Kingston: McGill-Queen's University Press, 2008) at page 259.

120 King, *The Inconvenient Indian* at page 158.

121 Ibid. at page 247.

122 See Kerry Wilkins, "Conclusion," in *Advancing Aboriginal Claims: Visions/Strategies/Directions*, ed. Kerry Wilkins, 288–312 (Saskatoon: Purich, 2004).

123 Beverley McLachlin C.J.C., "Respecting Democratic Roles," *Constitutional Forum* 12 (2002) at page 18.

124 Andrew Griffith, "Diversity among Federal and Provincial Judges," *Policy Options*, May 4, 2016.

125 For a summary of judicial accountability, see Beverley McLachlin C.J.C., "Judicial Accountability" (presentation, Conference on Law and Parliament, November 2, 2006). For a detailed account of "regulatory mechanisms" for judges in Canada, see Adam Dodek and Richard Devlin, "'Fighting Words': Regulating Judges in Canada," in *Regulating Judges: Beyond Independence and Accountability*, ed. Richard Devlin and Adam Dodek, 76–104 (Cheltenham, UK: Edward Elgar Publishing, 2016).

126 Kent Roach, *The Supreme Court on Trial: Judicial Activism or Democratic Dialogue?* (Toronto: Irwin, 2016); Macfarlane, *Governing from the Bench* at pages 161–72; *Corbiere v. Canada*, [1999] 2 S.C.R. 203 at para. 116.

127 Macfarlane, *Governing from the Bench*, at page 55.

128 Christopher Manfredi, "Fear, Hope and Misunderstanding," in Wilkins, *Advancing Aboriginal Claims*.

129 J.A.G. Griffith, *Politics of the Judiciary* at page 314.
130 There is a limited exception in that judges can take judicial notice of undisputed historical facts and conduct research into such facts: *R. v. Sioui,* [1990] 1 S.C.R. 1025 at page 1050.
131 *Rules of the Supreme Court of Canada,* Rule 59(3).
132 *Reference re Remuneration of the Judges of Provincial Court (PEI),* [1997] 3 S.C.R. 3 at para. 82.
133 Macfarlane, *Governing from the Bench* at pages 93–99.
134 *Rules of the Supreme Court of Canada,* Rule 42(4), (5).
135 *Rules of the Supreme Court of Canada,* Rule 71(5).
136 *R. v. Marshall,* [1999] 3 S.C.R. 533.
137 *Wewaykum Indian Band v. Canada [No. 2],* 2003 SCC 45.
138 Michael Ignatieff, "Afterword," in *From Recognition to Reconciliation: Essays on the Constitutional Entrenchment of Aboriginal and Treaty Rights,* ed. Patrick Macklem and Douglas Sanderson (Toronto: University of Toronto Press, 2016) at page 509.
139 *RCAP,* vol. 2, *Restructuring the Relationship,* Chapter 4, section 6.4, recommendations 2.4.29 to 2.4.41 at pages 591–618.
140 Miguel Martinez, *Study on Treaties, Agreements and Other Constructive Arrangements between States and Indigenous Populations,* UN Doc. E/CN.4/Sub.2/1999/20 (June 22, 1999) at paras. 306–11.
141 Ibid. at para. 254.
142 For the lack of action on the RCAP recommendations, see Assembly of First Nations, *Royal Commission on Aboriginal Peoples at 10 Years: A Report Card,* 2006, http://www.cbc.ca/news2/background/aboriginals/pdf/afn_rcap.pdf; see also "Sharing the Land, Sharing a Future" (RCAP 20th Anniversary Conference, organized by Queen's University School of Policy Studies and the National Centre for Truth and Reconciliation at the University of Manitoba, November 2–4, 2016), http://www.queensu.ca/sps/rcap20.
143 James Anaya, *Report of the Special Rapporteur on the Situation of Indigenous Peoples in Canada,* UN Doc. A/HRC/27/52/Add.2 (July 4, 2014) at paras. 15–31.
144 Aboriginal Affairs and Northern Development Canada, *The Community Well-Being Index: Well-Being in First Nations Communities, 1981–2011* (Ottawa: AANDC, 2015).

Cases Cited

Note: Cases shown in bold are the short form of the case name used in the text of this book. The complete name is given below against each case together with its citation.

A

Adams – *R. v. Adams,* [1996] 3 S.C.R. 101.
Ahousaht Indian Band v. Canada, 2009 BCSC 1494, aff'd 2011 BCCA 237; 2013 BCCA 300.
Alberta v. Elder Advocates of Alberta Society, [2001] 2 S.C.R. 261.
Alderville Indian Band v. Canada, 2014 FC 747.
Anonymous, (1722) 24 E.R. 646 (P.C.).
A.G. Canada v. A.G. Ontario, [1897] A.C. 199 (P.C.).
A.G. Canada v. Canard, [1976] 1 S.C.R. 170.

B

Badger – *R. v. Badger,* [1996] 1 S.C.R. 771.
Baker Lake v. Minister of Indian Affairs, [1980] 1 F.C. 518 (F.C.T.D.).
Bear Island – *Ontario v. Bear Island Foundation,* [1991] 2 S.C.R. 570.
Behn – *Behn v. Moulton Contracting Ltd,* 2013 SCC 26.
Blackwater v. Plint, 2005 SCC 58.
Blueberry River – *Blueberry River Indian Band v. Canada,* [1995] 4 S.C.R. 344.
British Columbia v. Okanagan Indian Band, 2003 SCC 71.
Buffalo v. Canada, 2016 FCA 223, leave to appeal to SCC denied, No. 37280, March 9, 2017; reconsideration denied, June 22, 2017.

C

Calder – *Calder v. British Columbia,* [1973] S.C.R. 313.
Calvin – *Calvin's Case,* (1608) 77 E.R. 377 (Court of King's Bench).
Campbell – *Campbell v. British Columbia,* 2000 BCSC 1123.
Canada v Craig, 2012 SCC 43.
Canada v. Fontaine, 2017 SCC 47.
Canada v. Lameman, 2008 SCC 14.
Canada v. Lavell, [1974] S.C.R. 1349.
Canada v. Mikisew Cree, 2016 FCA 311; leave to appeal granted by SCC, No. 37441, May 18, 2017.
Canada v. Musqueam First Nation, 2008 FCA 214.
Cape Breton v. Nova Scotia, 2009 NSCA 44; leave to appeal to SCC denied, CanLII 71470, 2009.

Capital Cities Comm. v. C.R.T.C., [1978] 2 SCR 141.

Carter v. Canada, 2015 SCC 5.

Chartrand v. B.C., 2015 BCCA 345.

Cherokee Nation – *Cherokee Nation v. Georgia,* 30 U.S. 1 (1831).

Chippewas of Sarnia – *Chippewas of Sarnia Band v. Canada,* (2000) 195 D.L.R. (4th) 135 (Ont. C.A.), leave to appeal to S.C.C. denied, 205 D.L.R. (4th) vii.

Chippewas of the Thames – *Chippewas of the Thames First Nation v. Enbridge Pipelines Inc.,* 2017 SCC 41.

Clyde River – *Clyde River (Hamlet) v. Petroleum Geo. Services Inc.,* 2017 SCC 40.

Coastal First Nations v. B.C., 2016 BCSC 34.

Corbiere v. Canada, [1999] 2 S.C.R. 203.

Côté – *R. v. Côté,* [1996] 3 S.C.R. 139.

Council of the Haida Nation v. B.C., 2017 BCSC 1665.

Cowichan Tribes v. Canada, 2017 BCSC 1575.

Cunningham – *Alberta v. Cunningham,* 2011 SCC 37.

D

Daniels – *Daniels v. Canada,* 2016 SCC 12.

Delgamuukw v. B.C., (1981) 79 D.L.R. (4th) 185 (B.C.S.C.).

Delgamuukw v. The Queen, [1995] 5 WWR 97 (BCCA).

Delgamuukw – *Delgamuukw v. B.C.,* [1997] 3 S.C.R. 1010.

Derrickson v. Derrickson, [1986] 1 S.C.R. 285.

Drew v. Newfoundland, 2006 NLCA 53.

E

Earl of Rutland's case, (1608) 77 E.R. 555.

Ermineskin v. Canada, 2006 FCA 415.

Ermineskin – *Ermineskin Indian Band v. Canada,* 2009 SCC 9.

F

Fejo v. Northern Territory of Australia, [1998] HCA 58.

First Nations Child and Family Caring Society of Canada v. Canada, 2016 CHRT 2.

G

Gitxaala Nation v. Canada, 2016 FCA 187.

Gladstone – *R. v. Gladstone,* [1996] 2 S.C.R. 723.

Gladue – *R. v. Gladue,* [1999] 1 S.C.R. 688.

God's Lake – *McDiarmid Lumber Ltd v. God's Lake First Nation,* 2006 SCC 58.

Grassy Narrows – *Grassy Narrows First Nation v. Ontario,* 2014 SCC 48.

Grassy Narrows (trial) – *Keewatin v. Ontario,* 2011 ONSC 4801.

Guerin – *Guerin v. The Queen,* [1984] 2 S.C.R. 335.

H

Haida – *Haida Nation v. B.C.,* 2004 SCC 73.

Hamilton Health Sciences Corp. v. H.(D.), 2014 ONCJ 603; revised reasons 2015 ONCJ 229.

Horse – *R. v. Horse,* [1988] 1 S.C.R. 187.

Horseman – *R. v. Horseman*, [1990] 1 S.C.R. 901.
Howard – *R. v. Howard*, [1994] 3 S.C.R. 299.

I

In Re Eskimo, [1939] S.C.R. 104.

J

Johnson v. McIntosh, 21 U.S. 543 (1823).
Jones v. A.G. of New Brunswick, [1975] 2 S.C.R. 182.

K

Kahkewistahhaw First Nation v. Taypotat, 2015 SCC 30.
Kanthasamy v. Canada, 2015 SCC 61.
Kapp – *R. v. Kapp*, 2008 SCC 41.
Kitkatla – *Kitkatla Band v. B.C.*, 2002 SCC 31.
Kokopenace – *R. v. Kokopenace*, 2015 SCC 28.
Ktunaxa – *Ktunaxa Nation v. B.C.*, 2017 SCC 54.

L

Labrador Metis Nation v. Newfoundland, 2007 NLCA 75.
Lax Kw'alaams – *Lax Kw'alaams Indian Band v. Canada*, 2011 SCC 56.
Little Salmon – *Beckman v. Little Salmon*, 2010 SCC 53.
Long Plain – *Long Plain First Nation v. Canada*, 2015 FCA 177.
Lovelace v. Canada, (1981), U.N. Doc. A/36/40 (U.N. Human Rights Comm.).
Lovelace v. Ontario, 2000 SCC 37.
Lower Nicola Indian Band v. Trans-Canada Displays Ltd, 2000 BCSC 1209.

M

Mabo – *Mabo v. Queensland (No. 2)*, [1992] HCA 23.
Manitoba Métis – *Manitoba Métis Federation v. Canada*, 2013 SCC 14.
Maple Lodge Farms v. Canada, [1982] 2 S.C.R. 2.
Marshall I – *R. v. Marshall*, [1999] 3 S.C.R. 456.
Marshall II – *R. v. Marshall*, [1999] 3 S.C.R. 533.
Marshall/Bernard – *R. v. Marshall/ R. v. Bernard*, 2005 SCC 43.
Martin v. Chapman, [1983] 1 S.C.R. 365.
Mikisew Cree – *Mikisew Cree First Nation v. Canada*, 2005 SCC 69.
Miller v. Secretary of State for Exiting the European Community, 2017 UKSC 5.
Mississauga of Scugog First Nation v. NAATGWU, 2007 ONCA 814.
Mitchell – *Mitchell v. M.N.R.*, 2001 SCC 33.
Mitchell v. Peguis Indian Band, [1990] 2 S.C.R. 85.
Morton v. Manzari, 417 U.S. 535 (1974).
Musqueam Indian Band v. Glass, 2000 SCC 52.
Musqueam Indian Band v. Canada, 2004 FC 579.
Musqueam Indian Band v. British Columbia, 2005 BCCA 128.
Musqueam Indian Band v. British Columbia, 2005 BCSC 1069.
Musqueam First Nation v. British Columbia, 2012 BCCA 178.
Musqueam Indian Band v. Musqueam Indian Band (Board of Review), 2016 SCC 36.

N

Nacho Nyak Dun – *First Nation of Nacho Nyak Dun v. Yukon,* 2017 SCC 58.
Native Women's Assoc. v. Canada, (1992) 57 F.T.R. 115, aff'd (1992) 145 N.R. 253 (FCA).
Neskonlith Indian Band v. Salmon Arm, 2012 BCCA 379.
Nikal – *R. v. Nikal,* [1996] 1 S.C.R. 1013.
Norwegijick v. Canada, [1983] 1 S.C.R. 29.
N.T.C. Smokehouse – *R. v. N.T.C. Smokehouse Ltd,* [1996] 2 S.C.R. 672.
Nunatakavut Community Council v. Canada, 2015 FC 981.

O

Ontario v. Beaudrey, 2006 ONCJ 59.
Ordon Estate v. Grail, [1998] 3 S.C.R. 437.
Osoyoos Indian Band – *Osoyoos Indian Band v. Oliver,* 2001 SCC 85.

P

Pamajewon – *R. v. Pamajewon,* [1996] 2 S.C.R. 821.
Paul – *Paul v. B.C.,* 2003 SCC 55.
Paulette v. The Queen, (1973), 42 D.L.R. (3d) 8 (NWTSC); [1977] 2 S.C.R. 628.
Peter Ballantyne Cree Nation v. Canada, 2017 SKCA 5, leave to appeal to SCC denied,
    No. 37485, June 22, 2017.
Powley – *R. v. Powley,* 2003 SCC 43.
Province of Ontario v. Dominion of Canada, (1895) 25 S.C.R. 434.

Q

Quebec v. Moses, 2010 SCC 17.

R

R. v. Blais, 2003 SCC 44.
R. v. Clark, 1999 CanLII 13543 (ON. LST).
R. v. Day Chief, 2007 ABCA 22.
R. v. Dick, [1985] 2 S.C.R. 309.
R. v. Drybones, [1970] S.C.R. 282.
R. v. Henry, 2005 SCC 76.
R. v. Ignace, (1998) 156 D.L.R. (4th) 713 (BCCA).
R. v. Ipeelee, 2012 SCC 13.
R. v. Machekequonabe, (1897) 2 C.C.C. 138, 28 O.R. 309 (Ont. Div. Ct.).
R. v. Morris, 2006 SCC 59.
R. v Oakes, [1986] 1 S.C.R. 103.
R. v. S. (R.D.), [1997] 3 S.C.R. 484.
R. v. Sutherland, [1980] 2 S.C.R. 451.
R. v. Syliboy, [1929] 1 D.L.R. 307 (N.S. Co. Ct.).
R. v. Williams, [1995] 2 C.N.L.R. 229 (BCCA).
R. v. Williams, [1998] 1 S.C.R. 1128.
R. v. Williams and Taylor, (1981), 34 O.R. (2d) 360 (ONCA).
Re the Queen v. The Secretary of State for Foreign and Commonwealth Affairs, ex parte
    The Indian Association of Alberta, [1982] 3 C.N.L.R. 195 (H. of L.).
Reference Re Offshore Mineral Rights of B.C., [1967] S.C.R. 792.

Reference re Remuneration of the Judges of Provincial Court (PEI), [1997] 3 S.C.R. 3.
Reference re Secession of Quebec, [1998] 2 S.C.R. 217.
Rio Tinto – Rio Tinto Alcan Inc. v. Carrier Sekani Tribal Council, 2010 SCC 43.

S

Saik'uz – Saik'uz First Nation v. Rio Tinto Alcan Inc., 2015 BCCA 154.
Sappier – R. v. Sappier, 2006 SCC 54.
Sga'nism Sim'augt (Chief Mountain) v. Canada, 2013 BCCA 49.
Sikyea v. The Queen, (1964) S.C.R. 642.
Simon – Simon v. The Queen, [1985] 2 S.C.R. 387.
Sioui – R. v. Sioui, [1990] 1 S.C.R. 1025.
Skeetchestn Indian Band v. B.C., 2000 BCCA 525.
Snuneymuxw First Nation v. Board of Education – School District #68, 2014 BCSC 1173.
Sparrow – R. v. Sparrow, [1990] 1 S.C.R. 1075.
St. Catherine's Milling – St. Catherine's Milling and Lumber Co. v. The Queen, (1888),
    14 A.C. 46 (P.C.).
Sundown – R. v. Sundown, [1999] 1 S.C.R. 393.

T

Taku – Taku River Tlingit First Nation v. B.C., 2004 SCC 74.
Taku River Tlingit v. Canada, 2016 YKSC 7.
Thomas v. Norris – Thomas v. Norris, 1992 CanLII 354 (B.C.S.C.).
Tsilhqot'in – Tsilhqot'in Nation v. B.C., 2014 SCC 44.
Tsilhqot'in v. B.C., 2007 BCSC 1700 (trial).
Tsilhqot'in v. B.C., 2012 BCCA 285 (B.C.C.A.).

U

U.S. v. Jicarilla Apache Tribe, 564 U.S. 162 (2011).
U.S. v. Winans, 198 U.S. 371 (1905).

V

Van der Peet – R. v. Van der Peet, [1996] 2 S.C.R. 507.

W

Wakatu v. Attorney General, [2017] NZSC 17.
Wewaykum – Wewaykum Indian Band v. Canada, 2002 SCC 79.
Wewaykum Indian Band v. Canada [No. 2], 2003 SCC 45.
White and Bob – R. v. White and Bob, (1965), 50 D.L.R. (2d) 613 (B.C.C.A.) aff'd [1965]
    S.C.R. vi (note).
William v. Riverside Forest Products Ltd, 2002 BCSC 1199.
Williams Lake – Williams Lake Indian Band v. Canada, 2018 SCC 4.
Worcester v. Georgia – Worcester v. Georgia, 31 U.S. 515 (1832).

Y

Yorta Yorta v. Victoria, [2002] HCA 58.

Index

abolishment of, 38–40, 97, 138. *See also* Aboriginal title; *Constitution Act, 1982*, Section 35; extinguishment of rights; infringement of rights; justification for infringement of rights (*Sparrow* test)

Aboriginal rights, recognition: constitutional recognition (s. 35), 7, 85; continuity doctrine, 86–87; date of contact, 59; distinctive culture test, 88–89, 91, 204; pre-existence requirement, 85–86; proof of practices at date of contact, 22, 59. *See also* reform pressures by Aboriginal peoples

Aboriginal title: about, 104–8, 114; asserted vs established rights, 150; burden of proof, 102–4; communal nature, 16–17, 29, 92, 105–7, 181; compensation for infringement, 112–13, 115; constitutional protection (s. 35), 93, 106; continuity doctrine, 64, 95, 103, 104; critical commentary, 94, 107–8, 110–11, 200–2; Crown title and sovereignty, 93–95; date of European sovereignty, 59, 92, 103, 104, 114; duty to consult and accommodate, 173; exclusive occupation, 22, 92, 104, 106, 114, 181; existing vs Crown interests, 94; federal committee on BC land claims (1927), 37–38, 96; fee simple interests, 105, 201–2; fiduciary duties, 99; for future generations, 105, 106, 107–8, 112, 114–15; generic rights, 92, 105; history of law on, 94–102; inalienability except to Crown, 105, 106, 107, 114; *Indian Act* ban on fundraising, 7, 36, 37, 96; Indigenous laws, 101, 181; infringement if justification, 92, 94; inherent limits and restrictions on uses, 105, 107–8, 114–15; joint title, 104; judicial law making, 202–4; justification test for infringement on, 108–13, 115; key questions, 85, 196, 200; land titles registries, 106; as legal property right, 99; Marshall decisions, 35, 63; in modern treaties, 123–24; notice of claims, 202; oral evidence, 103; ownership

rights, 105; "postage stamp" (territorial vs specific sites), 101–2, 104, 114; proof of title, 102–4; recognition under Royal Proclamation, 33–35; reconciliation with non-Aboriginal people, 20–22, 109–11; remedies, 108; source in prior occupation, 93, 106; in spectrum of rights, 85, 89, 92–93; successor group, 103; sufficient occupation, 104; *terra nullius* theory, 8, 51, 63, 71; test for title, 104; and treaties, 94–95, 116–19; uncertainty factor, 113, 115; UNDRIP provisions, 187–88; uses for land, 105; White Paper (1969) abolishment of, 38–40, 97, 138. *See also* British Columbia, Aboriginal title; *Constitution Act, 1982*, Section 35; justification for infringement of rights (*Sparrow* test)

Aboriginal title, cases. *See Calder* (1973); *Delgamuukw* (1997); *Marshall/ Bernard* (2005); *Tsilhqot'in* (2014)

accommodate, duty to. *See* duty to accommodate

act of state doctrine, 60, 66. *See also* sovereignty of the Crown

activism, Aboriginal. *See* reform pressures by Aboriginal peoples

activism, judicial. *See* Supreme Court of Canada (SCC), judicial law making

Adams (1996), 112

administrative law: about, 163–64; consultation process vs outcome, 145, 167–68; delegation of consultation, 169–70; duty of fairness, 145, 170; duty to consult, 144–45, 173; reasonableness, 167. *See also* duty to consult

ADRIP (American Declaration on the Rights of Indigenous Peoples), 187, 192, 194

AFN. *See* Assembly of First Nations (AFN)

agreements: about, 91; Australian model, 171; delegation of self-government powers, 64–65; duty to consult as preparation for, 145; impact and benefit agreements (IBAs), 159–60, 163, 171; influence of *Haida* decision, 166;

modern treaties, 49, 137; negotiations, 137, 209–11; third parties, 163. *See also* negotiations; treaties, modern
Alaska settlement, 199
Alberta: Métis settlements, 220n45, 227n7; special courts, 184
Alcantara, Christopher, 210
Alfred, Gerald Taiaiake, 56–57
Algonquin Nation, 49, 95, 124
American Declaration on the Rights of Indigenous Peoples (ADRIP), 187, 192, 194
Asch, Michael, 65, 119
Assembly of First Nations (AFN): lobbying, 40; negotiations and power imbalance, 209–10; against privatization of rights, 198; residential schools compensation, 50
assimilation: Hawthorn Report (1966), 38, 138; historical background, 31–32; *Indian Act*, 36–37; White Paper (1969), 38. *See also* historical background, displacement and assimilation (1800s to 1969); residential schools
Attawapiskat reserve, 41
Australia: agreements, 171; Indigenous laws, 180, 182–83, 186; *Mabo*, 60; Native title, 180, 201; a source of Aboriginal law, 27; sovereignty of the Crown, 60; *terra nullius* theory, 8; UNDRIP status, 189–90
Australian Law Reform Commission, 180, 182–83, 186

Badger (1996): duty to consult, 172; fiduciary duties, 74, 112; honour of the Crown, 80, 125, 191; interpretation of treaties, 136, 238n64; justification for infringement, 112, 172; legal nature of a treaty, 125; numbered treaties, 134, 136
Bakan, Joel, 213–14
bands and band councils: delegation of self-government powers, 64–65, 70; federal funds, 65; fiduciary duty of the Crown, 77–78; First Nations terminology, 12; *Indian Act* provi-

sions, 36–37, 64, 180; Indigenous laws, 177, 180. See also *Indian Act*; reserves
Bastarache, Michel, 212
Bear Island (1991), 134–35
Behn (2013): collective and individual rights, 152–53, 172, 197–98; duty to consult, 152–53, 172
Bennett, Carolyn, 190
Bentham, Jeremy, 24
Berger, Thomas, 3–4, 19, 35, 40, 42, 97, 98
Binnie, William Ian Corneil, 7, 34, 59, 118, 120, 128–29, 131, 160, 169, 205–8
Black, Conrad, 8
blood quantum, 13
Blueberry River (1995), 76
Borrows, John, 21, 34–35, 94, 111, 133, 176–78, 182, 183, 188, 201; *Canada's Indigenous Constitution*, 183
Britain. *See* United Kingdom
British Columbia: Aboriginal rights ignored by governments, 7–8; consultation policy, 158; critical commentary, 140–41; Gustafsen Lake standoff, 41; Indigenous laws, 177; proposal for reorganization of existing groups, 71; self-government referendum, 58; special courts, 184; third order of government issue, 68–69; Treaty of Oregon, 59, 103
British Columbia, Aboriginal title: critical commentary, 140–41, 200–2; date of British sovereignty (1846), 59, 102, 103; Douglas treaties, 95, 121, 125, 137, 200; historical background, 94–98; justifications for dispossession of land, 9; key questions, 200–1; lack of land surrender treaties, 95, 121, 142; modern treaties, 36, 49, 98, 137, 140–41, 210; MST Partnership, 205; Musqueam role in legal developments, xi–xii, 18–19, 204–5; parliamentary committee on land claims (1927), 37–38, 96; political will, 210; power imbalance in negotiations, 210; private property rights, 200–1; treaties, 94–96, 121. See also *Delgamuukw* (1997); *Tsilhqot'in* (2014)

federal government; fiduciary duty of the Crown; honour of the Crown; provincial governments; sovereignty of the Crown
Cunningham (2011), 135
customary law. *See* Indigenous laws

dams, hydroelectric. *See* pipeline and hydroelectric developments
Daniels (2016): fiduciary duties, 73; Métis definitions, 12, 197; RCAP recommendations quoted in, 48
date of contact test: about, 59, 103; critical commentary, 88–89, 91; "frozen rights" approach, 67, 88, 89, 91–92, 114, 204; for Métis (pre-control), 59, 90–91; for rights (date of contact), 59; for title (date of British sovereignty), 59, 92, 103. *See also* distinctive culture test (*Van der Peet* test)
decolonization: recommendations, 50–51, 71, 94. *See also* Aboriginal rights, recognition; Indigenous laws, recognition; justice for Aboriginal peoples; reconciliation
Delgamuukw (1997): about, 99–100, 114; Aboriginal title, 99; assertion of Crown sovereignty, 59; broader public good for infringement, 109–10; "clear and plain" intention to extinguish rights, 100; compensation for infringement, 112, 159; complexity and cost, 99–100, 206–7; consultation spectrum, 147; critical commentary, 107; duty to accommodate, 159; duty to consult, 147, 160; duty to obtain consent, 160; encouragement of litigation and modern treaties, 141; fiduciary duties, 74; first principles vs case law, 100; human costs of litigation, 206–7; Indigenous laws, 178, 181; inherent limits on uses, 107; justification for infringement, 109–10, 200; oral history evidence, 91, 100, 103, 178; ownership vs jurisdiction over land, 94; provinces not to extinguish rights and title, 61–62; reconciliation, 209;

self-government, 67; settlement of foreign populations, 110, 202; and sovereignty, 59–60
demographics of Aboriginal peoples, 9
Deschamps, Marie, 151–52, 209
development of resources. *See* resource development
Dickson, George Brian, 99
Dickson, Jamie, 81
discovery doctrine, 63, 66, 71, 83, 84, 93
discrimination and race, 4–5, 8
dispossession of Aboriginal peoples: about, 6–10, 28; broader public good for infringement, 109–10, 115, 213; colonialism, 7–10; defined, 6; duress and threat of force, 9; inadequate resources, 206; justifications for, 8–9, 28; *terra nullius* theory, 8, 63, 71. *See also* colonialism; infringement of rights; justification for infringement of rights (*Sparrow* test); treaties
distinctive culture test (*Van der Peet* test): about, 86–89, 114; benefits for Aboriginal peoples, 92; burden of proof, 88, 91; critical commentary, 88–89, 91–92, 196; date of contact, 87–88, 114; evidence of distinctive culture, 87–88; exclusion of post-contact activities, 91; "frozen rights" approach, 67, 88, 89, 91–92, 114, 204; integral to the distinctive culture, 67, 87–89, 91, 114; judicial law making, 204; Métis rights, 90–91; precise claim identified, 87–88; *Van der Peet* trilogy, 87. *See also* date of proof; justification for infringement of rights (*Sparrow* test); *Van der Peet* (1996)
doctrine of act of state, 60, 66
doctrine of continuity. *See* continuity doctrine
doctrine of discovery, 63, 66, 71, 83, 84, 93
doctrine of precedent, 26, 213
doctrine of tenure, 93
dominium and *imperium*, defined, 58–59. *See also* sovereignty of Aboriginal groups

extinguishment of rights: about, 6–7, 86, 116; burden on the Crown to show extinguishment, 86; *Calder*, 97–98; by "clear and plain" intention (*Sparrow* test), 86, 97–98, 99, 100, 114, 203; constitutional protection of rights (s. 35), 6–7, 86, 199; defined, 6; judicial law making, 203; in modern treaties, 139; regulation as not extinguishment, 86; by treaties, 116, 133–36

extinguishment of title: about, 97–98, 116; *Calder*, 97–98; by "clear and plain" intention (*Sparrow* test), 93, 97–98, 99, 100, 114, 203; constitutional protection of rights (s. 35), 6–7, 86, 93, 199; critical commentary, 133–34; *Delgamuukw* (1997), 61–62; extinguishment by federal government, 92–93; by federal government, not provinces, 93; judicial law making, 203; in modern treaties, 139; by treaties, 116, 133–36. *See also* treaties

Family Homes on Reserve Act, 17
federal government: "the Crown," 14–16; delegation of self-government powers, 57, 58, 68–69, 70; division of powers, 61–62; extinguishment of rights (before 1982), 93; inalienability of title except to Crown, 106; interjurisdictional immunity principle, 62; jurisdiction over Indians (s. 91), 11–12, 61–62; parliamentary committee on BC land claims (1927), 37–38, 96; primary jurisdiction, 28; restructuring of Aboriginal department, 220n50; UNDRIP status, 189–91. *See also* the Crown; duties of federal and provincial governments; Harper, Stephen, government; Trudeau, Justin, government; Trudeau, Pierre, government

fee simple interests, 105, 201–2. *See also* Aboriginal title; land ownership

fiduciary duty of the Crown: about, 72–78, 81–82, 84; Aboriginal title, 99; ad hoc relationships, 73–74; adverse effects, 74, 78; best interests of others, 72–73, 77, 78; burden on government,

112; cases, 74–78; constitutional duty (s. 35), 111, 203; critical commentary, 81–82; Crown's control over specific interests, 73–74, 77, 78, 79, 84; duty to consult, 153; and honour of the Crown, 77, 79, 81–82; judicial law making, 203; justification for infringement of rights, 109, 111–12, 115; loyalty, 72–73, 81; non-Aboriginal interests, 200; per se relationships, 73; proportionality, 112; as "settled law," 73, 82; specific Aboriginal interests, 73–74, 77, 78; statutory limitations, 77–78; test for ad hoc duties, 73–74; vulnerability to Crown's control, 74, 78. *See also* honour of the Crown

fiduciary duty of the Crown, cases: *Badger*, 74, 112; *Blueberry River*, 76; *Ermineskin*, 77–78; *Guerin*, 74–75; *Haida*, 77; *Manitoba Métis*, 78; *Osoyoos Indian Band*, 76; *Sparrow*, 75, 111; *Tsilhqot'in*, 112; *Wewaykum*, 76–77, 200; Williams Lake, 78

final agreements, 123. *See also* treaties, modern

First Nations: definitions, 12; demographics, 10; legislation, 23. *See also* Aboriginal peoples; bands and band councils; *Indian Act*

First Nations Elections Act, 23

First Nations Land Management Act, 23

fishing rights: about, 89; agreements and government programs, 92; commercial fishing, 87, 90; date of contact, 91; distinctive culture test, 87–88; *Gladstone*, 89; justification for infringement, 110, 112; *Marshall/Bernard*, 100–1; Natural Resources Transfer Agreements, 122; regulation of, 86–87; *Sparrow*, 86–87, 89. *See also* resource development

Flanagan, Tom, xi, 12, 34, 71, 107, 133–34, 198–99

forestry rights: about, 89–90; commercial aspects, 89; culturally modified trees, 62; duty to consult on asserted rights, 147–50; duty to consult on future adverse effects, 154–55, 157;

Helin, Calvin, 165
Hinkson, Christopher, 189
historical background: about, 22, 30–32, 54–55; four stages of history, 30–32, 54–55, 120; imperial law, 26; separate worlds (to 1500), 30–31; a source of Aboriginal law, 27. *See also* continuity doctrine; imperial law; Indigenous laws
historical background, contact and co-operation (1500 to early 1800s): about, 31, 32–35, 54, 120; covenant chain (two-row wampum), 33–35, 57, 185; imperial law, 26; Indigenous laws, 179; Marshall decisions, 35, 63; *Mohegan Indians* (1704–73), 33, 54; nation-to-nation relationships, 57, 139; peace and friendship treaties, 32–33, 54, 120, 126–27; Royal Proclamation of 1763, 33–35, 119. *See also* imperial law; Royal Proclamation of 1763
historical background, displacement and assimilation (1800s to 1969): about, 31–32, 36–39, 54, 120–23; Aboriginal title, 94–97; assimilation, 31, 179; federal committee on BC land claims (1927), 37–38, 96; Hawthorn Report (1966), 18, 38, 124, 138; *Indian Act*, 36–37, 54; *Manitoba Act* (1870), 37, 69, 78, 80; treaties, 36, 54, 116, 120–23; White Paper (1969), 38–39, 54. See also *Indian Act*; residential schools; treaty rights; treaties; treaties, historical and numbered (to 1920s); White Paper (1969)
historical background, negotiation and renewal (1970 to present): about, 32, 39–55; constitutional reform failures, 41–46; court successes, 52–54, 55; modern treaties, 49, 54–55, 123, 139–41; peaceful solutions, 40–41; RCAP hearings and report, 46–48; reform pressures by Aboriginal peoples, 39–41; TRC hearings and report, 49–51. See also *Constitution Act, 1982*; *Constitution Act, 1982*, reform attempts; Royal Commission on Aboriginal Peoples (RCAP); treaty

rights; treaties, modern; Truth and Reconciliation Commission (TRC)
honour of the Crown: about, 72, 78–82, 84; *Badger*, 80, 125, 191; broad purposive approach, 80–81; compensation for infringement, 112–13; consultation spectrum, 156; critical commentary, 81–82; delegation not allowed, 162–63, 170; duty to consult, 149, 150, 151–52, 153, 162–63; and fiduciary duties, 77, 79, 81–82; *Haida*, 77; historical background, 78–79; judicial law making, 203; justification for infringement, 111; *Manitoba Métis Federation*, 78; treaties, 118, 125–26, 136–37, 142; uncertainty of, 81, 82; UNDRIP's influence, 187, 191, 194. *See also* fiduciary duty of the Crown
Horse (1988), 135, 136
Howard (1994), 134, 135
Howard, Albert, 213
human rights. See *Canadian Human Rights Act;* Charter of Rights and Freedoms
hunting and trapping rights: about, 90; *Behn*, 152–53; commercial rights, 90, 122; duty to consult, 150–51, 153; *Horse*, 136; *Little Salmon*, 151–52; *Marshall/Bernard*, 100–1; Métis rights, 90–91; *Mikisew Cree*, 150–51; Natural Resources Transfer Agreements, 122; provincial laws not to single out Aboriginal people, 62; treaty interpretation, 126, 136; *Tsilhqot'in*, 90, 101–2; visible, incompatible use test, 200
hydroelectric developments. *See* pipeline and hydroelectric developments

Idle No More, 40–41, 49
Ignatieff, Michael, 20, 58, 216
impact benefit agreements (IBAs), 159–60, 163, 171
imperial law: continuity doctrine, 26, 64; defined, 26; Indigenous laws validity in absence of colonial laws, 33; as part of federal common law, 26; as source of Aboriginal law, 26. *See also*

continuity doctrine; Mohegan Indians; Royal Proclamation of 1763

imperium and *dominium*, defined, 58–59. *See also* sovereignty of Aboriginal groups

Indians: definitions and terminology, 10–14; demographics, 10; federal jurisdiction (s. 91), 11–12, 15. *See also* Aboriginal peoples; First Nations

Indian Act: about, 36–37; amendments and replacements, 36; ban on cultural practices, 7, 36; ban on fundraising for land claims, 7, 36, 37, 96; and *Canadian Human Rights Act*, 5–6; critical commentary, 36; definitions and terminology, 10–14; federal delegation of self-government powers, 57, 64–65; *Indian*, as term, 11; and Indigenous laws, 180; individual and collective rights, 6, 17, 29, 197; legal benefits of Aboriginal ancestry, 17; marriage to non-Aboriginal, 186; and modern treaties, 123; non-status Indians, ix, 12; provincial jurisdiction, 62; provisions in, 7, 36–37; a source of Aboriginal law, 23; taxation, 5. *See also* historical background, displacement and assimilation (1800s to 1969); residential schools

Indigenous laws: about, 22–23, 174–78, 193; Aboriginal rights and title, 101, 193; and *Canadian Human Rights Act*, 5–6; collective rights, 197–98; and common law, 178–82, 193; community values, 178–79, 193; continuity doctrine, 180–81; critical commentary, 184–86; defined, xii, 3, 12–13, 175, 193; examples, 176–78; gender equality, 6, 180; key questions, 174, 185–86; knowledge systems, 179–80; lack of state authority, 176, 179, 193; law commission report, 183; legal pluralism, 176; *Marshall/Bernard*, 101; *Mohegan Indians*, 33; proof of title, 101; remedies and compensation, 178; rule of recognition, 174–75, 179; as a source of Aboriginal law, 22–23; sources of Indigenous laws, 176–77,

193; *Thomas v. Norris*, 17, 179; traditional medicine as a right, 90; TRC recommendations, 174–75, 184, 186, 193; validity in absence of colonial laws, 33

Indigenous laws, recognition: about, 20, 22–23, 174–76, 180–82, 193; areas not likely to be recognized, 179; in Australia, 180, 182–83; benefits, 182; continuity doctrine, 20, 64, 83, 180–81; critical commentary, 184–86; examples, 180, 193; and *Indian Act*, 180; key questions, 185–86; law commission report, 183; objections to, 182; objectives of Aboriginal law, 19–22, 29; rule of recognition, 175–76; TRC recommendations, 174–75; UNDRIP provisions, 188

Indigenous peoples: defined, xii, 12. *See also* Aboriginal peoples

individual and collective rights. *See* collective and individual rights

infringement of rights: about, 6–7, 108–11; compensation, 112–13; constitutional justification (s. 35), 108–9, 111; critical commentary, 108–9, 110–11, 169; cumulative impacts of development, 169, 196; defined, 6; justification test to allow, 86, 108–13; UNDRIP provisions, 188–89. *See also* justification for infringement of rights (*Sparrow* test)

interjurisdictional immunity, 62

interlocutory injunction, 148

International Convention on Civil and Political Rights, 186

international law: about, 26–27, 186–95, 194–95; ADRIP, 187, 192, 194; dualist theory, 186; key questions, 174; marginal role of, 26–27, 193; a source of Aboriginal law, 26–27; sovereignty of Aboriginal groups, 56–57; treaty interpretation, 127; UNDRIP, 186–92, 194. *See also* Australia; New Zealand; UNDRIP (United Nations Declaration on the Rights of Indigenous Peoples) (2007); United Kingdom; United States

198; fee simple interests, 105, 201–2; modern treaties, 123; provincial registries, 106; rights in Aboriginal title, 104–6, 114; sovereignty vs ownership, 58–59, 94. *See also* Aboriginal title

land titles registries, 106

Law Commission of Canada, 183

law in Canada. *See* Aboriginal law; legal system, Canadian

law in other jurisdictions. *See* international law

The Law of Nations (Vattel), 8–9

Lax Kw'alaams (2011), 89, 207, 208

Leacock, Stephen, 32

legal community: Aboriginal ancestry, 19, 214; Canadian Bar Association resolutions, 184; contributions to Aboriginal law, 52; critical commentary by, xi; influence on SCC, 19; law schools and courses, 19, 51, 183–84; legal scholarship, 19, 52, 184; success of Aboriginal law, 52–53, 55; TRC recommendations, 19, 51

legal system, Canadian: about, x–xi, 176; Aboriginal participation, 82, 214, 216; adversarial nature, 207–8, 214; central authority, 178; decolonization recommendations, 50–51, 71, 94; derogatory attitudes, 100; dualist theory, 186–87; fiduciary duties, 72–74, 81–82; and Indigenous laws, 178–80, 184; individualistic approach, 72–73, 179; and international law, 186; knowledge systems, 179–80; legal pluralism, 176; reconciliation with Indigenous laws, 174–75; rule of recognition, 175–76; sovereignty as political fact, 59–61; special courts, 184; specialist tribunal proposed, 216; value and policy considerations, x–xi. *See also* Aboriginal rights, recognition; courts; fiduciary duty of the Crown; honour of the Crown; Indigenous laws, recognition; litigation; Supreme Court of Canada (SCC); Supreme Court of Canada (SCC), judicial law making

legislation: about, 23–24; administrative tribunals for consultation, 164; dele-

gated powers, 23, 64–65; fiduciary duty limitations, 77–78; First Nations, 23; on future events, 24; interjurisdictional immunity, 62; jurisdiction for, 23–24; limitation legislation, 208; public input, 215; as a source for duty to consult, 144–45; a source of Aboriginal law, 23. *See also* federal government; *Indian Act*; legal system, Canadian; politics; provincial governments

L'Heureux-Dubé, Claire, 88

Liberal governments. *See* Martin, Paul, government; Trudeau, Justin, government; Trudeau, Pierre, government

limitations, statutes of, 208

litigation: about, 206–11; adversarial nature of, 207–8, 214; benefits for Aboriginal people, 213–14; complexity and cost, 99–100, 101, 206–7, 213; critical commentary, 206–8, 213–14; and duty to consult, 145, 166; historical background, 18–19; human costs, 206–7; inequality of resources, 205–7, 208–9, 212–13; injunctions, 148; key questions, 211; limitation legislation, 208; limited to parties, 210; mixed results, 207; negotiation on continuum with, 209–11; process not designed for good policy, 214–15; remedies for breach of duty to consult, 164–65; treaties preferred over, 118; unreasonable delay, 208. *See also* courts; evidence; legal system, Canadian; negotiations

Little Salmon (2010): consultation procedures, 163; duty to accommodate, 159–60; duty to consult, 80, 146, 149–50, 151–52, 153, 172; duty to obtain consent, 160; honour of the Crown, 80, 151–52, 153; modern treaty, 128–29, 134, 151–52, 172; participation for reconciliation, 209; third party land grant, 151

local government, 16, 58

logging. *See* forestry rights

Long Plain (2015), 162

Lovelace v. Canada (1981), 186

Luxemburg, Rosa, 198

Mabo (1992), 60
Macdonald, Sir John A., 31
Macfarlane, Emmett, 214
Mackenzie Valley pipeline, 40
Macklem, Patrick, 4
Mandamin, Leonard, 175
Manitoba Act (1870): about, 37; honour of the Crown, 37; land grants to children, 37, 69, 78, 80
Manitoba Métis Federation (2013): constitutional basis for sovereignty of Crown, 23; fiduciary duties, 78, 80; honour of the Crown, 37, 78, 80–81, 82; individual vs collective rights, 197; land grants to children, 37, 69, 78, 80; negotiated acceptance of sovereignty, 69; numbered treaties, 134; supremacy of Constitution, 23
Manuel, Arthur, 191
Maritime provinces: lack of land surrender treaties, 95, 100; *Marshall/ Bernard*, 100–1; Mi'kmaq people, 33
Marshall, John, 35, 63, 66
Marshall decisions (1820s and 1830s, US), 27, 35, 63, 95
Marshall I (1999), 127–28, 204
Marshall II (1999), 215
Marshall/Bernard (2005), 100–1, 102, 104, 126, 181
Martin, Paul, government, 48–49
Martin, Sheilah L., 25
McEachern, Allan, 100
McHugh, P.G., 52, 82
McLachlin, Beverley: on Aboriginal title, 95–96, 98, 99, 100; on the Charter and Aboriginal rights, 108; on consultation spectrum, 156–57; on continuity doctrine, 64, 180; on distinctive culture test, 88; on historical treaties, 134; on judicial law making, 24, 213; on justification for infringement, 110–11, 213; on reconciliation, 20–21; on social change, 213; on sovereignty, 69; on treaty interpretation, 127
McNeil, Kent, 102, 107–8, 109, 135, 181
Meech Lake Accord, 44–46, 48
men. *See* gender equality

Métis peoples: about, 90–91; acceptance by modern community, 11–12, 91; ancestral connection to historical community, 11–12, 91; definitions, 11–12, 91, 196–97; demographics, 10; federal jurisdiction (s. 91(24)), 11–12, 15, 196–97; lack of government registry, 12; self-identification, 11–12, 90–91
Métis rights and title: about, 90–91; Alberta settlements, 220*n*45, 227*n*7; anomaly between Métis and Indian rights, 91; *Daniels*, 12, 197; definitions of Métis, 11–12, 91, 196–97; distinctive culture test (*Van der Peet* test), 86–91; fiduciary duties, 73; fur trade, 91; honour of the Crown, 37; key questions, 196–97; lack of government registry, 12; *Manitoba Act* (1870), 37, 69, 78, 80; multiple identities, 12; Natural Resources Transfer Agreements, 122; *Powley*, 90; pre-control test (date of effective British control), 59, 88, 90; proof of pre-control practices, 22, 59, 103. See also *Manitoba Métis Federation* (2013)
Mikisew Cree (2005): consultation spectrum, 157–58; Crown's power to "take up" land, 136–37, 150; duty to accommodate, 159; duty to consult on established rights, 146, 150–51, 153, 155, 172; duty to obtain consent, 160; duty to participate in consultation, 161; historical treaties, 131, 135, 136–37, 172; honour of the Crown, 136–37, 150, 153; justification of infringement, 136–37, 150; notice of proposed actions, 157–58
Mi'kmaq people, 33, 66, 125, 128
Mills, Aaron, 178–79
Mitchell (2001): continuity doctrine, 86; evidence, 91; honour of the Crown, 79; self-government, 68; sovereignty authority, 59
modern treaties. *See* treaties, modern
Mohawk people, 41, 46, 56–57
Mohegan Indians v. Connecticut (1704–73), 18, 33, 60, 65–66

More, Thomas, 8

Morris, Alexander, 121–22, 136

MST Partnership, 205

Mulroney, Brian, government: Charlotte-town Accord, 44–45, 211; Meech Lake Accord, 44–46, 48

municipal government, 16, 58

Musqueam people: role in legal developments, xi–xii, 18–19, 204–5. *See also Guerin* (1984); *Sparrow* (1990)

Nacho Nyak Dun (2017), 119, 129

Napoleon, Valerie, 178, 179, 206–7

nation-to-nation relationships, 57, 139. *See also* self-government

Native Rights in Canada, 18, 97, 124

natural resources: Indigenous laws, 177–78. *See also* fishing rights; forestry rights; hunting and trapping rights; Indigenous laws; resource development

Natural Resources Transfer Agreements, 122

negotiations: about, 137, 209–11; and duty to consult, 145, 161–62; influence of *Haida* decision, 166; limited to parties, 210; litigation on continuum with, 209–11; power imbalance, 209–10; treaty renewal, 137. *See also* agreements; litigation; treaties, modern

New Brunswick. *See* Maritime provinces

New Democratic Party, 42

New Zealand: differing understandings of the parties, 35; fiduciary duties to Māori, 73; a source of Aboriginal law, 27; UNDRIP status, 189–90

Newfoundland: test for distinctive culture, 91. *See also* Maritime provinces

Newman, Dwight, 165, 166

Niagara, Treaty of, 33, 119

Nikal (1996), 111–12, 146–47

Nisga'a people: Aboriginal title, 96–98; self-government powers, 65, 68–69. See also *Calder* (1973)

non-Aboriginal people: broader public good in infringement, 109–11, 115; Crown as representative of, 28; notice of title claims, 202; race and dis-crimination, 4–5, 8; reconciliation as balance with Aboriginal rights, 21–22, 29, 199–202; rights, 4; sources of legal occupancy, 10. *See also* historical background; justice for Aboriginal peoples; reconciliation; third parties

non-status Indians, ix, 12. *See also* Aboriginal peoples

Northern Gateway pipeline, ix, 53, 164, 167

Nova Scotia: peace and friendship treaties, 120. *See also* Maritime provinces

N.T.C. Smokehouse (1996), 87

numbered treaties. *See* treaties, historical and numbered (to 1920s)

Obed, Natan, 165–66

obiter dicta (said in passing), 26, 100

Ojibway, 130, 135, 137

Oka crisis, 41, 46

Ontario: Caledonia land dispute, 41; covenant chain (two-row wampum), 33–35, 57, 185; Crown's power to "take up" land, 137; Ipperwash crisis, 41; modern treaties, 124; Robinson treaties, 120–21, 135; special courts, 184; Williams treaties, 122–23

oral history: *Delgamuukw*, 91, 100, 103, 178; as evidence, 103, 178, 207; Indigenous laws, 177–78; treaty interpretation, 128; *Tsilhqot'in*, 102

Oregon, Treaty of, 59, 103

Organization of American States (OAS), ADRIP, 192, 194

Osoyoos Indian Band (2001), 76

ownership of land. *See* land ownership

Pamajewon (1996): continuity doctrine, 64; self-government, 67; self-government and date of contact, 84

Paul (2003), 212

peace and friendship treaties, 32–33, 120, 126–27. *See also* historical background, contact and co-operation (1500 to early 1800s)

peaceful solutions for historical grievances: about, 20; AFN lobbying, 40–41; constitutional lobbying (1980s),

41–42; covenant chain (two-row wampum), 33–35, 57, 185; hydroelectric and pipeline developments, 40; Idle No More, 40–41, 49; objectives of Aboriginal law, 19–22, 29; peace and friendship treaties, 32–33, 120; reform pressures by Aboriginal peoples, 40–41; treaties, 133. *See also* Indigenous laws, recognition; justice for Aboriginal peoples; reconciliation; reform pressures by Aboriginal peoples

Penikett, Tony, 65, 140

Penner Report, 57

pipeline and hydroelectric developments: consultation procedures, 164; duty to consult on future adverse effects, 154–55; James Bay, 40, 98, 123; Kinder Morgan, 52; Mackenzie Valley, 40; Northern Gateway, ix, 53, 164, 167; peaceful solutions, 20, 40–41, 53; Trans Mountain, 15, 164. *See also* resource development

pluralism, legal, 176, 185

Poelzer, Greg, 65, 210–11

politics: about, 211–17; Aboriginal responses to White Paper, ix, 39–40; benefits of, 211–12; and judicial law making, 213; judicial law making after political failures, 52, 55, 212, 214; justification for infringement of rights, 110–11; key questions, 211; political will, 210, 216–17; RCAP recommendations, 211–12. See also *Constitution Act, 1982*, reform attempts; federal government; legislation; provincial governments

Powley (2003), 90

Price Paid (Sellars), 9

Prince Edward Island. *See* Maritime provinces

privatization of rights, 196, 197–99

provincial governments: "the Crown", 14–16; delegation of self-government powers, 57, 70; division of powers, 61–62; extinguishment of title not allowed, 93; inalienability of title except to Crown, 106; increasing role of, 15, 61; infringement of rights by, 15;

interjurisdictional immunity, 62; jurisdiction over Aboriginal rights and title, 15–16, 61–63, 83; land title systems and Aboriginal title, 106; legislation in areas of jurisdiction, 62; legislation not to single out Aboriginal people, 62; power to "take up" land, 15, 136–37, 150; special courts, 184; *Tsilhqot'in*, 62. *See also* the Crown; duties of federal and provincial governments

Quebec: Charlottetown Accord, 44–45; James Bay Agreement (1975), 40, 49, 98, 123; Meech Lake Accord, 44; Oka crisis, 41, 46; peace and friendship treaties, 120; sovereignty as a political act, 59; test for distinctive culture, 91; treaties, 125

racism and discrimination, 4–5, 8

RCAP. *See* Royal Commission on Aboriginal Peoples (RCAP)

recognition: rule of recognition, 175–76. *See also* Aboriginal rights, recognition; Indigenous laws, recognition

reconciliation: about, 20–22, 29; balance of Aboriginal and non-Aboriginal interests, 29, 199–202; broader public good for infringement, 109–11, 115, 213; critical commentary, 111; definitions, 21–22, 29, 50, 55, 174–75, 199; duty to accommodate, 159; duty to consult, 151–52, 157; Indigenous laws, 174–75; judicial forbearance, 129; judicial law making, 202–4; justification for infringement of rights, 21, 109, 111, 199–200; by litigation, 206–8; by modern treaties, 119; objectives of Aboriginal law, 19–22, 29; source in s. 35, 111; sovereignty as political fact, 66–67; TRC recommendations, 50, 174–75; by treaties, 22, 142. *See also* Aboriginal rights, recognition; Indigenous laws, recognition; justice for Aboriginal peoples; peaceful solutions for historical grievances

Red Paper *(Citizens Plus)*, 40, 138

reform pressures by Aboriginal peoples: about, 39–41; AFN lobbying, 40; constitutional lobbying (early 1980s), 42–46; Idle No More, 40–41; peaceful solutions, 40–41; response to government policies, 39–41, 49; violent incidents, 41; White Paper responses, 39–40

regulatory bodies: discharging Crown's duty to consult, 153

reserves: delegation of self-government powers, 64–65; fiduciary duties, 76–77; *Guerin*, 99; historical background, 31, 116; *Indian Act* provisions, 36, 64, 180; Indigenous laws, 180; legislation on, 23; proposals for privatization, 198–99. *See also* bands and band councils

residential schools: about, 37, 49–50; compensation and apology, 49–50; historical background, 31; *Indian Act*, 37; TRC report, 37, 49–51, 55. *See also* Truth and Reconciliation Commission (TRC)

resource development: broader public good for infringement, 109–10, 213; cooperation, 148; cumulative impacts of development, 169, 196; duty to consult on asserted rights, 147–50, 165; duty to consult on future adverse effects, 154–55, 157, 165; fee simple interests, 105, 201–2; inherent limits on uses of Aboriginal land, 105, 107–8, 114. *See also* fishing rights; forestry rights; hunting and trapping rights; pipeline and hydroelectric developments

Resource Rulers (Gallagher), 52–53

Reynolds, Jim: legal background, xi–xii, 204

rights, Aboriginal. *See* Aboriginal rights; Aboriginal title

Rio Tinto (2010): about, 153–55; adverse effects of future action, 154–55, 169; consultation procedures, 164, 167; critical commentary, 167; duty to consult on asserted rights, 147–48, 153–54; duty to consult on future actions,

152, 153–55, 169, 172; inequality, 169; remedies for breach of duty to consult, 164

Roach, Kent, 111, 118

Robinson treaties, 120–21, 135

Rothstein, Marshall, 81, 82

Rowe, Malcolm, 25

Royal Commission on Aboriginal Peoples (RCAP): about, 46–48, 55; critical commentary, 48; four stages of history, 30–32; groups as "political and cultural entities," 13; historical treaties, 130–35; inadequate living conditions, 206; inherent right to self-government, 58; lack of implementation of recommendations, 48, 55, 215; legal challenges to treaties, 131–32; mandate and structure, 46–47; report (1996), 47–48

Royal Commission on Aboriginal Peoples (RCAP), recommendations: about, 47–48; decolonization of law, 71; economic and social inequities, 47–48; extinguishment of rights in modern treaties, 139; funding for more opportunities, 211–12; institutional changes, 47–48; modern treaties, 119; nation-to-nation relationship, 57; new Royal Proclamation, 47, 132; proposed government response, 216–17; renewal of historical treaties, 119, 132–34; reorganization of existing groups, 47–48, 70–71; residential schools, 49; self-government, 58, 67–68, 70–71, 84, 195–96; shared sovereignty (treaty federalism), 57; specialist tribunals, 216; TRC establishment, 49

Royal Proclamation of 1763: about, 33–35, 119; assertion of Crown sovereignty, 119; *Calder*, 34; covenant chain (two-row wampum), 34–35, 57, 185; critical commentary, 34–35; differing understandings of the parties, 35; honour of the Crown, 80; not a source for title, 93; recognition of Aboriginal rights and title, 33–34, 119; treaty federalism theory, 119. *See also* historical background, contact and co-operation (1500 to early 1800s)

Saganash, Romeo, 190
Saik'uz (2015), 201
Sappier (2006), 89–90, 181, 197
Saskatchewan: special courts, 184
SCC. *See* Supreme Court of Canada (SCC)
scholarship on Aboriginal law. *See* Aboriginal law; legal community
Scott, Duncan Campbell, 31
Section 35. See *Constitution Act, 1982*, Section 35
Section 91. See *Constitution Act, 1867*
self-determination: definitions, 56–58; UNDRIP provisions, 187, 188. *See also* self-government; sovereignty of Aboriginal groups
self-government: about, 56–58; critical commentary, 65; definitions, xiii, 56–58; delegation of powers under legislation and agreements, 64–65; distinctive culture test (*Van der Peet* test), 67; federal delegation of powers, 57, 58, 68–70; federal policy statement (1995), 64–65, 83; inherent rights, 58, 69; judicial law making, 203–4; key questions, 195–96; modern treaties, 65, 123; nation-to-nation relationship, 57; *Pamajewon*, 67, 84; Penner Report, 57; reorganization of existing groups, 70–71; sources of, 58; third order of government issue, 68–69, 84; UNDRIP provisions, 188. *See also* sovereignty of Aboriginal groups
self-government agreements. *See* agreements; treaties, modern
Sellars, Bev, 9
settlement lands, 116. *See also* treaties, modern
shared sovereignty, 57. *See also* sovereignty of Aboriginal groups; sovereignty of the Crown
Simon (1985), 125–26
Sinclair, Murray, 50
Sioui (1990), 118, 125, 128, 238*n*64
Slattery, Brian, 61, 106, 107

Smith, Melvin, 42, 43, 107
sources of Aboriginal law. *See* Aboriginal law, sources
Southin, Mary, 200
sovereignty of Aboriginal groups: about, 56–59; cases, 67–69; continuity doctrine, 64, 70; covenant chain (two-row wampum), 33–35, 57, 185; critical commentary, 70–72; date of British sovereignty for Aboriginal title, 59; date of contact for Aboriginal rights, 59; date of effective control by Britain for Métis, 59; definitions, 56–58; under international law, 56; key questions, 56, 195–96; land ownership compared, 58–59; Marshall decisions (1820s and 1830s), 35, 63; nation-to-nation relationship, 57, 139; *Pamajewon*, 67; pre-existence of Aboriginal sovereignty, 63, 66–67, 98; shared sovereignty, 68; third order of government issue, 68–69. *See also* continuity doctrine; Royal Proclamation of 1763; self-government
sovereignty of the Crown: about, 56–63, 83; act of state doctrine, 60, 66; British sovereignty's impact on Aboriginal sovereignty, 63–64; cases, 65–67, 83; constitutional basis, 23; continuity doctrine, 63; covenant chain (two-row wampum), 33–35, 57, 185; critical commentary, 70–72; Crown title, 93–94; date of British sovereignty for Aboriginal title, 59; date of contact for Aboriginal rights, 59; date of effective control by Britain for Métis, 59; definitions, 56–58; delegation of self-government powers, 64–65, 70; discovery doctrine, 63, 66, 71, 83, 84, 93; infringement of Aboriginal rights, 94; under international law, 56; key questions, 56; land ownership, 58–59, 94; Marshall decisions, 35, 63; *Mohegan*, 65–66; nation-to-nation relationship, 57, 139; *Pamajewon* (1996), 84; as political fact, 59–61, 66, 83; provincial jurisdiction, 61–63; provincial powers, 83; as reconciliation, 21; Royal

traditional laws. *See* Indigenous laws

Trail of Tears, 35

Trans Mountain pipeline, 15, 164

trapping. *See* hunting and trapping rights

TRC. *See* Truth and Reconciliation Commission (TRC)

treaty rights: about, 36, 116–19; Aboriginal rights vs treaty rights, 117–18; benefits of treaties, 117–19; community well-being, 137–38, 210–11; duty to consult, 145, 150; evolution of rights, 126, 128, 135–36; extinguishment of rights, 116; extinguishment of rights not possible (s. 35), 7; judicial law making, 202–4; justification for infringement, 117–18; key questions, 116; Natural Resources Transfer Agreements, 122; as reconciliation, 21–22, 142; treaty federalism theory, 119, 230*n*105; UNDRIP provisions, 188, 189; White Paper (1969) recognition of, 39. *See also* justification for infringement of rights (*Sparrow* test)

treaties: about, 36, 116–19, 142–43; benefits of treaties, 117–19; compared with litigation, 118; critical commentary, 124–25, 130–34, 206; honour of the Crown, 79, 84, 118, 125–26, 129, 136–37, 142, 150, 153; interpretation, 118, 127–29, 135–36, 238*n*64; key questions, 116; legal nature of, 124–27; nation-to-nation relationship, 139; as reconciliation, 21–22; specific to Aboriginal group, 118, 127; symbolic importance, 138–39, 142; treaty renewal, 137. *See also* duty to accommodate; duty to consult; honour of the Crown

treaties, historical and numbered (to 1920s): about, 36, 120–22, 130–39, 142–43; community well-being, 137–38, 142, 210–11; content, 121–22, 131; critical commentary, 130–39; Crown's power to "take up" land, 7, 15, 136–37, 150; differing understandings of the parties, 35, 130–31, 134, 136, 139, 189;

extinguishment of rights and title, 121; hunting and fishing, 131; inequality and unfairness, 130–31, 133–34, 142, 189; interpretation, 118, 127–29, 135–36; key questions, 196; legal validity of, 134–35; Natural Resources Transfer Agreements, 122; reserves, 36, 121–22, 131; symbolic importance, 138–39; transcripts of negotiations, 130, 136; translators, 130, 134; treaty renewal, 137; treaty-making process, 121–22. *See also* historical background, displacement and assimilation (1800s to 1969)

treaties, historical and numbered (to 1920s), specific: about, 120–22, 142; Douglas treaties, 95, 121, 125, 137, 200; numbered treaties, 36, 121–22, 134–37; peace and friendship treaties, 32–33, 120, 126–27; Robinson treaties, 120–21, 135; Treaties 5 to 11, 205; Treaty 3, 130, 135, 137; Treaty 6, 126, 135, 136; Treaty 8, 95, 121, 131, 132, 135, 136–37; Treaty 11, 132; Williams treaties, 122

treaties, modern: about, 49, 55, 119, 123–25, 139–43; BC treaties, 140–41; community well-being, 137–38, 142, 210–11; complexity and cost, 123, 129, 140, 143; critical commentary, 139–41, 143; development of law, 123–27; duty to consult, 137, 151–52, 153; economic logic of, 139–40; examples, 49; extinguishment of rights, 116, 139; interpretation, 128–29; James Bay Agreement (1975), 40, 49, 55, 98, 123; modified rights and title, 118; *Nacho Nyak Dun*, 119; negotiations, 209–11; as reconciliation, 119; as renewal of existing treaties, 119; for self-government, 65; settlement lands, 116; specific to groups, 123; Tsawwassen Final Agreement, 123–24. *See also* Aboriginal title; extinguishment of rights; *Little Salmon* (2010)

treaty federalism, 57, 230*n*105. *See also* sovereignty of Aboriginal groups

Treaty of Niagara, 33, 119
Treaty of Oregon, 59, 103
tribunals, administrative, 164
tribunals, specialist, 216
Trudeau, Justin, government: about, 52; ADRIP, 192; principles for Aboriginal relations (2017), 191; review of government practices, ix–x, 52; TRC recommendations, 50–52; UNDRIP status, 52, 190–91, 194
Trudeau, Pierre, government: Aboriginal responses to White Paper, ix, 40; constitutional reform, 41–43; "just society" program, 38, 195; proposal to terminate treaties, 123, 138. *See also* White Paper (1969)
trust relationships. *See* fiduciary duty of the Crown
Truth and Reconciliation Commission (TRC): about, 49–51, 55; on law as "tool for dispossession," 7; report (2015), 50–51, 55; residential schools, 37, 49–51; treaty federalism theory, 119, 230*n*105
Truth and Reconciliation Commission (TRC), recommendations: about, 50–51, 55; burden of proof for title, 102; decolonization of law, 50–51, 71; education on Aboriginal law, 19, 51; Indigenous laws, 174–75, 184, 186, 193; limitation legislation, 208; reconciliation, 50, 55; reorganization of existing groups, 71; Royal Proclamation of Reconciliation, 51, 175; self-government, 71, 84; treaty making, 119; J. Trudeau's acceptance, 50–51; UNDRIP implementation, 51, 55, 187, 194
Tsawwassen agreements, 49, 123–24
Tsilhqot'in (2014): about, 101–4, 114, 200–1; Aboriginal title affirmed by SCC, 101–2; collective rights in title, 105–6, 197; complexity and cost, 101, 102; consultation spectrum, 155–57; continuity doctrine, 103; critical commentary, 110–11; Crown title and sovereignty, 93–94; duty to consult and accommodate, 109, 150; duty to

obtain consent, 161; encouragement of litigation and modern treaties, 141; established vs asserted rights, 150; exclusion of private lands from claim, 200–1; fiduciary duties, 112; future generations, 105, 107–8, 112; honour of the Crown, 150; Indigenous laws, 178, 181; inherent limits and restrictions on uses, 107–8; interjurisdictional immunity principle, 62; justification for infringement, 108, 109–12, 160–61, 213; negotiations, 209; oral and written evidence, 102; "postage stamp" (territorial vs specific sites), 101–2, 104, 114; provincial powers, 69; reconciliation, 208; settlement of foreign populations, 202; successor group, 103; test for Aboriginal title, 104; test for justification of infringement, 109
Tsleil-Waututh Nation, 205
two-row wampum (covenant chain), 33–35, 57, 185

UNDRIP (United Nations Declaration on the Rights of Indigenous Peoples) (2007): about, 186–92, 194; adoption status, 189–91; ADRIP compared with, 192; collective rights, 16; critical commentary, 189–91; duty to obtain consent, 161, 188–89, 191, 194, 196; good faith, 161, 187; historical background, 49; honour of the Crown, 191, 194; justification for infringements, 191; specialist tribunals, 216; TRC recommendations, 51, 55, 187, 194
United Kingdom: Aboriginal appeals to the monarch, 14, 42–43; British sovereignty's impact on Aboriginal sovereignty, 63–64; continuity doctrine, 20, 64; "the Crown," 14–15; discovery doctrine, 63; dualist theory, 186; fiduciary duties, 72; honour of the Crown, 78–79; imperial law, 26; peace and friendship treaties, 32–33, 126–27; rule of recognition, 175–76; a source of Aboriginal law, 27; sovereignty as political fact, 59–60

United Nations Declaration on the Rights of Indigenous Peoples. *See* UNDRIP (United Nations Declaration on the Rights of Indigenous Peoples) (2007)

United States: Alaska settlement, 199; blood quantum and tribal membership, 13; *Cherokee Nation*, 95; discovery doctrine, 63; federal powers over self-government, 58; *Johnson v. McIntosh*, 63, 107; Marshall decisions (1820s and 1830s), 27, 35, 63; peace and friendship treaties, 32–33; privatization of reservation lands, 198–99; right of entry, 220n55; a source of Aboriginal law, 27; trading across the border, 68, 90; Trail of Tears, 35; Treaty of Oregon, 59, 103; UNDRIP status, 189–90; use of treaty land, 107; *Worchester v Georgia*, 63

The Unjust Society (Cardinal), ix, 10, 40, 124, 131, 138

Utopia (More), 8

values, Indigenous, 178–79, 193. *See also* Indigenous laws

Van der Peet (1996): broader public good for infringement, 110, 213; continuity doctrine, 64; critical commentary, 88–89, 91, 110; date of contact, 114; distinctive culture test, 67, 87–89, 88–91, 114; flexibility in analysis, 89; Indigenous laws, 179, 181; self-government, 67; sensitivity to Aboriginal perspectives, 207; test for Aboriginal rights, 114. *See also* distinctive culture test (*Van der Peet* test)

vetoes in consultations. *See* duty to obtain consent

Vickers, David, 101, 111

voting rights, Aboriginal, 5

Walkem, Ardith, 207

Wedderburn, K.W., x

wetiko and Indigenous laws, 179

Wet'suwet'en people: Indigenous laws, 181. See also *Delgamuukw* (1997)

Wewaykum (2002), 76–77, 200

Wewaykum No. 2 (2003), 215

White and Bob (1965), 125

White Paper (1969): about, 38–40; abolishment of special rights, 38–40, 97, 138; Aboriginal responses to, ix, 39–40; critical commentary, 40; historical background, 31; recognition of Aboriginal title, 39; Red Paper (*Citizens Plus*), 40, 138

Widdowson, Frances, 213

Williams Lake, 78

Williams treaties, 122

Wilson, Bertha, 13, 47

Wilson-Raybould, Jody, x, 190

windigo and Indigenous laws, 179, 184

women. *See* gender equality

Worcester v. Georgia (1832, US), 63